Two panoramic views of the Abbeville Public Square soon

after the erection of the Confederate Monument in 1906.

OLD ABBEVILLE

Scenes of the Past of a Town Where
Old Time Things Are Not Forgotten

by

Lowry Ware

HERITAGE BOOKS
2016

HERITAGE BOOKS
AN IMPRINT OF HERITAGE BOOKS, INC.

Books, CDs, and more—Worldwide

For our listing of thousands of titles see our website at
www.HeritageBooks.com

Published 2016 by
HERITAGE BOOKS, INC.
Publishing Division
5810 Ruatan Street
Berwyn Heights, Md. 20740

Copyright © 1992 Lowry Ware

All rights reserved. No part of this book may be reproduced or transmitted in any form or by any means, electronic or mechanical, including photocopying, recording or by any information storage and retrieval system without written permission from the author, except for the inclusion of brief quotations in a review.

International Standard Book Numbers
Paperbound: 978-0-917890-05-5
Clothbound: 978-0-7884-6446-1

About the Author

Lowry Ware is a native of Abbeville County, and he now lives on the farm between Hogskin and Chickasaw Creeks near Due West where he was born and has spent most of his life. He graduated from Erskine College and the University of South Carolina where he earned a PhD in history in 1956 and was elected to Phi Beta Kappa.

After teaching for a year in Connecticut, he taught history at Erskine College for thirty three years. During his graduate study he worked at the South Carolina Department of Archives and History, and he has continued his interest in historical research. Among the organizations he holds membership in are the South Carolina Historical Association, the South Carolina Historical Society, and the South Caroliniana Society. In 1982, he co-authored (along with James W. Gettys) a bicentennial history of his denomination, *The Second Century, A History of the Associate Reformed Presbyterians, 1882-1982*, and at the same time he completed *A History of Erskine College, 1839-1982*. In 1990, the *South Carolina Historical Magazine* published two of his articles which were based upon research in the history of the Old Abbeville District.

The Fifth Abbeville Court House, 1872-1908

Preface

For at least a decade I have searched for materials about the history of Abbeville District (later County) with the view of writing a traditional narrative history of that subject. Three disastrous fires in the 1870s destroyed many of the public records of this area, and I had to look for information in many sources. In this search, I was frequently impressed by accounts of life in the town of Abbeville. They included contemporary records, but were primarily reminiscent accounts of persons and events in its history, and they reflected the atmosphere of the town.

Abbeville may well have been the typical Southern town that its citizens thought it was. Two themes run through its history. Its citizens, or at least the most memorable of them, had a strong sense of pride or honor. Abbevillians, even those who were not the most favored, preferred a genteel life style. At the same time there were recurring incidents of violence. In choosing to emphasize these themes, I am well aware that I have neglected other important aspects of the history of the town. For the most part, I have selected accounts which I found interesting as well as important.

I have chosen to limit my emphasis to "Old Abbeville," which means that I have not covered such important subjects as the coming of the railroad and the cotton mill to the town in the 1890s. These two events brought unprecedented growth in the population of the town in the decade from 1890 to 1900 from about 1,300 to almost 3,800. They also brought the beginings of the modern town with changes in the life styles of Abbevillians. The subjects which I have treated after 1900 illustrate the persistence of the old patterns of life which have made Abbeville distinctive .

In the articles which I have collected, the original text is rendered in italics, and in some cases I have abridged the account. When I have omitted portions of the orginal, I have indicated this with ellipsis marks. The authors of the various selections have very different writing styles, and this requires the reader to adjust accordingly. For example, the writers for the 19th century Abbeville newspapers, as well as other authors of an earlier day, often used the British spelling of words such as *defence* or *offence* instead of the American spelling. I have not "corrected" or changed the spelling in such cases, nor have I indicated that this is incorrect by inserting [*sic*] in these instances. The variety of authors enables the reader to see Abbeville life from different perspectives. I have purposely kept my own comments as brief as possible to allow the readers to interpret the sources for themselves.

Preface

In some areas of the life of "Old Abbeville" where I could find no relevant articles, I chose to write my own treatment. Limitations of space and sources prevented me from covering others which might have been both interesting and important.

Traditionally, the local historian set aside a section which dealt with the leading families of the town or region. Although I have not done this, a glance at the index will indicate those families which played prominent roles in social life of Old Abbeville. I have also included materials which might be of particular interest to genealogists and other students of family history.

Also, I have made a special effort to include some account of the life of the blacks in Abbeville's history and to integrate them in the story. During most of its past, they were a majority in the population of the town.

Robert Henry Wardlaw, Isaac Branch, Addison F. Posey, and the other local authors, whom I have chosen, shared with most of their fellow citizens a love of and conscious identification with the history of their town. In a number of instances, I have used accounts from the Abbeville newspapers and from non-Abbeville publications. I wish to make special acknowledgement to *Life Magazine* for permission to print the poem by Joseph Auslander, to Ralph Ellison for his letter about his grandfather, and to the South Caroliniana Library for the reminiscenes of Robert Henry Wardlaw, the broadside of Ben Lane Posey, and the 1882 Gray's map of Abbeville. I would like to express my thanks to all who have helped me in my research and writing, to Jane Harrison for the use of some of her pictures, and, particularly, to Rose-Marie Williams who generously proof read the whole and gave me many useful suggestions.

Lowry Ware

CONTENTS

I	Early Abbeville	1
II	Wardlaw Family Traditions of Early 19th Century Abbeville	6
III	Abbeville and Its Two Most Famous Men	21
IV	Grandfather's Stories of Abbeville in 1825	25
V	Reminiscences of an Ex-Abbevillian, Addison F. Posey	
	Abbeville Forty Years Ago (1876)	27
	The Great Whiskey War of 1843	30
	The McLarens	32
	Major James Alston	35
	The Hendersons	36
	Robert B. Hamilton	40
	The Hanging of Kindred Kitchens, 1836	42
VI	Abbevillians in Duels	44
VII	Abbeville and Its Slaves, Paternalism and Fear	49
VIII	Fatal Stabbing in a Carriage Shop	54
IX	The Golden Age of Fine Abbeville Homes, 1850-1880s	58
X	The Lesley-Hoyt-Simonds-Burt-Norwood-Calhoun-Stark House	62
XI	A Walking Tour of the Abbeville Business District, 1857	66
XII	Dr. Togno and the Rock House	68
XIII	Trinity and the Sacred Heart	71
XIV	The Great Secession Meeting, November 22, 1860	75
XV	The Legend of the Cradle and the Grave of the Confederacy	77
XVI	Life in Abbeville During the Civil War, the Story of a Young Boy, John E. Gardin	84
XVII	The Five Lost Colonels	92
XVIII	An Abbeville Lady Visits General Lee in Virginia	95
XIX	Mrs. Davis in Abbeville	96
XX	Jefferson Davis in Abbeville: General Basil Duke's Account	98
	General Ferguson's Account	100
	An Account from the Viewpoint of One of Dibrell's Men	102
	Experiences of Two Kentucky Officers at Abbeville	104
	Postmaster General Reagan on Abbeville	105
	A Rebel Reefer in Abbeville, April-May, 1865	106
	The Confederate Treasure Train in Abbeville	110

Contents

XXI	The Occupation Garrison in Abbeville, 1865-66	115
XXII	Reconstruction Scenes: "Big Alfred" Ellison and His Grandson, the Novelist	118
	The Guffins and the County Robbery Case	121
	The Great Fires of 1872-73	125
	Love and Infidelity: the Houston Scandal	129
	Big Tuesday, August 22, 1876	132
XXIII	Abbeville at Leisure in the 1870s and 1880s: Baseball Comes to Town, 1873-74	136
	Parson Mountain as a Summer Resort, 1883	137
XXIV	Scenes of Violence from 1880 to 1900: The Killing of Pem Guffin	139
	The Benedict Homicide, 1884	142
	The Lynching of Dave Roberts (1882) and the Rescue of Charles Hall (1896)	145
	A Shocking Tragedy. Sheriff Kennedy, U.S. Marshal Dansby, and William Kyle of Massachusetts Killed	148
XXV	Days of Celebration and Dedication: The Eureka	151
	Confederate Monument	152
	New City Hall and Opera House	153
	The New Court House	157
	The Shadow of the Dispensary	160
XXVI	Hope and Tragedy: The Stories of Harbison College and Anthony Crawford	162
XXVII	Abbeville Artists	173
XXVIII	All American Hero, Tom Howie	177
XXIX	Roll of Abbeville Citizens (Male), May, 1859	179
	The Citizens of Abbeville, April, 1884	183
XXX	Naming of Streets (1883) & Business Directory (1894)	187
XXXI	Abbeville Presbyterians	189
XXXII	Abbeville Methodists	197
XXXIII	Abbeville in the Federal Census Schedules The Census of 1850—Village of Abbeville	210
	The Census of 1860—Village of Abbeville	219
XXXIV	Abbeville Town Officers, 1833-1989	231
	Index	237

I. EARLY ABBEVILLE

Despite its name, Abbeville was not founded by French settlers, but by the Scotch-Irish who settled most of the area around it. Local tradition held that in 1785, Dr. John de la Howe bestowed that name on the new county and thereby upon its court house site. According to this story, de la Howe was one of the commissioners appointed to locate the court house for the new county which was being set off in the westernmost part of the lower Saluda division of the old Ninety Six District. It has been speculated that he had been born at Abbeville, France, but it is known only that he came from France. Others have supposed that he was memorializing the Huguenot colony at New Bordeaux Township which had been settled in 1764 at the mouth of Long Cane Creek and thus within the new county's borders. De la Howe, although living in Charleston, had close friends among the New Bordeaux French, and in a short time he moved his permanent residence to his estate (today De la Howe School) which lay between Long Cane Creek and Little River, some twenty miles below and to the west of the site of Abbeville Court House.

The new court house and the village which grew up around it was located on land which in the 1780s belonged to Andrew Hamilton and which he purchased from Andrew Pickens. It had not been originally granted to Pickens, but to one Agnes Moore, a member of the Scotch-Irish party which was supposed to be settled at the head waters of Long Cane in the Boonesborough Township in the 1760s. Following the death of Andrew Hamilton in 1835, the first of his four tracts of land was described in the equity court as *the 100 acres originally granted to Agnes Moore and by Robert Moore and his wife Agnes conveyed to Andrew Pickens and by him conveyed to Major Hamilton whereon the village of Abbeville is now situated. A considerable portion was sold off in lots by Major Hamilton.* South Carolina *Colonial Plats*, Book 18, page 497, December 22, 1767, indicated that it lay just to the west of Pickens' spring.

The *Charleston Records*, Deed Book V-5, page 495 recorded a deed from Robert Moore and his wife Agnes to Andrew Pickens, Esq., May 5, 1772 of 100 acres for ten shillings current money. The plat shows that the whole top of the ridge on which the later village was located was crossed with a path and a road which led to Andrew Pickens' home on the east.

In 1792, the South Carolina legislature authorized the construction of a powder magazine and public arsenal at Abbeville, and Governor William Moultrie appointed Major John Bowie as the magazine and arsenal store keeper. He also appointed Richard A. Rapley and Andrew Hamilton to oversee the construction of a 24 by 32 feet arsenal and a 10 by 12 feet magazine at the cost of 700 pounds sterling.

Twenty two years later, both the magazine and the arsenal were so

Early Abbeville

decayed that a legislative petition from Abbeville declared that they were in "a situation very contiguous to the other public buildings and in that part of the village most populous of all others." It said that rather than a protection, the building (the powder magazine) had now become dangerous since it was within twenty feet of a private residence and there was nearby a row of private houses "at least a hundred yards long." The petition requested that the magazine be removed to a more suitable location which Andrew Hamilton was willing to supply. The twenty three signers of the petition may have included persons who were not immediate neighbors, but it almost certainly included those who were. As such, it marks the earliest list (1815) of Abbevillians:

Patrick Noble	A. Hamilton
Joseph Noble	Chas. C. Yancey
Thomas Aron (?)	A. C. Hamilton
Talo. Livingston	Jas. Wardlaw
H. A. Jones	Henry Livingston
Wm. Robertson	Jacob Sossimon
Thos. Livingston	Thos. W. Tallman
Thos. Spierin	James Taggart
R. H. Wardlaw	Moses Taggart, Jr.
Moses Taggart	J. Allen
D. Wardlaw	Alex. Bowie
William Lomax	

The next list of the inhabitants of Abbeville Court House was printed in the *Abbeville Medium*, January 10, 1872 when "Citizen," probably Dr. Isaac Branch, recalled the residents in 1822, the year when he arrived from Vermont, as follows:

James Wardlaw	James Moore
Moses Taggart	Wm. McMillen
Alexander C. Hamilton	Samuel Branch
Thomas Livingston	Dr. E. S. Davis
Andrew Hamilton	Jacob Sossimon
Alexander Bowie	John Finley
Patrick Noble	Charles Dendy
Henry Livingston	Wm. Robertson
John Allen	Lemuel White
John McLaren	

As early as October, 1816, the Grand Jury of Abbeville District in its presentment to the State advanced *the necessity of incorporating the village of Abbeville in order to preserve more effectually the peace*

Early Abbeville

and happiness of the citizens in general at all times , but more particularly during the sitting of court as much disturbance prevails among the disorderly at such times to the great inconvenience of many orderly persons.

However, the village of Abbeville was not incorporated until 1832 when the South Carolina legislature set off its boundaries as one mile to the east, south, west and north of the court house. The first intendent or mayor was Moses Taggart, the long time Ordinary (judge) of Abbeville District.

The *Abbeville Whig and Southern Nullifier,* the town's pioneer newspaper which was published by Samuel A. Townes, carried the first ordinances of the new town in March 28, 1833. There were four: the first provided for a list of all free white males over eighteen years in age which would be used to set up patrol duty; the second provided that the same persons would be used in road duty or pay a duty of $6; the third established regulations for licenses for shows or exhibitions within town limits; and the fourth provided for licenses for the retail of spirituous liquor or taverns.

The *Greenville Mountaineer,* September 10, 1836, gave the following picture of Abbeville four years after it was incorporated:

The village or town of Abbeville lies in latitude 34 10' North of the equator, on an elevated plane, surrounded on all sides, except the West, by hills from which issue springs of the purest water in the world. These springs are numerous and large, and the water from them running with rapidity to the rich bottom lands of Long Cane Creek, a distance of five miles from the village, which consequently is remote from the deleterious influence of stagnant water or vapor. The village is equi-distant from the Savannah and the Saluda Rivers, 18 miles above the line which divides Edgefield from Abbeville District, and 15 miles below the old Indian boundary line which divides Abbeville from Pendleton (now Anderson) *District. Part of the village stands on a mulch-red clay and the other part on a sandy soil and red clay bottom. These soils are fertile and produce an abundance in the finest growth of vegetables.*

The village contains 438 inhabitants, white and black--190 of whom are children, viz., 75 white male adults, 63 white female adults, 37 white male children, 43 white female children; 43 black male adults, 67 black female adults, 45 black male children, 54 black female children: 29 of the population are of the following ages; 1 black female 100--1 white female 95--1 black female 85--2 black males 85--1 white female 76--10 black females upward of 60--6 black males upward of 60--4 white females upwards of 60. These old persons and the children constitute just one half of the population; the remaining 219 are between the ages of 15 and 60, all in the enjoyment of good health, this 12 August, 1836. Where can this be

Early Abbeville

beaten or equalled in the State of South Carolina?

The village consists of 34 dwelling houses, 2 tan yards, 3 tailor shops, 5 carriage making shops, 1 cabinet maker's shop, 1 silversmith's shop, 2 shoe maker's shops, 1 saddler and harnessmaker's shop, 1 blacksmith, 1 tin shop, 1 paint and glazing shop, 6 large dry goods stores, 2 groceries, 5 taverns, 1 Methodist Episcopal church, 1 male academy (closed), 1 female academy (closed), 1 market house, 1 arsenal, 1 magazine, 1 court house, 1 jail, 1 temperance society, 1 Sunday school society, 1 female library society, 3 clergymen, 3 physicians, 7 lawyers, 1 Justice of the Peace, 4 notaries, 1 clerk, 1 commissioner, 1 ordinary, 1 sheriff and several military titles. The religious of the village are Presbyterians and Methodists.-- Communicated.

The earliest official list of the residents of the town which has been preserved is the following list which Francis P. Robertson compiled for the South Carolina State Census of 1839. It contained the freeholders (all white) with the number of free persons in each household.

1. Widow Jane Allen-- 20
2. B. L. Posey-11
3. R. H. Wardlaw-15
4. T. C. Perrin, Esq.--11
5. James Wardlaw, Esq.-3
6. Joseph J. Wardlaw-2
7. J. A. Calhoun-6
8. W. C. Black, Esq.-2
9. Wm. Atkison-3
10. Thomas Wightman-3
11. John White-10
12. Samuel Goff-4
13. Widow Jane Stithmire-4
14. James Shillito-4
15. Dr. F. Branch-18
16. Samuel Branch-13
17. Rev. George Moore-7
18. Rev. James Moore-6
19. James A. Creight-10
20. Dr. Isaac Branch-6
21. Thomas Jackson-10
22. Charles Dendy-8
23. Dr. J. F. Livingston-9
24. John Taggart-6
25. Donald Douglass-9
26. John McLaren-10
27. J. C. Kingsmore-8
28. John Russel-7
29. Hutton Douglass-7
30. Pamelia Alford-2
31. James Alston-5
32. Johnson Ramey-12
33. Moses Taggart, Esq.-2
34. Sarah Downey-9
35. Patrick Noble-9
36. Wm. Baker-8
37. D. L. Wardlaw, Esq.-9
38. A. Burt, Esq.-5

Total- 299

When a branch railroad line was planned from Hodges to connect Abbeville with the Greenville & Columbia Railroad, there was an impetus to expand the village from the immediate vicinity of the court house and jail. A town council was elected which set about cutting new streets and opening up the Magazine Hill area to settlement

Early Abbeville

For example, the *Abbeville Banner*, November 25, 1852, carried an advertisement by S. McGowan, Isaac Branch, H. A. Jones, John McIlwain, H. S. Kerr, and Wm. Hill which read *anxious for the improvement and welfare of Abbeville village, and desirous of stimulating the spirit of improvement which is now rennovating our town* [we] *offer at private sale about twenty lots, suitable for private residences or business purpose. All are subdivisions of that high and commanding region known as the "Magazine Field." All are about one and a half acres and are located on a high ridge equidistant from the public square and the new depot of the G. & Cola. R. R.* Those who wished to see a survey of the development were directed to "the plan of the village, filed in the clerk's office." This "plan of the village" unfortunately was destroyed by the great courthouse fire two decades later. A copy was filed as one of the exhibits in the equity suit over Andrew Hamilton's estate in 1835. Although the equity papers were saved from the fire, the survey has been lost from those records.

In 1852, a new ticket was elected to the council with the pledge to spend its resources to improve the public square and public buildings. Little however could be done for lack of funds until 1857 when a public meeting called upon the State legislature to amend the town charter to give its authorities the power to tax property. This was secured and in 1857, T. W. McMillan, apparently the first town marshal or police, was given the contract to build a storm sewer (then called a blind ditch) of rock and brick to carry off the rain water from the public square. He also put up curbing and put down sand and gravel upon the side walks and on the square which had in the past been miry and muddy following rains. McMillan also planted rows of elms and maples in the square which had previously been entirely open. A series of new ordinances forbade residents or visitors from hitching their horses to the little new trees, restricted townspeople from allowing cattle to roam the streets, and required residents who did such work in the streets as cutting fire wood to clean up the refuse afterwards. Observers often commented in 1858-60 on how much improvement these changes brought to the public square.

In fact, except for the changes in the buildings which fronted on the public square, it remained basically as it was from 1858 to 1919 when the town decided to pave a large portion of it as well as the main streets which led outward from it. In the summer and fall of that year the Southern Construction Company of Chattanooga, Tenn. put down, after the trees were cleared out of the square, 9,000 feet of brick paving in the square and 7,000 feet on the street leading to the depot (Washington), Trinity, Vienna, Church, South and North Main Streets. The old rock curbing was taken from the square and replaced with concrete curbing around the park which was located in the center.

II. WARDLAW FAMILY TRADITIONS OF EARLY 19TH CENTURY ABBEVILLE

By Robert Henry Wardlaw from his "Reminiscences and Random Recollections," a typescript volume in the South Caroliniana Library.

Wardlaw was born in the village of Abbeville in 1807, and he had lived there until he wrote out these memoirs in 1885 and 1886. During most of that time he was a merchant on the public square. No family was more intimately involved in the formative years of the village than his family. His account was written for his family. The ellipses (. . . .) mark where I have chosen to omit portions from Wardlaw's original.

My father [James Wardlaw] *owing to the scarcity of schools in that day enjoyed very little of the opportunities of an education. . . . I am under the impression that his school term was less than a winter session. . . .* [yet] *he made such attainments that he became a land surveyor. He was deputy to Maj. John Bowie who was Clerk of the County Court. My father staid* [sic] *at the Court House and attended to all the business, Maj Bowie who lived six miles in the country came in about once a week to sign such papers as required his signature.*

I am not certain at what time father became the deputy of John Bowie, Clerk of the County Court, probably about 1790. He married 9 June 1796 to my mother Hannah Clarke. His first settlement was on what he called the McIntire tract of 100 acres which he after the marriages of Thos. C. Perrin and Sister Jane and myself and your mother, Eliza Bowie, both of which took place in 1830, gave Jane Perrin one third, myself one third, retaining the balance himself. His house stood near the spot on which T. C. Perrin built the house now [1885] *occupied by Jas. S. Cothran.*

. . . Here his first child Eliza Alice was born 7 July 1797, she died 7 years old. John Quay, stepfather of my mother, built on the Donaldson tract the house of hewed logs which my father bought from Quay in which he always afterward resided and in which his other seven children were born. David Lewis Wardlaw born 28 March 1799 being the first native of Abbeville Village. (Some thought that Maj. Hamilton's daughter Betsy afterwards Mrs. Alston was the first native of the village, but my father told me that though older than Bro. Lewis she was born on Norris Creek about 2 miles from the village).

This house added to and improved is still standing and was lately the residence of Judge Thos. Thomson and belongs to some of his family. From my father's conversation I learned some facts which I here state that you may better know the state of the country. He said

Wardlaw Traditions

our whole country was covered with wild pea vine, cane and other vegetation which afforded sufficient pasturage for horses and cattle, that it was the custom to give the horses very little if any food but were belled or hobbled and turned out to forage for themselves in the woods and that frequently then he spent a good part of the forenoon in hunting up the horses to put them to the plough, and that this hunt frequently took a considerable time, when the horses had strayed off further than was expected. The woods which were burnt off every winter destroying the undergrowth so completely that a wild turkey could be seen 100 to 200 yards through the open woods and a deer at a greater distance. . . .

On one occasion of hunting my father in riding through the [deer] drive came suddenly on a Negro man belonging to old Maj. Hamilton who had for some time been a runaway and as my father had his gun the Negro readily submitted to him, but as father had no intention of using his gun and fearing that the Negro might attempt to dodge him as he was on horseback as they passed the many thickets on the way. So my father adopted the following expedient. He made the Negro take off his suspenders and with them tied his hands behind his back. Then unbuttoning the waist band of his pants the fellow had to hold up his pants so that they would not fall and hobble him, by taking hold of them with his hands behind, then mounting he drove the runaway before him home and to his master.

. . . .I will add a little more, developing father's character. Since my recollection there were 3 or 4 houses which as they were built in the same manner as the dwellings I surmised were built by John Quay from whom my father bought. These were a store house, an office, a two story smoke house and I believe a kitchen all built of large hewn logs. This store house was used by father and since my recollection by two Yankee brothers Lot and Saml. Seth Newall from Connecticut and afterward by John Jack Barnett from Georgia from Washington or near there. William West kept the store for Mr. Barnett who married his cousin Miss Jack (May) of whose children were Thos., Saml., Ann Eliza, Isabel, Sarah and Little ---- and Mary and perhaps others. In this store house my father for a while sold goods and as at the time every store kept spirits particularly W[est] I[ndies] Rum to accomodate customers. The store was attended to mostly by Uncle David Wardlaw and old Mr. Taggart afterwards our District Ordinary.

. . .My father had been elected by the Legislature Clerk of the District Court of Genl. Session and Common Pleas when the county courts were abolished and the district courts were established. His commission to the office was during good behavior. He went into office 1 Jany. 1800 and continued clerk till 1838 when he resigned his office 1st November, 1838. . . .

My father was very exact in all the duties of his office and particularly scrupulous in keeping his books and papers free from mistakes, blots, etc. . . . My father by a careful perusal of the laws passed by our legislature was informed on the statute law. I heard A. Burt, Esq. who was capable of judging say that father was better acquainted with the statute law of South Carolina than any other man he ever saw. . . .When John C. Calhoun was appointed Secretary of War for the U. S., he found the office in such confusion that it was with great difficulty that any paper ever of importance could be found when called for. He had studied law at Abbeville and known my father well and something of his office. After his appointment as Secretary of War, he came on a visit to S. C. and spent some days in looking into father's system. He was so well pleased with it that after his return to Washington he adopted it.

Genl. Andrew Pickens . . . lived at or very near to the Block House which stood on the branch only a few hundred yards below the R. R. Depot of the branch R. R. from Hodges to Abbeville. Saml. Watt (afterwards Squire), father of Mrs. R. A. Gilmer and grandfather of my wife. . . . then a young unmarried schoolmaster was boarding in Genl. Pickens family. This must have been sometime before the Revolutionary War (I cannot say when) for it was before he was married as above stated. He came from Ireland, landed in Charleston 8 Oct. 1768, married Janet daughter of John Lesley the date I cannot give but the third child Rosey Ann (afterwards wife of Andr. Bowie and then Robt. Gilmer) was born 15 Oct. 1780.

. . . This brings me back to the Block House. It was built on the east side of what is still called the Block house branch, by the Whigs of the surrounding country for protection in cases of incursions by the Indians or raids of the Tories. A number of anecdotes of events that occurred at or near were related to me in my younger days but the impressions made by them are so indistinct that I cannot pretend to repeat them except two. The Block house was occasionally at least garrisoned by a few Whigs. . . . When the Block House was built I have no means of ascertaining. It was strongly built of logs and pierced with loopholes from which the inmates could fire on an approaching enemy. . . . I will now give my early reminiscences of our Town of Abbeville. I will begin by mentioning the names of the most prominent inhabitants of the place who at my earliest recollection lived here with their families. In name first my father as with me he always stood first. Then Maj. Andrew Hamilton, Henry Livingston, father of Dr. John F. Livingston and Mrs. Jane L. Allen, Moses Taggart, afterward Ordinary of Abbeville District. James Kyle, who was father of Wm. Hunter Kyle, Mrs. David Lesley (Louisa), Jas. W. Kyle, my playmate in boyhood, Jane Kyle, Margaret, wife of Rev. Wm. McWhorter, Taliaferro usually called Toliver Livingston who preceded M. Taggart as Ordinary, Capt. Wm. Robertson, father of Dr.

Wardlaw Traditions

Frank M. Robertson of Charleston and his brother Peter R., the darkest white I think I ever saw. To that were after a time added Dr. Eli S. Davis, son in law of Maj. A. Hamilton. Thos. K. Talman, father of M. O. Talman, old John Finley and others.

Of the houses or rather residences now still standing there were only four or five that were built before my recollection. These are first my father's house in which I was born and lived with him for some twenty months after I was married 5 July 1830 and in which my son Andrew B. was born. . . .

Second, Mrs. Archer's house is also dear to me as in it I recited to Alpheus Baker my first lesson in Latin and in it I was married. . . .The third of these houses is formerly the residence of Gov. Patrick Noble now owned by J. Allen Smith, but now occupied by John Flynn. The fourth of these houses is the Presbyterian parsonage [torn down in 1885 to put up new manse].

. . . .[Of the houses no longer standing] *the first or oldest house as I was told was the one known in my early days as the old Red House which some of my sons will recollect as being the residence of the McLarens in which was for a long time the post office. This Red House stood not exactly on the corner but near it on the Public Square, on the site now occupied by the Brick Hotel and stores built by John Knox. I was informed that house was used as a tavern a part of time, at other times as a dwelling. I think I have heard that Maj. Hamilton* [lived there] *and afterwards his son William who married into the family of the Chiles, relative of your Uncle Thos. Chiles Perrin. Mrs. Wm. Hamilton was a woman of high character. She died here and was buried in Long Cane Cemetery. . . .The other occupants of the Red House some of whom I knew personally though I cannot name them in consecutive order were George Whitfield, Toliver Livingston, Capt. Wm. Robertson, and his brother Peter. . . .*

Maj. Hamilton was I think generally looked upon as the Patriarch of our place. . . . He lived just on the spot known since the Hampton Campaign of 1876 as Alston's Corner. Alston, Hamilton's son-in-law, built his residence further back on the lot. . . .[Of Hamilton's sons] *John either to improve his education or for some other cause went to England and spent some time in London, but it was money thrown away as he never attained any higher eminence than that of a common old field school master. . . . Wm. or as he was called Bill Hamilton was wild and dissolute. He went off to the Indian Nation and settled on the Etowa. . . . Archy I think went off in the same direction. The only one of Maj. Hamilton's sons who attained to respectable standing was Capt. Alexr. C. Hamilton who became Sheriff. . . . She*[Caroline Frances James Lesley] *was a daughter of James Lesley, I believe built the house lately occupied by Rev. J. L. Martin as the Presbyterian Manse who was killed in a duel by Boshell.*

Wardlaw Traditions

She married Van Ness of New York and settled in California. She visited her Uncle David Lesley and had with her a son Tom [and a Chinese servant]. . . .*Henry Livingston, father of Doctor John Livingston and Mrs. Jane L. Allen,* [lived] *in a Red house which stood on the spot now occupied by the store house of White Brothers . . . .The house was later moved back and used as a kitchen and a new frame house was built on the corner on the same site, but was much larger and was used as a hotel and boarding house after it came into the possession of Mr. John Allen. . . .* [who] *married Miss Jane (or as she was us usually called Jinsey) Livingston.*

. . . Mrs. Allen bought the lot which had been occupied for a long time by old John Finley and joined the house which John Finley had built on it to the one which had been his own residence, and it was then quite a capacious house.

. . . He [John Finley] *kept a small retail liquor shop and in order that he might legally sell by the drink he had to take out a tavern license and to give bond he had two spare beds and a supply of horse feed for the accomodation of his customers. Finley literally complied with the terms of the license so far as the two beds were concerned and kept some provender on hand which generally went to supply the needs of his cows. . . . on one occasion a traveler in some way stopped with Finley to stay all night and Finley being seldom troubled in that way exerted himself to show the man every possible attention. Mrs. Finley got him up a good supper, and in order to effect this supper was somewhat delayed. Finley proposed to his guest that as there was preaching in the Methodist church that night they should go. His invitation was accepted and they got to the church rather late as the sermon was then being preached. They got seated and Finley carrying out his kind attention rose and addressing the preacher said mister there is a stranger here who came too late to hear your text, please repeat it. This the minister did and went on with his sermon.*

.Next above Finley's lot was that of Mr. Jas. Kyle who came with his wife I think from Pennyslvania. He was a quick tempered man and kept a small store and a hotel in the same house which was occupied afterwards as a hotel by Saml. L. Watt, Wm. H. Kyle, David Douglass, B. L. Posey, and Phil Rutledge and in which B. L. Posey committed suicide. I recollect Mr. Kyle well, especially I remember his giving me a stone ware bottle which for some time I carried milk to school. . . .

Mr. Kyle was shot and killed by Peyton Randolph. It has been so long since this occurrence that I cannot tell the tale as I would like to do and may probably be mistaken in something. . . . I recollect that I was walking through the yard just about dark [when] *I distinctly heard the report of a gun on the public square, and as firing of guns especially at night was not so common as now, it made an impression on my mind. This was just about dark and no doubt the report of the gun which killed Kyle as was confirmed by the proof on the trial of Randolph for murder. I think it was before I got into the house upon the report of the gun I heard the rapid footsteps of some person as if running along the road passing by father's.*

From my recollection of the facts it appears that Randolph had been deer hunting and coming by the village went to Kyle's store which was a room in the front of the house, and R.[Randolph] having perhaps too much whiskey behaved so that a quarrel ensued and he was ordered out, perhaps put out. On going out he seized his loaded gun which in going in he had left outside; he fired though the open door at Kyle who was in the store, but outside the counter. It was a fatal shot, and I think Kyle's death immediately ensued.

A posse to purse the criminal was soon gathering in the house of a man named Pickens who lived where Robert Richey now lives. It was supposed to be the first point to where Randolph would go. Randolph lived at Pickens and was connected with the family or it was thought he was. In the meantime whilst the village party were getting ready to go in pursuit, Alex Bowie (the chancellor) went up to Mrs. Jack (his mother-in-law) and gathering a few men from the immediate neighborhood determined that they would also attempt to arrest R. This party also made Pickens' house the point upon which they directed their first movements. By arrangement one of them went to the door of the kitchen and discovered Randolph sitting before the fire with his gun lying across his lap.

Randolph discovering the state of things immediately rose and fled through the opposite door. He was pursued and the others being summoned by a pre-concerted signal or halloo soon repaired to the scene. Sam Jack or Wm. Lesley the pursurer (I don't remember which) in running came unexpectedly across a clothes line hanging in his way and caught a fall. However, they soon had R. arrested. I should say that this party had proceeded with as much caution and silence as possible, hence their success.

About the time that they had Randolph securely in their clutches, the village party was heard approaching at a considerable distance; so loud was their talk etc. that they would probably have given Randolph the alarm and sufficient notice for him to effect his escape. These facts about the arrest I learned from A. Bowie one of the successful party.

Randolph was put in jail that night. On his trial at the next session he was found guilty of manslaughter and was sentenced to be branded with the letter M on the ball of the left thumb. I was too young to know much about this but I suppose that by the sentence the execution was to be executed on a fixed day and hour before the expiration of the session of the court. This much I remember--At one door of the court house I saw old Jack belonging to Maj. John Chiles

Wardlaw Traditions

the sheriff with a pan of charcoal into which the branding iron was inserted, keeping the iron red hot by blowing the burning coals with a hand bellows, and soon after I saw the smoke of the hissing burning ascend from the hand of the prisoner which was tied to the prisoner's dock.

As soon as the sentence was executed and the prisoner discharged, he hurried to Dr. Jones' office then in a room of the old Red house. By arrangement previously made, the Doctor having everything ready, cut out the brand and burn and dressed the wound. This was the last I knew of Peyton Randolph until years afterwards I heard the story from my father. About 1832 (it was during the Nullification time) father and sister Caroline went to visit my sister Amanda Bonham living in Wilcox County, Alabama. Uncle David and some other friends who had moved from Abbeville living in that neighborhood. [James Wardlaw saw Randolph at a store there, and Randolph recognized him.]

. . . After Jas. Kyle, Saml. Watt was next in possession of the lot. He with his sister, Mrs. Kyle, kept the store for a while. He built the first part of the store house in which he did business first under the firm name of Watt & Grisham, afterwards Watt & Bowie (My wife's brother John). During his mercantile life he had Saml. W. Bowie (of this I am not certain) and Jas. S. Bowie as clerks in the store. I have heard your Uncle Jas. Bowie say that as clerk he had every morning to carry out some thirty pieces of pot ware and arrange it near the front door on the floor of the piazza and take them in at night. I don't recollect certainly whether this store house was or was not occupied by any one till it was in the hands of J. S. & L. Bowie, but am under the impression, in fact I know that Leander Bryan sold goods there a year or less. The store was conveyed by S. L. Watt to J. S. & L. Bowie and after additions and improvements by them to R. H. & W. A. Wardlaw. When Bro. W. A. Wardlaw went to Charleston in the cotton business, I continued to carry on the business of selling goods and took my son Jas. A. into co-partnership under the firm name R. H. Wardlaw & Son and continued until the store and goods were burnt 19 Jan., 1858. I sold the site to the Bank of State of S. C. The Bank now stands on the site of my old store. . . .

The upper boundary of the Kyle lot (to use the old name) included the post office built by H. W. Lawson. . . . Next above the Kyle lot was the Taggart lot, an old "rickety concern" consisting of a tavern, store house and etc. A piazza was in front of each of the buildings extending from H. Livingston's or Allen's to the upper end of Taggart's.

. . . The first wedding that I ever attended was that of Mr. Taggart's second daughter Polly to Thos. Perrin's son Rob't. Perrin who lived at Winter Seat just beyond Hard Labour Creek. This Thos. Perrin was a *cousin of Thos. C. Perrin. Just as Dr. Barr concluded the ceremony a loud report (the old swivel probably) was heard in the public square just in front of the house. It was timed I suppose by a signal given by some one watching through a window.*

. . .Whilst I was in cultivation of the field which comprehends the lot which Col. Marshall bo't from me and built his dwelling, Mr. Taggart had a yoke of likely oxen, but they had contracted the habit of throwing down fences and leading other cattle into any field they might choose. One morning on my way to the village, I went through the field and found that these oxen had thrown down my fence and followed by a number of cattle were playing sad havoc with my corn. I was the more provoked as they passed Maj. Alston's field afterwards owned by T. C. Perrin which had no fence worthy of the name and had thrown down my fence which was good.

. . .I will now speak of the public buildings of the place, and first of the Court House. I know of no other person, Elijah Wilson excepted, who can say as I now do, that I have seen five court houses. The first one was a wooden frame building standing a little higher up the public square than the subsequent ones. Of this house, I don't recollect much but a few things, but a few things are fixed in my memory. I recollect that during a summer there was a school kept by a school marm Maria Neddiman.

When another court house was built the material of this wooden house was bought by B. C. Yancey, Esq. and erected into a building on the Blue Hill. It afterwards passed through several hands and was at one time owned and occupied by my teacher, Alpheus Baker.

. . .Benjamin Yancey was a distinguished member of the Abbeville Bar and died at Orangeburg on his return from a visit to Charleston.

The second court house was built of brick and was upon the whole a pretty good court house. It would have lasted many years no doubt had the trustees whose superintendence of its construction not been cheated by the contractor. These trustees were men of the place not skilled in architectural knowledge and themselves drafted the plan. When the house had reached the second story windows, it became known to them that the workmen instead of using lime mortar according to contract was using kaolin of which there were several beds in the neighborhood and this substance so nearly resembled lime in appearance that the trustees had not detected the fraud played upon them. When they did, they had the wall pulled down, but unfortunately did not go low enough. For after it was built up again and stood for years, the walls bulged out because [they] were too weak to sustain the superstructure and threatened disaster. This rendered it necessary to build another.

The third court house was planned by Robt. Mills, an architect of skill and he was then living in Abbeville, he superintended its erection.

Wardlaw Traditions

C. Humphries was the contractor. It was built in 1829, perhaps not completed until the next year. It stood as near to the first brick court house as was convenient, a little further down the Square. This was the best built and handsomest court house and in my opinion the best that we have had with one exception that it was too small. It had however a great defect, in digging the foundation, one corner of it passed over where there had formerly been a gully and they did not go deep enough and it resulted in some years in that corner sinking so as to make a crack in the wall to an considerable height. When this court house was condemned by being unsafe on account of the crack, it was decided to build another. . . . After this another, the fourth court house was built which was the one burnt about 1872 in one of our disastrous fires and with it most of the books and public records in the Clerk's office. I am not sure as to the other offices in the building.

The fifth court house thus rendered necessary was erected I believe on the same foundation as the fourth and is still in use [1886]. Of these last two I cannot speak with satisfaction as to the details which have escaped my recollection, why I cannot say as I have resided here all the time. I know that neither of them displayed any architectural beauty and that the last serves its purpose pretty well.

Robert Mills, the architect of the third one above mentioned, came from Columbia to this place and taught with his wife's assistance a female academy in the building which stood on the spot now occupied by the Roman Catholic Church. About the time the third court house was built, he moved to Washington City [D.C.], and was employed in the erection of some of the public buildings in that city. He also increased his reputation in planning and carrying into successful execution the raising and placing the statute on top of the Washington Monument.

In these court houses a number of trials for capital crimes were conducted, and the result in a good many cases was a conviction followed in most of them by execution by hanging. I witnessed the execution of three or four of these criminals. The first of these was John O'Brien which took place in Novr., 1818, I think (it was the day after Mr. John Allen and Miss Jane L. Livingston were married). O'Brien was there for some crime I don't remember and Turner a mail boy for robbing the mail. On their escape from the penitentiary, they each stole a horse and fled to S. Ca., crossing the Savannah River at Barksdale's Ferry. A few miles on this side of the river they overtook a man seeming to be a traveler and falling behind they concerted to rob him. O'Brien was riding with heavy stirrups. He loosed the buckle of one of his stirrups, holding the strap in his hand and his foot in the stirrup to appear as attached to the saddle. They then rode up one on each side and O'Brien struck him on the head with the stirrup and killed him. They took him into the woods a short distance, rifled his *pockets, and found $2.50 cts. I think I can remember the small amount was less than $3.00.*

They then tried to escape. The body was soon found and suspicion being fixed on these two men, old Squire Josiah Patterson, a Justice in the neighborhood, soon had a warrant in the hands of William Truit, his active constable, who was soon in pursuit. He followed them to Orangeburg District and discovered they had separated, each taking his own road. The other was also soon overhauled. They were brought back and lodged in the Jail and it not being considered safe, a guard was placed in and around the Jail to insure their safe keeping. On his arraignment, O'Brien pleaded <u>Guilty</u>, and of course Turner had a separate trial. Truit by his energetic pursuit of the criminal got quite a reputation and became a man of respectability and influence and acquired property.

Geo. McDuffie was Turner's lawyer and his management and eloquence succeeded in acquitting him. When the crime was fresh there was great feeling and indignation in the community manifested against the criminals, and had Turner been tried at the same Court I think he would probably been also condemned. But McDuffie succeeded in continuing the case till the next term of Court and in the meantime the feeling of indignation had subsided for a youth supposed to be led into the crime by an old offender. One victim had already been sacrificed to justice. When the trial came on, McDuffie gave out to the full his powerful eloquence. I was in the crowd in the court house and heard at least a portion of his speech. It was grand. I remember a sentence or so, but any attempt to repeat or imitate him would be a failure. I heard that McDuffie himself said that on the preparation of the exordium and peroration he had spent a good part of the interval of six months that intervened between the courts. If it did not lay the foundation, it at least added very much to his fame. Turner settled in Edgefield Dist. and I saw Dr. S. W. Bowie wearing a coat which he said Turner had made for him as he (Turner) whilst in the penitentiary had worked at the tailor's trade.

O'Brien was an old offender and had according to his confession made frequent escapes from prison, if not in Ireland as to which I have forgotten, but certainly Canada and the United States. It was understood that he (O'Brien) intended to make a full confession as to his various crimes which it was supposed would be interesting. It is said that Dr. Moses Waddel came up from Willington to write out his confession and if so it would probably have been worth reading. But he found out that he had been anticipated by a printer named Davenport from Cambridge or 96 who had moved to this place and did some work as a job printer. Davenport wrote out his confession from his own mouth, but promised not to divulge it till after his execution. Davenport printed it in pamphlet form and as soon as the execution took place a young man (Gibson Wooldridge) who was present in the large crowd sold a large number at 25 cts. each as fast as he could hand them out. O'Brien was a fine specimen of the physical and was thought to be strong. It was said that he sneered at the idea that our jail could hold him. Perhaps nothing but the constant watchful guard secured his confinement. It was generally believed that there was a solemn promise or agreement between O'Brien and Mr. Taggart [the sheriff] and his son so that the Doctors should not get his body, and they succeeded concealing his grave so well that it was not discovered until a year or two after when the Academy was being built it was discovered by a negro. The grave was in the hollow just above the spring of the Academy now Mrs. Kitty Perrin's spring. The place of execution was up the same hollow near where Dr. Livingston's steam mill stood till burnt down. The Taggarts faithfully fulfilled their promise by watching and subterfuges to induce the belief that the body had been conveyed to some distant and secret place.

. . .This execution of O'Brien I voluntarily witnessed, but that sufficed me for sights of that kind. However, not with my own consent I had to attend three others. These were Foster for stealing Negroes, Cornelius Matthews for horse stealing and Kindred Kitchens for murder and it occurred thus.

Foster stole some negroes, was pursued and overtaken at a camp where they had stopped for the night. Attempting to run, he was fired on with a gun, his arm broken, and he was captured, brought back, tried, condemned and sentenced to be hanged according to law as it then stood. When the day of execution arrived, I had no intention of going, but Bro. Jos. was anxious to go. To this my father would not consent unless I would go to take care of him.. At Joseph's earnest request, I took him up behind me on horseback. At that day there was no such thing as a scaffold fixed with a drop, but the custom was to haul the prisoner to the gallows in a cart, and his hands being pinioned, the noose adjusted around his neck, and the cap pulled over his face, the horse was then led or driven forward, and the culprit was by the rope connecting the noose around his neck to the gallows being securely fastened thereto was literally dragged out of the cart and swung off into eternity.

On this occasion by some unfortunate accident, the noose became unadjusted and slipped so as not even to produce immediate suffocation, and I myself heard Foster swinging utter an exclamation. To remedy this mishap, Captain Hamilton then sheriff had the body held up till he adjusted the noose. Just then, I had leaned my face down on my horse's neck to shut out the dreadful sight. Some person speaking to me said that the boy behind me was about to faint.

While I was Deputy Clerk, I got from the mail a packet containing

Wardlaw Traditions

a bail writ for debt sent by a member of the Laurens Bar for the Clerk to sign and enter and at once to deliver to the Sheriff for his service (at the suit of Limoi Madden vs. Cornelius Matthews) as soon as it was entered in the Sheriff's office, the deputy summoned me as a posse to assist in the arrest of the defendant. Finding out he was at the Billiard Room, we went there and arrested him. Matthews not being able to give bail as he was a stranger here, having come here from Laurens only a few days before, was lodged in Jail. By outside assistance, he escaped from Jail and on the same night stole a horse from Col. Patrick Noble and a saddle from Col. Eldred Simkins of Edgefield who was stopping with Col., afterwards Govr. Noble.

The next day Saml. Branch was sent in pursuit of him and without any difficulty was able to follow his path as he was notable both by the horse and his garb as he had on a calico hunting shirt of such glaring colours as would probably attract the attention of almost every one whom he passed. Branch overtook him somewhere in Georgia, and having secured him with handcuffs, he brought him back. On the way he lodged him one night in the jail at Augusta, Ga. and the next at Edgefield, S. C. When our Court came on, Col. Noble was very unwilling to have a man hung for stealing his horse and would gladly have him let off for horse stealing and punished for the saddle, but he had no control of the matter. Matthews was tried for horse stealing, convicted and sentenced to be hanged. I was a member of the volunteer company which was detailed to guard over Matthews to the gallows. . . . [Wardlaw was present in 1836 at the hanging of Kindred Kitchens, but he provided little detail. For a much more detailed story, see the account elsewhere by the Ex-Abbevillian.]

. . . On the lot once owned by Govr. Noble now by J. Allen Smith, at my earliest recollection there stood a stable built by heavy hewed oak logs, the floor and ceiling made of the same sort of logs. This was, as I was told, the first jail in the place that I ever heard of and had been no doubt removed from its original site to the spot which it then occupied. It was then only one story and had four rooms and I think [was] *a safe prison if the openings were well secured. I remember seeing a horse's head poked out of the small square window which no doubt had been secured by crossed iron bars. I have no recollection of knowing how long it was used as a jail.*

For the next one was built before I can recollect. This was a three story brick building with four rooms on each floor, the lowest or first floor intended for the Sheriff's use, the second was the debtors' room, so called, and the third contained the prisoner's cells. For greater security two of these rooms or cells were lined with iron bars crossed at short distances apart and riveted together forming small squares covered or concealed by the plastering. A number of escapes of

Wardlaw Traditions

prisoners occurred, and I remember it became necessary to repair and make it more secure. New window sills brought from Augusta of sandstone just such as composed the back stairs to the house occupied by Dr. W. C. Wardlaw. A gully threatened such encroachments on the back of the foundation so that a stone wall had to be built to protect it. This jail was used for a good number of years. It was situated on or near the spot now occupied by the range of law offices in the rear of the present court house. It was thought better to remove the jail from the public square. A new one was built superseding this and is the one still standing and in use [later the Abbeville museum].

At the early days of our village, there were three magazines for powder in the State, as I was informed, one in Charleston, one I think, in Camden, and this one in Abbeville for the use of the western part of the State. This last one was a brick building with a smaller one enclosed within it if my memory is right. How much powder was kept in it I do not know. It was only issued under the Governor's orders, and the only use that I heard of was militia service in firing artillery salutes, etc. Maj. Hamilton was magazine keeper for many years and had to go in occasionally to turn over the kegs in order to keep the ingredients of the powder from settling to one part of the keg. I recollect that the old man was very particular not to permit any one to enter upon the brick floor who had tacks in his shoes for fear he might strike fire and produce an explosion. A small salary probably about $100 a year [was paid] *to the magazine keeper. Hamilton was succeeded in office by Wm. Hunter Kyle, but I am not sure whether the change took place before the removal of the Magazine from the public square. This building stood just across the street leading by Mrs. White's to the public square and opposite the stores of White Brothers.*

The village grown up around it, the danger of letting it remain in the heart of the place was thought to be so great that the Legislature on a proper showing made an appropriation to have it removed and bought a lot since and now called Magazine Hill with the street leading from it to Main Street, and there erected another building for the same purpose with an arched building inside. When the contractor reported the job finished, the trustees here had some officer or architect from Columbia to come and examine the building before they would receive it. Those commissioners and the architect went to examine it when he observed that there was a piece of scantling looking as though accidentally left there reaching from the arch of the inner house to the wall of the outer house. He ordered this to be taken away, which was done, and it was soon manifest that upon this scantling the arch rested for support, and they barely made their escape when it tumbled down.

Of course the job had to be done over. There being no other

Wardlaw Traditions

public land about the place, and this Magazine lot belonging to the State, it was used as a place of execution and two men were hanged there, one white man named Bell for an infamous crime and Cornelius Matthews for horse stealing as before mentioned. Some time after the rumor got started that the Negroes were trying to get into the Magazine to get powder, and it had at least this foundation that it was evident that some brick had been removed from the back end of the house as though to make an entrance.

Of course this produced some excitement, and as a matter of prudence it was determined that the young men should in turn keep a secret watch about the Magazine and certain roads at night. During this excitement it was the lot of Lewis Taggart and myself to watch the Magazine. We took a faithful pointer dog with us to watch the Magazine and had such confidence in Banco's watchfulness and that he would give us a whine as notice of the approach of anyone that we wrapped our cloaks around us and lay down in the broom straw with our dog at our feet. When daylight came, we found that we had been sleeping just on the grave where Matthews had been buried. The Negroes had their excitement too before this. A white squirrel had been seen in the woods very near the same place which their superstitious belief declared to be Matthews' ghost.

In hunting, Jeff Douglas, then a resident of the village, shot and killed this squirrel and brought it to the village and as it was very unusual to see a perfectly white squirrel it was looked on as a great curiosity. The ammunition in this magazine was moved to some other magazine and afterwards the lot was sold. I am not sure who was the purchaser at the sale ordered by the State authority, but I know that Dr. J. W. W. Marshall had built a good residence near Smithville which he took down, hauled the timber, etc., and it is erected on this lot. The residence was burnt down some years since. The outbuildings were not consumed in the conflagration, and one of them was fitted up and repaired and used by Dr. Marshall and family as a dwelling till the beginning of the year 1886. Magazine Street is still a public street built up with residences.

The only other of these old public buildings that occurs to my mind as worthy of mention was the Arsenal for the storage of arms belonging to the State. This was a frame building about 30 feet square and had only one high room, the side ceiling or walls of which had a great many pegs or wooden pins in it one inch to suspend muskets, etc. besides such as were enclosed in boxes from time to time received. It was I presume built about the same time as the Magazine and was placed in charge of the Magazine keeper. On removal of the contents, it was sold and purchased I think by Timothy D. Williams who remodeled it by giving it two floors having inserted joists into the walls and used it for some years as a body shop. The site was on the

Wardlaw Traditions

lot afterwards owned and occupied by Charles Dendy and was a little farther back from the street than the rear end of the brick building on the corner of the public square which was erected by Dendy.

Near to this Arsenal the gentlemen of the village erected what was called a Ball alley on which to play the game called Fives. The alley was made by erecting perpendicular poles of considerable height one side of which was made straight by turning in, to these poles plank were nailed with their edges touching so as to present an even and smooth surface. The game was played by an indefinite number equal on each side and consisted of striking with the hand an elastic ball against the alley from which it rebounded and in like manner alternately returned until one side missed by which the opposing side made one in the score. When good players were engaged in the contest they kept the ball up for some time. It was an athletic and exciting game and was very popular. The yard occupied all the space between the alley and the street and was in constant use every afternoon.

Being a boy I did not engage in the game when the men were playing, but we boys frequently set up a game on our own hook. There were quite a number of these ball alleys through the District, one at nearly every store. On public days it was not unusual that our ground was occupied by men from the country most of the day. Fives was a good game, but like all such games it had its day. I have not known of a game for many years. I don't recall any betting on it, but suppose that such as are called sporting men did bet.

III. ABBEVILLE AND ITS TWO MOST FAMOUS MEN

1. General Andrew Pickens' Block House

When Dr. John H. Logan published his *A Hisltory of the Upper Country of South Carolina* in 1859, he designated it as "Volume I" which indicated his plan to write an additional volume. He was a native of Abbeville District, and in 1856 while he was editing the Abbeville *Banner*, he collected a number of manuscripts dealing with local history which dealt with Andrew Pickens and the Block House during the American Revolution. He was unable to complete a second volume, but some of these materials were published later in the "Logan Manuscript" in *Historical Collections of the Habersham Chaper, D. A. R.*, III. Among those which dealt with Pickens were two letters written by Pickens' grandson, F. W. Pickens, later the Governor of South Carolina during the Civil War, as follows:

"Logan Manuscript," pp. 94-95. F. W. Pickens to Chas. H. Allen, 26th March, 1848.

My grandfather [Andrew Pickens] *... in 1765 moved and settled at the place where the Block House is standing near Abbeville C. H. He built the Block House about 1768--perhaps 1767--and made it a resort for the neighbors to fly to in order to protect themselves from the Indians, he always taking the command. He owned all the lands about the place where the present village stands, and I think sold to Maj. Hamilton who was also a gallant soldier of the Revolution.*

Maj. Alston [Hamilton's son-in-law] *must have the papers and the deeds, which will show when he* [Andrew Pickens] *sold, and left for Hopewell in Pendleton* [District]. *But my notes indicate he left Abbeville in the year 1787. . . .*

When he built the block house the neighborhood was a great resort for Indians who brought their ginseng, pink root, deer and bear skins and beaver, in large quantities; and he owned afterwards a warehouse opposite Augusta, near where the bridge now rests in Hamburg, to which place he sent all these things obtained from the Indians. He also sent droves of beef cattle to Philadelphia from both Abbeville and from Pendleton afterwards.

During the war [American Revolution] *his house near the Block House was burned down by the Tories, and his family lived for weeks in the woods near Abbeville, fed by their own Negroes secretly.*

F. W. Pickens in a letter to J. H. Marshall, 4th Nov., 1847 gave additional details about one of those slaves. From "Logan Manuscript," pp. 101-104.

... his [Andrew Pickens] *body servant, Old Dick... was a faithful African, and had followed him through the Indian wars as well as the*

Andrew Pickens

British, and actually fought by his side; and my father told me that Gen. Pickens, his father, often said Old Dick was as brave a man as ever faced battle.....He was with Gen. Pickens through the war. When the Tories burnt Gen. Pickens' house, near the Block House, (at a time when he was off in the army) and drove the family to seek shelter and protection in the woods, for days, Dick and other servants furnished them with supplies, and nursed them, some of the children actually having small-pox, and one of the sons died with it.

Gen. Pickens always allowed Dick to the day of his death every privilege. He ever wore a long knife in a leather sheath, and belt by his side; and not even Gen. Pickens' sons were permitted to rebuke or cross Dick, and he said what he pleased. Gen. Pickens was the only man Dick always treated with profound deference.

The "Logan Manuscript," p. 108 related another anecdote about Pickens in Abbeville during the Revolution in a tradition told by Andrew Shillito, a descendant of the White family:

Gen. Pickens' old neighbor who he kicked a little was one of King George's most loyal subjects, and he made it his especial business, so soon as he heard of any victory the British had gained, or any advantage the British or Tories had got of the rebels, as he called the Whigs, he could not be easy until he had told his news at Gen. Pickens' and John White's. What news he had to tell the day of the kicking I do not remember; but the General happened to be at home, and as soon as the old fellow got through with his good news, he began to boast of his King, of the discipline and bravery of his army, and said that King George had never been conquered--that it was in vain for the rebels to contend with him, for they would "be kilt." The general could not listen to him any longer; he rose up, took the old fellow by the hand, led him to the gate, and kicked him down the hill to the block house branch, some hundred and thirty or forty yards.

Andrew Shillito also related a tradition which dealt with a more tragic incident, "Logan's Manuscript," pp. 76-78.

After the surrender of Charleston, the people, however, being still in the old Pickens Block House for fear of the Indians, they fell short of corn, when the following men were sent with wagons to Coroneaco [sic] Creek,[now Coronaca in Greenwood County] famous for its corn, to get a supply--Hugh Porter (father of Alexander Porter, once a pastor of Cedar Spring Church, now in Ohio), Jared Liddle, Enos Crawford, Andrew White, Matthew Thomson, James Beard, and one Smith--the last three lads--Finley, and one of the brothers of Andrew Pickens, (The names of his brothers were John and Joseph)--and

John C. Calhoun

yet others, names not recollected. They had crossed McCord's Creek early in the morning (and were to have been followed from the fort by a guard detailed for that purpose, commanded by one Anderson, who afterwards moved to Anderson District, and became a Colonel of militia, when his cowardice on this occasion showed him unworthy of any command), and when ascending the hill leading up to where West Croman [Cromer] *now* [in 1857] *lives, they were attacked by a party of Tories under one John Crawford.*

They shot three of the Americans on the spot--Enos Crawford, Hugh Porter, and one of Pickens' brothers. It may have been that Pickens was killed by the Indians after they reached the Nation, which gave rise to the report that one of them was burnt. They took the rest of the party prisoners, and carried them North across the Saluda-- for James Beard said afterwards, that if the guard under Anderson had pursued them the prisoners could have been retaken when crossing that river.

Andrews Rapley, an English born lawyer whose large plantation was located at a place which he called "Cornacre," later filed a claim with the South Carolina Legislature that in 1781, he had supplied *44 bushels of Indian corn for the use of men on duty at Genl. Pickens' Block House.* He also filed a claim for *28 indigo plank (half wore) for the public service in erecting a Block House at General Pickens's Plantation.* Both of these claims were attested by Lt. Matthew Finley. Finley himself filed claims *for service as officer of a guard kept at General Pickens' Block house by order of Capt. Robert Anderson from the 13th of Oct., 1781 until July 18, 1783...* [and he received] *30 pounds* [English money] *for carpenter work done at General Pickens' Block House.*

2. John C. Calhoun as a Young Lawyer in Abbeville, 1807-1808

The most famous American who once resided in Abbeville was John C. Calhoun who was born less than a dozen miles from the village and began his law practice there. Later he served in the U. S. Congress, as Secretary of War under President Monroe, as Vice President, and as Secretary of State under President Tyler, but he earned the greatest acclaim as a U. S. Senator. He has been ranked as one of the six greatest Senators in American history.

W. Pinckney Starke in his "Account of Calhoun's Early Life" in the 1899 American Historical Association's *Annual Report* wrote (p. 85) *He* [Calhoun] *left Charleston about the 1st of June, 1807, and returned to Abbeville village, where he expected to establish himself as a lawyer....Immediately after the attack on the Chesapeake, June 22, 1807, the farmers of Abbeville district called a public meeting...*

John C. Calhoun

[at which] *the committee of arrangements selected him to draw up and present the resolutions to the citizens of Abbeville. . . .*

For the first time in his life he rose to his feet before his assembled countrymen. Standing 1 or 2 inches above 6 feet, the gaunt, erect, young man, then in the 26th year of his age, presented that marked visage known to many in the audience, and for the first time flashed upon them the intense light from those dark brown eyes. No report has reached us of this important speech except through tradition.

That it was effective we know from the results which followed. The people of Abbeville district had long entertained an objection to being represented in the legislature by lawyers. For many years no one of that profession had ventured to offer himself as a candidate for political honors. Now, however, with general acclaim, the people of his native district called for John Caldwell Calhoun and elected him to the legislature at the head of the ticket.

Another incident relating to Calhoun's life in Abbeville was told by Alexander Bowie and was included by John Belton O'Neall in his *Bench and Bar in South Carolina*, II, 391-92, as follows:

While Mr. Calhoun was a practicing lawyer at Abbeville, there were a number of young men, students of law, in the offices of Calhoun & Noble, B. C. Yancey and George Bowie, viz.: Nathaniel Alcock Ware and Robert Cunningham in the first, Charles Yancey and Tyler Whitfield in the second, and the late Chief Justice Lipscombe of Alabama and myself in the last. In the summer evenings we were accustomed to assemble in Mr. Calhoun's piazza for conversation, Mr. Calhoun and Mr. Yancey leading the conversation, of course. To the young men, these were rare occasions for improvement. The street in front of us presented an inviting spot for a foot race, being smooth and level.

On a certain evening (I don't know from whom the suggestion came), it was agreed that we should pair off, and have a succession of foot-races. All were then for the sport. Yancey was pitted against Calhoun, Ware against Noble, Lipscombe against Whitfield, and Charles Yancey against myself.

None of us doubted that Mr. Yancey, being more accustomed to athletic exercises than Mr. Calhoun, would distance him in the race. To our surprise, it resulted differently; Mr. Calhoun came out ahead. I do not remember how the race resulted between Whitfield and Lipscombe; but I well remember that I was beaten by Charles Yancey. The most amusing contest of the evening was that between Ware and Noble. Both were exceedingly clumsy; each did his very best; there was much grunting and puffing. Their progress was so slow that there was a general burst of laughter when they came out an <u>incontestible tie.</u>

IV. GRANDFATHER'S STORIES OF ABBEVILLE IN 1825

(*Press & Banner*, July 10, 1889, written by either Addison F. Posey or Dr. Isaac Branch)

The present location of Abbeville was selected for two reasons: first to be near a big spring, a great consideration in those days, second, because Major Hamilton owned most of the land here. The county commissioners first selected a site three miles from the present location, at the Holy Rock, which is said to be the center of the county, and would have been a more desirable site than the present one.

The first court house was a wooden building and stood a little above the present one. In 1825, it was pulled down and moved over to the Blue Hill and occupied by Alpheus Baker. The second court house was built of brick two stories high. The Clerk's and Sheriff's offices were in front; the doors in the main building opened on the north and south sides. During court an officer was stationed at each door. The jury rooms were upstairs, with a stair case leading from the Judge's stand up to those rooms. The contractor who built the house used, instead of lime for mortar, kaolin which he found near Mr. W. H. Parker's, it did not last long and had to be taken down. In 1828, the third court house was built, which many of our citizens remember. It [The fourth was built in 1854.] was burnt in the big fire of 1872.

In 1825, Major Hamilton, the father of Mrs. James Alston, lived in a small house near where the new hotel now stands. Mr. James Wardlaw, father of Judge Wardlaw, built and lived in the house in which Mr. Thomas Thomson now lives. Moses Taggart, grandfather of Col. M. O. Talman, kept a hotel on the site where Messrs. Visanska and Cannon's stores now are. For many years he acted as Ordinary for Abbeville County. Mr. Kyle, father of Mrs. David Lesley, kept the hotel which extended to the bank building from Mr. Taggart's lot. Where the bank now stands was a store kept by Watt and Bowie, and for many years after by Mr. Robert Wardlaw; next to that John Finley had a dwelling and store; John Allen kept a hotel on the corner; Dr. Wetherel lived in the house now owned by Mrs. Lucy White; Isaac and Samuel Branch's shop where White Brothers' new store stands; Mr. Chalmers' lot was owned by Thomas C. Owens; Jim and John Shillito occupied a shoe shop on Mr. Hammond's lots; Eli S. Davis, father of the blind minister [see page 198], built Mr. Noble's house. For many years he was a member of the legislature. At that time there were no other houses on this side of the street.

Thos. Dendy lived near Dendy's Corner. The Arsenal was near where Col. H. T. Wardlaw's law office is. In it guns, swords, pistols, and flags were kept. The powder was kept in a small brick building

Grandfather's Stories

on the spot where Dr. J. W. Marshall's house now stands; it was called the Magazine, from which the hill derives its name. The office now used by Col. H. T. Wardlaw was built and occupied by Judge Wardlaw and Gov. Noble. Law Range, where the office of Parker, McGowan, and others now stands, was the first jail lot. A brick office where Mr. Russel's [Russell] store now stands, was used by John McCraven, a lawyer; next door to this was a store built by William Pinchback, over the store was the bar room of the town; next to this, where the wooden part of the Knox building is, was a home called the "Red House." One room in the building was John C. Calhoun's first law office. The McClarens, a Scotch family, lived in this building and kept the post office for many years. On Washington Street, Sossimon kept a silversmith shop.

Circus and shows always exhibited on the lot where Mr. Russell's livery stable now stands. **The Whig**, the first paper ever published in Abbeville, was printed on the lower floor of a small wooden building on the corner lot. The **Press & Banner** is now printed on the second story of the same spot, the first **Banner**'s office was a small wooden building in the rear of Mr. Allen's Hotel, opposite Mrs. Lucy White's; Henry Allen publisher, Henry Knox printer. On the Episcopal church lot was a gin house owned by Mr. Moses Taggart. There was small log store in front of Mr. Thomson's.

All the houses built at this time were of hewn logs. The house now owned by Mr. Brooks was built by Mr. Moses Taggart, for many years owned by B. Y. Martin and Capt. James Perrin. Mr. L. W. White's house was built by Dr. Arnold. The carved mantels was looked upon as a wonderful piece of work. He sold it to Judge Wardlaw and bought the log school house on Mrs. K. C. Perrin's lot. He added to this, then sold to Dr. Livingston who improved the building very much. The house was burned a year ago. Between the present houses of Messrs. Quarles and Allen Smith was Mr. Alexander Bowie's law office (He moved to Talladega, Ala.). This office was afterwards occupied by Samuel Townes, lawyer and first editor of the **Whig**. William Lomax, father of Mr. James Lomax, built and lived in the first house on Mr. Quarles' lot. Patrick Noble, Esq. lived in the house now owned by Mr. Allen Smith. He was afterward Governor of the State. The first house on the Presbyterian lot was built by Mr. Wm. Yancey, afterwards owned by Mr. Bowie and Dr. Joe Wardlaw.

The first academy was built on the lot now owned by Mrs. K. C. Perrin, in which Mr. Alpheus Baker taught, assisted by Mr. Doggett, an Irishman; flogging was the order of the day. Mr. Baker was a classmate of Daniel Webster, he was famous as a good Latin and Greek scholar. The first church built in Abbeville was by the Methodist denomination, about opposite Mrs. Miller's Hotel.

V. REMINISCENCES OF AN EX-ABBEVILLIAN, ADDISON F. POSEY: No. 1, Abbeville Forty Years Ago (1876)

Abbeville Medium, April 12, 1876

On the 2d of February, 1834, I became a citizen of Abbeville C. H. I was then a boy thirteen years old and was carried there by my father, who removed from another locality. My recollection of Abbeville as she then appeared are among the most vivid of my youth. I have been absent [he moved to Greenville, Alabama in 1851] a full quarter of a century. . . . Abbeville town in 1834 contained about three hundred whites. The court house, a respectable brick building" built in 1829" so labeled, stood on the east side of the center of the square; the three story brick jail stood east of the court house about sixty feet, and on a line with the edge of the square.

Around the square were the following buildings, commencing at the northwest corner and running south: Taggart's Hotel, Kyle's Hotel and Allen's Hotel, all wooden buildings. The former was purchased by B. L. Posey, who subsequently bought out Kyle and kept both as a hotel during his life. Attached to the Kyle house on the south was a one story building owned and operated by J. S. and L. Bowie, merchants, who subsequently enlarged it and sold out about 1840 to Messrs. R. H. and W. A. Wardlaw. Next below with the intervention of an alley stood a two story unoccupied building, and next was Allen's Hotel, the best of the block. Mr. Allen subsequently purchased the house and lot adjoining and by an addition united them for the accomodation of his guests. Mr. John White occupied the corner of Allen's Hotel as his storehouse and lived in a cottage on the same spot afterwards covered by his residence. He also moved a log shanty on the corner of the square and replaced it by the storehouse so long afterwards, and, perhaps yet, occupied by him.

Going down the street [South Main] the next was a residence occupied by John Finley, with a front shop occupied by Elford Owen, silversmith; next a vacant house afterwards owned and occupied by Dr. Thos. B. Dendy; next the residence of Dr. Eli S. Davis, subsequently owned by Messrs. Burt, Cunningham and Noble; next was the residence of Mrs. Shillito; next Thos. Jackson and Jas. Shillito ended the row. Then crossing the street and going back; first was the residence of Dr. Franklin Branch, then the brick residence of Samuel Branch, then the residence of Jas. S. Wilson, then Gen. John Bowie, then Dr. Isaac Branch, then Thos. P. Spierin's residence and law office, and next on the corner of the street and square, Charles Dendy.

Then turning to the right stood the Arsenal well supplied with

Abbeville in 1834

muskets on the southeast corner of the square. Then at a right angle stood the law offices of Wardlaw & Perrin, Patrick Noble, Esq. (brick office), and John A. Calhoun, next to the jail. A vacant space was subsequently filled with Thos. Jackson's carriage shop. Above the jail was Jas. S. Wilson's brick storehouse, and next door was a one story brick office bearing on the door "J. McCraven, Attorney at Law," who had just died and it was closed for a long time--was subsequently occupied as a tailor's shop and afterwards owned and occupied by John Cunningham and Edward Noble, Esqs., as a law office; next was a long two story building occupied, I think, by McMorries, merchant; next was the McLaren residence in which was a tailor's shop and the post office, kept by Uncles "Sawney" and Robin, and on the corner of the square nearby and belonging to the same, was a one story building occupied by Robert Cochran, who dealt out "sperits by the small."

Turning down the street leading east [Washington], *the next building was the Methodist church, a one story affair, not ceiled overhead, about 30 x 20 with a multiplicity of windows, innocent of a glass or the attempt to it. . . . Another building further on, and the end of the row, was logs, who owned it I never knew and cannot remember an occupant except Hut Douglass when he was town marshal. Crossing the street was a harness shop owned by one Hendricks, who left soon after to return, not in consequence of "something consarning leather." Next was the shoe and harness shop of the revered and honored Rev. James Moore, and in the rear was his residence; then followed along a vacant lot until you reached the square on the right of which afterwards stood the Marshall House. There stood there then the most uncomely one story building in America. It was labelled "Whig Office," and closed were its doors. The true rendering was that in that building had been published The* **Abbeville Whig or Southern Nullifier,** *defunct institution.*

Turning up the street [North Main] *stood a medium sized house occupied by McMorries as a private residence. It had been used as a hotel, and had a one story dining room about sixty feet long. . . . The proprietor of the Marshall House of necessity ended this establishment. Next above was the residence of Jas. S. Bowie, subsequently and perhaps now of Thos. Thomson, Esq.; then above the female academy, then a vacant lot and next, the elegant residence of David L. Wardlaw, Esq., afterwards Judge. Far off in the distance could be seen the residence of Wm. C. Black, Esq., afterwards owned and occupied by Dr. J. F. Livingston.*

Crossing the street [Main] *the first house on that side was the residence occupied by, I think, Langdon Bowie, the same afterwards owned and occupied by Dr. J. J. Wardlaw; to the right in the oak grove stood the residence occupied by Moses Taggart, afterwards B.*

Abbeville in 1834

Y. Martin and *Col. J. M. Perrin.* Then going towards the square, next came the residence of *Patrick Noble, Esq.*--afterwards Governor-- subsequently owned by *John Cunningham* and *H. A. Jones, Esqrs.*; next was the residence of *John A. Calhoun, Esq.*, and on the square next stood a hip roof building owned and occupied by Major *James Alston,* who on the erection of his finer building about 1840 removed the old one and the spot then covered was a part of the flower garden. I have now gone around the public square and streets as I remember them in 1834, and a few additions will complete the **residential** situation.

Old Mr. *James Wardlaw* lived in the grove on the street leading to Georgia, and which is no doubt now occupied by some of his descendants. Col. *T. C. Perrin* lived over the branch on the Warrenton road and *Robt. H. Wardlaw* lived in the grove opposite. Major *Burt* and lady boarded at Allen's Hotel, and he occupied an office in *John White's* lot.

The public officers were *James Wardlaw,* Clerk of Court, and *Moses Taggart,* Ordinary. . . . *Wm. C. Black* was Commissioner in Equity, and *Robert Gilmer,* Sheriff. The latter died in the Spring of 1834, and *John Taggart* was appointed his successor, and subsequently elected.

The lawyers at the bar were *Wardlaw & Perrin, Patrick Noble, Armistead Burt, John A. Calhoun, Wm. Lomax* and *Thomas P. Spierin.* Messrs. *Perrin & Perrin* alone survive. The merchants were Messrs. *J. S.* and *L. Bowie, John White, Jas. S. Wilson,* and *M. McMorries,* all dead except Mr. *White* and *McMorries*--the latter living a year ago in Galveston, Texas. The practicing physicians were Drs. *Frank Branch, Isaac Branch* and *Lewis Taggart.* . . . Dr. *Eli S. Davis* had a fine repute in medicine, but when I knew him he only acted for special friends. He had turned his attention to Federal politics and had connections with the White House that beat any doctor's fees. He removed his family to West Tennessee, and the last seen of him was about 1835 when he passed through with $40,000 of Gen. Jackson's money to invest in Western lands.

Who were the "bucks" and "belles" of 1834? I am not the best witness, but am inclined to think Abbeville was scarce of them both. I remember Miss *Eleanor Cottrell,* afterwards Mrs. Dr. *Taggart,* and Miss *Susan McLaren,* afterwards Mrs. *McBryde,* both of whom are dead. I could name some others that may be living and widows, and in the hope they are, I have respect of their holy horror of facts and figures indicating ages. I can spot the "bucks" and "belles" from 1840 to 1850, every one of them, knew every man that courted a woman and every woman that disposed of a man and how she did it. Democracy [the Democratic party] reigned supreme, there was no politics to discuss; there were no literary societies to engage the men's

Whiskey War of 1843

attention, and personal affairs and gossips were all we had to talk about. If therefore many people knew more of other people's business than they did of their own, it was unavoidable and reasonable under the circumstances.

No. 2, The Great Whiskey War of 1843

In 1858, Judge John Belton O'Neall wrote a temperance group the following observation about Abbeville: *I regret to say that I saw more evidence of drinking to excess in Abbeville than at any other place on my circuit. I confess that I grieved more for such excess . . . for this town is very near to old Long Cane Presbyterian church, where some of the most honored men worshipped, and where the Rev. Mr. Barr long spread before them the words of soberness and truth. The descendants of the Pickens, Calhouns, Nobles, and Wardlaws are in this town; and to them, how revolting must be such scenes as were seen the first week in October.*

In the **Press & Banner,** April 26, 1876, Addison F. Posey described a confrontation which the temperance forces had with the "wets" fifteen years earlier in Abbeville in *the great Whiskey War of 1843. . .*[when] *in the spring of that year, the dealing in liquor by the small, and almost all of it, had retreated from the public square, and had fallen into the hands of "the great Sanhedrim"* [a nickname which Posey commonly used for Silas Anderson, the bar keeper of Washington Street]*and another of like mental and moral calibre, in another alley.*

They had been selling under licenses granted upon simple application, corn and fodder was missing, chickens would disappear, and the Negroes were drunk all the time, and the town was twice within an ace of being burned down by accident of drunken white men. There was a public alarm, which resulted at an attempt at self-defense through the law. Two tickets were run for the town council-- the "wet" and the "dry." The wet ticket meant that any man should sell whiskey who paid for the privilege; and the dry ticket meant that nobody should have a license to retail if it could be avoided. I do not remember who ran on the wet ticket, but the dry, which carried by a considerable majority, was Dr. J. F. Livingston, Intendant, Isaac Branch, Addison F. Posey, Joseph A. Hamilton, and David Lesley.

On the expiration of the licenses to retail, the council refused to grant them to anybody on any terms. The next public day found Abbeville Court House without anything to drink, and the "boys" from the country, with a due proportion in town, were not prepared for so great a dry period and were terribly excited and put to it. But a sail [whiskey wagon] *from Pickens hove into sight, and being hailed, answered that she had thirty gallons at forty cents per gallon, and*

Whiskey War of 1843

which soon found a ready cash customer. A company of cavalry was organized, 29 in number. . . .

The barrel was placed in the centre of the public square, the head knocked out of it, and a blue bucket and tin cup procured. The company drank at half mount, then at a signal mounted and rode up to Judge Wardlaw's, and went down in a trot in platoons to James Shillito's, and returning in single file at a gallop each leaped the barrel, and on to Judge Wardlaw's again. Returning "at will," they formed a hollow circle around the barrel and drank again; then remounting, the same revolutions were gone through until late in the afternoon, about six drinks each being distributed.

During the above described scenes, the "wet" men in town were very often exultant, and often approached the councilmen, to be seen standing, in doors and doctor shops, and tapping them on the shoulder, remarked, "Didn't we tell you so, that you couldn't stop free men from exercising their inalienable rights?" But the council stood firm like knights with visors down and arms at rest.

The "Sanhedrim" came to them at once with a peremptory demand for a license, which they answered by a peremptory refusal. The "Sanhedrim" sold anyway, and for eight days the council indicted him every day. At the end of ten days, however, he came at them with a lawyer in front of him, proving a sign of "entertainment for man and beast," including drinkables; that the ex-church had been subdivided into three apartments [this was the first Methodist church on Washington Street] ; to wit, one for the drinking saloon, one for the host, and one for the traveler; also that he had stalls for two or more horses. He bore also satisfactory bond and the written recommendation of four freeholders that "the Sanhedrim" was trust worthy, in the required particulars.

The council held a debate with closed doors, and after a short parley, surrendered to the "great Sanhedrim" and gave him a license. The man in the other alley, however, was not prepared for such legal compliance, and he prepared to fight it on some other line, to be determined.

So on Monday morning he called together a council of his friends, and the subject of his situation and their rights was discussed. War was agreed upon; but whether upon the whole council or only the most offensive members, or some one else in the principle of vicarious atonement, was open for discussion.

Dr. Livingston, the intendant, was the first discussed. Not much was said in his favor, except it was hinted that that cane he carried had a spear in it, and the apparent fullness in his vest was produced by the brace of pistols. It was also stated by one who knew, in his younger days no man dared confront him in anger.

Dr. Isaac Branch was next. An orginal Yankee, he was so noted, *but he was one of the most combative ones ever known thereabouts, and he pulled down 200 pounds, and was known to have splendid muscle action, and was afraid of nobody.*

The next in order was Gus Hamilton who was unanimously voted as strong as a lion, ready to fight at the drop of a hat, and never knew when to quit fighting. So he was exempted. The next was Addison F. Posey. It was agreed that he was the softest case of the lot in strength--would no doubt give the best fight he had; and at this point a member sprang to his feet and said that Posey had loaned him money in a tight, and two others added that he had kept them out of jail, and his [exemption] was voted by acclamation.

The next and the last was David Lesley, whose size was medium, he was an elder in the church, was Judge of Ordinary and a peace officer, was an advocate of the Maine law and had said hard things about liquor and drunkards, and a whipping was the device against him. "Who will do it? "I will give ten dollars," said one. "I will do it," reported another, and just at this point, a $10 bill was seen to fall on the table, which was grabbed and pocketed by the party accepting, who made his way to the Court House, in front of which Judge David was standing, with a dozen others, and the first thing the Judge knew he was staggering from a blow of an unknown Goliath. Recovering he ran up and struck him a blow in the pit of the stomach, which totally overthrew him for the time, and the next moment found Goliath down and David astride him and pressing his throat almost to strangulation.

The excited crowd tendered him opened knives and insisted on his cutting his throat or cropping his assailant; but the Judge's magnanimity prevailed, and he arose, inviting his opponent to arise and go. On recovering his feet, Goliath drew from his pocket a knife unopened and inflicted a severe wound on the Judge's forehead, and fled.

The excited crowd pursued him, but his wind and bottom soon carried him beyond their reach. The alley men and their adjuncts beat a rapid retreat, and this ended the whiskey war.

No. 3, The McLarens

Press & Banner, May 24, 1876

There lived in 1834 as well as long before and afterwards, this well known family. . . . They must have been there many years, as John, Jr. was called a bachelor when I first knew him (and died in that line), and I often heard him say he was a boy when they left the "old country," Scotland, from whence they came.

They lived in the oldest house in town, on the northeast corner of

The McLarens

the square antedating, so it was said by a decade the first "rebellion"--that old hip roofed house, which if my information is correct, has been destroyed in a general conflagration of that side of the square within the last eight years. The original building was of logs, to which were added an inside and outside frame, until its walls were as thick as of ancient castles upon the Clyde. . . .

My account of them is that there were three brothers in Scotland, to wit: Adam, John, and Robin--the former only married, and the Abbeville widow was the mother of his children, to wit: Adam, Jr., John, Jr., Janet, Agnes, Eliza, Susan, and a Mrs. Williams and Mrs. Baker, the last named having married and left before my day. The brothers John (better known as "Sawney" or "Uncle Sawney") and Robin were tailors, and came to Abbeville in the teens of this century and opened a shop. If their cut or make were ever "artistic" in the modern sense, there was a sad falling off before I ever saw any of it. No "latest fashion" picture adorned their walls, but they got plenty of work, and they worked early, worked long and worked late, and saved what they made. Robin would not own a thing; John had to take it all. All that Robin asked for the inner man was three meals a day and three half gills of whiskey in divisions of half of an hour before each meal, and as that was the usual mode of procuring the article in "those days," the practice was for Sawney to receive the amount in a cup and take one half himself, or near as he could divide it, and set it at a certain place in a corner and go back to the shop, and then Robin would go in and take his and return without a say. . . .

For the outer man, Robin asked only enough of the coarsest white cloth to make him pants to fit like a bandage from the ankles up and a long round-about coat of the same material. He wore a Scotch cap and heavy brogan shoes, and had no use for linen goods, cravat or gloves. . . .Robin was a round man, heavy and low in stature, and walked with a stoop, and his steps were as long as the conformation of the man would permit. His Scotch was so broad as to require an interpreter, and he never offered it outside of the family and furnished the least possible amount demanded, and that "york" or "nark.". . .

Sawney, however, did most things better, was a good talker, and of intelligible Scotch, too, and though wearing coarse cloth, sometimes half wool, it was in better style. He knew many things, was a genial old fellow, a good manager, and together they soon had a good start. No one living could get Robin to take more than his three half gills per day, but Sawney, besides his half with Robin, was ready to "take a wee dhrop with you" (so sizing it as to never get drunk), but the man who "took" with him, excepting nevertheless and always Robin, could never be found. Sawney died about 1841, was post master, and had held that position many years, and discharged the duties most pleasantly.

The McLarens

The family were Presbyterian and had great respect for and attachment to the church, and the females were members of Upper Long Cane, and John, Jr. not infrequently accompanied them, but Sawney and Robin. . . read not Bibles nor went to church--and only such theological practice as St. James accords, and confining and concentrating all that upon their deceased brother's widow and children, and most religiously, faithfully, and heroically did they do that. They left Adam in Scotland, poor and struggling to feed his wife and eight children, six of them girls, and the first thing they did after procuring the means was to send money and bring them over; and the father dying soon after, his dependent family fell on their hands, but never was there safer ground touched.

Sawney and Robin not only took care of them, but provided for their future. They sent Adam and John to "Baker's School" and paid for it; sent the girls to the most accomplished teachers, and put silks, satins, and gold on them to equal any. They graduated Adam, Jr. in medicine, and by the combination of the influence of the Bakers with Daniel Webster [Alpheus Baker, Abbeville's school master, had been a classmate of Webster's at Dartmouth College]and Maj. Alston and Dr. Eli S. Davis, direct power with the headquarters of Gen. Jackson, they sailed him into the position of Assistant Surgeon, U. S. A. under a commission dated March 2, 1833, and he was soon after on his own bottom advanced to full surgeon, and Uncle Sawney told me in 1838 that "Oddam was thrying for Surgeon Gineral and hooped to get it." I don't think he did, but he reached an enviable position, and was always to be found in the military family circle of Scott and Taylor. Soon after entering upon his duties he was stationed near Boston, was introduced into the "charmed circle" there by Daniel Webster, and soon after led captive and to the altar the accomplished and rather wealthy Miss Townsend, a grand-daughter of Elbridge Gerry.

McLaren died about four years ago, still connected with the army. He was tall and had regular features, unlike John, a piercing black eye, and a melodious voice tinctured with just enough Scotch to make it rich and creamy.

Dr. McLaren did not take sides with the South during the late war, nor did he owe South Carolina anything and Abbeville but little; yet he treated the Palmetto Regiment in Mexico with marked consideration and tendered his service to the Abbeville boys in any way that he could serve them, and I venture that if any of them fell during the late struggle into prisons and hospitals within his reach, all the aid and consideration he could afford was rendered. . . .

I cannot dismiss this reminiscence without a word of the females. No family known to me ever furnished three more beautiful women than Eliza, Agnes, and Susan. Eliza was the least so, but she had a voice as melodious as music borne across the waters and a smile most

Major James Alston

bewitching; Agnes had hair as black as the raven, and eyes "purely dark and darkly pure." I saw her at 30 a beauty, again at 40 a beauty, and again beautiful at 50, and at 65, if living, I venture she is still so. Susan was as queenly a woman as ever touched the earth in my presence, and as she tripped along, the earth, walls, and rocks seemed to answer back the reflection from her cheeks and glance.

No. 4, Major James Alston

Press & Banner, May 17, 1876

Among the celebrities of old none will be better remembered by older citizens than Major James Alston. He was a branch of the distinguished and wealthy family, so well known in the early and middle history of South Carolina. He was, however, a a native of North Carolina, and his end of the family was poor in his childhood. His opportunities in early life were limited, and he was not in general acceptance an "educated man." He inherited or made himself (my recollection is the latter) several hundred dollars and removed, while a young man, to Elbert County, Georgia, and engaged in merchandise, with a partner who ran off with the funds and left him bankrupt. His own personal character, however, was unimpeached, and during the War of 1812, or the Seminole War of 1817-18, he received from Gen. Jackson the appointment of paymaster or quartermaster, with the rank of major, which he afterwards bore--and came out having honestly obtained several thousand dollars ahead.

Soon after his success in war, he found in Abbeville a lady to whom he was happily united in marriage and she having a small estate added to his, enabled him to commence planting on a small scale, and by economy, none better knew that "a penny saved is a penny made," their estate grew until when I first knew him in 1834, he was in fine circumstances, and at his death in 1850 or not long after, the estate was exceeded only by Joel Smith, George McDuffie, Dr. Samuel Marshall, and Williamson Norwood, in Abbeville, and having only one child, like McDuffie, she ranked second in wealth, and were she the subject, I would say, in other respects, second to none.

A marked feature in the character of Major Alston was that he never entirely forgot a friend, nor entirely forgave an enemy or injury. He was ever after his promotion the friend of Gen. Jackson, and during the Nullification and the Force Bill, as well as long before and afterward the man who in his presence said anything reflecting personally upon the character of Gen. Jackson, and politically they had to tread lightly, had to fight him then and there. . . .

The Major looked at men to estimate how much money they could make and how much they could lay up out of their makings. . . . He

The Hendersons

was fair and honorable in his dealings, if he owed you anything he asked no remission and paid you to the minute, and if you did not the same, he would tell you of it.

He lived happily in his family life [he was the son-in-law of Andrew Hamilton], *was a good husband, affectionate father and humane master, and more than an average friend. Major Alston was a high toned man of fine sense and good judgment, would not do a mean thing nor tolerate it in others. He was tall and stout with a military bearing. His chief defect out of which any others grew, was his over-estimate of money. He was sober, moral, and seemed to have a respect, at a distance from the church, for religion; and it was supposed, and charitably suggested, that his neglect to attend church was not contempt for the teachings, but he was too honorable to receive benefits without compensation, and he did not care to make the investment.*

No. 5, The Hendersons

Press & Banner, April 19, 1876

Any reminiscences of mine of Abbeville of old would be grossly imperfect and partial, that omitted the two Hendersons, Francis senior and Francis junior--father and son. My account of the former is that he was born in Scotland and made his way to London when a young man, whether with or without family prestige, I know not. He became, however, an officer in the Bank of England, and must have occupied a fine social position to have met there on a visit to her relatives, the beautiful, accomplished, and wealthy Miss Laurens of Charleston, S. C.

She was the only child and heir of Col. John Laurens who fell in a skirmish in South Carolina at the close of the Revolutionary war. Col. John was the only surviving child and heir of his father, Henry Laurens, and was the aide and special friend of Gen. Washington. The elder Laurens during the colonial government obtained from the Crown a large and select grant of land on the Reedy Branches, which must have embraced twenty thousand acres [actually between five and six thousand] . . . . The property was left in trust, or as was better understood, as entailed property. . . .

[Francis Henderson, Sr., on the other hand] *was the ugliest man in Abbeville or elsewhere, five feet four inches high, shaped like a barrel, with not a feature to plead in extenuation. He was not even intelligent in general or specially; and if he was a businessman he had the poorest way of showing it in his own transactions; if he had ever known much, he had forgotten it in less time than any man I ever knew. He had but little confidence in anybody and less in himself. He*

The Hendersons

was a lawyer's client, and never moved without him; wouldn't sign a receipt for ten cents without the inspection and approval of his attorney. He was the most polite man ever seen, and it was a sore affliction to be in close and constant proximity to him. Meeting him in the morning you had to shake hands and tell him how you were, and at every encounter during the same day you had to stop and tell him how you were "by this time." I never knew but one to get rid of him, (and only a deduction,) and that was young Adolphus Williams, who boarded in the same house, and who thought his afflictions beyond any other, as he had to shake hands and explain at every meal. On one occasion, he replied: "Mr. Henderson, I thank you for your solicitude, and am happy to inform you that I am in excellent health, and if you will take it for granted until further notified, I promise to report the slightest change to the contrary." He escaped afterwards with three tips of the beaver each day.

But the point to reach is that Miss Laurens, with fortune, fame and rank at her feet, waved them off and married little ugly Frank Henderson. This must have occurred about the year 1800. They lived together about a year, during which young Frank was born. (I suppose he was born in London and it was so understood in Abbeville, as I several times heard him say his vote was challenged at Cedar Spring in '30 or '32 for evidence that he was 'civilized.') The husband and wife spent the second year, or a part of it, in Paris, and quarreled and filed bills and cross bills for divorce, with evidence that looked ugly for both. I do not know whether the battle was in England, France, or South Carolina; no dissolution of the marriage tie was granted, but the child was awarded to the father, and also the trusteeship of the estate, the wife being allowed an annuity of $1800, and the balance of the income divided between the father and the son.

My understanding is, that the father placed his son in Scotland with his relatives and came himself to the United States to manage the estate, making his residence at Newport, R. I., where he again married and raised a family, spending the winter in Charleston and Abbeville, leasing and renting the property. The wife remained in England and was living at an advanced age 26 or 28 years ago. Frank, Jr. was graduated at Edinburgh College and afterwards went through and graduated also at one of the first German colleges and traveled a year or two. He then came to Charleston and read law with James L. Pettigrew or another and was admitted [to the bar] after a most brilliant examination and the highest hopes entertained for him.

But just at that seemingly propitious period, he learned of the existence of his mother, whom he supposed had died at his birth, and the message was too much for him; his proud heart broke, and though caring not for the bowl he sought refuge in it from thence until the grave closed over him. When I first saw him in 1834, he

The Hendersons

appeared to be between 30 and 35 years of age, and had reached his quart per day; in 1840 he could "run" it, and to the end there was no difficulty in disposing of it. He made Abbeville his home and never left it but three times that I remember--twice he spent the summers at Flat Rock, N. C., and about 1836 he went to Washington. His father was trying to get reimbursed for a large sum expended by the elder Laurens in support of the first "rebellion," and supposed his presence would aid it. During his stay he was a guest of President Jackson at the White House.

Frank, Jr. boarded with the McLaren family, (as also his father during his stay), and was as regular in his habits as David Lewis Wardlaw, but they were, unfortunately, not so well ordered. He arose at 9 o'clock a. m., took a cup of strong coffee, a hot roll and butter, boiled mackerel, ham and eggs or steak, (he cared not for chicken). Then he would sit or walk until 11 o'clock a. m., and then take his seat near a table, and after having filled a glass half with spirits and half with water (never used sugar) he would read and sip an hour which carried him to dinner time, when he would go in on nearly a bee line and make a hearty meal; then at 4 o'clock p. m. he would read and repeat the morning potations until supper, eating again; then after giving supper one hour, he would read and run down a pint by bed time, which would leave him in a condition requiring a little aid (always at hand with the well-paid servants) in getting rid of his boots, etc.

The statement explains him from about 1834 to about 1842. Afterwards he weakened rapidly and required aid at the end of the day sittings, and on the "quarter stretch" he had to read and drink mostly in bed. He went under in 1847. How a man could drink so much, so persistently, and so long is a puzzle. My explanation is this: he in the first place inherited a perfect physical development, strengthened by the school and college discipline in Europe, and he was free from all irregularities and habits taxing the system until perhaps 27 years of age with the basis of a good constitution established: again, he always ate his meals and slept; and drank only the purest spirits, and never before breakfast or on an empy stomach.

He usually purchased by the bottle or the demijohn, and whoever had the best "Otard" or "Dupuy" found a good customer. He drank mostly in his room, but sometimes with Robert Cochran whom he liked; and his seat was at a table in the back room. He was polite and courteous and approachable for a proper enquiry, but accessible only to a few. I remember to have heard at the time of his being accosted on his way into Cochran's by an impertinent fellow who mistook him. . . from his neat dress and having seen him standing in a tailor's shop, for a "jour," and addressed him as such which cost him a horizontal position and a bleeding head from a lance wood cane.

The Hendersons

He always dressed in fine taste, of the finest material, and had no use for cotton. He would in his better days have passed for handsome, but for his projecting eyeballs, the most so I ever witnessed.

Notwithstanding his habits, he kept up with the current literature of the day, and was as nearly an encyclopedia or walking library as ever came within my reach. . . .He had visited all the great cities and points in Europe, and had seen, or was familiar with, all the potentates, politics and leaders of the day in Europe. He knew but little on this side of the water and cared less. His American politics were a friend to Jackson.

Although he never married, Francis Henderson left a descendant who became a conspicuous figure in the 1876 Hampton campaign. Edward Henderson was born to a slave woman who belonged to John McLaren, Francis Henderson's landlord. Long after Edward Henderson had died, which was in 1886, Hugh Wilson in the *Press & Banner*, March 27, 1907, in discussing the "Laurens Lands," recalled that the legal settlement between Francis Henderson and the Laurens family was that if young Francis left no heirs the property would revert to the Laurens family. He commented, "Captain Ed Henderson of this county, if he had been born in wedlock, would have inherited the estate, and this inheritance would have made him rich." Edward Henderson was so light skinned that when he appeared in Columbia before the Congressional Committee investigating the Election of 1876, he was asked whether he was a "white man" or a "colored man." On that occasion he said that before emancipation he belonged to John McLaren who raised him. In 1880, the Census list showed that Hattie McLaren, his mother and a mulatto 75 years of age, lived in the household of Edward Henderson, a carpenter whose family included a wife and two daughters.

In 1876, Edward Henderson was one of the blacks who cast his support to the Wade Hampton campaign. He served as the captain of the "colored Democrats" who wore blue shirts and joined in the parades in that campaign in which white Democrats from the countryside wore red shirts. In 1878, by a narrow vote the Abbeville County Democrats refused to accept Captain Henderson's company as a Democratic club, although they declared their willingness to accept its members as individuals. Wade Hampton appointed him as one of the county's jury commissioners in 1877, and he served in that position for eight years.

No. 6, Robert B. Hamilton

Press & Banner, July 5, 1876

Probably a few old citizens of 1834-40 may call to mind a tall young man full six feet and two inches high, well formed and probably as fine a specimen of physical development as Abbeville ever produced . . . and whose power and genius were equal to his looks. He was a great unknown and undeveloped--a son of Capt. Alexander Hamilton who long lived and died on the high hill one mile northwest of the town, and who died in the winter of 1835-36, highly honored and respected, and who in his time had filled the office of Sheriff and represented the District in the legislature one or more times. Robert Burns was his full name, and so chosen by his father, of Scotch extract. . . . He was the pet of a large and perhaps the handsomest family ever raised in Abbeville, the pride and hope of his father. Alpheus Baker who fitted and primed him for college told me he had the power had he willed it, or had it so been willed, to have "climed the hill of fame and planted his banner on its highest peak."

He was in Yale College between 1830-34, and by inheritance an anti-Nullifier, his father being a leader of that ring at home; but he found so much hostility to South Carolina and Calhoun, that himself and another from another section of the State, took up the cudgels in debate, and which ended in actual cudgels a regular encounter in which South Carolina more than maintained itself against heavy odds. For this they were expelled, or commanded to make concessions not suitable to them and they came home.

He commenced reading law, but soon fell in love with a milliner's beautiful girl and wanted to marry her, which was so shocking to the family pride and so likely to cause the death of his father that he yielded and sought refuge in "the bowl" first, and then absence afterwards, to break the spell. His father gave him several hundred dollars and he took passage westward in the stage coach in the Spring of 1834, like the mariner upon an unknown and untried sea without chart or compass. He belonged to a family whose temperament rendered stimulants maddening, and upon taking an amount that would have produced "happiness" to many, it was nothing short of madness to them.

The first point he halted at was Milledgeville, Ga., where two drinks required the officials and posse comitatus to catch him, and for which he had to pay. He then went to Savannah, where three drinks required the police and military, for he was resistful and dangerous and strong and sinewy as a lion--and it cost him again. He then took passage to New York, and on arriving there was the guest of Capt. Daniel Baker of the marines then in post. Baker was an Abbeville man to this extent, had lived there several years and married one of the Miss McLarens, and was a special friend of the Hamiltons. Robert

Robert B. Hamilton

got on a spree in New York, and raised a thunder-storm among the police, upsetting them like nine-pins and wounding one or two badly, and making good his escape to the vessel, he seized a cutlass and placed himself in the hatch-way or gang-way, or elsewhere, ready to kill one or two of the first adventurers. Baker coming found the position warlike and stationary and pled "crazy" for his friend, which induced them to retire after placing sentinels on land, with a promise to inquire into that next morning. During the night, Baker in a life boat got him into a vessel ready to sail to Gibralter, and the next morning found him under sail for that port.

Arriving there he remained a while and then sailed in an English vessel for China, where he remained several months. He then sailed to the Island of St. Helena, where he spent a month visiting every day and musing over the grave of Napoleon, whom he worshipped. . . .At St. Helena his money gave out and he worked his passage on vessels back to New York, where he borrowed money and reached Charleston on his way back home, but there learning of the death of his father, in part of grief at the absence or loss of his son, he changed his mind. Not a word or line had reached his family after he had sailed from New York eastward and that was learned from Capt. Baker. His aptitude enabled him to become proficient on a vessel, instead of returning he engaged on a vessel for Rio Janeiro, He remained there a long time and at sea between small ports and made and spent all he made, when a war broke out between Peru and Chile and he entered on a vessel as a midshipman but I forget which side he took.

He came back to Abbeville in 1839 after five years absence, read law and perhaps was admitted to practice. He claimed to be free of former habits, and proposed a marriage joyous to his relatives, but not so to hers, by reason of doubts of the stability and soundness of his reform. The marriage was consummated and the fears of the latter were soon realized by his return to stimulants and madness. He died in 1840, the victim of circumstances or himself; and light should be the tread on his ashes by men of genius, for he was one of them.

If you will stroll down to the old block-house or where it used to stand and going down parallel with the large branch below the union with the spring branch, you will find on two rocks a boar's head and a lion's paw, chiseled by him on granite in 1831 with a razor blade and mallet. . . . and following a short distance you will find chiseled by the same artist and poet on the smooth surface of a rock overhanging a waterfall--I venture it is still there, though perhaps moss covered-- what may inspire your courage and console you in calamity:

"Freedom like this purling rill
When opposed is prouder still."

No. 7, The Hanging of Kindred Kitchens, 1836

Press & Banner, July 26, 1876

I witnessed a hanging once in a grave yard about four hundred yards west of the public square. It was in 1836, and the subject was one Kindred Kitchens, probably the worst man that ever lived in Abbeville. He had murdered an old man [John Hinton] of or near eighty years old--his own age was between thirty and forty years. The victim was acting as bailiff for Tribble's Beat and I think it occurred at Tribble's store.

The old man's offence was levying on Kitchens' horse while he was in the grocery. He retook the horse by violence, seized the old man by the hair and drew his knife across his throat, almost severing his head from his body, leaped the fence near by, dropping the knife reeking with blood, and escaped. He was afterwards captured, tried and condemned to rope stretching.

To tell all the bad deeds imputed to this man would fill pages and thrill the blood to write or listen to them. The most brutal was on one occasion coolly sharpening his knife to the keeness of a razor, and gauging the point between his fingers, seized his wife, telling her that he was going to see how near he could come to killing her without doing it, and with her feeble frame in his powerful grasp, he drew the knife from ear to ear, touching without cutting the jugular vein. . . . Yet this poor creature clung to him when all others turned their backs and spurned him, did all she could for his defence before the law and made the last appeal on her knees before Gov. McDuffie, whose presence she reached on foot and wearied to exhaustion. No one would sign her petition nor loan her a horse for that errand. On the fatal day she was present to receive his remains and give them a decent interment.

This writer then a half-grown man wanted to see a hanging and especially to see that man hung, and to make sure work of it, as soon as the gallows were erected, two days before, selected as his seat a sapling within ten feet, and before the crowd assembled--not less than two thousand came, placed himself in the top as a squirrel or opposum would have done. I recollect an over anxious boy got very tired in holding his position for two hours before the centre of attraction and escort arrived, and then a full hour occupied by religious services and the speaker entitled to the floor.

The latter announced himself "prepared to go" and "wanted to see and shake hands with all he had quarreled with and fought," and they went in shoals. I thought it would take all day. Only one stood back, his brother in law, Nat McCollister, and seeing him he called him up and they made friends (each bore upon his person not less than twenty scars inflicted by the knives of the other).

This ceremony over, the speaker drew from his pocket some poetry

Hanging of Kindred Kitchens, 1836

which he asked the privilege of reading and which met no objections--all about his wife and children. Prefacing his lines, he said: "Genteel men I'm gwine to die and leave you. I have been a bad man in my time and am sorry for it. I haven't treated my wife right in many respects, and she's one of the best weemun God ever made and has been a mighty good wife to me, and I hope some of you will find it convenient to take her for she is a good woman and handy and no mistake."

The lines began:
"And its dear wife I love you well
  And all the children too.
I hope your soul in Christ may dwell
  And all the children's too."

I can't call to mind the succeeding lines, but the above was repeated as a chorus to the other "verses." The production was lengthy, and the author had to be reminded that only a few minutes remained, when he was advanced a step forward and higher, the rope adjusted and after three blows (the first two missed) from a mallet in the hands of Sheriff Taggart, a pin was knocked out, a few movements of the body, then closed the worsted experience of Kindred Kitchens.

VI. ABBEVILLIANS IN DUELS

The cruel practice of dueling was uncommon in the upcountry, but records of a number of instances involving Abbevillians have survived. The first of these was the Bochelle-Lesley duel in the summer of 1808. Dr. Bochelle does not seem to have ever resided in the village of Abbeville, but James Lesley was a member of a well-known family which lived in the village and on lands close to it on the road to Pendleton. His brother David would later become the Ordinary of the district and build the landmark home where the Burts hosted Jefferson Davis in May, 1865. R. H. Wardlaw in his memoirs said that James Lesley built the house which in the late 19th century was used as the Presbyterian manse.

R. H. Wardlaw spelled the doctor's name as Boshell, but the account of the duel in the Pendleton *Messenger*, (August 20, 1808) spelled the name as Bochelle. A Lesley family tradition said that while the doctor was treating a distant relative of James Lesley, he made some remarks which implied the youth was of a low social class. James Lesley, a young Abbeville lawyer, took offense, and the two had words which led to blows. Dr. Bochelle challenged Lesley to a duel. Lesley was aware that he might lose his life, and, since his wife was expecting their first child, he made his will before the duel. *Well aware that what estate I now have after paying my just debts will not be more than sufficient for the maintenance of my beloved wife Eliza and for the education of a child if she should after my death have one to live,* he provided that it be sold to his father William and his friend Dr. Thomas Casey *for the benefit of my wife unless she remarries. Should I have a child, I have perfect confidence* [he wrote] *that its amiable mother will apply everything to the best advantage for giving our child a good education which I consider inestimable.*

The duel took place on August 9, 1808 on the Georgia side of the Savannah across from Fort Charlotte. Neither party's first fire was effective, and before the second fire Lesley's friends made proposals for a compromise, but Dr. Bochelle would not accept them. In the second fire, Lesley did not fire, and Bochelle's shot broke Lesley's rib, and, though attended by Dr. Casey, Lesley died eight hours later. James Lesley's wife sometime later gave birth to a daughter, whom she named Caroline Frances James Lesley. His widow and daughter moved away from Abbeville, and the daughter married a Mr. Van Ness from New York who later became mayor of San Francisco.

A second duel involving Abbevillians was related as one of the traditions of the town by the Ex-Abbevillian (Addison F. Posey) in the *Press & Banner,* June 7, 1876, in relation to his tribute to Dr. A. B. Arnold. He said that all Abbevillians, wealthy and poor, had great confidence in the abilities of Dr. Arnold. The incident related below is

Abbevillians in Duels

not dated, but clearly was earlier than 1836.

I will relate here a matter with which Dr. Arnold was connected before my day. It was current forty years ago [1836] upon the streets of your town, so talked about and never questioned in my hearing, and "I tell the tale as it was told to me." I can't date the event and it bears a good margin as wide as the old jealousy between Georgia and South Carolina growing out of their rival champions, Crawford and Calhoun.

When Dr. Arnold lived in town, there lived also in the old McLaren's building a wealthy family named Wooldridge, and there boarded a man named Tom Wooldridge. He was sent to the great high school at Sparta, Ga., taught by the father of the late Hon. Howell Cobb. He there fell in love with a lovely woman (and what man, except hereinafter could blame him), and found a rival in a fellow student named Moffett, and as usual in "those days," the former having precedence in favor, the latter challenged the former to fight a duel, but the former, having Falstaff's ideas of honor, and the fear of death before his eyes, not only surrendered the girl, but apologized for loving her, and for peace and safety came home.

The girl still not showing favor to Moffett after his disgrace of Tom, he followed him to Abbeville Court House and challenged him again, through his friend and second, the late Gov. McDonald of Georgia, if my recollection is not at fault. The cartel was written in the Taggart building and received in the Hotel de McLaren. It put Tom to bed and he sent for Arnold, not as a "friend," but as a physician. Arnold came and Tom told him honestly what was the matter. The Doctor gave his patient a stimulant and told him he would get him out of the difficulty--wrote a note which he had Tom sign acknowledging the receipt of their note, and referring the "whole matter to my friend Dr. A. B. Arnold."

In about an hour, the Doctor returned and told Tom the "arrangements" which were--"At Petersburg this day week, 6 o'clock, a. m., pistols at ten paces." Tom swooned declaring he couldn't go; to which the Dr. replied, "That's alright; all you have to do is to default and that will give me a chance at them. Georgia shall not crow on this soil."

At the appointed hour, the doctor was there, and contrary to his expectations, Tom was on hand and ready to take the peg, which he did (the latter) insisted on and did, and at the first fire received his adversary's ball in the elbow going out at the shoulder, and sent his into the forehead of his adversary who fell and expired instantly. It is said that Tom then left and was uneasy until he had himself landed at Vienna, while the Doctor remained on the field until all others had gone and returned with measured steps.

The third recorded duel was between two young lawyers from

Abbevillians in Duels

Abbeville and nothing is reported about its origin. The *Anderson Gazette*, March 22, 1844, carried the following brief account:

Duel on Saturday the 16th--two miles above Hamburg between Col. John Cunningham and Samuel McGowan, Esq., both of Abbeville, weapons, U. S. Yaugers and distance 30 paces. Mr. McGowan was severely wounded the first firing in the back of the neck (it was thought not to be mortal). The meeting was near a public highway and witnessed by 200-300. Louis T. Wigfall was Cunningham's second, and B. Y. Martin was McGowan's.

Perhaps the most sensational duel was the encounter between Ben Lane Posey, who was later founder and editor of the *Independent Press*, and Dr. Warren Lomax in July, 1851. Posey was a Mexican War veteran who seemed to love controversy. Apparently he had gained the dislike of Frederick Selleck, the acknowledged hero of the Palmetto Regiment, and the Colonel of the regiment, J. Foster Marshall, and this enmity continued even after their return to Abbeville.

Bad feelings reached a climax when some of Selleck's friends blackballed Posey from a formal dance in Abbeville to which other eligible young men were invited. Posey's family was quite respectable. His father had been sheriff of Laurens District and later a prosperous hotel keeper in the village of Abbeville, and young Benjamin Lane studied at the South Carolina College. It was rumored, however, that Posey had lately been seen with a young slave girl in his carriage.

Posey considered the matter a calculated insult, and he challenged the chairman of the invitations committee, Dr. Warren Lomax, to a duel. The latter accepted and chose Selleck as his second, Posey secured a young friend from Edgefield to attend him. The men involved spent the night in Lowndesville and met the following morning on an island in the Savannah near Moseley's Ferry. Posey proved his courage by drawing first blood with a shot into Lomax's arm which disarmed him.

To explain his position in the matter and to vent his distaste for the Abbevillian whom he considered behind the insult, J. Foster Marshall, he published the following handbill:

To the Public, by Benjamin Lane Posey. Abbe. C. H., July 28th, 1851.

It becomes my unpleasant duty to detail the circumstances that gave rise to the late scandal that was bruited about, against me, and which led to the duel between Dr. Lomax and myself. I was aware of the existence of a coterie in this place, who were interested in depressing me, and who watched me with a jesuitical cunning, ready to snap at any indiscretion that might be perverted to my injury. About a month ago, a trifling incident gave them a handle, which for a while, they worked successfully. I will give a candid statement of the facts....

A Negro boy (Lewis) who belongs to my brother, and who is hired at Due West, has a wife at Dr. Lomax's. His father, mother, and sister (Harry, Chloe and Mahala) live in this place. My brother was about to remove to Alabama and take them, leaving Lewis on account of his wife. Before parting with them forever, he (Lewis) wished to give them a dinner. These were all that were to have been invited, except Dave, his fellow workman and his wife.

For certain reasons that shall be sub-rosa, Dr. Lomax insisted that a nice little girl that belonged to John McLaren, should be invited, and accordingly she was. The old man was too unwell to go, and the women had engaged a vehicle for themselves. On the morning of the dinner, they failed to get the expected vehicle, and were much grieved at the disappointment. To relieve their disappointment, I took them in my buggy, to wit: Chloe, an old woman about sixty five; Mahala, a married woman more than half that age; and McLaren's little girl. Chloe and Mahala are women of exemplary characters, and have always been treated with the greatest care and kindness by my family. They both were my nurses, and I feel justified in being kind to them, though I incur, thereby, the harmless censure of the sickly squeamish. When I am sustained by my own self-approval, I care not a straw for other men.

I gave a seat to the little girl, because she was to have gone with the women by previous arrangement, and (God save the mark) that Dr. Lomax also should not be disappointed. Lest this language might injure the little girl, I will say, that as far as I know, and believe, she is as chaste as the temple of virtue-- Dr. Lomax had invited me to take dinner with him on that day, and I was going without reference to the Negro affair. But they wished me to go with them [for protection] from an officious patrol. I was hospitably received and entertained by Dr. Lomax and his mother, and returned in the evening. It has been the habit of Dr. Lomax's family and mine, to attend the festivals of our favorite Negroes, and to be entertained by each other on such occasions. And to make a full confession, I attended in 1848, with at least twenty gentlemen, an excellent barbecue, given exclusively by Dr. Lynch's Negroes, at his plantation. These are the facts; gentlemen harpies, make the most of them.

When the 4th of July ball was in agitation, Dr. Lomax came to me, and begged me to attend the meeting, and aid in getting up the ball. I declined, as I told him, because I expected to be in New York on that day, but I promised if anything kept me here, to give my aid. On the next day he came again, and urged me to attend the meeting, but I pleaded other engagement. Ball matters remained in status quo, until the evening of the 4th. I applied for a ticket, more from duty than *anything else, and was amazed at the announcement that the junior managers, (Dr. Harrison excepted) had given orders to refuse me one. I knew that the senior managers were merely ornamental, and had properly nothing to do with it. But a junior manager told me that a senior manager was implicated.*

When I learned that they had attempted to degrade me, by declaring that I was unfit to attend the ball in which they were allowed to participate, and as I believed to gratify unworthy feelings, I determined to have adequate revenge, and accordingly sought satisfaction, by inflicting upon the person of Dr. Lomax--chairman of the committee-- an indignity which he has since resented, as the representative of the committee, and in his own defence, by meeting me on a field of honor. He did, and intended me a grievous injury, and grievously has he answered for it. I buried all my resentment toward him, when I drew his blood. I rejoice at the accident that saved his life, and wish him a speedy recovery. It has been my object in the above details to spare his feelings, as far as compatible with truth and my own vindication.

I was preparing on the 24th, to demand satisfaction of two others of the managers, but have been dissuaded from it. At the request of Edward Noble, Esq., I awaited the decision of gentlemen of high authority in such matters. It was referred to Col. Cunningham, Col. McGowan and Edward Noble, Esq. They gave me their decision in writing, which was, that the managers had given the insult as a body, and that Dr. Lomax has, as the representative of all, given full satisfaction. In deference to their judgment, and from a reluctance to push my advantage, to vindictiveness, I shall pursue them no further. I hope, however, that they have received a salutary lesson, and that it may make them wiser and better men.

I suspected Jehu Foster Marshall of being the Cataline of the conspiracy, and before leaving for Augusta to meet Dr. Lomax, I left the manuscript for a hand bill, in which I had given a quietus to the said Jehu Foster. Hearing that facts were coming to light, he called on Mr. Kerr, protested his innocence in the refusal of my ticket; disclaimed any desire on his part, that I or any one else should be excluded, and solemnly averred to Mr. Kerr, Dr. Branch, and before others, that the first that he knew of my exclusion, or any intention to exclude me, was when Lomax applied to him for advice, after our difficulty. On this, they suppressed the publication, and addressed me the reasons, which I accepted as satisfactory, and tendered, through them, my acceptance of his denial. . . .The whole matter. . . is now before the public. . . and I willingly submit to their censure or approbation.
                                              Benjamin Lane Posey

VII. ABBEVILLE AND ITS SLAVES, PATERNALISM AND FEAR

Like other towns in the Slave States, Abbeville found that town life presented special hazards to the control of its resident slaves. In part, it was a problem of numbers, for it is relatively certain that more slaves than whites lived in the village. The 1850 Census listed 881 slaves as owned by Abbeville residents as compared to a white population of 331, but it also noted that an indeterminate number of this total lived outside of town on plantations owned by Abbevillians.

Some of these town slaves were particularly favored, and their stories were the ones most frequently remembered. For example, in the excerpts printed in Chapter III, there were the accounts of Andrew Pickens's slaves and the favored position allowed his body servant Dick. There were numerous other examples. In the WPA *Slave Narratives* recorded in the 1930s, William Hunter of Arkansas said (Vol. 9, Pt. 3, p. 367) that *my mother came from Abbeville, S. C., a Negro trading point.* [Slaves were sold frequently at the public sales in front of the court house in estate settlements.] *When she was put on the block, my father went to McBride* [John McBryde was apparently his owner.] *and asked him to buy that woman for him a wife. He said she was a mighty pretty young woman. McBride bought her. . . . My mother was mixed with the white race. She was a bright woman.*

When in 1876, Addison F. Posey wrote about the most memorable inhabitants in the village of Abbeville in the 1830s, one of the ones he recalled most warmly was "Aunt Jinny Branch," an elderly slave who technically belonged to Andrew Hamilton, but who lived with Isaac Branch. She was a "character" around town who regaled young and old with her experiences in Charleston during the British occupation in the Revolution. Her death in 1840 was chronicled in the Abbeville District Coroner's Book. When she did not return to Dr. Branch's one evening, the whole village conducted an organized search and found her body on Charles Dendy's lot (later Dendy's Corner)

Another favored black was J. Foster Marshall's Israel who served the Captain of the Palmettoes (Abbeville's company in the Mexican War) as his devoted body servant in Mexico. While in Mexico, Israel married a Mexican woman, and Marshall gave him the option of staying in Mexico. Israel decided to return to Abbeville and continued in Marshall's service into the Civil War years when he was with his master until Marshall's death in Virginia.

Perhaps the most revealing picture of how the Abbeville gentry treated their "favorite servants" can be found in the public broadside which Benjamin Lane Posey, a bitter rival of Marshall's, issued to explain the cause of the Posey-Lomax duel. This is reprinted in the previous section.

The one local black of the ante-bellum years who later attained

Abbeville's Slaves

national distinction remembered unusual favors there. Henry McNeal Turner, one of the first black chaplains in the Union army and one of the founding figures of the African Methodist Episcopal (A.M.E.) Church, was brought to Abbeville from Newberry as a small boy some time in the 1850s. His mother was a free black, Sarah Greer, the daughter of David Greer. In Newberry in 1849, she was able to get a white woman to teach young Henry (then 15 years of age) the alphabet and how to spell simple words. Later when they moved to Abbeville, she employed another white woman to teach her son every Sunday until the woman was threatened with imprisonment. It was against the law of the State to teach slaves to read and write, and, although Henry's mother was a free black, the threat stopped the teaching. However, according to Turner's biographer, he was engaged as a servant in a law office in Abbeville where he learned to read and write "more accurately." Also, he recalled that the lawyers encouraged him in his efforts to become more literate.

After Bishop Turner had become a celebrity, he returned to Abbeville on several occasions. The *Press & Banner*, July 11, 1884, reported that *Bishop Turner of the A M E Church spent last Sunday in our town. In the morning he attended preaching in the Methodist Church, where, over forty years ago he was baptized and received into the church. At night he preached in the colored Methodist church. Several of our white citizens went to hear him, and they all speak highly of his sermon. While it was eloquent, it was adapted to the comprehension of his audience. He is a natural orator. He was born in Newberry. In early life he came to Abbeville and served an apprenticeship in a carriage factory.*

The trial of a slave who belonged to J. Foster Marshall's brother Dr. S. S. Marshall in 1857 (*Abbeville Banner*, October, 1857) indicates to what length some wealthy slave masters would go to aid a valued slave. *The trial of the boy Josh, belonging to Dr. S. S. Marshall, for the murder of Andy, belonging to Mr. Abram Lites, was held in this village on Tuesday last before Wm. M. Hadden, Esq., the magistrate, and resulted in his conviction of manslaughter. The prosecution was conducted by Gen.* [Samuel] *McGowan, and the defence by Col.* [James L.] *Orr* [at that time the Speaker of the U. S. Congress as well as the husband of Dr. Marshall's sister Sue], *who each delivered elaborate speeches on the occasion. The boy was sentenced to six months imprisonment, and to receive 600 lashes, to be given twice a month, 50 lashes at each time.*

The account elsewhere of the events which led to the fatal stabbing of Samuel Branch in his carriage shop in 1840 gives details on slave discipline as well as the protective feeling of one master who thought his slave was being abused.

At the same time that some masters indicated paternal concern for their slaves, the town as a whole showed continuous concern for slave unrest. The first ordinances which were approved by the town included one which enrolled all free males of age in a slave patrol. Although there were a number of instances in which masters were killed by their slaves in Abbeville District, the town experienced only one threat of a slave uprising.

Samuel Agnew, a Due West youth who was then a student at Erskine College, on April 22, 1851 recorded in his diary: *Hear of a "rising" among the blacks in Abbeville. Some 15 in prison, to rise when the State secedes. One of Mrs. Allen's sons discovered it 2 weeks ago, and has ever since been watching its progress with a wary eye, keeping the secret locked in his breast.* A few days later, he noted that *Pa* [his father, Dr. Enoch Agnew] *is summonded as a juror in the "slave insurrection case" which is to be tried next Monday.* On April 28, 1851, he wrote *Pa went in to the court-house today, to the Negro trial. Didn't hang any of them.*

The *Abbeville Banner*, May 3, 1851, carried the following story: *For several reasons, we omitted, in our paper of last week to state anything in relation to the arrest and confinement in Jail of three Negroes on suspicion of endeavoring to organize an insurrection. They were tried on Monday last and found guilty in legal parlance of 'counselling to run away,' and sentenced as follows--Austin, the slave of Mrs. Allen, and Asa, the slave of T. E. Owen, each to receive one hundred and fifty lashes and leave the State; and Taffy, the slave of John White, to receive twenty five lashes and be discharged.*

There was no evidence of anything against Taffy, except that he was in bad company, into which he was drawn by liquor which the others kept; but there is no doubt but that the other two meditated setting on foot an insurrection, and had they not been detected, serious consequences may have followed. Public opinion is very much excited against Austin and Asa, and demanded their suffering the highest penalty of the law; but the jury, composed of gentlemen of character and intelligence, did not feel warranted, from the evidence, in finding a verdict to that effect. The indictment was brought by Samuel McGowan, Esq., on the part of the Town Council, and defence sustained by Messrs. Wilson and Noble on the part of the owners.

Taffy was not the only Abbeville slave susceptible to liquor, a problem for many Abbevillians, white and black, free and slave. On October 30, 1857, the *Independent Press* editorially commented that intemperance was on the increase among the Negroes of Abbeville *and they most assuredly have facilities for procuring liquor which did not exist formerly. We have been credibly informed that there are several places within the corporate limits where liquor is positively retailed by Negroes. We have also been informed that there is no*

Abbeville's Slaves

difficulty whatever in the way of their obtaining it, that at any time they can procure orders signed by white men to the grocer. We advise masters to look into this if they do not wish their Negroes ruined. This is infinitely worse than downright abolitionism.

The problem persisted. In the *Abbeville Banner*, January 15, 1860, James M. Perrin wrote *For more than twelve months past drunkeness has been a common evil among our Negroes. Scenes of riot and debauch have occurred in our streets, and even the sanctity of our churches has been invaded. These abuses have called loudly for reform. The powers of the Town Council have been invoked, but it was found that whilst it was found that they could punish the offender, they were powerless to reach the source of the evil.* The result was that a number of "worthy and respectable citizens" formed the Abbeville Vigilance Committee and directed Perrin to inform such merchants as Messrs. J. and N. Knox that they should close down their cellar door at sundown and not open it again until sun up the next day, sell spirituous liquors to no Negro on any man's order, and sell to no "irresponsible worthless white man." He acknowledged that "some of the good people of the country" complained when their orders were no longer honored. Perrin's reply was, *To you in the country it is a small matter to ride a few miles to purchase in person the liquor you wish. To the citizens of this village it is a matter of vital importance to have their Negroes sober and obedient.*

Ironically, the citizens of the country were at the same time complaining that the town people were buying chickens from their slaves and thus encouraging them to steal their master's chickens and use that money to buy liquor.

Before the turn to vigilantism in 1860, the town of Abbeville had tried to deal with the problems of slave management in the courts. For example, the *Independent Press*, October 14, 1859 reported two rather dissimilar cases: *One of the cases was an indictment against the captain of a Patrol for shooting and wounding a Negro who was attempting to escape. In charging the jury his Honor stated the law to be that the Patrol had no right to use a deadly weapon, except in a clear case of self-defence. The defendent was convicted, but as the wound was slight and there were mitigating circumstances, he was sentenced to pay a fine of only five dollars.*

Another case was the indictment of two of the most respectable physicians for disinterring the dead body of a Negro for the purpose of dissection. They plead guilty to the indictment, and alleged in extenuation of the defence, that it was done with the design of advancing their professional knowledge--the Negro having been the patient of one of them, and his disease presenting some peculiar symptoms, they wished to make a post-mortem examination. The judge imposed a nominal fine of one dollar each.

Abbeville's Slaves

In the Spring of 1860, the fear of slave unrest caused less concern with the law against shooting runaways. The *Independent Press*, May 25, 1860, carried a story that a cave had been discovered in the upper part of the District which appeared to have been occupied by runaway Negroes. It had cooking utensils, fire, and provisions. A watch surprised two runaways. Both ran and were shot with the result that one was killed.

The outbreak of war brought tough new restrictions on slaves in the town of Abbeville. The *Independent Press*, July 26, 1861, reported a town ordinance *that after the 4th Sunday of July all Negroes who live outside the corporate limits are forbidden to enter town to attend church except with the special permission of their master or to congregate on the streets before or after preaching nor will be allowed to come into town after night except by special permission and must leave immediately upon the accomplishment of their errand.* Violators would be jailed, and their masters would have to pay their fines before they could be released.

VIII. FATAL STABBING IN A CARRIAGE SHOP

In 1840, the South Carolina Legislature determined that the district coroners begin to keep record books with the testimony which was taken at inquests. Since these records were kept in the homes of the coroners, nearly all of them were later lost. In fact, the book kept by William Means, coroner for Abbeville District, may have been the only one which has survived. It is now in the South Carolina Archives.

The first case recorded in this volume is one in which an inquest was held over the body of Samuel Branch on July 20, 1840. Branch had been stabbed to death by Jesse Adams in an altercation in his cabinet shop which resulted from a quarrel over the punishment of a slave Branch was renting from Adams.

Samuel Branch was one of three brothers who first came as mechanics to Abbeville in the early 1820s from Vermont. His two brothers, Franklin and Isaac, later returned to Vermont where they took medical training and then came back to Abbeville as physicians. They were active in the organization and early years of the Methodist church in the village, although Isaac later joined the Presbyterians. Both were present along with four other doctors to examine the body of their brother for this coroner's inquest. Later, Franklin moved to Florida, but Isaac lived the rest of his life in Abbeville and played a prominent role in its religious and social life.

In the incident detailed in the coroner's book, Samuel Branch had rented a slave boy from Adams, and he had attempted to use him in his carriage shop. When he ordered the boy to run and get things for him, he would not run, so one of Branch's assistants undertook to whip him.

The slave got free and ran back to his owner to seek his protection. Adams brought him back to the shop to find out why he was being punished. One witness, James Simpson, testified that *I was at Branch's Shop in the piaza when Adams came with the Negro, and asked Branch if he wanted to have anything to do with a runaway Negro. Branch came to the door where Adams was standing and addressed himself to the Negro, and said "have you been runaway? I never have missed you." Adams then asked Branch what was the difficulty between them. Branch then said that Holliday* [one of his assistants] *had attempted to whip him for some misconduct, and gave him a few stripes with a cowhide and the Negro caught Holliday and swore that he would not be whipped by him. The Negro then denied taking hold of Holliday, and Branch said,"Will you tell Holliday so?" He said he would, and Branch then called Holliday.*

Nothing was then said until Holliday came, except that Branch then said that a Negro never made anything off him by running away. When Holliday came, Adams asked him what had been the difficulty between him and the Negro. Holliday then reported what Branch had

Fatal Stabbing

told Adams. The Negro denied taking hold of him, but said he took hold of the cowhide. Holliday said you did and I can show the print of your black hand on my coat. At that time Branch stept up and took hold of the Negro and said you have got to have a floging, and pulled him (the Negro) into the room. Adams then said you shall not unless you whip him by law.

The fullest account of what happened next was given by R. McLain who also worked in Branch's shop: *On last Friday morning about 11 o'clock I was at work in Mr. Branch's shop and heard a noise in the front room. I quit my work and went to the window and saw Mr. Branch, Mr. Adams and a Negro boy, each of them (Branch & Adams) pulling at the boy and telling each other to let him go. Adams then said he would not let him go, for he was his boy. Branch said that he was his boy this year, and that he* [Adams] *had no authority over him. Adams still held the boy and Branch telling him to let him go. Adams put his arm around Branch and threw him and the boy down. Mr. Branch said will you gouge me and scratch me and Adams said he did not do it but could do it if he wanted to. Branch told him that he did do it and again told him to let the boy go for he intended to whip him. Adams asked him what he was going to whip him for, and said the boy could not serve two or three masters. Mr. Holliday stept up and told the reason he wanted him whipt, and asked Adams if he would stand the like. Adams said no he would not stand it at all. Mr. Holliday said all he wanted was to give him a moderate whipping. Adams then asked Branch what he was going to whip him for. Branch said he intended to whip him for disobeying his orders. Stating that while working on Mr. Weems' carriage he sent him to the shop three times in a hurry telling him to run and he would not do it. They both held on to the Negro and Adams asked why he used such violence. Branch said he was afraid the Negro would run away. Adams said there was no danger while he was there. Branch told Adams that the Negro had told him* [that his owner had told him] *if he (Branch) attempted to whip him to run home and he would protect him. Adams denied telling the Negro so.*

Branch said it was not worthwhile to contend any long about it, for whip him he would. Adams said he should not unless he done it according to law. Branch told him he would call three disinterested men, and when they said he had whipped the Negro enough, he would quit. Adams agreed to this. Branch then called Mr. Baker [Alpheus Baker, the town's schoolmaster], *Mr. Cunningham* [John Cunningham, a lawyer], *and Mr. McLaren* [John McLaren, the postmaster]. *He took the Negro into the next room, took off his shirt and tied him. Branch then gave him 25 cuts with the cowhide pretty severe and went to Mr. Cunningham and asked him something concerning the law for whipping Negroes. Mr. C. replied 39 lashes is*

Fatal Stabbing

the end of the law. Mr. Branch went back and gave the boy 12 cuts more. While Mr. Branch was talking with Mr. Cunningham, Mr. Adams walked out with Mr. Hill and staid out until Mr. Branch had gave the Negro the 12 cuts.

When Adams came back, Branch was untying the Negro. Adams said he wished he had it in his power to give him as much as he had given the Negro. 'I would give it to you with more free will than you have given it to the Negro,' at the same time abusing Branch and damning him for the meanest man in Abbeville. Branch ordered him out of his house; Adams said (I think) that he would stay as long as he pleased. Adams called him a damned son of a bitch and shook his fist in his face.

Branch turned round to the harness table and looked as though he was hunting something to strike him with, but could find nothing. He stepped into the other room and picked up a piece of ash wood. Adams said come on with your stick, I can whip you with your stick, but before he went after the stick, he told Adams if he said that again (alluding to his calling him a damned son of a bitch and shaking his fist in his face) that he would strike him. Adams followed him toward the door and stopt, and Branch stept inside of the door and raised his stick. Adams advanced toward him and told him to strike away shaking his fist at him. Branch struck him with the stick, then dropt it and run, Adams after him to the far end of the room when he caught him. I went to the window and saw Mr. Markey holding Adams arm to prevent him from hurting Branch.

Several persons gathered in, one caught Markey and pulled him away. They then turned toward the window where I was, and I saw Adams kick Branch severely in the right side, Branch hollowing 'take him off.' Before they turned round towards the window and while Markey was holding Adams' arm, I heard Adams say 'will you hold me and let him stab me?' I did not see that he held him so as to prevent him using his limbs. When Adams kicked Branch, he nearly lifted him off the floor. I saw Adams with his left arm round Branch's body, holding Branch's left arm, his right arm round Branch's shoulder and arm and with his (Adams') right hand he wrested the screw driver which Branch had in his left hand from him and struck it into his breast. Hill then caught Adams, he still striking at Branch and at one time cutting his pantaloons in the back.

Another witness, Kinney Thomas, told much the same story of the fatal blow, and he added a few details: *I heard Mr. Branch order Mr. Adams out of his house, and went into the back room, and brought out a piece of timber with which he approached Adams and drew it over him, something was then said about a former dispute when Adams shook his fist in Branch's face and called him a trifling scoundrel or something like it. Branch then struck Adams and*

Fatal Stabbing

dropping the timber retreated into the back room. Adams pursued him and caught him at the work bench. I ran into the room as quick as I could, though I was behind some of the company. I saw Adams have hold of Mr. Branch and surrounded by three others. Mr. Holliday, John Branch [Samuel's fifteen year old son], *and one other which they called Mr. Markey. John Branch had a piece of timber in his hand. Mr. Holliday had hold of Adams, when Adams said 'God damn it gentlemen, will fifteen or twenty of you stand and see a man stabbed and beat to death?' I then assisted Mr. Jordan* [Samuel Jordan] *and Mr. Hill* [Richard Hill] *in parting them, when I saw for the first a weapon in the hands of both Adams and Branch. Adams being the strongest man took the weapon from him. Branch then attempted to get to the work bench to sit down, when I saw Adams strike at Branch with the weapon. I saw nothing more.*

Alpheus Baker testified that as Adams stabbed Branch, he "told him he was a dead man," but Branch replied "No, I am not much hurt." John E. Allen testified that *he heard Mr. Adams say after the affair had happened that 'he wished to God he (Branch) would die.' Some one sitting by told him he had gone too far, when Mr. Adams said he would call back the expression.*

Three days later, a coroner's jury found that the fatal blow was *by the hand of Jesse S. Adams, at the said Samuel Branch's workshop in the village of Abbeville on Sunday the seventeenth day of the same month and year.* James Alston was the foreman, and the other jurors were James S. Wilson, D. Douglass, James Moore, Samuel Goff, James Creight, Andrew Hamilton, B. M. McFarlin, John White, Edmund Cobb, B. L. Posey, John McIlwain, John Hunter, Joseph Runnels, and James Shillito.

The Highland Sentinel (Calhoun, S. C.) of November 5, 1840 reported that Jesse Adams had been acquitted of the charge of murder of Samuel Branch following a three-day trial in Abbeville. Attorneys for the prosecution were Col. Wardlaw, Solicitor J. J. Caldwell and Major Burt; those for the defense were Col. John Cunningham, J. H. Wilson, Esq., and Gen. Waddy Thompson.

Two decades later when Jesse S. Adams died in his 70th year, the obituary in the *Independent Press,* March 23, 1860, gave the following even-handed assessment of his life: *He was a 'plain, blunt man' in all his intercourse with his fellow man. No concealing of sentiment; was well known to his neighbors, and appreciated as belonging to the old school of hospitality--which was only understood by those who met him under his own vine and fig tree, where the true spirit of hospitality is displayed. He was a member of the Presbyterian church, though no enthusiast upon the subject of religion.*

IX. THE GOLDEN AGE OF FINE ABBEVILLE HOMES
1850-1880s

In July, 1880, when the dwelling of J. Townes Robertson was burned, the *Press & Banner* (July 28, 1880) observed that, *From 1850 to 1860 a majority of the fine houses of the town were erected, and within the past decade, from 1870 to 1880, it seems that nearly the whole of them have been destroyed by fire.* During the three decades before 1890, visitors saw Abbeville at the peak of its wealth and beauty. For example, a Pennsylvania reporter in 1869 wrote of the village, as follows:

It lies nicely along the top of a ridge, and it has in it some fine dwellings with very handsome grounds attached; the residence of planters whose plantations are in the surrounding country, but who, on account of its greater convenience, sociability and healthfulness, prefer to live in the village. The destructive fires would come later.

In its account of the Robertson fire, the *Press & Banner* said, *Colonel Robertson's dwelling was one of the two largest and most expensive dwellings in town, and occupied a commanding eminence, surrounded by an elegant growth of trees of every variety. . . . This will be remembered as the dwelling of the Hon. J. Foster Marshall erected in 1850 soon after his return from Mexico.* This date was probably in error, for on May 10, 1847, an Abbeville lady had written, *Capt. Marshall was a lawyer and had just completed the building of the largest and most beautiful dwelling house in the village* (*Abbeville Medium*, March 3, 1904).

Perhaps the saddest loss of a fine home by fire came three years earlier in 1877. When it was built in 1858, the residence of Thomas C. Perrin, the President of the Greenville & Columbia Railroad, was described in vivid detail in the following account in the *Independent Press*, September 24, 1858:

Beautiful Mansion. We had the pleasure a few days since of visiting, in company with the architect, Mr. F. Cownover, the beautiful private residence of Mr. Thos. C. Perrin, Esq. which has just been completed. It is one of the finest and most commodious mansions in the State, and is truly an ornament to our village. It is situated on the level platform between the Presbyterian church and the Female Academy, and at a convenient distance from the Main Street to which it presents an imposing front. To give some idea of its size, we would state that it extends 76 feet in the front and 85 in the rear, and is 54 feet in height; that it contains 28 rooms in all, and has 19 fireplaces.

A broad flight of steps, in front, extends from the ground to the portico, which is supported by fluted columns, and leads into an airy and commodious entry, which is decorated overhead with a beautiful ceiling of stucco work. Upon the right, opening into this entry, are two spacious drawing rooms, separated by sliding doors; these are richly ornamented with stucco work, and with beautiful mantle pieces

Golden Age of Abbeville Homes

of Italian marble, and are provided with glass doors opening upon the portico. On the left of the entry are the parlor and dining room, separated also by sliding doors. Attached to the dining room is a speaking trumpet connected with the kitchen; and adjoining is a well appointed serving room, provided with pipes of hot and cold water, suitable cupboards and other conveniences. Upon this floor is also a commodious chamber, with a bathing room attached and supplied with pipes of hot and cold water; a very commodious library room, and convenient pantries.

A wide stairway with a beautiful railing of mahogany leads to the upper story. This contains six or seven large and airy chambers, each with a dressing room attached. In this story is also a bathing room; and porticos in front and in the rear add much to the comfort and convenience of its arrangements.

From this story a stairway leads to the attic, where is kept the reservoir of water from which the various pipes are supplied; and thence to the observatory on the top of the building. This is a glass frame-work, of octagonal shape, opening upon the flat tin roof, and commands a fine view of the surrounding country.

The basement story is of brick, and contains sleeping apartments, storerooms, and other rooms appropriated to various purposes; and is very commodious and well arranged.

The whole building reflects great credit upon the taste and liberality of the proprietor and the skill of the architect, Mr. Cownover. The stucco work is a beautiful specimen of art, from the hands of Mr. [Joseph D.] Daly, who to the skill of the artist adds that of an accomplished architect. The painting was executed by Messrs. Corbett and Ard; and the various doors and wainscoting exhibit some excellent specimens of groining and marbling.

The building throughout, in each passage and room, is lighted with gas; and nearby is the house containing the furnace for its manufacture, and the spacious gasometer for its reception.

The *Independent Press*, February 4, 1859, informed its readers that Abbeville's building renaissance had attracted a foreign architect, as follows:

A Plan of Abbeville. Dr. Togno informs us that Mr. August Bernelle, an architect and a landscape gardener just from Paris, having fixed his residence among us, contemplates making a plan of our village and environs. So people need not be surprised to see him take dimensions, etc. of their respective properties and buildings.

On April 1, 1859, the *Press* reported that it had *been shown by Mr. Joseph D. Daly, the architect, the plans for the fine Brick Range of stores to be erected by Mr. R. J. White on the burnt district, and also some beautiful designs of private mansions prepared for James M. Perrin, Esq., Gen. A. M. Smith, and others of our citizens.*

Golden Age of Abbeville Homes

A week later the same paper made the following observation:
The private residences of our village present many objects of attraction to the eye of a stranger with their surroundings of fine shrubbery and beautiful flower gardens. The beautiful and tasteful residence of Wm. H. Parker, Esq. which will soon be completed presents a fine specimen of architectural skill and is a model of good taste. It was constructed by Mr. F. Cownover from designs by Mr. J. D. Daly, and as well in the plan as in the execution reflects the highest credit upon those so employed.

The *Press & Banner*, February 14, 1877, carried a sad account of the destruction of the T. C. Perrin mansion when *this ornament and pride of the village, surrounded by the most superb gardens of choice evergreen and trained shrubbery to be found anywhere in the State" was consumed by fire. Unfortunately, "Mr. Perrin commenced to insure his house before it was finished and since then has paid the insurance premium regularly for twenty years until last Wednesday at 12 o'clock when he allowed the insurance to expire.* There was no suspicion of arson, in the words of the newspaper report, *it seems the fire originated from a spark in the roof, the shingles being dry and the wind blowing a stiff breeze.*

The house built for J. M. Perrin, one of the "Five Lost Colonels" was burned in 1887 along with the Abbeville Presbyterian Church. The *Press & Banner*, April 6, 1887, carried the following story:
At three o'clock while W. T. Buck and Will Cobb, tinners and painters in the employ of H. W. Lawson & Co. were at work painting and repairing the roof of Judge McGowan's house [Samuel McGowan had purchased the Perrin house and lived there along with his son-in-law, W. Christie Benet], *Mr. Cobb noticed smoke coming through the shingles in a story below, but not under them, to which he called Mr. Buck's attention. Seeking to investigate the cause, they immediately slipped down the roof from where they were to the roof below, from which the smoke came. In raising the scuttle or trap door in the roof they saw that the building was on fire. Dense smoke and hot air came out of it when opened. It being impossible to reach the tower from whence they came, Mr. Buck and Mr. Cobb jumped down the scuttle through the smoke, not knowing where they would land. They rushed down stairs and gave the alarm, the family being at dinner at the time.*

The tinners and the painters had commenced that morning to paint the roof and to do whatever repairing was necessary. They carried their soldering furnace to solder leaks in the tin, and had finished that part of the work by eleven o'clock, placing the furnace on the tower at that time, with very little fire in it, and they had not used it since that time. They had been painting since eleven o'clock, and were together on the tower when the fire was discovered in a part of the house in which they had not been, and which is immediately over the ironing

Golden Age of Abbeville Homes

room.

Rising from the table Judge McGowan took several torpedo fire extinguishers, and threw them on the fire, but they were useless to stop the flames. . . . In about half an hour after the alarm of fire, the cornicing to the roof of the Presbyterian church took fire and ineffectual efforts were made to extinguish it. Fifteen minutes later the tower blazed, and in a little while the whole tower was in a bright blaze. . . .

Judge McGowan's house was the finest private residence in the upcountry, and was the pride of Abbeville. It was built by Col. James M. Perrin in 1859 and 1860. Exclusive of the high gable roof and still higher reaching tower, but counting the basement, it was four stories. The cost of its construction is not definitely known, though some say it was thirty thousand or more. Others place its cost at twenty five thousand.

. . . . The Presbyterian church was of brick, covered with tin. It was built in 1854, at a cost of $4,000--Dr. J. F. Livingston and David Lesley, contractors. The Presbyterian church was not insured, but the McGowan house and furniture was insured for $8,500. Samuel McGowan and his son W. C. McGowan put up another fine house on the site which was later owned for many years by the W. D. Barksdale family. In 1989, it was given to the Abbeville County Historical Society for restoration and preservation.

X. THE LESLEY-HOYT-SIMONDS-BURT-NORWOOD-CALHOUN-STARK HOUSE

This house has long been the symbol of Abbeville, and its history has illustrated that of the town. Located on a conspicuous site astride a slight ridge at the junction between North Main Street and Greenville Street, it still commands the attention that it has attracted through much of its one hundred and fifty year existence.

It was built by David Lesley, a prominent lawyer and planter, at about the time when he became the Ordinary (judge) of Abbeville District in 1841. The Lesley family were pioneer settlers in the country a few miles west of Abbeville along a stream named for them. By tradition, they founded the Upper Long Cane Cemetery, and the oldest marked graves in it are members of their family.

David Lesley was not listed as a householder in the town in the State Census of 1839, so that it was not until after that year that he moved into the town of Abbeville. His wife Louisa, the daughter of James Kyle, was a native of Pennsylvania; and according to Lesley family tradition while on a trip to the North, the Lesleys saw a house in the Hudson Valley which they particularly liked. So they sent their slave carpenter, Cubic, on horseback to examine the house, and he built their new house by its plan.

David Lesley was an elder in the Upper Long Cane congregation which was about a mile north of Abbeville, and before he died in 1855, he had played a leading role in building a brick sanctuary for the Presbyterians who lived in town. This church was across Main Street on the site later occupied by the First Baptist Church. David Lesley was a devoted Presbyterian, and in 1835 he became the first lay commissioner to represent the South Carolina Presbytery in the General Assembly of his denomination. He was also an avid prohibitionist and twice was elected to the town council on a "no license" ticket. His role in the "Whiskey War of 1843" is chronicled in the previous article by Addison F. Posey. The Lesleys had no children, but they raised his wife's niece, Louisa Jane Kyle, and at other times her nephew, Andrew Kyle, lived with them.

In 1855, the Rev. Thomas Hoyt, the pastor of the Upper Long Cane congregation, bought the house, and the Hoyts lived there until 1860 when the Rev. Hoyt was called to the pastorate of the First Presbyterian Church of Louisville, Kentucky. The Hoyts had four small children, and Mrs. Hoyt's older sister and mother also lived with them. The latter owned some twenty slaves which she brought from Sumter to Abbeville. One of these slaves was Alfred Ellison who became town marshal (policeman) of Abbeville in the 1870s.

In 1860, Andrew Simonds of Charleston became the third owner of the house. In that year, Simonds married his cousin Sallie, the daughter of John A. Calhoun, a nephew of John C. Calhoun and a

Lesley-Burt Stark House

wealthy planter (in 1860, Calhoun owned 155 slaves and about 2,000 acres). In 1860, Abbeville was selected as the site of the first upcountry branch of the Bank of the State of South Carolina, and Simonds was put in charge of it. In 1862, Simonds sold this house and moved to a plantation below the town near where his father-in-law lived. In the *Abbeville Press*, February 20, 1863, there appeared the following ad: *$5 REWARD. Strayed from my house, one and a half miles from the village on the Snake Road, a Brown colored Terrier Pup, about 6 months old--answers to the name of JEFF. The above reward will be paid on his delivery to me, or to the Bank at Abbeville. Andrew Simonds.*

Armistead Burt, the fourth owner of the house, only lived in it about six years, but ever afterwards the house was called "the Burt house," or sometimes "the Burt Mansion." An Edgefield native, he had grown up in Pendleton, and by 1862 he had become the Intendent (mayor) of Abbeville and one of its most respected lawyers. He had represented the District in the state legislature and in the Nullification Convention. From 1843 to 1853, he had served in the U. S. Congress. He owned a plantation, Orange Hill, near the Savannah River.

Burt was largely self-taught, but he was widely read, and he was noted for his caustic wit and his success in the court room. His friend Benjamin F. Perry said that many a culprit owed his life or liberty to Burt's skill as a defense lawyer.

Burt married Martha Calhoun, said to be John C. Calhoun's favorite niece. In March, 1839, Calhoun wrote his daughter about a trip to Abbeville to attend the wedding of E. P. Noble and Sarah Calhoun. He wrote, *The wedding took place at Mr. Burt's. The party was large, with really a beautiful array of fine looking fashionable girls, far more so, than I could have expected in Abbeville. The supper was tasteful, as you would expect from your cousin* [Martha Calhoun Burt], *who you know has a good deal of ambition, and no small share of taste* (*Calhoun Papers*, XIV, 593).

Burt's career, like that of almost all successful South Carolina politicians, was linked to the support of John C. Calhoun and his policies. This was particularly necessary in Abbeville. In 1847, a Virginia lady, who had married into an Abbeville family, wrote her brother back home that, *they* [Abbeville ladies] *are strangers to the enthusiasm and party spirit so often displayed among all ranks and both sexes in Virginia, all nearly, being united in their admiration of and devotion to John C. Calhoun; and their only hopes, wishes and plans (political) being centred in him, there is no room for disagreement or argument.* When it was noticed that Armistead Burt was not present at the bedside of Calhoun at the latter's death in Washington in 1850, Burt found it necessary to explain publicly. He

Lesley-Burt-Stark House

wrote the editor of the *Abbeville Banner* that he had been worn out from nursing his wife's famous uncle, when "in the coldest weather [I] slept in his room on a matrass [sic] on the floor" (reprinted in the *Edgefield Advertiser*, August 7, 1850).

The Burts made the house the center of social life in Abbeville, despite the wartime atmosphere. They were considered the most handsome couple in the town. Martha Burt was said to have one slave girl whose chief duty was to keep the wide walks freshly raked, and others who tended the shrubs and flowers which had been planted by the Episcopal minister, the Rev. Benjamin Johnson.

Judge Robert E. Hill in his memoirs said that the common people of Abbeville found both of the Burts rather overbearing or haughty, but they were quite hospitable to their friends. Mrs. Varina Davis on her flight south from Richmond in April, 1865 had not stopped at any point with old friends or for longer than a few days until she arrived at the Burts on April 18. She stayed until twelve days later, and only reluctantly did she leave two days before her husband and his entourage arrived at the Burts' house. The Confederate president came to Abbeville hoping to catch up with his family, and he clearly intended to stay there for some time.

Several generations of Abbevillians argued that the last meeting of the Confederate cabinet was held at the Burt house on May 2, 1865. Sometimes the people of Washington, Georgia challenged this claim with the assertion that their town was due the honor of being the site of the "last meeting of the Confederate cabinet." In the late summer of 1903, following a particularly heated exchange between proponents of the two towns, the two sides agreed to submit the question to the decision of the last living cabinet member, ex-Postmaster General John H. Reagan of Texas. R. R. Hemphill, the editor of the *Abbeville Medium* and himself a Confederate veteran, took a somewhat bemused view of Reagan's verdict. In August 6, 1903, Hemphill reported that Reagan as "the great umpire stated that the last cabinet meeting was in Richmond."

In fact, although Jefferson Davis only stayed in Abbeville from 10 a. m. until about midnight on May 2, 1865, what happened in Abbeville was quite important. The war cabinet meeting with his military leaders was far more important than any meeting with his remaining cabinet members. Jefferson Davis neglected to mention even briefly the meeting in Abbeville in his *Rise and Fall of the Confederate Government*, but it is quite clear in other accounts and in his letters that it played a key role in his final acceptance of the fall of the Confederacy. What he heard from the brigade commanders and from the troops themselves left him with a bitter feeling, and an hour before he was scheduled to leave Abbeville he wrote Burton Harrison that he thought his family was, *safest when fartherest from me. I have*

Lesley-Burt-Stark House

the bitterest disappointment in regard to the feeling of our troops, and would not have any one I love dependent upon their resistance against an equal force.

Since Armistead and Martha Burt had no children, they did not suffer the human loss of many of their neighbors, but the outcome of the war left them somewhat impoverished. For example, a few years into the post-war era Burt told a correspondent of the *New York Tribune* who interviewed him in Charleston that gentlemen like himself "in the old times would never drink brandy that was less than 30 years old, and now they can afford nothing better than the meanest corn whiskey." In 1868, when Mrs. Burt's health failed, the couple moved from their house to the Marshall House, a hotel on the north side of the public square. Within a year, Mrs. Burt died.

The fifth owner of the house, James A. Norwood, also belonged to the group of nearly ruined ante-bellum planters. In 1860, Norwood was the second largest slave holder in the District with 194 slaves and nearly 2,000 acres in the rich Flatwoods section west of the town. Norwood died in 1875, and for the next dozen years the house was the residence of his widow, the former Sarah Hester, and her children, Sarah (Sallie) Norwood Calhoun and her husband, Edward B. Calhoun, and her two unmarried sisters. Like the Stark family which later lived in the house, Sallie and Ed Calhoun's only children were twin daughters, but unlike the Starks, they had two sets of twin daughters. They lived in genteel poverty, and the house fell into such a state of dilapidation at the turn of the century that when it was pointed out to a group of Northern financiers who were in Abbeville to assess their investment in the new cotton mill, their sole comment was that the house needed some paint.

The house and its four-acre lot were purchased by J. S. Stark in 1913. Mr. Stark was a well-to-do land owner, livery stables operator, and banker, and the Stark family restored the house and grounds as a showplace in Abbeville. The Starks with their twin daughters, Fannie and Mary, were active in all facets of the life of Abbeville, and the house became the "Burt-Stark House."

In 1971, the surviving Stark sister, Mary Stark Davis, offered her historic home to the Abbeville County Historic Preservation Commission which had been set up to maintain such properties. Somewhat later she donated the contents of the house as well. Until her death at the age of 103, "Miss Mary" continued to host a stream of tours and individuals who visited in her venerable house. The house is now maintained by the Historic Preservation Commission with generous help from the county and city of Abbeville.

XI. A WALKING TOUR OF THE ABBEVILLE BUSINESS DISTRICT, 1857

Independent Press, September 25, 1857

Our town has during the past week presented quite a business air, and a spirit of life and activity seems to pervade all departments of business. The cotton wagons, laden with produce, are beginning to come in from the country; and gay equipages with bright eyed lassies, in search of the various novelties of the season, are thronging our streets. Come one, Come all; as our merchants are prepared, both to buy and to sell.

Their name is legion, and to inspect a tithe of their various attractions would give a good morning's task to the active young shopper.

Passing up from the Court House on the right, we first reach the fine brick corner store of Messrs. Wier & Lythgoe, who have just received an extensive stock from New York, which they are selling on the most liberal terms. We may next call at the agency of the **Bank of Newberry**, where we will find our worthy Intendant, ready to dispense justice, discuss a question of finance, or grant a pecuniary accomodation. If we can resist the temptation of making a call at the Jewelry Establishment of Mr. H. T. Tusten, we may pass on to the grocery where the Messrs. Knox are prepared to furnish a little of everything in their line. Just beyond stands the spacious new store of Mr. McLaren, now occupied by Messrs. Cobb, Hunter, & Co., where bales of bagging, coils of rope, and any number of barrels and boxes show what these gentlemen are doing for their customers. Our friend the Postmaster may next have for us a few crumbs of the intellectual feast which he dispenses daily to a waiting public, and we at length arrive at the corner store, which has been handsomely fitted up for the reception of the new goods of Mr. Wm. C. Moore, which have been carefully selected in New York by himself, and which competent judges pronounce to be an admirable assortment.

Standing at the corner and looking down Washington Street, we may take a "bird's eye" view, if nothing more, of the various tailoring establishments of Messrs. Alexander & Ives; the boot and shoe shop of Mr. Roche; the "barber shop;" Mr. Davis' livery stables, and in the distance, the Abbeville Hotel by Mr. Hughey.

Crossing over to the Marshall House, which has just been opened by a new proprietor, Mr. Edmund Cobb, under the most favorable auspices, we may find the Messrs. Winstock at the corner store, prepared to exhibit a most extensive stock of ready-made clothing, just from New York. Just over the way, we see friend Gray, No. 1, Granite Range, of the firm of Chambers & Marshall, ever at his post, and ready to extend a cordial greeting to all who may honor him with a call. We will next visit the tastefully arranged Jewelry

Business District, 1857

establishment of Mr. M. T. Owen, and then drop in at the "Drug Store," where Dr. Jordan is receiving from New York an extensive and well selected stock. Next door stands invitingly open the fine store of Messrs. Israel & Brussels, where the well fitted shelves and loaded counters show the extent and completeness of their stock. Just beyond opposite his large grocery establishment, stands friend Kerr with a bland smile playing upon his countenance; ready either to buy or sell, to give the highest price for produce or to sell with the cheapest. Let us give him a call and then solace ourselves with a glass of soda water at Messrs. Branch & Allen; where we may be tempted to subscribe for one of their recent publications.

*Passing the well known Ramey Hotel, we arrive at the large and long established store of Mr. R. H. Wardlaw & Son, whose enlarged experience and fine taste enable them to satisfy all customers. Here is also established the agency of the **Bank of Charleston**. Just beyond Mr. J. A. Allen is disposing of a fine assortment of fancy and staple goods at reduced prices; and still further on Mr. Westfield may be found ready to serve one in search of a superior stable or harness. At the opposite corner, a large pile of empty boxes labeled "J. & R. J. White" show that these gentlemen have received their extensive fall supply from New York, which they are selling low.*

By continuing our walk down the street, we might visit the tailoring establishments of Mr. Martin and of Mr. Shillito; the tin factory of Mr. Lawson; the marble yard of Mr. Chalmers, the harness shop of Mr. Golding; the carriage manufactories of Messrs. Christian & Deale and of Mr. Taylor, or retracing our steps may be rewarded by a reconnaisance of the extensive cotton gin factory of Messrs. Enright & Starr; or if not fatigued may find it a pleasant ramble to the steam mill of Dr. Livingston.

XII. DR. TOGNO AND THE ROCK HOUSE

Independent Press, February 11, 1859

Died in the Village [Abbeville] *Saturday night, 5th inst., Dr. Joseph Togno, aged about 65 years.*
He was a native of Corsica, and when quite young an officer in the French Navy. He came to Philadelphia in early manhood; there took the degree of Doctor of Medicine, and acquired distinction in his profession, both as a practitioner and as a writer. Having been disabled by a paralytic affection, he retired from active practice, and was for a while engaged as vaccine agent, and as a Professor of Modern Languages in the Virginia University. Afterwards, he removed to Wilmington, N. C., and zealously entered upon the cultivation of grapes and fruits.
In 1854, he selected a farm in the neighborhood of this place for the prosecution of his favorite schemes, and here established his vineyard and orchard. With small means, he accomplished much, and he seemed to be just on the eve of remunerative success, when he was struck by apoplexy, or disease of the heart.
He was a man of varied acquirements, possessing a good memory well stored, communicative as he was full. He was robust, patient of privation, joyous in society, and ever anxious to be useful. He adapted himself to conditions and pursuits widely diverse, and in all was busy and cheerful. He loved the country of his adoption, but by instinct he was a Bonapartist, devoted and unswerving. Educated a Catholic, he became, by sincere conviction, a liberal Protestant, and his conduct was habitually controlled by the spirit of the Christianity which he professed and felt--full of charity.
Dr. Togno called his home *Montevino*, and with that as his pen name, he addressed numerous letters to the Abbeville newspapers in which he promoted the cultivation of the native grape known as the scuppernong and in which he carried on a running battle with the more zealous advocates of temperance. He exhibited his scuppernong wine at the Charleston Exposition and elsewhere.
He was a distinctive figure. As Mrs. Frances Marshall described him, *I remember him as being a man short and stout with a bushy head of hair which he grew quite long. He kept to the mode of dress of his country, wearing a very short jacket with full baggy pants.*
However, the distinctive achievement of Dr. Togno was probably the house which he built, known to later generations as "The Rock House." In the 1870s, G. A. Douglass bought the house, and the following (*Press & Banner*, June 15, 1931) is a description of the house at that time as remembered by the Douglass family:
The house was built of rock blasted from the place and the walls are about a foot in thickness with the rock of ordinary size and the

Dr. Togno

between space filled in with small rock. The whole lower floor of the house was without flooring and the walls were without windows except for two in the back which were iron barred. The bars were stout square bars standing upright and were imbedded in the walls. The front of the house was without an opening on the lower floor, all this space being used as a wine cellar, a cool even temperature being necessary for the making of a good wine. A trap door in an upstairs room was the method of entering the cellar. The entrance to the upstairs was made by a flight of stairs from the outside and a small gallery after the French style of architecture which was without covering. There were two rooms and a hall upstairs and above this was a small cupola or observation tower which had a window on all four sides, affording the doctor a clear view over all his vineyard. A double door in the wine cellar was made of two thicknesses of heavy plank and this was studded thickly with heavy home made square nails. This door was opened from the inside and was held by the cross bar of lumber, about a four by four, fitted into the walls by a space left vacant and was further held with a heavy padlock.

A place of this kind would not be perfect without a ghost and the Douglass children heard from many of a ghost which walked around the place. It seemed that a Mr. Gaston when cutting lumber at the back of the place was struck by a tree and killed. He was buried on the grounds and ever after was said to stray around and cause the Doctor to frequently shout from the observation windows at the intruder.

The *Independent Press*, May 6, 1859, carried the following story on the "Sale at Montevino:"

Montevino, as is known to many of our readers, is distant from our village about a mile and a half in a southeasterly direction, and near the residence of John H. Wilson, Esq.-- from which the tract was originally purchased. A gentle ascent leads to the top of a bold eminence, which commands a fine view of the adjacent fields and forests. Here upon the Southern declivity of the hill, the late Doctor had planted a flourishing vineyard which was now budding in all the luxuriance of the blooming spring. Near by he had also planted some choice fruit trees, beds of strawberries and rare flowers. . . . Fronting the vineyard on the north he had erected a substantial mansion built of granite from an adjacent quarry; the basement of which formed his capacious wine cellar, whilst above were collected his valuable books and treasures of art.

The library was a large one and comprised some rare medical, scientific and literary works, in French, Spanish, and Italian, as well as many valuable English works. The French, Spanish and Italian were for the most part "caviare to the general [public]," but we had among the purchasers, Col. James E Calhoun of our District, whose proficiency in these languages is well known, and who availed himself of the present opportunity of adding to his already large collection of rare and valuable books.

The books generally sold well, though some of the rarer works, we thought, fell far short of their true value. A copy of "The Vatican Illustrated" in five volumes (the only copy we believe in this country) brought about sixty three dollars--"Dante Illustrated" about $40, and besides these were sold other valuable works of art illustrating the genius of Raffaelle, Canova, and others. The valuable medical works and the rare anatomical plates were not sold on account of the slim attendance by the [medical] fraternity on the occasion, and the sale of the larger portion of the works in foreign languages was also deferred to a more favorable opportunity.

The wine sold well, the "Sparkling Catawba" of the vintage of 1856, sold for about $4 per gallon; and the Burgundy and Scuppernong wines of the same year sold from $3 to $4 per gallon. The wines of succeeding years sold at prices equally high in proportion. The stock on hand consisted of about 200 gallons and readily found purchasers.

The vineyard at Montevino is still in successful cultivation. Mr. Wilson, the Executor of the Estate, has continued the services of the Messrs. Bernelle, in the superintendence of the vineyard during the present year, and they promise themselves a fine yield.

The Lesley-Burt-Stark House
Site of last Confederate War Council, 2 May 1865

Trinity Episcopal Church
Built 1859-1860

XIII. TRINITY AND THE SACRED HEART

The oldest church sanctuary in Abbeville is Trinity Episcopal which was built in 1859-60. It replaced the first Episcopal church, a wooden building which was put up in 1843 and taken down in 1859 and moved to Willington.

Most of the earliest settlers in Abbeville were Presbyterian, but there was no Presbyterian church in the village until 1855 when a brick chapel was built on the site now occupied by the First Baptist Church. It was a part of the Upper Long Cane church until 1868 when it became a separate congregation. In 1783, the Presbyterian leaders in the area considered the region between the Savannah and the Saluda such Presbyterian territory that they met at General Andrew Pickens' block house to divide the territory into four congregations. Of these, Upper Long Cane, was less than two miles from the court house, and for half a century it was Abbeville's Presbyterian church.

In 1826, Methodist circuit riders organized the first congregation in the town of Abbeville, and it built a small wooden church on Washington Street. When the congregation outgrew this church, it was sold to Silas Anderson who embarassed the Methodists by turning the former church into a drinking establishment (see "The Great Whiskey War of 1843").

In 1842, Thomas Parker, who had moved his family from Charleston to a nearby farm, organized Trinity Episcopal Church, and in the next year it built its first sanctuary. In 1846, there were 34 members of Trinity, and it grew so rapidly that in 1855 the total had grown to 91.

On February 25, 1859, the *Independent Press* reported that a meeting of the pew holders of Trinity had approved a committee's report on plans to build a new church and "whilst the subscription in the congregation, and the District have been most generous, the aid from abroad has been truly generous and praise worthy."

On June 24, 1859, the same newspaper made the following report on the new building:

The ceremony of laying the cornerstone of the new Episcopal church in our village was performed with becoming solemnity on Monday morning last at 10 o'clock by the Rt. Rev. Thos. F. Davis, D. D., the Bishop of the Diocese in the presence of the attending clergy and quite a number of spectators. Seats had been provided in the pleasant shade of the trees in front of the present edifice. . . [following the laying of the corner stone] *prayers were then offered by the Rev. B. Johnson* [the rector], *and the 100 Psalm of David was then sung to the tune of "Old Hundred"--after which followed the addresses of the Bishop, and the Rev. Thos. S. Arthur of Greenville. . . .*

The plan of the new church was prepared by Mr. G. E. Walker

Trinity Episcopal

architect, of Columbia. It is a beautiful design in the Gothic style, and has received the enconiums of all who have seen it. The church will occupy the site of the present edifice. It will be a large and imposing edifice, and will when completed be truly an ornament to our village.

Two weeks later, the paper carried the following notice:

To the Contractors. The undersigned will receive proposals until the 28th day of July next, to build a NEW GOTHIC CHURCH on the site of the present Trinity church. The Building Committee will furnish all the brick necessary to complete the church. The contractor will be required to furnish everything besides the above to complete the church.

    Jno. A. Calhoun
    J. F. Marshall
    A. M. Smith
    Ed. Noble
    Wm. H. Parker, Building Committee.

On July 29, 1859, the *Independent Press* reported that the contract had been awarded to Blease & Baxter of Newberry for about $10,000. It also reported that the spire would be 130 feet high, that the builders would begin laying brick by September 1, and that the congregation hoped to be in the new building by the next Spring.

This expectation was overly optimistic, and the new building was not finished until the next Fall. On November 9, 1860, the *Independent Press* published the following account of the dedication of the new Trinity:

The church is a beautiful Gothic structure, and is one of the handsomest edifices in the upper country; reflecting great credit in its design and construction upon the architect, Geo. A. Walker of Columbia, and the contractors, Blease & Baxter of Newberry. The symmetry of its exterior, and the convenience of its interior arrangements have been very generally admired. Entering by the ample doorway, a spacious centre aisle and two side aisles, conduct to well-cushioned seats, and to the rear of the building. On either hand are the large Gothic windows of stained glass, through which the "dim religious light" falls in rays of many a fantastic hue; whilst in the rear is the beautiful chancel with its soft carpeted floor, its stuccoed ceiling, and rich stained glass window. This window has been much admired, and is one of the finest in the state; representing the figure of Christ bearing his cross, and surrounded with many appropriate devices.

An attractive feature of the chancels is the beautiful marble slab of the communion table, a handsome present to the church from the generous donor, Mr. J. D. Chalmers of the village. Mr. Chalmers has furnished other specimens of his skill in a fine marble baptismal fount

Sacred Heart

and an exquisitely polished tablet, which has been erected to the memory of the late Thomas Parker, the founder of Trinity church.

In a recess to the right of the reading desk has been placed the new organ--a sweet toned instrument from the well known establishment of Mr. John Baker of Charleston. The organist is Prof. Aichel of the Cokesbury Masonic Female College, assisted by a fine choir of young ladies and gentlemen [the Rev. Johnson, the rector, was then acting as President of the Cokesbury College].

The church bell is a present from the Hon. J. Foster Marshall and is a fine specimen of Southern manufacturing skill from the well known foundry of Messrs. John Alexander & Co. of Columbia, S. C.

The interior decorations of the building, the cushions, the curtains, the carpet, etc. have been furnished by the ladies of the congregation. ...The painting of the interior of the church has been executed by Mr. John Corbett of our village, and for taste and finish the graining and frosting could scarcely be excelled.

In June, 1861, the Diocese of South Carolina met in its annual convention in the new Trinity church where the Bishop in his annual address took obvious note of the war with the Union as he declared, *Our brothers and our children are in the field. Our youths with whom heretofore we have only sported, have sprung up into armed men. ...Our cause is right and God is true. Let us show the world that we can trust both.*

In late January, W. A. Lee, the editor of the *Independent Press* and a member of Trinity, had written from Sullivan's Island that "Mr. [Oscar] Aichel is our Drummer and on last Sunday you would not have recognized the organist of Trinity, as he rolled a 'rub-a-dub' for our Dress Parade." In less than two more years, among those members of Trinity who had lost their lives to the Confederate cause were two members of the building committee, J. F. Marshall and A. M. Smith.

The other church in Abbeville which combines beauty and age is the Catholic church, Sacred Heart. The following account was printed in the *Abbeville Medium* (October 29, 1885) at the time of its completion:

The church has just been completed and is one of the handsomest ornaments of the town, situated on Main Street and convenient to all parts of the village. It is cruciform in shape, built of brick, with slate roof and a steeple surmounted by a handsome gilt cross. The walls are cemented outside and jointed and painted in imitation of Vermont stone with freestone trimmings. It is 65 feet in length and 32 in width with a seating capacity of 150. The style of architecture is Norman-Gothic. The basement is 16 x 34 feet. The beauty of the exterior is surpassed by that of the interior. The open truss roof with timbers is handsomely painted. The panels are of pine finished in natural

Sacred Heart

colors. The walls are plastered and calsomined a French grey color. The pews are finished in natural pine, with ends of cypress all oiled and varnished.

A special feature is the beautiful stained glass windows. Of these, nine are in the body of the church, three in the front, three in the tower and three in the sanctuary over the altar. Over the vestibule is a large rose window, in the center of which is a dove bearing an olive branch. The three in the sanctuary are of artistic beauty. One of these contains a life size figure of the Sacred Heart of Jesus. On either side of this is a window of the Blessed Virgin and St. Joseph. The altar is made of wood painted white and trimmed with gold. It will be adorned with elegant candlesticks and vases, gifts from different fields in the North. Above the altar is a groined arch ceiling terminating in a larger arch from which is suspended an elegant sanctuary lamp.

The church has an interesting history. The lot on which it was built was purchased some years ago mainly through the efforts of John Enright, an old resident of our place and a devout Catholic who was liberally aided by all our citizens. He did not live to see his intention of building a church realized. His work, however, has been carried out by his youngest son, Thomas G. Enright, who died on April 23, 1883 and bequeathed all the earnings of his short life to this object. By good management on the part of his executors, Edward Roche and Hugh McElrone, the estate realized nearly $4,000 and this amount judiciously expended has been sufficient to erect one of the most beautiful little churches in the State. The cornerstone of the building bears the name of the donor and is a fitting monument to his memory which will keep it fresh for many years to come.

The plans of the church were drawn by E. Fogette of Spartanburg, and have been faithfully carried out by J. W. Nichols of Greenville, under the supervision of Father Monaghan, Rector of the church. ...[Nichols had built the Presbyterian church at Greenville]. The altar was built by J. W. Barnett and is very handsome. It is made of native wood and beautifully trimmed in gold.

XIV. THE GREAT SECESSION MEETING, NOVEMBER 22, 1860

Robert R. Hemphill in *Abbeville Medium*, May 2, 1907

I remember the great Secession meeting in Abbeville in 1860 which was an introduction to the War Between the States. It was on the twenty second day of November and a great multitude was in the town. Augustus M. Smith was Marshal of the day. W. M. Rogers and J. F. Livingston were his assistants. The procession formed in the public square and escorted by about 500 minute men marched to the grove near the Southern depot where the mass meeting was organized by electing T. C. Perrin, President; Judge D. L. Wardlaw, Col. John A. Calhoun, Dr. J. W. Hearst, Capt. John Brownlee, and Dr. John A. Logan, vice presidents, and James C. Calhoun and George McDuffie Miller, secretaries.

Hon. A. G. Magrath of Charleston was the first speaker and I remember his first sentence was "The time for speaking has passed and the time for action has arrived." He rolled his "r's" in fine style. He was a very handsome man and made a capital speech urging immediate action on the part of South Carolina at any and every hazard. [The Abbeville people remembered this speech and were appalled when less than six years later, Magrath in his petition for amnesty implied that he never had been very much in favor of secession in 1860.] *He was followed by Hon. M. L. Bonham who also favored immediate action. Resolutions were unanimously adopted favoring secession of the state.*

A Committee of Twenty was appointed to select nominees for the Convention which met December 17, 1860. While this Committee was out, speeches were made by Samuel McGowan, W. C. Davis, and J. N. Cochran. The following gentlemen were elected to the Convention: Edward Noble, John A. Calhoun, Thomas Thomson, John H. Wilson, and D. L. Wardlaw. Called upon for an expression of views, each one endorsed the resolutions adopted which were published in the county newspapers. The speeches, however, were crowded out and lost to the generations that came after.

It was not however the official action of the mass meeting that I now undertake to record. It is the small and commonplace incidents of the day. I came down with several students from Due West which was rather a conservative community, a place where the war spirit had not reached. Four of us did not join the procession but stood on the sidewalk where the post office now is. Near us was a great watch hung out as a sign that H. T. Tusten was in business there. W. W. Lindsay and I. L. Grier of Due West, Robert Yeldell of Alabama and I kept together during the day. Yeldell would not march in the procession because he was afraid of giving offense to Samuel Jordan,

Great Secession Meeting

a kinsman, who held strong Union sentiments. We could not get near enough to hear much of the speeches and so we sat down on the ground and watched the firing of a cannon at intervals during the meeting. It was all new to us and we wondered how anyone could stand before artillery. In time, however, we learned the lesson. The last I saw of Yeldell, he was a lieutenant in an Alabama artillery company with the army near Yorktown in 1862. I. L. Grier was killed at the battle of Gaines' Mill. W. W. Lindsay was mortally wounded at Snicker's Gap in Virginia, November 2, 1862 and died on the 20th day of the same month, and only I escaped to tell the story.

There was a man in the crowd that day from Turkey Creek on the Saluda side of the District. His name was Wesley A. Robertson. He was up in years, well past the military age, slender in figure, with keen eyes, and full of good humor. When Judge Wardlaw in his speech inquired what would we do if a revenue cutter of the U. S. Navy would come into Charleston harbor to collect duties on imports, W. W. Perryman made some interruption and Robertson shouted. "I'd wade in and sink her, blank her, sink her." He never heard the last of it while the war went on. He was not the kind of man to help get up a fight and back out of it. He and his boys went to the front. He did all his age and strength would allow as a member of Co. G, Orr's Rifles, the famous command. In the winter of 1863-1864 when camped near Orange [Virginia.], he was sent up in the mountains upon light duty to look after commissary suplies. Returning from his detail when he came in sight of the regiment, he wore a high crowned, white stove pipe hat and was mounted on a skewbald or calico horse. He was greeted with the cry, "sink her, blank her, sink her," and received with the warmest welcome. No joke of his comrades ever disturbed his equanimity and the pleasure of his comrades in seeing him on this occasion was particularly enhanced by the fact that he had in his commissary wagon a barrel or two of eggs for Co. G., which he had received from the pretty mountain girls for telling their fortunes. He always told them something good and pleasant. After the close of hostilities, he went west and died in Texas in 1894.

I write this narrative to keep in the minds of our people a son of Abbeville past the vigor of young manhood and gray haired, who fought a good fight and risked all for his home and friends.

Wesley Robertson may have been "a rough sort of fellow," but in 1860 he owned 48 slaves and about 500 acres of valuable farm land. He qualified to rank as a planter of the second rank, at least. However, his property was unlikely to gain him admission into Abbeville society since it was inherited from a stepfather who was a free black, Reuben Robertson of Turkey Creek. (See this writer's article on the same, *South Carolina Historical Magazine*, October, 1990).

XV. THE LEGEND OF THE CRADLE AND THE GRAVE OF THE CONFEDERACY

From the New York *Sun*, as reprinted by the *Press & Banner*, August 25, 1886. This article is very readable, although it is contains obvious errors (such as the dates) and folklore (such as the story of the hijacking of the Treasure train).

Abbeville, S. C. On a cold drizzly day in February [April], 1865, a train drew up at the depot here with a mysterious car attached. With it came several agents, who busied themselves in hiring teams for the transportation of the contents of the car. Abbeville is about twenty miles from the Savannah river, which divides South Carolina from Georgia, and is the terminus of the branch of the Greenville & Columbia Railroad that runs off about twelve miles from Hodges to this village. Consequently, the only way to reach the Georgia frontier is by horse power.

By 10 o'clock that night enough horse teams were secured, and they began loading from the mysterious car. The goods rolled out were in stout little kegs of phenomenal weight, and though the packages were small, they taxed the strength of the able bodied Negroes detailed for the work. At length the loading was accomplished, and amid the flash of lantern and the cracks of whips and the cries of the driver, the long line of teams pulled up out of the muddy railroad yard up the sloppy hill, through the village streets, where curious crowds had gathered to watch them pass, and disappeared in the darkness on the winding "snake road" that leads to Georgia.

When the teams had gone about ten miles, forty or fifty masked men rushed upon the astonished drivers and caretakers, held them mute under the muzzles of pistols, and proceeded to unload the wagons of their stout little kegs. A cloth was spread upon the ground, and around it assembled the ring, with flickering torches held aloft, while deft hands stove in the heads of the kegs and poured their contents into a heap. It was gold--bright, yellow, glittering gold pieces by the thousands! The hungry eyes behind the masks gleamed with avarice. It was a weird, mystic scene, like a page from some Arabian romance. The abysmal silence of the forest, broken only by the rearing and plunging of the frightened mules, the shriveling ring of light varying as the torches were moved to and fro, the surrounding gloom, the anxious faces of the Negro drivers, gazing with startled eyes and gaping lips upon this fantastic spectacle, the eager circle of masks, and last, the solid pile of sovereigns, the centre of the whole-- all formed a panorama which those who saw will never forget.

With all possible haste the money was divided up between the masked men, and in fifteen minutes they were gone. So was the gold.

Confederate Cradle and Grave

Nothing remained but the empty kegs and empty wagons, and the caretakers of this last remnant of the Confederate treasury sent the teams back to Abbeville, while they continued on their way to Georgia. What became of the money and who got it remains today a profound secret, and will probably never be learned. My information about the forest scene was derived from one of the Negro drivers of the teams to whom a masked man had thrown a tin bucket full of gold in exchange for a commodious carpetbag, and he showed the gold in confirmation of the story.

A few days after this, stray squads of Wheeler's cavalry began to wander through the town. Sherman's army had passed through Georgia and through a part of South Carolina a little lower than Abbeville, and was now sacking and burning Columbia. The broken forces which opposed Sherman were taking the back track a little higher up, and seeking to reach the pinelands of Georgia.

One evening about sundown [actually 10 a. m.], Jefferson Davis reached Abbeville. Judah P. Benjamin was with him and two other members of his Cabinet, I think, but who they were I do not now remember. Abbeville is a long, straggling town, of one street, being built on the crest of a hill, until it reaches a point where it branches off into the upper or western part. Just in the fork is situated what used to be the residence of Armistead Burt, who was before the war a Congressman of South Carolina. Mr. Burt is dead now, and the house is in strange hands. The house itself is a square, unpicturesque, three story building, surrounded by what used to be lovely grounds and orchards. Jefferson Davis and his Cabinet proceeded to the house of Mr. Burt, where they were hospitably received.

No public demonstration was made on the arrival at the depot or on the public square of Abbeville, except that which was made by some half dozen furloughed soldiers or citizens who happened to be standing together at the Marshall House corner. As the president was driven near to them, they raised their hats and gave a single cheer for the Confederate chieftain, whose only recognition of the salute was the raising of his own hat. His face betrayed the deep feeling and extreme anxiety which he felt for the safey of the Government on which he had placed his heart and the success of which he had so earnestly devoted all the powerful energies of his great mind.

A strange coincidence! Has it ever been noted before? I believe not. Here was about to be performed the last official act of the Confederacy, while hardly a stone's throw from the spot was Secession Hill, the grove which gave birth to the war. Just four years previously, this ampitheatrical hill, shaded by oaks and other giant trees, was filled by a sea of excited faces, all looking toward a stand constructed against three tree trunks at its foot, and containing the leading men of the State.

Confederate Cradle and Grave

It was the first of the Secession meetings. Speaker after speaker dilated in glowing terms on the necessity of severing the relations of the State with the Union, and every word was cheered to the echo. At length the venerable Judge Wardlaw, a man whose decisions had been quoted throughout the land, and who held a place in the front ranks of jurists, rose and solemnly warned the people against the rash act they were taking. He told them plainly they would be crushed, that they had not a single chance, and that, aside from arguments about their political rights, it would be better for them to remain in the Union, with disadvantages, than to fight and be forced back at the point of the bayonet, with all the evils that war and defeat would entail. Judge Wardlaw was hissed off the platform. The people were determined on their course. But such of them as now survive are convinced of the wisdom of his counsels.

The almost deserted condition of Abbeville on that bleak February day, when Jefferson Davis sought the hospitable shelter of Mr. Burt's residence, bore mute but eloquent witness to the prophetic words of Judge Wardlaw. In gloomy loneliness Davis and his Cabinet assembled in one of the sitting rooms. They held their last consultation, discussed plans that were discussed only to be abandoned, and finally decided the end had come, and that they had better try to escape. Then they examined such papers as they had with them, and when the hour of twelve struck, the ashes of nearly all these papers were smouldering in the glowing coals of the big wood fire. The question then came up as to the disposal of the seal of the Southern Confederate States. It was plain that it ought to be destroyed; but how could they do it? Time pressed. They should be on their weary flight for safety even now. There was an old covered well in Mr. Burt's yard, and into this Mr. Benjamin threw the seal. It has since caved in and filled up, and now the seal of the late Confederacy is safe under fifty feet of ground and exactly in what spot there lives no man who can tell.

The sequel is known. A week or so after this meeting Mr. Davis was captured in Georgia. Mr. Benjamin escaped to England. --New York Sun.

Hugh Wilson, editor of the Press & Banner, added his comments:

Many of the facts stated in the above paragraph are true. They are inaccurate in some particulars.

Mr. Davis, the President of the Southern Confederacy in his retreat across the country after the fall of Richmond, arrived in Abbeville the 1st day of May, 1865, about 10 a. m. and left about 12 p. m. He had with him five of his Cabinet officers, Gen. Breckinridge, Mr. Benjamin, Mr. Mallory, Mr. Reagan, and Gen. Lawton. Mr. Davis was entertained by the Hon. Armistead Burt whom he had known as a Congressman in Washington. General Lawton was entertained by

Confederate Cradle and Grave

Judge Monroe, a refugee from Kentucky. The other four members of his Cabinet were entertained at the Hon. Thomas C. Perrin's house. The last Cabinet meeting was not held in Mr. Perrin's house, but a council of war was held in the house of Mr. Burt.

At this meeting Mr. Davis who had with him two brigades of cavalry commanded by Generals Vaughn and Duke urged that a stand should be made at this point, that a reorganization of the army might be attempted, and the Confederacy not entirely abandoned, at least until such terms might be secured from the United States Government as would protect the life and property of the supporters of the Southern Confederacy. He was, however, overruled by the council after free consultation. General Breckinridge occupied the library of Mr. Perrin as his office, and was engaged until a late hour at night in preparing and signing discharges for such soldiers who applied for them, and there were many.

This incident is related of the meeting: Mr. Davis after stating his views, asked General Duke if his troops could be relied on to make a stand at or near Abbeville. General Duke replied he feared not. The same question was asked of Generals Vaughn and Bragg, and the same reply received from each. Mr. Davis then rested his head against the back of his chair, and covered his face with his unfolded hankerchief. Mr. Burt arose, took Mr. Davis by the arm, and conducted him to his chamber.

About twelve o'clock of the same night, the presidential party resumed their retreat. Reaching the house of the Rev. J. O. Lindsay, D. D., near Mt. Carmel, Mr. Davis found Mrs. Davis who had preceded him that far and was waiting for him. [Here Wilson added some legend of his own.] *Mr. and Mrs. Davis drank a cup of coffee with Mr. and Mrs. Lindsay before taking their departure, and so Mr. Davis took his last meal in Abbeville County with Dr. Lindsay, just before they crossed the river into Georgia.*

Secession Hill, where it seems the policy of the State to secede was definitely fixed, is less than a half mile from and in sight of both the above mentioned houses.

Between these houses and Secession Hill lived Charles Henry Allen's family in what was known as the Alston house. His son, James Clark Allen, was the first man to lose his life in the war. Hurriedly passing from one room to another in their barracks in the Moultrie House on Sullivan's Island, February 13, 1861, he ran against the point of a comrade's bayonet, which entered his eye and pierced his brain. So the first dead soldier was brought home and lay a corpse in his father's house in sight of Secession Hill and within view of the house where the Confederate Cabinet and their generals first acknowledged their inability to rally their remaining soldiers for resistance to the Union forces and to fight for Southern independence.

Confederate Cradle and Grave

The members of the Cabinet, except Mr. Benjamin, were very much dejected, but he, with good humor, took great interest in the flowers and strawberries, and discussed their beauties and excellence with the ladies of the house in a free and cheerful manner.

Mr. Benjamin asked Mr. Perrin (T. C.) for a hachet to deface the Confederate seal. As they were preparing to leave for Washington, Ga., and all was confusion, Mr. Perrin suggested that he would soon cross the Savannah River and why not commit it to the river's keeping, to which he assented. The seal was not thrown into an old well in Mr. Burt's yard, and could not have been, because there is not and has never been any other well than the one out of which the family now get water. In this a member of the family now living in the house concurs. Mr. T. C. Perrin was chairman of the delegation to the Secession Convention from Abbeville, and as such, the county being first alphabetically, he signed his name to the Ordinance of Secession first after Hon. D. F. Jamison, the President of the Convention.

The above account of the part taken in the meeting on Secession Hill by Judge David Lewis Wardlaw is nearly correct as far as it goes. Although he warned and implored the people to beware even with tears streaming down his cheeks, yet he always said that his destiny should be cast with theirs, and so great was the confidence and love of the people for him that they elected him one of the delegates to the Secession Convention, and he was the author of the Ordinance of Secession [commonly attributed to his brother, Francis H. Wardlaw, then of Edgefield].

Wilson added several additional comments in connection with D. L. Wardlaw's role in the Secession meeting. In the deliberations of the Committee of Twenty One, the committee which was charged with nominating the Abbeville delegates to the State Convention which were held in the depot, *it was ascertained that eleven of the twenty one would vote against the nomination of Judge Wardlaw. They were not satisfied with him because of his well known opposition to what was then known and styled "separate state action." It was, however, through the personal influence of Judge Cothran, with his friend and kinsman C. W. Sproul, whom he induced to change his vote, that Judge Wardlaw received the nomination, even by a bare majority vote.* ...When Judge Wardlaw as one of the nominees addressed the crowd, *although he was greatly respected personally because of his much learning, great ability, his uniform correct and honest deportment through a long and useful life, when attempting to speak, he was hissed and jeered. The manifestation was not intended as personal, but it was evidence of the excited condition of the country, when the people would not listen to reason. The crowd was tumultous, and the venerable old man, who was wiser than the rest, was forced to succumb. At last, as if in a supreme monent, with tears*

Confederate Cradle and Grave

in eyes that were not accustomed to weep, and with the emotions of a heart which felt more than it could express, he said:

"Has it come to this, my neighbors and friends, that I who was born among you, and have always lived with you all these years, am to be denied the right to speak to you?"

Every heart was thrilled. The people stood upon the benches, and crowded around the speaker's stand. In the commotion, Prof. E. L. Patton, a native of the District and current President of Erskine College ..who was so well known as the most modest and unassuming man in the county, became so excited that he elbowed his way through the crowd toward the speaker's stand, and, with fire and determination, with gesture and vehemence which could not be described, and in a voice which was distinctly heard above the din and confusion, said:

"Judge Wardlaw shall be heard."

The utterance and the act was like an electric shock. Quiet was restored for a moment. During a temporary lull, Mr. Noble, who was a recognized leader in the Secession movement, appealed to the audience to hear the Judge.

Quiet being still further restored, Judge Wardlaw proceeded with his speech, and in endeavoring to impress the force of his words, said: "Suppose South Carolina should endeavor to secede alone, and the United States government should send a frigate to Charleston and blockade your harbor, what would you do?"

Voice from the crowd, "We'd wade in and sink her."...

Appropos this incident, Wilson wrote, *we have heard Judge Cothran , who in the Spring of 1861 was a young lieutenant on the South Carolina coast, relate the following:*

When the regiment [Orr's] to which he belonged was afterwards stationed on Sullivan's Island, the officers of Company B, of whom he was one, had their headquarters in one of the houses fronting on the beach from which the vessels then blockading the port of Charleston were in full view. Very often in the afternoon some of the men of Company B and Gompany G, also an Abbeville company, would assemble on the piazza and on the steps to discuss the stirring events of the times. On one occasion, after a pause in the conversation, West Robertson, a member of Company G who had been most vociferous in advising Judge Wardlaw how to get rid of the blockading squadron...,said: "I am getting tired of seeing them saucy ships a riding out there beyond the bar."

Lieutenant Cothran--"Robertson, do you remember a little incident that occurred at Abbeville Court House on the day of the Secession meeting, when a good old man and a wise one, attempted to remonstrate with the people and point out to them some of the difficulties that might be expected if the mad course then insisted on

Confederate Cradle and Grave

was insisted on?"
Robertson, "Yes, I do; the old man was Judge Wardlaw, and they treated him shamefully."
Lieutenant Cothran--"Do you remember that when he said in case of war the port would be sealed up by the presence of a U. S. frigate?"
Robertson--"Yes."
Lieutenant Cothran--"Do you remember when the Judge asked what we would do about it, the reply he received and by whom?"
Robertson- "Yes, I do, and I was the fool who cried out to him, 'We'll wade in and sink her.' I had never seen the sea then, nor a ship or I don't reckon I would have said what I did. One thing certain, I don't feel near as much like doing it now as I did then, and I reckon there are others pretty much in my fix."

Hugh Wilson did not question the *Sun* 's view that the Abbeville Secession meeting was the "birthplace" of Secession. To those who believed this legend, it was a fact which was so self evident that it needed no documentation. When it was pointed out by outsiders that it was not the first district meeting to endorse immediate secession or even to select its delegates for the State Convention, it was said to be more influential on later district meetings. However, the only daily newspapers in the State, those in Charleston and Columbia, failed to carry even a short notice about the Abbeville meeting of November 22.

In fact, no single district meeting in the State could be said to have a decisive influence elsewhere. Every delegate chosen in each of them was in favor of immediate secession, and, if there were persons who opposed this action, they stayed away. Even Judge Wardlaw had come to believe that the only course left.

Skeptics who learn of this claim that the November 22, 1860 meeting was the birthplace of Secession find it hard to understand why its proponents advanced it with such fervor. Perhaps it was because the war which resulted was the decisive event in the town's history, and they wanted to think that the town had played an essential role in the determination of its own fate.

Wilson did not question another local tradition which is the hijacking of the treasure train, perhaps because it was so fanciful. If it had any validity, it referred to the hijacking of the wagons which carried the private treasures which had been stored in Richmond banks and which had accompanied the Confederate treasure train. This occurred near Danburg, Georgia.

XVI. LIFE IN ABBEVILLE DURING THE CIVIL WAR
THE STORY OF A YOUNG BOY

John E. Gardin, "The Story of a Young Boy During the Civil War," *Press & Banner,* October 30, 1925.

We were obliged to leave Charleston some time in 1862, as our home was on the line of fire from the battery on Morris Island. We first refugeed to Williston, Barnwell County, then to Camden, to Columbia and finally reached Abbeville.

My boyhood days in Abbeville were very happy ones, and I still remember with a thrill of pleasure many incidents that occurred during that time. On arriving in the village, my grandmother under whose care I had been since my second year, assumed the position as governess in the family of Colonel Jehu Foster Marshall who was killed August 29, 1862 at the Second Battle of Manassas. We were taken as a member of the family and made to feel at home. The family consisted of Mrs. Marshall and six sons and daughters, William, Samuel, Foster, Quitman, Ida, and Mary. William Marshall was at an early date in command of a company of State Infantry located on Sullivan's Island. . . .

It was a happy family, although Samuel also went to war. He returned though a few months later with one of his fingers shot off. Here was a hero indeed. Sam had a time with all the pretty girls of the town trying to coddle and nurse him. His wound however soon healed, and he again returned to the front. This time he stayed away for over a year when he was brought home on a stretcher, shot through both legs. The poor fellow was laid up for some time, but this also had its compensations and he recovered only too soon, forcing him to return to the ranks. He remained at the front until the close of the war.

Foster, the third son, was crazy to go and could hardly await the time when his age permitted him to do so. This goal was finally reached and Foster went to Charleston, where he fell into the hands of a recruiting sergeant for the Marion Artillery. . . . Foster had his uniform and other equipment all ready and never lost an opportunity to be seen on the streets in his splendor. Alas, though for fame, before he was able to join his regiment, the tragedy of Appomattox occurred. Thus ended Foster's military aspirations.

I have already mentioned that there were two girls in the family, Ida and Mary who as well as a cousin, Willy Barcolow, were constant companions.

The house was a large colonial mansion with a number of large fluted columns reaching to the roof. The house was set in a beautiful formal garden of the period with an imposing background of majestic

Boy's Life in Abbeville During the Civil War

red oak trees. The garden was encompassed on three sides by a fancy picket fence with undulating lines. Inside this fence extended along its entire length was a most remarkable piece of topiary work about fifteen feet high consisting of mock orange trees, trimmed to represent an arcade. In all my travels throughout the world, not excepting the famous garden of Versailles, have I seen anything to equal it. (Now owned by the Robertson family)

The gardener who was the creator of this wonderful work was an old Negro, named Israel, who was never addressed other than with his sobriquet, Uncle. In the minds of the younger generation, Uncle Israel was an invaluable adjunct to the community. He was the owner of a very sharp pocket knife, probably the only pocket knife in the whole village. This knife had an historic career as it was borrowed by every boy in the neighborhood and only returned when the edge was entirely worn off, much to Uncle Israel's disgust. Next door to the Marshalls lived the DeBruhl family who were closely related, and the intercourse between the two families was very intimate.

As already mentioned the youngsters of both families, including myself, were constant companions. The older Marshall children despised us and placed us in the infant class although their age exceeded ours by only a few years. The reason for this was the military age was the basis for all calculations as far as the youth of the country were concerned, and the nearer the approach to that goal, the more important the individual.

The school system at that time was entirely disrupted and the only schooling we received was under the care of my grandmother who was a remarkable woman. ... Later on, a member of the Charleston College staff, Professor Porcher, opened a school in a small abandoned shack on the Blue Hill in the neighborhood of the Calhoun place. However, it was only as a matter of courtesy that it was called a school. The Professor was an indiscriminate disciplinarian. Armed with a ten foot hickory, he never hesitated to slash into the bunch on the occasion of the slightest disturbance in the ranks, and the just as well as the unjust had to suffer. Notwithstanding this promiscuous severity we all liked him, strange to say. The reason for this was probably because he never seemed to care whether we had learned our lessons or not.

The great stunt during school was the filling of the water bucket. To this service five or six boys were detailed. The spring was located about two miles to the south of the school house and the time consumed to bring the bucket back filled and sometimes not filled was never less than two hours.

During the Chinquapin season the water detail sometimes never got back. The little school house and the surrounding territory was the scene of many a boyish prank and some of them would have wound up in a police court, had there been such a thing at the time. The youngsters certainly deserved severe punishment when their spirits deserted the bounds of discretion. I will never forget the consternation caused by the burning off of a ten acre tract of sedge, which had grown unusually rank and was good material for a blaze. It took the combined efforts of some thirty husky lads, stirred on by the indiscriminate application of the Professor's ten foot hickory, to save the schoolhouse from destruction. The meanest thing though that was done, was the undermining of the chimney, causing it to collapse while a Latin class was in session. Fortunately the chimney fell outward so no one was hurt but it put a stop to all schooling until the war was over.

The one thing that Professor Porcher hated was snakes and we never lost the opportunity to shove them under his nose. At the foot of Blue Hill the branch had to be crossed on two parallel logs and here one fine morning we coiled a huge black snake that we had killed. With glee in our miserable hearts, we awaited the coming of the Professor. He soon appeared but to our bitter disappointment he was not in the least perturbed and simply shook one of the logs with his foot, dropping Mr. Snake into the stream and then passed on. The old gentleman said not a word at the school and that was the worst punishment he could have inflicted upon us.

All was not glorious fun for the boys. They were made to suffer the same privations that were imposed upon their elders, only the boys were not so philosophic about it. One of the greatest hardships was the lack of light in the evenings, particularly during the winter. Tallow dips were used when obtainable and that was at times a very difficult matter. With the exception of one or two milk cows to a family all cattle had been requisitioned by the Government. Hog lard run into a cup with a wick made of a small piece of twisted cotton was frequently used. This method however had its disadvantages, as the greatest care had to be exercised to prevent the melting lard from spilling and besides the light was unsatisfactory.

Pine knots, which could be picked up anywhere, and large strips of fat lightwood were more popular. These were set up on end in the fireplace and in order to get the full benefit of this method of illumination, it was necessary to sit on the floor with the back turned to the light. This also had its drawbacks. The sticks had to be put at the proper angle, otherwise the room would be flooded with a sticky, sooty mess that carried ruin in its wake. Practice though soon made us perfect in the art. When parties were given, the invitations always read, "bring one or two or three candles with you," the number depended upon the number of guests from any particular household. These candles were made of beeswax and were worth their weight in gold. Many an invitation had to be declined because the family

Boy's Life in Abbeville During the Civil War

invited were not able to furnish the candles.

Real coffee and tea were two things we readily learned to do without. As a substitute for the former, sweet potatoes were used. These were sliced into small cubes and dried in the sun. For tea we had no substitute and did without, although I have since learned that in some districts the leaves of the Feverbush (Lindera Benzoin) were used after proper drying and proved satisfactory.

I would like to digress here for a moment to furnish a description of the funny little railroad we had running into Abbeville. The village was the terminus of a branch line connecting with the main line at Hodges about twelve miles distant. The locomotive was even in those days a comical sight--it must have been the first locomotive introduced into South Carolina ... The Abbeville specimen was only about twelve or fourteen feet long with the smoke stack projecting from the centre of the front of the boiler in a disjointed curve, upward. The cab was the only tribute to modern progress but it was a flimsy affair at that. The tender was a nondescript thing that did not seem to belong to the outfit. The passenger cars, of which there were two, were similar to those in common use at that time but they were small. A score of people would have crowded one of them to the limit, but there were never that many passengers.

The distance between Abbeville and the main line at Hodges was approximately twelve miles, but the running time between the two points ranged from one to two hours, depending upon how many times the engineer stopped to gossip with the farmers at the crossings. One day the train was unusually late in arriving at Abbeville and the explanation was that it stopped on the way to permit the passengers to kill an enormous chicken snake that was seen on the roadside. The specimen was about twelve feet long and was brought into Abbeville in triumph and exhibited on the court house steps for several days.

The rails were remarkable and the construction on the tracks most primitive. Evidently the U rail or the T rail had not been invented when that branch line was projected. The track consisted of eight inch beams, spiked to sleepers which were few and far between. The beams were projected by a strip of angle iron about two inches wide, nailed on the inside edge.

Our little train also served another purpose and the arrival of the train in the afternoon was anxiously awaited. It brought either glad or sad tidings from the army in the field. The former was evidenced by a long, joyous whistle while a series of short, mournful toots meant a defeat, or the death of some beloved citizen.

The closing days of the war were most exciting for the boys. One troop of cavalry after another came through the town on their way southward, either to meet or to avoid the rapid advance of federal forces on the way to the sea. The favorite camping place was in a

Boy's Life in Abbeville During the Civil War

triangular shaped grove to the east of Mr. Burt's residence. We became regular camp followers and assisted the soldiers in their manifold chores around the tents, receiving for a reward a box of cartridges, or a package of caps, or occasionally a worn out rifle or revolver. The greatest fun though, consisted of taking the horses to water at a branch about a mile distant.

Each one of us were given a mount and a string of six horses on a tethering rope. When all was set, the word was given and off went the cavalcade with a whoop and a hurrah, helter skelter, lickety split. We were all good riders and rarely had a spill, but many an exciting experience. A corporal and his squad were generally posted at the branch to see that the horses were properly watered and woe betide any one of the kids if he attempted to slouch the job. We had a great time and forgot home and everything else until the troop moved, to be soon replaced by another one and then the fun began all over again. What a glorious lot of cartridges and caps were given to us and we were thus again able to go hunting.

With the army caps however applied to the shotgun it was a rather ticklish business. The caps were three times the size of the gun nipple and when firing we were obliged to pay more attention to balancing the cap on the nipple than to the object we were aiming at, but, withal many a squirrel and many a dove was brought home as a welcome addition to the scanty larder. We manufactured the shot from the slugs that were attached to the cartridges by beating the lead flat, then cutting it into small squares and rolling the little pieces between two boards. This at least took the sharp corners and edges off.

The citizens of Abbeville were very proud when Mrs. Jefferson Davis took up her residence in the village with her young son about six or seven years old. She remained with us for about six weeks. . . .[actually two weeks].

But to return to Abbeville and the stirring events prior to the final scenes in the drama. There was a Confederate storehouse located in the town and when the first rumors of the impending end came, the officials in charge decided to distribute the contents of the store among the people. A huge scramble resulted and everybody got just what he did not want. I was fortunate in getting a huge piece of sole leather bigger than myself and had considerable trouble getting it home, where it was ultimately used in patching up what shoes we had. I certainly had no use for it as I had not worn a shoe for three years and my feet like those of every boy in town, were a mass of stonebruises, cuts, stubbed toe-nails, etc., but we did not mind. What did the boys care?

In this connection I recall a serio-comic episode while loafing around our favorite haunt, the blacksmith shop. A horse was being shod and in the process of forming a shoe small pieces of iron were

Boy's Life in Abbeville During the Civil War

cut off and thrown on the ground. Suddenly a pungent odor assailed my nostrils and the first impression I had was that my clothes were on fire. However I soon realized that I had stepped on a piece of red hot iron, but it took time to penetrate the leather like sole of my foot. . . .The soldiers continued to pass through town in increasing numbers, and it was painfully evident that they were more or less shy of discipline. Utterly demoralized at times, they were under no restraint by their officers at all, but just the same they behaved themselves and we were only too glad to share our provisions with them even though at times we were obliged to skip a meal.

One day a cavalcade rode into town and judging by the escorting toopers it was apparent that the individuals composing the group were important personages. It was then widespread around that the President had arrived. They took up their residence in the Burt Mansion and also in Mr. Perrin's house across the street. It was at Mr. Burt's that the last Cabinet meeting of the Confederacy was held. Horses saddled and bridled were tethered at the entrance to both houses and there was hurrying and scurrying by orderlies all day and all night.

The President arrived at 2 o'clock in the afternoon [it was actually 10 a. m.], *and it was then that I had my first look at him. I recall very vividly the lean haggard face of Mr. Davis who seemed to be the only one of the party who was composed, the others were all excited and talked without cessation.The President and party left at day break* [actually about midnight]. . . .

We now enter upon the beginning of the reconstruction period which produced a terrible condition of affairs. Safety of property meant nothing and even human life became a negligible quantity. The village was occupied by Negro soldiers, who soon made their presence felt. They were commanded by two white officers and it was generally conceded that they were pretty decent chaps and did all they could to keep their subordinates under control. This however was apparently impossible. With the encouragement that the soldiers received from the turbulent element in the surrounding country, it seemed as if all hell had been let loose. It was dangerous at night time to have a light burning in the room as it invited a shot out of the dark. This actually happened one night at Mrs. Marshall's house, when my grandmother entered one of the rooms with a lighted candle. Immediately a shot rang out and the slug buried itself in the ceiling. During the daytime, everything went on as usual but at night, danger stalked throughout the land.

When the boys came back there was constant friction. This was intensified when an order was issued from the commandant's office that all persons, male or female, over sixteen years old must take the Oath of Allegiance to the United States Government. William and

Boy's Life in Abbeville During the Civil War

Samuel Marshall, having only just returned from the service, naturally objected to this and here is where the trouble began. Occasional altercations had taken place with the two federal officers which culminated in an order to keep off the streets until they were ready to comply with the orders from Washington.

The intensity of feeling increased to such an extent that it became necessary to make complaint to military Headquarters in Columbia in the hopes of ameliorating conditions. Fortunately the pleas of the citizens were recognized as justified by the continued lawlessness of the Negro soldiers, and it was decided to substitute a white garrison for the colored one. In anticipation of the change two white soldiers, a sergeant and a private, were sent to Abbeville as an advance guard.

The Negroes realizing that their licentious behavior was nearing an end, became more troublesome than ever. It happened one Sunday afternoon when Mrs. Marshall and her son William were returning from church, they met a gang of soldiers with their female escorts on one of the sidewalks, which was raised somewhat above the level of the road. Instead of making room and allowing the two to pass, they became abusive and crowded Mrs. Marshall into the street. William promptly knocked the Negro down. This occurrence created a sensation in the village. The two older sons of Mrs. Marshall were furious and immediately proceeded to the commandant's offce to make a complaint. Here, however, they met with scant satisfaction; on the contrary, they were threatened with arrest for defying orders to keep off the streets.

The atmosphere was surcharged and after a conference with the neighbors it was decided that if it came to an outbreak the focal point of danger would be the Marshall mansion. It seemed therefore the better part of wisdom for the boys to seek asylum for the night elsewhere than at home, and subsequent events proved the wisdom of this decision. Evidently the white officers themselves recognized the situation and were fearful that perhaps further outrages would be perpetrated. They therefore ordered the two white soldiers at the Marshall home to remain on guard for the night. It is needless to say that this course was welcomed with a great sense of relief as there were no men around other than a few Negro servants, who though faithful enough, could not be depended upon in an emergency. One of these soldiers was stationed in front of the house and the other in the rear.

We had just concluded our evening meal, which as was usual in the summertime, was taken on the front piazza and were sitting around discussing the events of the day in a more or less agitated manner. Suddenly the front gate swung open and in marched a file of Negro soldiers, probably ten or twelve, and halfway up the garden walk they halted and several shots were fired point blank into the gathering. Fortunately no one was injured. In a moment all was confusion,

Boy's Life in Abbeville During the Civil War

women and children running in all directions. In the excitement all the small tables which were being used were upset and with them the large glass globes which served as protection to the candles. With that, everything was left in darkness and that undoubtedly was our salvation.

The white federal soldier who was placed on guard in the front of the house, disappeared mysteriously into space while the one in the rear came forward to see what the shooting was all about. Just as he entered the door leading into the hallway, several more shots were fired, one of which struck the poor fellow in the chest, killing him instantly.

I must not forget to mention that during the melee, plucky little Ida Marshall grabbed the gun of one of the Negro soldiers and tried to wrest it from his hands. The Negro soldiers who came to the house to arrest the boys, left precipitately when they discovered that they had killed one of their own men and that a white one. When this particular squad reached the village, the whole garrison fell into line and marched away into the darkness of the night. They were to have departed the next day anyway, but did not intend leaving that way.

The following morning the relief company arrived and on learning what had happened, immediately set out after the Negroes, They were overtaken about twenty miles from Abbeville but as to what happened when the two forces came into contact with each other will remain a mystery for evermore. The white soldiers returned to the village the next day, and after that life was more endurable.

XVII. THE FIVE LOST COLONELS

No story of Abbeville's past has been more highly revered than that of its "five lost colonels." Augustus Jackson Lythgoe, J. Foster Marshall, James M. Perrin, John Calhoun Simkins, and Augustus Marshall Smith were living on the upper end of the town's Main Street when the Civil War came, and each of them left a prominent or promising career to enter the Confederate army, attained the rank of colonel, and lost his life in battle or as a result of battle. Four of the five men were bound by ties of marriage and kinship.

Their loss became a symbol of the heavy losses suffered by the town, losses which had not been expected at the time of Secession. According to local tradition, at the memorable Secession meeting on November 22, 1860, when someone warned of war and bloodshed, Armistead Burt responded, as follows: *Why speak of war? Why speak of bloodshed? There will be no war. There will be no bloodshed. I will guarantee to drink all the blood that is shed in a wine cup, and a very small wine cup at that.* Perhaps the emotion of the times and particularly of that occasion led Burt to such a rash prediction. Nine years earlier when he was opposed to separate South Carolina secession, he had darkly warned the advocates of such a policy when he wrote the *Abbeville Banner*, May 17, 1851, *If you are not ready to lay down life and fortune, you are not prepared for secession. The North cannot and will not part with you, and the treasure she wrings from you, without a mighty struggle.*

Only three months after Burt had pledged to drink all the blood shed, Abbeville suffered its first loss in the accidental death of J. Clark Allen, February 13, 1861, on Sullivan's Island. During the next four years, the people of Abbeville District lost 346 men in Confederate service, and the town of Abbeville gave its proportionate share. The story of the five colonels illustrates this loss.

The first of the five to die was Augustus Marshall Smith who served as grand marshal of the famed Secession meeting, a planter who at the age of 34 was probably the richest young man in Abbeville. Smith was born at Stoney Point, the son of Joel and Isabella Marshall Smith, and his maternal grandfather was a brother to the father of J. Foster Marshall, another of the five colonels. When he married a daughter of Judge David L. Wardlaw, he moved to Abbeville. On his honeymoon, he and his bride traveled in the West, and in 1859 he returned to Arkansas and bought a tract of several thousand acres of land. He bought over a hundred slaves for his Arkansas plantation and hired an overseer. In the census of 1860, he was listed as the sixth largest slaveholder in Abbeville District with 135 slaves, real estate valued at $200,000 and personal property (chiefly slaves) valued at $250,000.

He went to Sullivan's Island in February, 1861 as the 1st Lieutenant

Five Lost Colonels

in Abbeville's Minute Man company which was captained by one of his brothers-in-law, James M. Perrin. In April, 1861, he entered the Confederate service as a major. On June 27, 1862, he was mortally wounded at the battle of Gaines' Mill and died three days later. On April 29, his wife had given birth to a son, Augustus W. Smith, later founder of a well known mercantile business.

A. M. Smith had drawn up a will (James M. Perrin was one of the executors) which provided that if he were killed during the war, his Arkansas estate would go into a fund to aid in the education of the poor. Unfortunately, when his family representatives were able to reach Arkansas, they found that the overseer had angered his neighbors and had been driven away, the 125 slaves there had been freed, his 450 bales of cotton had been burned, and the land was overrun by squatters. There proved to be no funds for the poor.

The second of the lost colonels to die was J. Foster Marshall who was killed at the battle of Second Manassas, August 29, 1862. He was the oldest of the five, 43 at the time of the Census of 1860 which valued his real estate at $128,700 and his personal property at $188,005 (chiefly his 95 slaves). Like A. M. Smith, he had extensive investments outside of Abbeville and the State, for he had a large plantation in Florida.

Fourteen years earlier he had been the captain of the Abbeville company which served in the Mexican War, and as a State Senator he had been a dominant figure in Abbeville District politics for years. When he stood for re-election in 1860, he declared that while he opposed separate secession, if Abraham Lincoln were to win, he would be for a Southern Confederacy "at all hazards." He was very active in the construction of the new Trinity church and was perhaps its leading benefactor. A conversion experience in 1858 led him to a confession of faith and membership in the church.

As a result of his Mexican War experience and perhaps because his sister had married James L. Orr, Marshall was second in command of the Orr's Rifles Regiment when it was organized in 1861 at Sandy Springs. After Orr was elected to the Confederate Congress, he resigned the command of the regiment, and Marshall became its commanding officer. His faithful slave Israel who had been his body servant in the Mexican War again acted in that capacity. The experiences of his family during the war and immediately after are related in John Gardin's account of his stay with them during the 1860s.

Augustus J. Lythgoe was the third of the colonels to die when he was mortally wounded at Murfreesboro, Tennessee, December 31, 1862. He was born in Aiken where his father had immigrated from England. Educated at the South Carolina Military Academy as a civil engineer, he had worked on the Blue Ridge railroad until it was

Five Lost Colonels

suspended. Then he came to Abbeville where he married Margaret Isabella Wier and went into the mercantile business with his brother in law, John A. Wier under the firm name of Lythgoe & Wier.

He enlisted in the 19th South Carolina Regiment, and because of his miltary training quickly rose from lieutenant to captain and by December, 1861, he was a lieutenant colonel. He saw action in Kentucky and Tennessee, and as a full colonel he was sent to Corinth, Mississippi in March, 1862. He was survived by a wife, a son and two daughters. All died without issue, for although the older daughter married, it was not until she was terminally ill.

The fourth of the colonels to die was James M. Perrin, who died on May 4, 1863. He had been mortally wounded the day before at the great battle of Chancellorsville. He was born on Hard Labor Creek 16 miles below Abbeville, the son of Samuel and Eunice Perrin. His father died when he was very young and he largely grew up in the home of Thomas Chiles Perrin, his oldest brother. He was educated at the South Carolina College, studied law and entered the Abbeville bar.

Perrin served in the Mexican War and rose to the rank of 2nd lieutenant by 1848. He was married twice. His first wife was Mary Smith of Stoney Point, Augustus M. Smith's sister, who lived for only six more years, and his second wife was Kitty Tillman of Abbeville. His first wife bore him three children, and his second wife had four children, the youngest born six months after his father was killed. One of the latter children was a boy who was born while his father was at Sullivan's Island. Fort Sumter had just been fired upon, and Captain Perrin when he received news of the birth of a son, named him James Sumter Perrin.

His older brother had one of the finest houses in Abbeville, and on the eve of the war, James M. Perrin built the fine house which was later owned by Samuel McGowan and was adjacent to the Presbyterian church. His brother owned 121 slaves at the time of the 1860 Census, and he owned 57 slaves. During 1860 he headed up the Abbeville Vigilance Committee which was formed to investigate "suspicious" vagabonds, chiefly peddlers, who were thought to be spreading sedition among the slaves.

J. M. Perrin was the captain of the first company which was formed in Abbeville at the time of secession, the Minute Men. After it had served at Charleston during the Fort Sumter campaign, it was disbanded, and Perrin raised another company which entered the Confederate service in July. He served in Virginia through the battle of Second Manassas when he was promoted to the rank of colonel. Elected to the South Carolina legislature, he returned home and served in that role until the end of January, 1863, when he returned to duty.

The last of the five colonels to die was John Calhoun Simkins who was killed July 18, 1863 in a Union assault upon Battery Wagner on the South Carolina coast. Simkins had married a daughter of Judge David L. Wardlaw and thus was a brother-in-law of Augustus M. Smith. He was also a brother-in-law of Governor Francis W. Pickens who had married his sister. Simkins was reared in Edgefield, and like J. Foster Marshall and James M. Perrin, he had served in the Mexican War. He entered the Palmetto Regiment at the age of 21 and rose to the rank of captain. He actually had a plantation in Newberry District, but he spent much time with his wife's family in Abbeville. He was there when the war broke out, and he soon became a captain in the 1st S. C. Infantry Regiment. By the time of his death in 1863, he had become a colonel.

XVIII. AN ABBEVILLE LADY VISITS GENERAL LEE IN VIRGINIA

General Robert E. Lee wrote his wife, November 1, 1863, the following: *I fear my daughters have not taken to the spinning-wheel and loom, as I have recommended. I shall not be able to recommend them to the brave soldiers for wives. I had a visit from a soldier's wife today, who was on a visit to her husband. She was from Abbeville District, S. C. Said she had not seen her husband for more than two years, and, as he had written to her for clothes, she herself thought that she would bring them on. It was the first time she had traveled by railroad, but she got along well by herself.*

She brought an entire suit of her own manufacture for her husband. She spun the yarn and made the clothes herself. She clad her three children in the same way, and had on a beautiful pair of gloves she had made for herself. Her children she had left with her sister. She said she had been here a week and must return tomorrow, and thought she could not go back without seeing me. Her husband accompanied her to my tent, in his nice gray suit. She was very pleasing in her address and modest in her manner, and was clad in a nice, new alpaca. I am certain she could not have made that....

She, in fact, was an admirable woman. Said she was willing to give up everything she had in the world to attain our independence, and the only complaint she made of the conduct of our enemies was their arming our servants against us. Her greatest difficulty was to procure shoes. She made them for herself and children of cloth with leather soles. She sat with me about ten minutes and took her leave-- another mark of sense--and made no request for herself or husband.

The *Press & Banner,* July 24, 1925, reprinted the above letter and identified the lady as Mrs. W. T. Penney (Mary Shillito).

XIX. MRS. DAVIS IN ABBEVILLE, APRIL, 1865

With General Robert E. Lee's surrender, Mrs. Varina Davis fled southward from Richmond with President Davis' private secretary, Burton Harrison, and a young midshipman, James Morris Morgan. From Charlotte onward they linked up with the Confederate "treasure train" which was guarded by a convoy of young midshipmen (mostly in their teens) who walked in columns on either side of wagons carrying the remaining Confederate specie as well as private collections of jewelry from the Richmond banks.

On the 13th of April, as Mrs. Davis left Chester (S. C.) where rumors of a Union raid caused her to stop less than an hour, she wrote President Davis that *I am going somewhere, perhaps to Washington, Ga., perhaps only to Abbeville. I don't know, just as the children bear the journey will I decide.* On the 14th, before he could have received her letter, Mr. Davis wrote her, *If you can go to Abbeville it seems best as I am now advised--if you can send everything there do so.*

Burton Harrison in an article in *Century Magazine* in November, 1883 wrote of the party's experiences in Abbeville: *Abbeville was a beautiful place, on high ground; and the people lived in great comfort, their homes embowered in vines and roses, with many other flowers everywhere. We had now entered the "Sunny South"* . . . . *Mrs. Davis and family were guests of the President's esteemed friends, Colonel and Mrs. Burt; and there, too, were the daughters of Mr. Trenholm* [Secretary of Treasury] *at the house of their brother.* On September 18, 1863, the *Abbeville Press* reported that a "Mr. Trennon [sic] of the firm [Trenholm &] Fraser & Co. of Charleston" had purchased the Marshall House for $25,000 to be used for refugees.

Harrison said that when Mrs. Davis was reluctant to continue her stay with the Burts for fear that their hospitality to the wife of the Confederate President might lead Union forces to burn the Burt home, Armistead Burt *replied that there was no better use to which his house could be put than to have it burned for giving shelter to the wife and family of his friend.*

On April 19th, Varina Davis wrote her husband from Abbeville that since leaving Richmond, *no such heartfelt* [her emphasis] *welcome has been extended to me as the one I received here--they will hear of no change of place for the present, and urge me with tears in their eyes to share with them what little they can offer. People call promptly and seem to feel warmly--Mr. Burt seems to feel tenderly to us, pets the children and does every kind thing in his power to me. Mrs. Burt is more than affectionate.* . . . *Jeffy D.* [Howell, her brother] *was taken ill on the cars* [they had come from Newberry to Abbeville on the railroad], *and is here sick at Mr. Trenholm's who lives just across the street.*

Mrs. Davis in Abbeville

On the 28th of April, Mrs. Davis decided to leave Abbeville "against her own convictions," she later wrote, "but agreeable to Mr. Burt's and Mr. Harrison's opinions." She wrote "my own dear old husband" from Abbeville on the 28th that *here they are all your friends, have the most unbounded confidence in you. Mr. Burt and his wife have urged me to live with them--offered to take the chances of the Yankees with us--begged to have little Maggie--done everything in fact that relatives could do.* In contrast, she wrote that *I have seen a great many men who have gone through --not one has talked fight. A stand cannot be made in this country, do not be induced to try it.*

Mrs. Davis added that *young Haskell insists on my going to his father's* [Charles T. Haskell's plantation, "Charlie's Hope," which was in the Flatwoods west of Abbeville] *in the morning to take lunch, and his carriage to Washington. He has been more than polite to me--so have all the people here--it is like old times.*

Burton Harrison described his search for a conveyance for the ladies in which he discovered General John S. Williams of Kentucky (later a U. S. Senator) who was but a few miles from Abbeville "recruiting his health." He learned that Williams had a large and strong vehicle. When he went out where Williams was, he found that he was at the home of a man "called queerly enough *Jeff Davis*," a well to do Abbeville farmer named Nathaniel Jefferson Davis. Williams let him have the vehicle and his horses with the provision that some one would accompany Mrs. Davis to Washington, Georgia and bring his horses back. Nearby, Harrison found the family of Judge Monroe of Kentucky had sought refuge, and three young Kentucky cavalrymen who had been on sick leave were willing to volunteer as escorts.

Mrs. Davis' stay in Abbeville led directly to the decision by Jefferson Davis to include Abbeville on his itinerary. In November, 1905, Mrs. Davis responded to another Kentuckian who was with her husband's party and who had written that it was at Abbeville that "the Confederacy went to pieces." Her version was:

The facts are these. Mr. Davis supposing his family to be with a friend, the Hon. Armistead Burt, in Abbeville, and not having seen them since before the fall of Richmond, naturally desired to bid his wife and children farewell before beginning his perilous effort to reach the Trans-Mississippi, he therefore came to Abbeville. However fearing to embarass him in his efforts to reach the Trans-Mississippi department, I sent a letter to meet him at the Saluda River by Col. Henry Leovy [of New Orleans, father-in-law of Judge Monroe], *an intimate friend, in which I begged him not to attempt to join us for even an hour; but to expect us, if we could accomplish the journey, to meet him in Texas. We hoped from the Gulf coast to get passage to Nassau, and thus to reach Texas.*

XX. JEFFERSON DAVIS IN ABBEVILLE: General Basil Duke

Five days before General Robert E. Lee surrendered his forces to General Grant at Appomattox on April 7, 1865, the Confederate president fled from Richmond. One month later, his journey south led him to Abbeville, May 2, six days after General Joseph E. Johnston had surrendered to Union General Sherman at Greensboro, North Carolina. For a summary of Jefferson Davis' hours in Abbeville, see pages 64-65 in Chapter X.

Bivouac Magazine, April, 1886, reprinted in *Abbeville Messenger*, September 7, 1886.

At Abbeville, South Carolina, Mr. Davis held a conference with the officers in command of the troops composing his escort, which he himself characterized as a council of war, and which I may be justified, therefore, in so designating. It was, perhaps, the last Confederate council of war held east of the Mississippi River, certainly the last in which Mr. Davis participated.

We had gone into camp in the vicinity of the little town, and, although becoming quite anxious to understand what was going to be done, we were expecting no immediate solution to the problem. We were all convinced that the best we could hope and do was to get Mr. Davis safely out of the country, and then obtain such terms as had been given General Johnston's army, or, failing that, make the best of our way to the trans-Mississippi.

The five brigade commanders each received an order notifying him to attend at the private residence in Abbeville where Mr. Davis had made his headquarters, about four o'clock of that afternoon. We assembled promptly at the hour indicated, and were shown into a room where we found Mr. Davis and Generals Breckinridge and Bragg. No one else was present. I had never seen Mr. Davis look better or show to better advantage. He seemed in excellent spirits and humor; and the union of dignity, graceful affability, and decision which made his manner usually so striking, was very marked in his reception of us. After some conversation of a general nature, he announced the purpose which induced him to join us together.

"It is time," he said, "that we adopt some definite plan upon which the further prosecution of our struggle shall be conducted. I have summoned you for consultation. I feel that I ought to do nothing now without the advice of my military chiefs."

He smiled rather archly as he used this expression, and we could not help thinking that such term addressed to a handful of brigadiers, commanding altogether barely three thousand men, by one who so recently had been the master of legions was a pleasantry, yet he said it in a way that made it a compliment.

After we had each given, at his request, a statement of the equip-

Jefferson Davis in Abbeville

ment and condition of our respective commands. Mr. Davis proceeded to declare his conviction that the cause was not lost any more than hope of American liberty was gone amid the sorest trials and most disheartening reverses of the Revolutionary struggle; but that energy, courage and constancy might yet save all. "Even," he said, "if the troops now with me be all that I can for the present rely on, three thousand brave men are enough for a nucleus around which the whole people will rally when the panic which now afflicts them has passed away." He then asked that we should make such suggestions in regard to the future conduct of the war as we deemed advisable.

We looked at each other in amazement and with a feeling a little akin to trepidation, for we hardly knew how we should give expression to views so diametrically opposed to those he had uttered as we entertained. Our respect for Mr. Davis approached veneration, and notwithstanding the total dissent we felt and were obliged to announce to the programme he had indicated, that respect was rather increased than diminished by what he had said. We recognized that his high and dauntless spirit abhored submission, not from personal considerations so much as because of the patriotic love he bore his cause and people.

I do not remember who spoke first, but we each expressed the same opinion. We told him frankly that the events of the last few days had removed from our minds all idea or hope that a prolongation of the contest was possible.

The people were not panic stricken but broke down and worn out after every effort at resistance had been exhausted. We said that an attempt to continue the war, after all means of supporting warfare were gone, would be a cruel injustice to the people of the South. We would be compelled to live on a country already impoverished, and would invite further devastation. We urged that we would be doing a great wrong to men, if we persuaded them to such a course. That if they persisted in a conflict so hopeless, they would be declared and treated as brigands, and would forfeit all chance of returning to their homes.

He asked why then were we still in the field? We answered that we were desirous of affording him an opportunity of escaping the degradation of capture and perhaps a fate which would be direr to the people than even to himself; in still more embittering the exasperated feeling between the North and South. We said that we would risk them in battle for that purpose, but would not fire another shot in an effort to continue hostilities.

He declared, abruptly, that he would listen to no suggestion which regarded only his own safety. Resuming his previous tone, he appealed with an eloquence which was sublime to every sentiment and

Jefferson Davis in Abbeville

reminiscence that might be supposed to move a Southern soldier, and urged us to accept his views. We remained silent, for our convictions were unshaken; we felt responsible for the future welfare of the men who had so heroically followed us, and the painful point had been reached, when to speak again in opposition to all that he urged would approach altercation. For some minutes, not a word was spoken. Then Mr. Davis arose and ejaculated bitterly that all was indeed lost. He had become very pallid, and he talked so feebly as he proceeded to leave the room that General Breckinridge stepped hastily up and offered his arm.

I have undertaken to narrate very briefly what occurred in a conference which lasted for two or three hours. I believe I have accurately given the substance of what was said by Mr. Davis in quotation marks. I have correctly reproduced it, or very nearly so. Generals DeBrell [Dibrell] and Ferguson and Colonel Breckinridge are still living. I think that their recollections of this somewhat remarkable occurrence will agree with mine.

Generals Breckinridge and Bragg took no part in the discussion. Both, however, after Mr. Davis retired, assured us of their hearty approval of the position we had taken. They had foreborne to say anything, because they were not immediately commanding the troops, and not supposed, therefore, to know their sentiments so well as we did.

General Ferguson's Account

When a controversy erupted between Abbeville and Washington, Ga. over their claims as the last site of a Confederate Cabinet, the Charleston (S. C.) *Sunday News* asked General S. W. Ferguson, then living in Charleston, to give his recollection "of what took place at Abbeville, S. C. and at Washington, Georgia." His reply was printed September 6, 1903, as follows:

President Duke was escorted from Charlotte, N. C. to Abbeville, S. C. by five brigades of cavalry, viz.: Duke's, Vaughn's, Dibbrell's, Williams' (the latter commanded by Col. W. C. P. Breckinridge), and my own, all under the command of Gen. Braxton Bragg. We marched generally by different roads, camping in the neighborhood of the President. I will first quote from my journal, kept at the time, then state some facts from memory.

"Cokesbury, May 3 [sic]

Had an interview with the President and Gen. Duke, at the camp of the latter. They moved on to Abbeville and I was left to wait at Cokesbury Junction until Gen. Dibbrell should come up, but about an hour later I was ordered by Gen. Bragg to move to Abbeville, at which place I reported to Gen. John C. Breckinridge, who directed me

Jefferson Davis in Abbeville

to camp on the road to the pontoon and to meet the President and Gens. Breckinridge, Bragg, Duke, Vaughn, and Dibbrell and Col. W. C. P. Breckinridge, commanding Williams' Kentucky brigade in council.

It was decided to push on more rapidly, starting that night at 11 o'clock, and that General Breckinridge should in person command all the cavalry. That the specie that we were guarding should be paid out to the men and officers present, and that brigade commanders should be allowed to furlough or discharge any officer or private at once upon application, or accept the resignation of any."

I have always been under the impression, and still believe that there was a meeting of the Cabinet at Abbeville after the Council of War. All circumstances point to it. All the Cabinet, who were available, were there; the crisis had come when the President was assured that the troops who were escorting him could not be depended upon to accompany him to the Trans-Mississippi. The agreement reached to parole and discharge officers and men, upon application, could surely not have been made by Gen. Breckinridge alone, and it is not likely that the President would have authorized it without consulting his official advisors who were on the spot.

Moreover, some disposition of the Treasure was arranged after the Council was concluded for I received a hurry order to furnish a wagon and team, to transport some of it, and not having time to get one from my quartermaster, emptied my headquarters wagon of its contents and sent that.

When, as stated in my journal, I reported to Gen. Breckinridge in Abbeville, I had a long confidential conversation, of what I had gathered from my scouts of the movements and strength of the enemy, and of the demoralization of our troops caused in great measure by a rumor which had reached them of the surrender of Gen. Johnston, in which surrender they believed themselves included. He told me that it was the intention of the President to spend two days at Abbeville; he agreed with me that this would result inevitably in his capture, and then said he would call the Council of War, and that he would, as Secretary of War, relieve Gen. Bragg of the command of the cavalry and take command in person.

This council of war was held in the house of Col. Burt, whose guest President Davis was. There were present the brigade commanders I have already named, also the President, Gen. Bragg, Gen. Breckinridge, and I think the other members of the Cabinet then in Abbeville and possibly some citizens of weight and influence.

Beginning with the junior in rank, and ascending, each commander in turn was questioned as to the number, condition, equipment, etc. of his command, and most particular as to how many could be depended upon implicitly to accompany the President to the

Jefferson Davis in Abbeville

Trans-Mississippi and there to continue the war. All the commanders vouched for their entire commands [this contrasts sharply with the other accounts], *that they would go with the President to the bitter end, until it came last to my turn, when I had to say most reluctantly that I had not a dozen men for whose crossing the Mississippi I would vouch.*

This statement was a surprise and a damper. My statements had weight, however, and a movement forward was begun at once. I was ordered to bring up the rear. The President and his party passed through my camp en route to the pontoon bridge at 11 o'clock that night, calm and dignified as always. With heavy heart I wrung his hand in what I feared would be a last farewell, realizing in its bitterness that our cause was indeed lost.

When Gen. Breckinridge and I crossed the pontoon bridge next morning, we found all the cavalry, which had marched the night before, there encamped. The specie for the troops was distributed, and the brigade at once paid off, except mine. The next morning when I moved out of camp on the march to Washington the strange spectacle of white flags all around the camps, tokens of surrender met my eyes. These were the commands that were to go to the Trans-Mississippi, hunting for some one to whom they could surrender.

My own brigade acted in a similar manner the next day, but, thank God, I had not vouched for them, but had really done them some injustice, for when the end came, more than one hundred and twenty remained true as steel, ready to follow the President wherever he might go.

The extract of my journal under the date of May 6, refers to the disbandment of my brigade, which took place the night before, when after they had received the cash alloted to them and were ordered to move forward, they refused to obey, claiming that they had been included in the surrender of Gen. Johnston.

An Account from the Viewpoint of One of Dibrell's Men

Press & Banner, March 23, 1866

An account in the Cincinnati *Enquirer* about the last days of the Confederacy led a writer in the Louisville (Ky.) *Courier* to declare that he *could vouch for its entire accuracy, especially of that portion which refers to what transpired at or near Abbeville, S. C., where we were located at the time. . . . I was a member of Dibrell's division of Wheeler's cavalry, and had some opportunities of knowing what was transpiring. . . .*[at Greensboro, his unit learned of Lee's surrender] *and were told that we were relied upon to guard Mr. Davis, his cabinet and archives to Charlotte, and keep off Stoneman, who was*

Jefferson Davis in Abbeville

hovering upon our right flank. . . . We reached Cokesbury after Duke, Vaughn and Ferguson had passed through; from thence we moved to Abbeville, where all were concentrated by noon of May 2.

In the meantime rumors had reached us of Johnston's surrender. . . At Abbeville, late in the afternoon of May 2, a consultation was held--the last military consultation in which the Confederate Government participated. It was a historic scene.

Mr. Davis presided with Gen. Bragg, who had become by the surrender of Lee, Johnston, Beauregard and Cooper, the senior General of the Confederacy on his right hand, and General Breckinridge, Secretary of War and Major General, on the other side of him. Next came Brigadier General S. W. Ferguson, a gallant and enterprising South Carolinian, a West Pointer, a pet of Beauregard and a favorite of Davis; next General George G. Dibrell, a plain, practical, sensible, middle aged Tennessee clerk and merchant, who was believed by his men, and had justly won his spurs by long, hard, skillful, devoted service; next on a little sofa, sat two young men-- Brigadier General Basil W. Duke, and Colonel William C. P. Breckinridge, well known among the troops from Kentucky in the Confederate army, and then, near Gen. Bragg sat Gen.[John C.] Vaughn of East Tennessee, a brave officer and an earnest man.

Each officer was called upon to state the condition of his command. Gen. Ferguson, sanguine himself, gave a too glowing account of his men, as the sequel showed, but still bad; he could count upon one hundred men fighting as well as ever--upon all for other duties and skirmish. Gen. Dibrell could not count on any fighting men in his brigade, except to save Mr. Davis and Gen. Breckinridge and every hour was diminishing his hold upon them, and I have heard that he declared, almost with tears, that he would not risk another life among his noble men except for that purpose, that the cause of the Confederacy was lost, and his duty now was to take care of his men.

Gen. Duke thought one hundred and fifty of his men would follow him anywhere, and that he did not believe the cause lost if all fell in as he did and would inspirit their men. Col. Breckinridge announced his own determination not to surrender until ordered by Mr. Davis and the Secretary of War, but that very few of his men shared that feeling, and he would not urge them to go any further. Gen. Vaughn and his command would accept whatever terms Gen. Johnston had; which was then not known to us.

Mr. Davis said that it was useless to keep men under arms who would not fight; criminal to risk the lives of men who would fight, to the bravery of them who would not--therefore the command must be winnowed--that he could have been at Shreveport by that day, but was not willing to leave the men who were still in the field. That he

Jefferson Davis in Abbeville

supposed that Gen. Johnston had surrendered--that all the army left in that department were the commands represented in that meeting--that of them not more than four hundred could be depended on any further. That he would attempt to go to Gen. Taylor, and if that army went to pieces, he would cross the river [the Rio Grande], and if the cause should be finally lost, he would feel that he had done all his duty as he best could. That, called to his place without intervention, he would continue to discharge its duties as long as possible, that his contest might have resulted disastrously, but, the cause was not lost; the blood shed during four years was not shed in vain, and under other auspices and abler leaders, would yet succeed.

After considerable discussion, it was agreed that Mr. Davis, with a small escort should go immediately to Washington, Ga., and then on such route as seemed best; that Gen. Breckinridge should take command of the cavalry there, and move that night across the Savannah River at Vienna, where there was a pontoon bridge. This was carried out, and at daylight we crossed the river.

Experiences of Two Kentucky Officers at the Abbeville Meeting

John W. Headley and Robert M. Martin were two young officers from Kentucky who had many adventures as special agents for the Confederacy. They were with the Davis party in Abbeville. See John W. Headley, *Confederate Operations in Canada and New York* (1906), pp. 433-435.

After passing through Unionville and Laurens C. H., a halt was made at Abbeville, C. H. Here President Davis and the members of his Cabinet were the guests of Hon. Armistead Burt, who served in the Congress of the United States before the war.

Early in the afternoon Col. Martin walked up to the house for a brief conference with Gen. John C. Breckinridge, now Secretary of War, whom he knew well to learn something of our probable destination. When Breckinridge was told of our recent trip to Canada and learned that we were splendidly mounted, he confided to Martin that he expected Mr. Davis to escape through the country to the West, probably to Mexico, and insisted that we should go as his guard and companions. We were both at first disposed to go, simply for the feature of romance that would attach to the journey and to have the prestige of guiding our chieftain to safety.

But the more that we discussed the trip, the weaker our inclination grew. It occurred to us upon calm reflection that ours had been a long and perilous career and that on such a journey it might be necessary to risk our lives again to protect Mr. Davis. It did not appear that we ever had anything at stake in the war except our love of the South and the gratification of a spirit of adventure. And now

Jefferson Davis in Abbeville

that our cause was lost, we ought not to assume a perilous service when so many others who were at least our equals were going directly home to Texas, and we believed could and would conduct Mr. Davis safely to Mexico. However, we concluded to do a reasonable part if our suggestions were agreeable.

It was our idea to have Mr. Davis take one companion of his own suggestion and we would escort him as far as Talladega, Ala. We ought to set out from Abbeville with him that night and cross the Savannah River about sunrise, at the ferry on the route to Athens, Ga., traveling at night [following a route north of Atlanta while the federal columns would follow the remaining Confederate party to the South].

We walked up to Mr. Burt's house about 5 o'clock and called for Gen. Breckinridge. He came out and we talked outside under a tree. Our plans and suggestions were promptly approved, and Gen. Breckinridge said that he intended to urge upon Mr. Davis, who was still reluctant to give up. He requested that Captain Martin should call again at 10 or 11 o'clock that night. Martin now took Captain Helm into his confidence. Helm had been a friend of Gen. Adam R. Johnson in Texas before the war and was with us on the expedition to western Kentucky in 1863. He cheerfully agreed to pick a safe companion and make the journey with Mr. Davis from Alabama.

At 9 o'clock that night every one was more at sea than ever. Until well authenticated rumors began to spread that a council of war had been held at which it had been determined that the troops would be surrendered, and the President and Cabinet would disperse. Martin went to see Gen. Breckinridge at 10 o'clock, and the rumor was confirmed, except that they would leave soon and all would continue the retreat to Washington, Ga. There had been no opportunity for Gen. Breckinridge to confer with the President upon his plan for escape, as his heart had been set on further desperate efforts to continue the struggle, to which Gen. Breckinridge was opposed.

Postmaster General Reagan on Abbeville

John H. Reagan in his *Memoirs* made only a very terse reference to his Abbeville experience, as follows:

When we reached Abbeville we were there joined by the remnant of five brigades of cavalry. The President had a conference with their commanders and sought to learn their condition and spirit. And here again we witnessed the raids made on the provisions by the citizens. I was forced to the thought that the line between barbarism and civilization is at times very narrow.

A Rebel Reefer in Abbeville, April-May, 1865

James Morris Morgan was an 18 year old midshipman who was a member of the escort party for the Confederate Treasure Train as well as a personal friend of Mrs. Davis and her younger brother, Jeff Howell, also a midshipman escort. The Treasure Train contained privately owned gold and jewelry from Richmond banks as well as the Confederate specie. Morgan's autobiographical account, *Recollections of a Rebel Reefer*, is an entertaining story which is questionable in details. For example, in the excerpt below, pp. 234-40, he has Davis' and his Cabinet arriving in Abbeville before Mrs. Davis, instead of almost two weeks later. However, he tells several stories either not told or only alluded to elsewhere.

The little command only had a short breathing spell at Charlotte, as the enemy were fast approaching and there was little time for them left in which to make a "getaway." Lieutenant [W. H.] Parker persuaded Mrs. Davis to trust herself to the protection of the midshipmen, and they again started on their sad and painful journey. The railways by this time were completely disorganized and they could only proceed as far as Chester, S. C., in the cars. There Lieutenant Parker commandeered some wagons which he loaded with the gold and Mrs. Davis and her family. They then started over the rough country roads for Abbeville, S. C.

What a distressing spectacle this train of three or four wagons, hauled by broken-down and leg-weary mules, must have presented, and what must have been the apprehension of that stately and serene woman, the wife of the President of a nation of Anglo-Saxons, as she sat, surrounded by her helpless children, on one of these primitive vehicles while the half-starved animals slowly dragged her over the weary miles. A platoon of the middies marched in front of the singular procession, acting as an advance guard. Another detachment followed the wagons, serving as a rear guard, and on either side of the train marched the rest of the youngsters. And not far away, on either flank and on their rear, hovered deserters waiting either for an opportunity or the necessary courage to pounce upon the, to them, untold wealth which those wagons contained. . . .

While Mrs. Davis and her escort of ragged boys were slowly plodding on their way, things began to happen in the beautiful village of Abbeville, where every residence was surrounded by a garden and which impressed one as a more fitting setting for a Mayday festival than for the scene of the disruption of a government. First, Senator Wigfall , the man who had received the surrender of Major Anderson's sword at Fort Sumter, arrived. He was the most malignant and unrelenting of all President Davis' political enemies. Before making Texas his home he had been a resident of Abbeville [he actually lived in Edgefield, although he also practiced law in Abbe-

Jefferson Davis in Abbeville

ville], *and he at once went to the house of Mr. Armistead Burt, an old friend, to ask for hospitality. Now it so happened that Mr. Burt had found means to send a message to Mr. Davis asking him, if he passed through Abbeville, to make his, Mr. Burt's house, his home. In less than forty-eight hours after Mr. Wigfall's arrival, who should appear at the house but Mr. Davis! Mr. Burt was placed in a most embarassing position for a few moments, but Mr. Wigfall relieved the tension of the situation by hastily taking his departure out of one door as Mr. Davis entered the other.* [Joe Lane in his recent biography of Louis T. Wigfall writes that the Senator visited friends in Abbeville on his own flight from Richmond to Texas, and he emphasized his long friendship with Armistead Burt.]

The next distinguished persons to arrive were President Davis' Cabinet, in an ambulance, with the exception of Mr. Trenholm, and the Secretary of War, Gen. Breckinridge, who preferred to ride on horseback. He made a great impression on me with his superb figure mounted on a large and fat charger, a rare sight in those days. The Cabinet camped in and around their ambulance which had stopped in the suburbs. I visited their camp and was somewhat surprised to see among these serious and care-worn-looking gentlemen the beaming smile on the round face of the rotund Secretary of State, Mr. Judah P. Benjamin. He was the picture of amiability and contentment. Mr. Trenholm, who had been taken seriously ill on the journey from Danville, had been left at a house on the road. Mr. Trenholm afterwards told me that Mr. Benjamin, up to the time he had left them, had been the life of the party with his wonderful fund of anecdote. ...Throughout this whole trying journey Mr. Benjamin smoked most fragant Havana cigars, much to the astonishment of his companions who wondered where he could have obtained such an unlimited supply of such a rare luxury.

Then Mrs. Davis arrived with her ragged and mud-stained escort, most of whom by this time were walking on their "uppers," or the bare soles of their poor bruised feet. On arriving at Mr. Burt's house she expressed to her host a fear that his house would be destroyed by the Union troops when they learned that she had been sheltered there. The grand old Southern aristocrat made her a profound bow and replied, "Madam, I know of no better use my house could be put to than to be burned for such a cause."

One of Mrs. Davis' children was quite ill, and it was sent over to the Trenholms' house where it could be more comfortable, as Mr. Burt's home was crowded with guests.

The midshipmen pushed on to Augusta, Ga., some eighty miles away, seeking for a safe place to deposit the treasure, and on their arrival were told to get out of there as soon as possible, as Sherman's men were expected at any moment; so back they trudged to Abbeville

Jefferson Davis in Abbeville

where the Secretary of Navy ordered them disbanded. These boys, averaging between fourteen and eighteen years of age, some of them nearly a thousand miles from their homes, the railroads destroyed, and the country filled with lawless men, were turned loose to shift for themselves. The money was turned over to the care of the soldiers. They took such care of it that to this day never a dollar of it has been traced! The lie that was circulated about Mr. Davis having got any of it was afterwards disproved by the poverty in which he and his wife lived and died.

When Mr. Davis was at Abbeville a very unpleasant incident took place which those who were present and afterwards wrote accounts of his flight from Richmond have avoided mentioning, I suppose because it was not to the credit of some of the Confederate soldiers. In the mountains of North and South Carolina near the Tennessee line there were bands of bandits who called themselves "guerillas." A false report reached Mr. Davis to the effect that these brigands, learning that a large amount of gold was being taken through the country protected only by a few little boys, had made a sudden descent from their mountain fastness and were rapidly approaching Abbeville.

On receiving the report Mr. Davis mounted his horse and rode out to a camp where some of the soldiers were bivouacked. The soldiers were drawn up to receive him and he made them a short address--very short. He told them of the report about the guerillas, and also told them that both Gens. Sherman and Johnston attacked this band wherever they found them on account of many atrocities they had been guilty of against both Union men and Confederates, and wound up his talk by asking the men if they would go out with him to attack these robbers and murderers. As he paused for a reply, a private pushed his horse to the front and said: "Our lives are just as precious to us as yours are to you. The war is over and we are going home!" And without the slightest semblance of order the gang--I can call them nothing else--dispersed, leaving those few gallant and loyal fellows who accompanied Mr. Davis until he was captured.

Before Mr. Davis left Abbeville I begged him to allow me to accompany him, but he told me that it would be impossible, as I had no horse, and that it was not in his power to procure me one. He spoke to me in the most fatherly way, saying that as soon as things quieted down somewhat I must make my way to the trans-Mississippi, where we still had a army and two or three small gunboats on the Red River, and in the meantime he would give me an official communication for General Fry, commanding at Augusta, asking him to attach me temporarily to his staff.. ..[Morgan did manage to secure a horse and reach Augusta, but he only stayed two or three days.]

General Fry advised me to return to Abbeville, as I had friends there, and being of no possible use where I was, I accepted his kindly

Jefferson Davis in Abbeville

counsel and returned.

The soldiers who had accompanied Mr. Davis had not surrendered at Appomattox, but now there was a stream of paroled men, and men who had deserted before the end had come in Virginia, passing through the once peaceful town. While these men committed no outrages, when they went into a private house to ask for food or shelter, they adopted a threatening attitude which was very offensive. Fortunately, a younger brother of Mrs. William L. Trenholm, a lieutenant in the South Carolina regulars, arrived, and while we could not prevent the crowds of hungry men from swarming over the lower floors of the house, where although not invited, they made themselves very much at home, we could and did keep them from invading the upper portion of the home where the ladies secluded themselves.

When the danger from our own men had passed, owing to their hurried exit from the town, we had immediately to prepare for another, Sherman's men who were very near and who were fast approaching, and the inhabitants were in mortal terror of the lawless crew known as Sherman's "bummers," who rode on the flanks of his army, accounts of whose fiendish outrages were on every tongue.

While we noticed no change in the demeanor of the slaves, still we had no means of knowing what their attitude would be when the Union troops entered the place, and this uncertainty caused us some anxiety.

In the house were two very large and very heavy chests of silver which Lieutenant Macbeth (Mrs. W. L. Trenholm's brother) and I determined to attempt to save by burying it. We were afraid to take any of the Negroes into our confidence, so we determined to do the work ourselves. We waited until midnight when every one on the premises was supposed to be asleep, and then, carrying our spades, we stealthily stole into the garden and proceeded to dig two large graves. The night was well suited for our work, as there was a moon but it was somewhat obscured by clouds. When we finished our task we entered the house and by great exertion managed to carry out the chests and bury them. As soon as they were covered with earth, it was evident, even in the dark, that the newly upturned ground would betray us. There was nothing left to do but to dig up the entire garden if our hiding place was not to attract the attention of the first passer-by, and this we at once proceeded to do. It was no light job, as the garden must have comprised nearly an eighth of an acre, and daylight came while the task was still uncompleted.

I suddenly looked up from my work and there, to my consternation, I saw "Nat," Mrs. Trenholm's butler, the slave whose loyalty to the family we had grave doubts about, leaning against the fence, on the top of which his arms were resting while he calmly watched what we were doing. I asked him how long had he been there, and he frankly

Confederate Gold in Abbeville

replied: "I'se been here ever since you gentlemen started work." I then asked him why he had not offered to help us, and he said it was because he thought we did not want any one to know what we were doing. Naturally it was too late to make any other dispensation of the silver, and we felt sure that it would be lost. That morning the advance guard of the Federals entered the village. Two or three soldiers came to the house and I saw "Nat" (standing over the very spot where the silver was buried) talking to them. Of course we expected a demand would be made for spades, but, be it said to "Nat's" honor, he never betrayed us. A few years after this incident occurred, I met "Nat" in Columbia. He was then a member of the legislature and one of our lawmakers.

The Confederate Treasure Train in Abbeville

Another account of the Confederate officials in the town in late April and early May, 1865, was made by Captain W. H. (William Hawar) Parker in his *Recollections of a Naval Officer, 1842-1865*, pp. 358-369. Parker was the officer in charge of the Treasure Train and its midshipmen escort on the flight southward. His description of its last days was, as follows:

During the march I never allowed any one to pass us on the road, and yet the coming of the treasure was known to every village we passed through. How this should be was beyond my comprehension. . . . I had sent a courier on ahead to Newberry asking the quartermaster to have a train of cars ready to take us on to Abbeville, S. C., a distance of some 45 miles, and upon our arrival we transferred the treasure to the cars and left the same evening at sunset. We arrived at Abbeville at midnight and passed the remainder of the night in the cars. Mrs. Davis and family left me and went to the house of the Hon. Mr. Burt, a former member of the U. S. Congress.

We formed a wagon train again here and set off across the country for Washington, Georgia. . . . Marcus Ammen, who was with the train, later said that he heard that it was intended to place the treasure in the new bank building in Abbeville, but the town officials opposed this. At Washington they again placed the treasure on railroad cars and went to Augusta. When the situation there became increasingly dangerous, on April 23rd the party returned to Washington, Ga.

We formed a wagon train again at Washington, picked up our ladies, and started for Abbeville. On the way we met Mrs. President Davis and family, escorted by Mr. Burton Harrison, the President's private secretary. They could give me no news as to the whereabouts of the President. I have forgotten where they told me they intended to

Confederate Gold in Abbeville

go. They had a comfortable ambulance, and two very finely fed horses, which I thought they would very likely lose. In crossing the Savannah river I remember saying to Captain Rochelle that if the money were mine I would throw it overboard rather than to be longer burdened with it. I had had it nearly thirty days; the midshipmen were suffering for shoes, hats and clothing, and the care and responsibility weighed upon me.

We arrived at Abbeville about the 28th, and here I stored the treasure in a warehouse on the public square, and placed a guard over it as before. I also kept a strong patrol in the town, which was now full of General Lee's paroled soldiers on their way to their homes. Threats were frequently made by these men to seize the money, but they always received the same reply.

Abbeville was on the direct route south, and all the trans-Mississippi troops passed through it, as well as others. The citizens had known but little of the sufferings of war. They were very kind and hospitable to us. On the night of the 1st of May, I was invited to a May-party, which I attended more to find out what was going on in the town than anything else. While there a paroled officer of General McGowan's brigade approached me and said he had information that the paroled men intended to attack the treasure that night, and he thought it his duty to tell me. I thanked him and went to my quarters, where I issued orders to double the guard and patrol. I had given directions as soon as I arrived in Abbeville that a train and engine should be held ready for me, with steam up, at all hours of the day and night. My intention was, if threatened by the enemy, to run by steam to Newberry, and then take to the dirt road again. Everything seeming to be in a state of quietude, I retired about midnight: leaving directions with the officer-of-the-guard to call me if anything occurred. I had quarters in a private house, and slept on the floor of the parlor where I could be easily aroused.

About 3 o'clock in the morning Lieutenant Peek the officer of the guard tapped at my window. I can hear him now: "Captain," said he in a low voice, "the Yankees are coming." Upon inquiry, I learned that a detachment of Federal cavalry had captured two gentlemen at Anderson about thirty miles distant the evening before. One of the gentlemen who had escaped and brought the news to Abbeville, as Mr. Peek told me, "thought the Federals would arrive about daylight."

I immediately called all hands and packed the money in the cars, and by daybreak had everybody on the train in readiness to move. I walked the platform in thought--for I had not quite decided to run. About sunrise we saw a company of cavalry winding down the hills in the distance, and I sent out two scouts who shortly returned with the information that it was the advance guard of President Davis' escort.

Confederate Gold in Abbeville

So I had judged rightly in returning to Abbeville. About 10 a. m. President Davis and his Cabinet rode into town and were well received by the population of Abbeville. It was a sad enough sight to me, I know. It reminded me of scenes I had witnessed in Central American revolutions!

By order of Secretary Mallory I transferred the treasure to the acting Secretary of the Treasury and was instructed by him to deliver it to the care of General Basil Duke, which I did at the railroad station. By Mr. Mallory's order I then immediately disbanded my command, and the Charlotte company marched off for home before I left the depot. The midshipmen left in detached parties, and an hour after President Davis' arrival the organization was one of the things of the past. . . . We had about thirty colored servants in the command, and they started for Richmond in a body. They went off in high spirits, singing a song in chorus, and all walking lame in the left leg as it is the habit of the colored population to do. I gave them all as much bacon, sugar and coffee as they could carry; and did the same to the midshipmen and the Charlotte company. The remainder was then divided into equal parts and distributed among the officers who remained with me.

Mr. Davis had with him four skelton brigades of cavalry, viz.: Duke's, Dibbrell's, Ferguson's and Vaughn's. Many of the men traveled with him, I believe, to get their rations. Some of them were throwing away or selling their arms, as they looked upon the war as over. There were many noble spirits among them who were ready, and anxious, to follow and defend the President to the death: but the force taken as an organization was demoralized.

President Davis went to the house of the Hon. Mr. Burt. After finishing my duties with regard to transferring the treasure, and disbanding my command, I called upon him. I never saw the President appear to better advantage than during these last hours of the Confederacy. He was captured eight days after this, near Irwinsville, Ga., about 175 miles from Abbeville. His personal appearance has been often described. I remember him as a slender man, of about 5 feet 10 inches in height, and with a grey eye as his most marked feature. His deportment was singularly quiet and dignified. At this time he showed no signs of despondency. His air was resolute; and he looked, as he is, a born leader of men. His cabinet officers, with the exception of Gen. Breckinridge and Mr. Reagan, stood, I thought, rather in awe of him.

Gen. Breckinridge presented his usual bold cavalier manner; but Mr. Mallory, Secretary of Navy, and Mr. Benjamin, Secretary of State, were much depressed and showed it. I do not recall Mr. Reagan--he was the Postmaster General, and acting Secretary of the Treasury. Mr. Trenholm, Secretary of Treasury, and Mr. Davis, Attorney

Confederate Gold in Abbeville

General, had been taken ill by the way and were not with the party.

In addition to the four brigades of cavalry the President had in company more Brigadier-Generals than I thought were in the army. Many of them had ambulances and wagons, and the train must have been several miles long. It seemed to me that it was half a day coming in. Referring to the Federal cavalry I have alluded to, it was said that it was marching on Abbeville, when it met Mr. Davis' escort and turned back. I never knew the truth of this report.

After shaking hands with President Davis, whom I found alone, I first gave him an account of my taking his family from Charlotte, and told him of my having met Mrs. Davis a few days before. He thanked me, and then inquired after my command. I told him I had disbanded it. He said: "Captain, I am very sorry to hear that." and repeated it several times. I told him I had but obeyed Mr. Mallory's order; that my command had been on the march for thirty days, and was without shoes and proper clothing. The President seemed to be in deep thought for a few moments, and I, wishing him clearly to appreciate my position, said: "Mr. President, I must beg you to understand that I acted upon the peremptory order of the Secretary of the Navy." He then replied: "Captain, I have no fault to find with you, but I am very sorry Mr. Mallory gave you the order." After seeing the escort I understood Mr. Davis' regret.

I told the President of my trip to Augusta, and of General Wilson's movements, and asked him what he proposed to do. He said he should remain four days in Abbeville. I then mentioned the affair of the previous night, and said I looked upon his capture as inevitable if he prolonged his stay. He replied that he would never desert the Southern people; that he had been elected by them to the office he held, and would stand by them. He gave me to understand that he would not take any step which might be considered an inglorious flight. He was most impressive on this point. The mere idea that he might be looked upon as fleeing seemed to arouse him. He got up and paced the floor, and repeated several times that he would never abandon his people.

I stuck to my text; said I: "Mr. President, if you remain here you will be captured. You have only a few demoralized soldiers, and a train of camp followers three miles long. You will be captured, and you know how we will all feel about that. It is your duty to the Southern people not to allow yourself to be made a prisoner. Leave now with a few followers and cross the Mississippi, as you express a desire to do eventually, and there again raise the standard."

The interview lasted an hour, and I used every argument I could think of to induce him to leave Abbeville; but it was in vain. He insisted that he would remain four days. Upon leaving the President, I found Messrs. Mallory and Benjamin awaiting me. The latter very nervous and impatient to continue the retreat. Mr. Mallory was more phlegmatic, but was of my opinion, that they would all be captured if they remained.

During the afternoon the soldiers packed the treasure in the wagons again, preparatory to moving. After it was taken away from Abbeville, which was on that night, I have no further knowledge of it.

. . . . I asked Mr. Mallory to come to my quarters for tea that evening, and about 8 o'clock Mr. Benjamin came in. He begged me to see the President again, and to urge him to leave. After some demur I consented to do so. I found Mr. Davis alone as before, and apologizing for my intrusion, said my intense anxiety for his safety must excuse it. I remained some time, and saw that he had a better appreciation of the condition of affairs in Georgia than when I had seen him in the morning. I proposed to him that he should leave Abbeville with four naval officers, (of whom I was to be one) and escape to the east coast of Florida. The object of taking naval officers was that they might seize a vessel of some kind and get to Cuba or the Bahamas; but this he rejected.

I left the President at 9 o'clock, and as I went out he sent one of his aides to call the Cabinet together. I went to my quarters, and not long after received a note from Mr. Mallory saying they would leave that night, and he notified me so that I might accompany them if I desired. As they were all mounted and I was on foot and could not get a horse, I was obliged to decline. About 11 o'clock the President and his escort left Abbeville for Washington, Ga. If I have given undue prominence to myself in relating the occurrences of this day at Abbeville it is only because I had just returned from Georgia, and was supposed to have a better knowledge of the conditions of affairs there than any one else about the President. <u>C'est tout.</u>

XXI. THE OCCUPATION GARRISON IN ABBEVILLE, 1865-66

A Tennessee soldier wrote in his journal on May 14, 1865, *passed through Abbeville at half past twelve, too full of soldiers* . . . [and he and his fellows] *pitched our tents four miles south of Abbeville.* On the 15th, he wrote, *I went back to Abbeville last night and got a supply of commissary stores, bacon, hams, flour, salt, sugar,* [Abbeville had a Confederate commissary at that time]. On the 16th, he noted, *Returned to the village last night, where I saw twelve Yankees who looked scared. Their mission, I hear, is to take care of the commissary stores there.*

The first post-war newspaper in the village, a two page sheet called the *Abbeville Bulletin*, in August 10, 1865, carried the following: *NOTICE. For the benefit of the Citizens and Garrison of Abbeville, S. C., the following Rules and Regulations will be adopted to preserve health and cleanliness. Each family will be held responsible for the good conditions of their yards. They will be policed three times a week--Monday, Wednesday, and Saturday; and all filthy substance collected will be placed in front of their respective premises, when it will be removed.*

The Health Officer will visit the premises of each family three times a week, and any party found guilty of not complying with this notice will be fined according to the nature of their case.
   George R. Black
   Lieut. 56 N. Y. V. V. & Health Officer

Two weeks later, August 24th, the same newspaper paid its compliments to the efforts of the Union officer, as follows: *OUR TOWN. Visitors cannot fail to notice the recent improved condition of our streets. Lieut. Black, the Provost Marshal, expresses the determination to keep the Village in a clean and healthy condition. Every day he has quite a number of freedmen, under a proper guard, sweeping the streets, filling mud-holes, building horse-racks, white washing the trees and boxing, and otherwise improving the appearance and sanitary condition of the town.*

The emphasis on improved sanitation may have helped prevent a large small pox epidemic. Small pox was brought to the village with the Confederate soldiers on their way home. The *Press & Banner*, May 12, 1886, related one story: *Last Monday was Memorial Day of the Confederate Dead. . . . the day was not generally observed in Abbeville, though one lonely Confederate grave was ornamented with flowers. That soldier sleeps under a cedar on the lot now belonging to J. F. C. DuPre, on the left side of the new street which leads to Fort Pickens. He was buried by two Negro men who had had small pox with no one else to witness the act. In 1865, that soldier, on his return from northern Virginia to his home was taken ill in this town with small pox. He and others similarly afflicted were quartered in an*

Federal Troops in Abbeville, 1865-1866

isolated house nearby. During his illness, he requested the attending physician, Dr. Parker, to write to his family and inform them of his fate. The Doctor's note of his name and their address was lost, and the dying request was never complied with. As near as we can learn, he was about thirty years of age. It is thought that he had come from Alabama.

The *Abbeville Press*, November 17, 1865, reported, *We regret to learn that a case of small pox has occurred in our village in the person of a Negro woman on the premises of Mr. D. R. Sondley. No explanation can be given of the origin of the disease. In the absence of a Town Council, it is necessary that precautionary measures at once be taken to prevent the spread of the contagion. A hospital should be immediately established, and a fund raised to meet the current expenditures.*

On November 24, 1865, the *Press* published a communication from Isaac Branch, M. D., as follows: *SMALL POX. A cruel and slandrous rumor is afloat that Mr. D. R. Sondley had the infant child of <u>Sarah</u> (who died of small pox) buried alive with its mother, and that he had driven all of her little children (six in number) from his yard. In justice to him, I feel bound to contradict the whole slander. The woman, <u>Sarah</u>, was very mysteriously taken quite ill with what turned out to be a case of small pox, of which she died in about ten days. As soon as it proved to be that disease, I took all possible pains to prevent its spreading.*

I forbad all access to her room, and no one but myself was permitted to see her. I visited her several times a day and administered every dose of medicine. She was doing remarkably well until the day before she died, when she gave birth to a six months child, which, also, exhibited a well marked case of the same disease. The child barely breathed until the next day when it died a short time after its mother, and the wonder to me is that it lived so long. They were both put into the same coffin by <u>four colored freedmen</u> and does any one suppose that they would have put a live child of their own color into a coffin? Mr. Sondley has her six children in his yard with his own, and is taking every possible care of them.

Sometimes the garrison won public acceptance. In September, 1865. "the most excellent band " of the N. Y. Veteran Volunteers played a number of well received concerts at the Abbeville Court House which included performances by local musicians. During the same time the band made an appearance at a mock ring tournament where Abbeville young men displayed their skills as horsemen, and a young lady was chosen as queen of the affair. Also, in the list of the marriages in the *Abbeville Press*, September 21, 1865, one was between Sergeant James H. Roosa, Co. A., 56th N. Y. V. V. and Miss Josephine C. Wilson of Abbeville.

Federal Troops in Abbeville, 1865-1866

The garrison made its mark in other ways. In the *Abbeville Press*, March 16, 1866, the district grand jury in its presentment noted that, *The Court Room, having been occupied by United States Troops, is very much damaged; the walls defaced, the chairs and the tables broken and destroyed, and the carpeting removed. . . .The Jail and premises are found in a state bordering on dilapidation. The sash and glass in the building are very much broken--the fencing around the lot entirely destroyed, and the meat house and stables stripped of weather boarding. The premises are now, and have been for some time, in the possession and occupation of the garrison of the place. Upon its removal, should it be soon, necessary repairs are recommended.*

A few weeks later (April 6, 1866) the same paper carried an account of a speech by Judge David L. Wardlaw at a public meeting when he gave the following favorable assessment of the U. S. garrison: *The Garrison at this place has been civil and inoffensive (I mean the white garrison--God forbid that I should speak so of the blacks by whom, at first, this community was afflicted). The white soldiers have done their duty with as little of harshness as could consist of that duty--they have been obliging and useful on the plantations when required to be there, and have given no cause for complaint.*

The same issue of the paper reported that the most recent garrison, a detachment of the 13th Maine Regiment under Lieut. Hall, was being replaced by a company of the 25th Ohio Regiment under Lieut. Biekerstaff. On May 11, 1866, the *Press* carried the news that the Ohio troops were being replaced by a company under Capt. Coan of the 15th Maine Volunteers.

Finally, the *Abbeville Press*, June 22, 1866, noted: *REMOVAL OF THE GARRISON. The garrison at this place under the command of Capt. Coan left our District on Monday last. They were a quiet and orderly body of men, in a high state of discipline, and furnished no cause of complaint during their stay with us. Still we rejoice that they are gone.*

XXII. RECONSTRUCTION SCENES

The Reconstruction years brought many changes in the life of Abbeville, and nowhere were these changes more dramatic than in the relationship of the former slaves and the white inhabitants. An example of the unusual changes is the story of Alfred Ellison.

1. "Big Alfred" Ellison and his Grandson, the Novelist

Among the slaves who were emancipated in Abbeville were those of Mrs. M. A. Ellison, the mother-in-law of the Rev. Thomas Hoyt, the pastor of the Upper Long Cane Church and the second owner of the Burt-Stark House. These slaves had been brought from Sumter to Abbeville, and were left in the town when the Hoyts moved to Louisville, Kentucky when the Rev. Hoyt assumed the pastorate of the First Presbyterian Church there in 1860.

Alfred and William Ellison were two brothers who became freedmen in Abbeville in 1865. The latter was, or soon became, educated, and he served as a school teacher during the Reconstruction and later. Alfred never learned to read or write, but his strength of body and character led to his appointment as town marshal in the Spring of 1871 and enabled him to keep that position for most of the next seven years.

The *Press & Banner* often made favorable comments on his services to the town. For example, on January 3, 1872, it noted that, *The peace of the village and the harmony of Christmas week were broken by two shooting scrapes . . . . John McCord, who had been arrested by Alfred Ellison, the town marshal, resisted the officer and discharged his pistol, without effect however, upon the marshal, who knocked him down, giving him a serious blow.* In November, it noted that Ellison "made an active and efficient officer."

On August 5, 1873, it reported on an altercation between Arthur Jefferson, a black county commissioner, and the marshal, when the former was *using a few more expletives than the marshal thought proper. Ellison, who is a powerful man, immediately disarmed Jefferson and threw him down, without any particular regard as to which part struck the floor first. . . . Alfred is usually able to take care of himself.* The *Press & Banner* on September 20, 1876, following a town election in which the white Democrats regained control of the local government, declared *the election of a town marshal takes place next Monday. We think justice and our best interests as a town demand that a coloured man get the place.* A week later, it reported that Alfred Ellison was re-elected.

On April 3, 1878, the same newspaper reported that, *It is alleged by some that it is a great shame that a Negro policeman should be allowed to carry a white man to the guard house while others contend*

"Big Alfred" Ellison

that it is a greater shame that a white man should conduct himself so as to put the Negro under the necessity of carrying him to the lock up.

Ellison served until September, 1878, when John Kirby, a white guard who had served with the Greenwood & Augusta railroad, was chosen to succeed him by a new Democratic town council.

Alfred Ellison spent the rest of his days in Abbeville as a truck farmer on a small farm on Magazine Hill just off Poplar Street. In 1883, when the town council adopted an ordinance officially designating the streets of the village, the Eleventh Section said *the street diverging from Poplar Street near Alfred Ellison's and leading to Pin Hook is called Pine Street.*

In the Spring of 1883, his brother William H. Ellison, *a fine looking, intelligent Negro who has been teaching school for some time in this county* was convicted of obtaining goods under false pretences. He was forced to pay a fine of $50. The *Press & Banner,* May 28, 1884, recounted what happened next, as follows: *In this condition of affairs he made a most earnest appeal to his unlettered brother, Alfred, who is a straight forward, hard working farmer and pledged him his pay certificate until the debt should be paid. Alfred came to his rescue, mortgaging his house to raise the money which was paid to the Court. William H. Ellison has been and is still a regular orthodox teacher, but he has never paid his unlettered brother one cent of the money he advanced for him.*

In later years, Alfred Ellison took part in local Republican meetings, and in 1895 he testified before a Congressional investigating committee which was concerned with alleged irregularities in the election between Republican Robert Moorman and A. C. Latimer, Democrat. Cross-examined by Coleman L. Blease, Latimer's attorney and later Governor of South Carolina, Ellison's testimony, in part, was:

Abbeville is my precinct. Been here nearly all my life. I voted. I registered. I had trouble in registering. I applied on the first Monday in April, but got one in May by paying twenty five cents for an affidavit. I got the registration ticket, but had to wait, on account of the Supervisor of Registration not doing his duty. . . .*[He] waited on ten white men and more, and I standing there holding my affidavit ready for him to register me. I was there between five and six hours, waiting.* . . . *No trouble for white men to get registration tickets. Colored men had trouble.* . . . *I voted for General Hampton in 1876, but I am not a Democrat.*

One of Alfred Ellison's sons, Lewis, moved to Oklahoma, and he named one of his two sons, Ralph Waldo Ellison. Like the man he was named for, Ralph Ellison became a distinguished writer, perhaps best known as the author of the American classic, *The Invisible Man.* In his boyhood, Ralph learned of his grandfather as a "respected

"Big Alfred" Ellison

patriarch" of the Ellison family, and he heard accounts of how his grandfather had others read the newspaper aloud for him. Despite his own inability to read, he could interpret the news accounts with more understanding than those who read them to him.

Ralph Ellison's aunt, Lucretia Ellison Brown, who had also moved to Oklahoma, instilled in the young boy and his brother the knowledge that they came from *an important family and should, therefore, bear . . . [their] inherited name with honor and pride.* To young Ralph, *this was like being told that we had inherited a great fortune which we would enjoy once we found its hiding place.*

As he wrote many years later, September 7, 1990, to this writer, *And while I took an abstract pride in being the grandson of the mysterious Alfred Ellison, he remained almost as abstract as the photographic image which I found among my father's possessions: A brown-skinned patriarch with veiled eyes and head of thick dark hair who faced the camera sporting a white goatee that was carefully trimmed in the then current style.*

I hasten to add, however, that my abstract sense of my grandfather's personality is by no means due to my having failed to meet him in person, rather it was because of the gap between our ages, my ignorance of my families' backgrounds, and the rapidity of change which marks American history. For shortly after my father's death, I did indeed meet my grandfather.

This was through an incident which came about (or so I was told years later), because Alfred Ellison had become curious about his recently deceased son's three year old brat of a boy. And so it was that I came to be taken to Abbeville by my older cousins, Tom and Maybell, who were the children of my grandfather's oldest daughter, my Aunt Lucretia Ellison Brown. I have no idea of the length of our visit, but it couldn't have been more than a month; because the adult in charge, my cousin Tom, was a Frisco Railroad brakeman. And since the Frisco made free passes available to its employee's relatives, he probably arranged for the trip to take place during his summer vacation.

Be that as it may, it was through Tom that I spent a few days with Alfred Ellison and my Aunt Bell and Uncle Jim, the two adult children who lived with him on the old home place. And it is thanks to that visit that I retain a child's vivid but spotty memories of the family's old home and its owner. These include its fireplaces that were so tall that a three year old could step beneath the mantles and peer up the chimneys, my Aunt Bell's cooking, and the huge feather bed in which I slept. I also remember the fresh fruit, melons, and vegetables that were gathered each day and heaped on the back porch to be carefully sorted and arranged for the market--which suggests that my grandfather was still active as a farmer.

The Guffins

I also remember Abbeville's huge moths, its butterflies, and the swarms of fireflies which an older neighborhood boy taught me to catch and store in a bottle, and the fun of watching them twinkle and glow through the glass at nightfall. But best of all there were the tall pecan trees, which were said to have been planted by my father, and with the fruit of which I was distantly familiar thanks to Christmas holidays when my Aunt Lucretia was sure to receive a gunny sack filled with that delicious share of her old home's bounty.

Since I remember my grandfather as being as taciturn as he appears in the photograph mentioned above, I have no idea as to what he thought of his grandson. He was said to have been quite proud of my father so I think that he found me acceptable. At any rate we got along fairly well, perhaps because we were united in our mutual grief. And my only unfavorable memory of the trip has to do with a violent nighttime storm. The next morning the air was quite clear and as I accompanied my Uncle Jim on a walk to assess the storm's damage, we came upon a nest of fledging birds that had been blown from their home in a tree.

<u>So around and about I had come</u>
<u>Upon that which I had started from.</u>

2. The Guffins and the County Robbery Case

Radical Reconstruction in Abbeville not only brought black ex-slaves into public positions, but it also gave positions to two new groups of whites: newcomers or "carpetbaggers" and scalawags, natives who cast their lot with the Republican party. Jeremiah ("Jerry") Hollinshead of Ohio first came into the state as a flag bearer in Sherman's army, and he came to Abbeville in 1869 as a federal revenue officer. In 1871, he was elected to the State Senate from Abbeville County, and he bought General Samuel McGowan's house on Magazine Hill. The most prominent of the scalawags were members of two families, the Guffins and the Tolberts, and it was primarily the former which aroused the antipathy of the white population during this period.

The three Guffin brothers descended from a family which had lived in the area for a century, but their ancestors had not shown any interest in public life. Their father, C. B. Guffin, served as superintendent of the Lethe or De la Howe School and farm before the Civil War, and two of the brothers, L. L. (" Lem") and L. P. ("Pem") served in the Confederate cavalry as scouts for Wade Hampton. By the Spring of 1871, Lem was the Abbeville Probate Judge, Pem was one of the county's members of the State legislature, and their brother Charles (C. W.) was Intendent or mayor of Abbeville.

The Guffins

The *Press & Banner*, April 7, 1871, reported the following: *ROBBERY OF THE COUNTY TREASURER'S OFFICE. As is known to most of our readers, the office of Mr. L. H. Russell, the County Treasurer, was entered on Thursday night of the past week, and money and county checks to the amount of $15,000 [some accounts placed the total as high as $25,000] abstracted. Both the door of the office and the safe were opened with false keys, and were found open on the following morning. A package of money containing $13,000 was overlooked by the burglar, and was not taken. Mr. Russell, with the aid of Chief Constable Hubbard, and other officers of the law, is sparing no effort to discover the guilty parties.* Russell offered a $500 reward and the State of South Carolina offered a $5,000 reward for the apprehension of the robbers and recovery of the money taken.

On April 14, the *Press & Banner* carried an update: *THE COUNTY TREASURY ROBBERY. We have no further developments except that the Messrs. Guffin: L. L., L. P. and C. W., have been arrested and charged with complicity in the robbery under warrants issued by Magistrate Solomons of Columbia and have given bond for appearance.*

Two weeks later, April 28, the *Press & Banner* said, *Under the order of Judge Orr, issued upon the exhibition of additional affidavits, alleging new circumstances of guilt as well as the inadequacy of the bond given, both in the amount and in the solvency of the obligers, the Guffins have been re-arrested and not giving bail were committed to jail. Albert Hamblin was also arrested under the same order for complicity in the robbery and required to give bail.*

On June 23, the *Press & Banner* reported the opening of the trial on June 19 of the three Guffin brothers and Hamblin for grand larceny, as follows: *Some forty witnesses for the State and the defence have been bound over in the case, and a formidable array of counsel have been secured. Messrs. McGowan & Parker assist the State and the accused are represented by Messrs. Burt, Thomson, and Hoge. The case opened on Thursday and will likely occupy next week.*

A week later (June 30), the same newspaper carried the following account of the trial: *The great case of the term after the protracted investigation which has occupied so many days was that of the State v. L. L. Guffin, L. P. Guffin, C. W. Guffin and Albert Hamblin, for the well known robbery upon the county treasury on the night of the 30th of last March. The case was entered upon on Thursday last and occupied the remainder of the week in bringing out the testimony for the prosecution and the defence. An idea of the amount of this testimony may be formed from the fact that the Judge's notes cover fifty five close written pages. Monday and one half of Tuesday of the present week were devoted to the argument which occupied nearly twelve hours.*

The Guffins

His Honor [Judge Orr] *gave greater latitude to the argument, he said, because so little of the time of the Court had been consumed in taking exception to the testimony.* During the argument the Court was densely packed, manifesting the general interest which had been excited, and is the first time in our observation, that the fair sex has honored the Temple of Justice with their voluntary attendance, whilst its priests were ministering at the altar. The attention and interest which were maintained throughout the argument afforded the highest testimony which could be given to the ability and zeal with which the case was argued by the legal gentlemen engaged.

The opening argument for the State was made by Col. Cothran, who was followed by Col. Thomson and Judge Hoge for the defence-- General McGowan replied for the State. Mr. Burt followed for the defence, and the argument was closed by the Solicitor, Mr. Perry, for the State. As the investigation had been most thorough and searching, the argument was elaborate and cogent, and the Judge closed with a clear and dispassionate review of the law applicable to the facts of the case.

The testimony for the prosecution was entirely circumstantial, and was remarkable for the number of circumstances relied upon. The most prominent of these were--that inquiry had been made of the Treasurer by one or more of the defendents a few days before the robbery, when he was going to Columbia--that application had been made to Messrs. Seal, Sign & Robertson for putty--that files had been procured by the defendents--that the keys of the treasury had been twice borrowed during the week of the robbery--that light on the same night had been seen in the Probate office--that a small piece of iron suitable for making a key had been missed from a blacksmith shop--that a vice at one of the defendent's residence had been brought into requisition, etc., etc.--and also great stress was laid upon the fact that neither the files, scissors nor vice were produced.

The defence admitted that the putty had been asked for, but stated that it was to be used for glazing--that files had been procured but that they were used, the smaller for cutting the rivet of a pair of scissors, and the others for sharpening the same and some saws, which they were about to use--that the keys had been borrowed, but only for a few moments during the absence of the Probate clerk who carried the keys of the office--that the light alleged to be seen was produced by the rays of a lamp, kept burning in a neighboring building, which was reflected from the door of the Probate office--that the vice in question was out of repair; etc., and as to some the defendents offered testimony to prove an alibi. In the argument, they denied that any robbery had been committed, but boldly charged that the County Treasurer had abstracted his own funds.

The case was committed to a jury of six whites and six colored with

The Guffins

Mr. James A. Norwood as foreman, and at a little before two o'clock, and after an absence of several hours, they returned with a verdict of not guilty.

So ended the great case.

In the meantime the County Treasurer, L. H. Russell, had relinquished his office presumably for failure to supply sufficient bond, and Governor R. K. Scott appointed J. F. C. DuPre as his successor. Neither Russell nor anyone further was ever charged with the robbery.

A native of Abbeville District who edited *The North Star*, a newspaper in LaCrosse, Wisconsin, B. W. Reynolds, gave a different view of the robbery case a few years later. His column, "Abbeville Correspondence," was reprinted by the *Abbeville Medium*, February 16, 1876. His views may have been discounted since he had left his Greenwood family because of his opposition to slavery and moved to the West some forty years earlier. However, he returned to Abbeville for some years in the 1870s, took part in Republican politics, and became disillusioned with the party. His honesty had always been admitted by even his political foes. He made the following comments on the Guffins and the robbery:

This family had some pretension to respectability formerly--one of the sons is a gentleman. But the assemblyman [Lem Guffin] *labors under the prejudice of being called a thief. This may be mere prejudice, but all the white people of this county, and many of the colored, believe it. The reason for this belief is this; a few years ago the treasury of this county was robbed of $25,000, and this man was known to have access to it. The treasurer accused him of stealing the money, and he laid it to the treasurer. The treasurer was not tried. He was. He employed Burt (a member of Congress before Secession), and asked him what he thought of his case. Burt told him if he had the money he could clear him, if not he could not. He was cleared.*

Pem Guffin was killed in an encounter in a bar room in 1880 and the story is dealt with elsewhere in this work. When Lem Guffin died near Charleston in 1899, the *Press & Banner*, May 31, 1899, took note of his death and made the following editorial comment:

In Reconstruction days the Guffins were well provided with office, and they were all powerful in the appointment of others. The Guffin family had lived in this community for a hundred years, and the old homestead had descended to succeeding generations, until it finally went out of the hands of the family at a comparatively late date.

The Guffin family had lived at peace with their neighbors from their earliest settlement in Abbeville, until the changed condition, when the younger generation then on the scene of action, went into politics [joined the Republican party]. *This act alienated former friends and neighbors of the family. The Negroes stuck to them with*

The Great Fires of 1872-1873

fidelity and whatever L. L. Guffin wanted for himself was given to him, and those whom he sought to set up were set up.

No man ever ruled any people more absolutely than he ruled the Negroes, and while the white people turned against him, he was true to his new political association.

He possessed, in a remarkable degree, political sagacity. His power in controlling his followers and his ability for quieting opposition, was notable.

3. The Great Fires of 1872-73

Three very destructive fires hit Abbeville and its public square in a period of a little over twelve months in 1872-73. The *Press & Banner*, January 24, 1872, described the devastating consequences of the first, as follows:

DESTRUCTIVE FIRE AT ABBEVILLE. LOSS, $70,000. *It is with feelings of profound sadness that we are called upon to record the incidents of the most destructive fire which has ever occurred in the history of Abbeville, and which has reduced the sightly proportions of some of its finest buildings to charred and blackened ruins. We have had a number of fires in different parts of our town before, but they have been partial in extent and involved comparatively trifling loss. Even the great fire of 1858 which swept away the "Posey Range," Mr. R. H. Wardlaw's store and Mrs. Allen's Hotel ...wooden buildings which were a relic of primitive architecture in Abbeville, and might well give place to more imposing and substantial structures.*

But, alas, the late destructive conflagration was not content destroying the frail tenements of wood, but consigned to crumbling ruins, our beautiful Hotel [the forty-room Marshall House]*, the pride and ornament of our town, and the large and commodious court house, with all of its public offices, and a large part of its public records. But after all we have cause to be thankful. There has been no loss of life, and the destruction of property might have been much greater....*

The extent of the area covered by the fire will be understood, when we say that it swept the whole Eastern side of the Public Square, from the Marshall House to the court house, and including these buildings -the wooden range adjacent to the Hotel--the bar-room, hotel, and store of Mr. John Knox--all the wooden buildings owned by Mr. Dennis O'Neill, and comprising the bar-room of Mr. L. H. Russell (the upper portion being used as a dwelling by Mr. Bowie and family), the confectionery of Mrs. Lomax, and the wooden tenement next to the Law Range-- the brick grocery store of Christian & Wilson-- and lastly the brick grocery store of Mr. B. O'Connor, at the corner next to the court house, occupied by Messrs. Kaplan & Sklarz.

The Great Fires of 1872-1873

The origin of the fire was in the back part of the kitchen in the rear of Russell's grocery--and was thus in the center of the wooden block with inflammable material on either hand. Whether the fire was accidental or not is unknown. We learn that there was no fire in the kitchen during the day previous, but it may have originated from a fire which had been used for washing, only a short distance in the rear of the building, and from which some sparks may have been blown, sufficient to ignite the house. . . .

Hugh Wilson, the *Press & Banner* editor who was a co-owner along with J. S. Cothran of the Marshall House, was in bed in his room in this hotel when he heard the alarm. He reported, *Rushing to the Public Square, I saw an excited crowd in the first paralysis and powerlessness of apprehension--knowing scarcely how or where to meet the raging flames. A light wind from the East blowing in the direction of the Marshall House seemed to threaten danger only in that quarter, and there hurried the crowd--some to assist in saving the building, others to aid the inmates in rescuing their property from the flames. The scene at the Hotel beggars description, and can only be realized by one who has seen half-clad men and helpless women in all the agony of sudden panic, when roused from their beds by the midnight cry of fire; collecting their household goods and all which are connected with the common uses and cherished associations of daily life, and seeking shelter away from their burning home. . . .*

But, alas, the extemporary organization, without any of the appliances of active, successful effort; engines, hooks, ladders, and buckets--was entirely unavailing to stay the conflagration.

The insurance generally bears but a small proportion to the property lost. The Marshall House, valued at some $15,000 was insured only to the extent of $3,000. . . . the aggregate loss will probably reach $70,000 upon which there was insurance to the extent of $12,000. . . . If the late fire should teach anything, it should be necessity of organization. Let us at least have a "Hook & Ladder Company." . . . We need organization, not merely to save our houses, but to protect property from plunder. The amount of pilfering was enormous and most reprehensible. . . .

On the Saturday following, Mr. George F. E. Wenck, the celebrated German artist, was upon the spot and transferred to canvas the "ruins," so that we may have a lasting remembrance of the appearance of the town on the day after the fire. With his practiced pencil he soon had a truthful and beautiful sketch of the "burnt district."

The same issue of the *Press & Banner* carried a story on the organization of the "Abbeville Hook & Ladder Company" headed by John Enright. Only ten months later, the new fire fighters were called upon to contend with another disastrous fire which the *Press &*

The Great Fires of 1872-1873

Banner, November 20, 1872, described, as follows:
ANOTHER DESTRUCTIVE FIRE IN ABBEVILLE; FOUR FINE BRICK STORES. PUBLIC RECORDS BURNT. *Again we are called upon to chronicle another of those disastrous conflagrations to which our town has more than once before been unfortunately subjected, and which breaking out about one o'clock on the morning of Sunday [the 17th] last, consigned four stores of one of its finest business ranges, with a large portion of their stock, to shapeless and unsightly ruin. One such calamity in the history of a town would seem to be too much for prosperous life, but Abbeville proudly lifts its head from the ashes of two great fires which the single year of 1872 has brought upon her, and points still to her stately business blocks, tasteful residences and commodious public edifices as proof that she is not dead yet. . . .*

The most serious loss and one that no money can replace is that of the public records in the offices of the Clerk, Sheriff, and County Commissioners. They were partially destroyed in the January fire, and now are totally consumed, not leaving a vestige behind. [Fortunately, this was not true of the Probate Court and Equity records.] *It is impossible to estimate the amount of trouble and inconvenience which this loss will occasion in long years to come, not merely to business and professional men, but to our citizens generally.*

The four stores burnt were on the Western side of the Public Square, extending from the McIlwaine building, owned by Mr. Hugh Wilson, to the New Post Office owned by Mr. H. W. Lawson on the South. The first store on the North was that of Mr. Thos. Robinson, occupied by Barnwell & Co. in the lower story for a general merchandise and grocery business, and the front room above by Mr. W. T. Branch as an insurance office, and the rear room above by Mr. A. M. Hill as a kitchen.

The next store was owned by Mr. Thomas Eakin, and occupied by A. M. Hill & Co. in the grocery and commission business; the upper room being occupied by Mr. A. M. Hill and family.

The next two stores were the property of the estate of Adolphus Williams, deceased, and the lower story of the first was used as a furniture store by J. D. Chalmers & Co., and that of the second as a drug store by Lee & Parker. Two of the rooms above these stores were used respectively, as Clerk's and Sheriff's, and County Commissioners' offices, and the others--one as an office by Dr. B. Rhett, being that formerly occupied by Drs. Wardlaw & Thomson as a dentist's office--and the other as a barber shop.

As to how or where the fire originated, there is a difference of opinion, some supporting it to be in the kitchen of A. M. Hill, above Barnwell & Co.'s store, and others in the store itself. It is difficult to account for its origin in either place, as it is said that the fire in the

The Great Fires of 1872-1873

store was extinguished at a late hour by one of Mr. Hill's family, and that the same was done in the store at the time of closing. It seems to be agreed that its starting was accidental, and that no apparent blame attaches to any one. . . .

The alarm extended to the Alston House, on the corner opposite and the inmates all had their furniture ready packed for a speedy removal. Lawson's New Post Office was subjected to even a fiercer ordeal on the South, as the flames beat even more intensely upon a thinner wall. Everything that human effort could do with the means at disposal was done. The ladder and buckets of the Hook & Ladder Company were called into requisition, copious streams of water were poured upon the heated roof and walls, and wet blankets were freely used. White and black, ministers, lawyers and merchants vied with each other in giving aid where it was most needed. Conspicuous among those who distinguished themselves at this point were Messrs. Lawson, Sign, Cater, assisted by Kennedy, Ellison, and a host of colored men.

Two months later, the *Press & Banner*, January 29, 1873, carried the news of a third terrible fire: *Again it is our sad duty to chronicle another destructive fire, being the third in the space of a little over twelve months, which has consigned to ashes another of our finest business ranges. On the 19th January, 1872, the Marshall House and the court house with the intervening buildings were swept off by the flames of the destroyer; on the 17th November last the Granite Range shared the same fate; and now again on last Monday evening, the 27th inst., Cothran & Wilson's New Range on Washington Street with the exception of the fine store occupied by Trowbridge & Co. . . . was consigned to dust and ashes. . . .The fire was clearly the work of an incendiary, prompted doubtless by the love of plunder.*

The *Press & Banner*, February 26, 1873, reported the dismal warning of the county grand jury in a current presentment in regards to the Probate Judge's office that, *There are in this office a large quantity of old Equity papers saved from the first fire of 1872, in a confused condition, and as they now are, do not so much as serve for common reference. These papers constitute the archives of Abbeville County. They are all that are left of the old landmarks.*

In the same issue, there was an acount of the only case brought against any one for arson in the three fires, as follows: *The most important and interesting case of the term was that of the State vs. Joe Moore for arson--the burning of Cothran & Wilson's new brick range the 27th of last month. The case was commenced by Messrs. Noble and Thomson, and the State was represented by Solictor Blythe and the Hon. Armistead Burt. The examination of the witnesses was long, thorough and critical and the arguments of the counsel for the State and defence were clear, logical, and eloquent. His Honor's charge to*

The Houston Scandal, 1875

the jury was a model of neatness and law. He adverted to the heinousness of the crime for which the prisoner stood indicted, and urged the jury to acquit themselves like men. The jury was wholly colored, the first instance of this kind in the history of our county. After remaining out three hours, the jury returned a verdict of not guilty.

4. Love and Infidelity: The Houston Scandal

Abbeville Medium, January 27, 1875

The most interesting and important case before the court last week was the trial of F. B. Houston for bigamy. The case came off for trial on Friday afternoon, General Samuel McGowan appearing for the defence, and Solictor Blythe and Robert R. Hemphill, Esq. for the prosecution. The court room was packed from the bar to the entrance and the most breathless attention was paid by the crowd. The indictment upon which the prisoner was arraigned charged that F. B. Houston married Ida Lawson on or about December 30, 1874, and that he again married Carrie Davis on or about January 2, 1875. A more diversified taste in the selection of wives was never before known in a civilized country.

Ida Lawson had long, auburn hair, clear white skin, light blue eyes, and a petite figure; Carrie Davis is as black as ebony, with a soft, oily expression and a kind of masculine front. The two wives are widely dissimilar in birth, in property, in education, and in social position. Ida moved in a respectable community, was petted and loved by indulgent parents, and was gratified in every wish. She was the light of the home circle, and the center around which domestic affections clustered. Carrie Davis was the daughter of colored parents--a descendant of Ham. She had never enjoyed educational advantages and moved in that circle to which God in his kindness had assigned her. Her notions of the world were contracted, and until she met Houston, she was in harmony with her surroundings.

The first scene of the last act of the terrible drama was enacted in the Court House last Friday. The spectacle was impressive. There sat Houston, in the presence of the dignified Judge and the incorruptible jury, to answer for his crimes against society and to receive the verdict of the violated law. He kept his seat throughout the trial, and looked like the personification of guilt and infamy. . . . Ida Lawson, the main witness for the prosecution, conducted herself in a lady-like manner on the witness stand, and told the tale of her trust and love in Houston with all the simplicity of truth. . . .She made a forcible impression upon the jury.

Carrie Davis, the second wife of the defendant, was put upon the

The Houston Scandal, 1875

stand. She was clad in the latest fashion, and wore a flaming red shawl and blue veil which ill comported with the sombre scene. Her evidence was clear and to the point, and fell with crushing weight upon the forlorn fool who had tampered with innocence and affection. The defendant was sworn but only added weight to his guilt by his hesitating evidence. After the evidence had all been taken, the case went to the jury--Mr. Hemphill opened for the State; General McGowan following for the defence, and Solicitor Blythe closing for the prosecution.

The speeches were short and full of fire. The case was then given to the jury, who, in about ten minutes, returned with a verdict. The most complete silence fell upon the crowded hall when the Clerk read, "We find the defendant guilty, R. E. Brownlee, Foreman." The first act in the play closed and the curtain fell--Houston to go back to jail to await his Honor's pleasure. . . ..Yesterday morning the last scene was enacted; with much the same house and the same painful attention. The Clerk waded through the indictment, and asked, "What have you now to say why sentence should not be passed upon you?" The prisoner said nothing. His Honor [Judge Thompson Cooke the son of a Methodist preacher] *spoke feelingly but effectively, as follows:*

"You have been convicted of the crime of bigamy. You committed the crime charged against you under circumstances of the most aggravated character. I can conceive in my own mind how persons of like skin might marry two women, but I cannot conceive of how a man of your color could connect yourself with a colored woman. Your conduct is exceedingly reprehensible. I do not think the Trial Justice [B. P. Hughes] *who performed the ceremony in this latter marriage is entitled to any credit for his work, and this community should look upon him with any favor because of this exercise of his office. As an official myself, I know that if any white woman should present herself for marriage with a colored man, I should question them very closely, so likely are persons so united to grow tired of each other, and to adopt much the same course you have adopted.*

You married a white woman of respectability and fine appearance, and then within three days after the marriage proved false to your vows and connected yourself with a colored woman. Now, I do not mean to say that you had no right to marry a colored woman--every man to his taste as the old woman said when she kissed the cow--but the two acts came so close together and were so incompatible in nature that I shall impose upon you the utmost rigor of the law. . . . I learn that you have two little brothers dependent upon you for their living; but you are not the proper person to mould the minds and form the character of the young. The sentence of the court is that you be imprisoned in the state penitentiary at hard labor for the period of five years."

The Houston Scandal, 1875

The detailed account of the main facts of this case may not prove uninteresting. . . .Ida Lawson's acquaintance with F. B. Houston began in the early part of March, 1874. At that time, he was an industrious, hard-working man and was well thought of by those who knew him, and Ida was a pure, guileless innocent child--the favorite in many circles and just blooming into womanhood. . . . They met frequently and were affectionate in all their association. After the first meeting in March of last year, Houston was a frequent visitor at the girl's home in Cokesbury, and was taken into the confidence of the family. He shared their hospitality and it was known by all the people that he and Ida would one day be husband and wife. The marriage was postponed from time to time because of Houston's professed inability to support his wife as he would wish her to be supported.

At length, however, the time was set, and in order that some little romance might attach to the event, a trip to Abbeville was planned, and on the thirtieth of December, in the year of grace, 1874, Ida, leaning upon the strong arm of her devoted lover, came to Abbeville to have the union consummated. The thirtieth was a dreary day. The rain fell in torrents and the streets of this place were almost deserted when the bridal party arrived. They left the train and came up into town. . . .they repaired to the shed in front of Seal, Sign and Robertson's mammoth carriage manufactory where the marital rites were performed by a Rev. Mr. Porcher [O. T. Porcher, a local Episcopal minister and teacher]. That was a scene for the painter's skill. There stood F. B. Houston and Ida Lawson, with only a rickety roof between their heads and heaven. . . .

[Three days later] *In Trial Justice Hughes' (colored) office on January 2, 1875, the same man who had promised eternal fidelity to Ida Lawson under the shed at the wagon factory was one of the principal actors. By his side and leaning upon his arm stood a dusky damsel. The trial justice, after the necessary questions, pronounced the pair husband and wife.*

This was not the first inter-racial marriage that Hughes had performed. The *Abbeville Medium*, July 16, 1873 reported, *Married by Trial Justice Benjamin Hughes, colored, on July 3, 1873--Newlin Mercer, white, of Batesville, Noble County, Ohio to Rena Bowie, colored, Abbeville.* This marriage lasted much longer than the Houston-Davis one did. Newlin Mercer was an ex-Union soldier who taught in the Bull Town colored school near Lowndesville for over two decades.

The *Medium* in October 29, 1879, carried an essay entitled "Miscegenation" from a writer who styled himself "Anti" and who the newspaper identified as a well known minister in the county. "Anti" noted that *miscegnation and drunkeness, leading to, and growing out of it, are the damning sins of the day.* He pointed out a strange

Big Tuesday, 1876

strange contradiction in the public's attitude. *But then it is spontaneous and not legalized miscegenation. The latter is regarded with abhorence by the very men who indulge in the former, without let or hindrance, and without loss of character. Society winks at and condones the first; but would be immensely horrified, at the slightest approach to the latter; hence society is largely responsible for this moral cancer.*

The *Medium,* October 13, 1875, reported that, after having been turned down once, F. B. Houston, who was sentenced for bigamy in January, 1875, was pardoned by Governor Robert K. Scott. Scott acted, it said, on a petition signed by General Samuel McGowan, T. B. Milford, W. H. Taggart, J. F. C. DuPre, and Jerry Hollinshead on the grounds that he was drunk at the time of the second marriage. Both of Houston's wives joined the petition as did Judge Cooke who recommended the pardon on the condition that Houston leave the state. Neither F. B. nor Ida Lawson remained in Abbeville, but Carrie Houston kept her married name and ran a cafe in town for many years.

5. Big Tuesday, August 22, 1876

Press & Banner, August 25, 1886

There is another day in the history of "Secession Hill" that will not be forgotten. That day has been called "Big Tuesday"--August 22, 1876. On that day D. H. Chamberlain [the incumbent Republican governor and candidate for re-election] *and other nominees on the State ticket had made arrangements to speak. Chamberlain and his crowd had rough days in Edgefield and Newberry. Abbeville was their third appointment, but they kept their coming a profound secret from the white people of the county, though it was known perhaps to every Negro in the county.*

To realize the situation, and to account for the intense feeling between the races, it will be necessary to remember that the Republicans had been in power for nearly eight years, and that in that time they had violated all of our ideas of justice, had gradually increased the taxes, and had raised the assessment of our property to such an extent that our people were really no longer able to pay them. . . . Bloody riots were of weekly occurrence and the torch of the incendiary did its destructive work at the bidding of mean white men. The people were, if possible, more excited and indignant than in 1860 . . . . With this condition of affairs the white persons were compelled to keep secret their movements and not divulge anything to the Negroes.

Under these circumstances the Democracy of this county was organized under the leadership of Col. J. S. Cothran. . . . It was

Big Tuesday, 1876

suggested that Chamberlain would come to Abbeville, and every ear was open to hear the first breath of a verification of such a belief. Arrangements had been made with the telegraph operators along the line of the Greenville & Columbia Railroad to inform Col. Cothran if Chamberlain should be on any train coming this way. About midday of Monday, August 21, 1876, the news was flashed over the wires that he and two associates were coming. Colonel Cothran immediately sent his couriers to every corner of the county with the intelligence... and with the request that the presence of every Red Shirt (red shirt being synonymous with Democrat) in the country was needed at Abbeville Court House by nine o'clock next morning, Tuesday, August 22, 1876. The newspaper report the next day estimated that five thousand mounted Red Shirts were, at the appointed hour, quartered on the outskirts of the village, ready to move at a moment's notice.

Excitement was intense, and each side mounted the full force of its following. Col. Cothran had his headquarters in the Law Range. Governor Chamberlain had his at Senator Hollinshead's house. It was a house on Magazine Hill which Hollinshead, an Ohio native, had purchased from General Samuel McGowan. *After consultation and holding a council as to the best and most advisable mode of procedure, it was determined to demand a division of time with the Republican speakers that day in their discussion of the issues of the day. Capt. J. N. King, A. B. Wardlaw, B. W. Barnwell, R. M. Sanders, and J. P. Phillips* (a week later the *Press & Banner* added the names of E. B. Gary and L. W. White) *were appointed as commissioners to bear the request to Chamberlain with the further instruction, if refused, to demand the right, and to insist upon a division of time, with force, if necessary. The request for division of time was finally granted.*

At ten o'clock the Democrats and the Republicans respectively formed processions, each being preceded by a band of music and flying banners. The Democrats were mounted, the Negroes moved first, marched defiantly to the stand, took position in front of it. Immediately afterwards the Democrats marched through the streets to martial music, with uplifted banners. The immense columns of determined men which extended further than the eye could see, formed an imposing scene for the immense throng of ladies, old men, and children that thronged every balcony and window on the public square and along the entire route of the procession . . . . Ten clubs with banners led by The Dark Corner Club of Edgefield and hundreds of Red Shirts that came from all parts of the county without organization, but joined the procession, all of whom were well mounted, and made a brilliant display.

Arriving at the stand the Democrats found the place densely packed by a great crowd of Negroes who occupied the seats. As the

Big Tuesday

column of Democrats, who were on horseback, came near the crowd of Negroes, they opened ranks, one side going to the right and the other to the left, and completely surrounded the stand and the Negroes by a cordon as determined as ever met an enemy.

Upon the stand was seated on the Republican side: Governor D. H. Chamberlain, Congressman S. L. Hoge, and Superintendent of Education J. K. Jillson. On the Democratic side: Hon. D. Wyatt Aiken, General S. McGowan, and Col. J. S. Cothran.

After speeches of an hour each and during the speech of the last Democratic orator, Col. Cothran, a number of Negroes rose to leave, whereupon, *the Red Shirts demurred. Drawing their pistols, they ordered them back, saying "Col. Cothran wanted to give them some good medicine which they needed and which they should take." This enforced delay was painful to them. . . following which Mr. T. N. Tolbert* [Abbeville's Republican chairman] *made a speech, during which time the ruling spirits of the day, Messrs. McGowan, Cochran, and Aiken, had taken leave of the grounds, and greater confusion and bad blood was apparent.*

At the final breaking up of the meeting, the colored flag bearers were advised to roll up their flags, and cease to do any further act to stir up strife. This they refused to do. On the way to the public square, their flags were waved defiantly, accompanied by irritating words, this was replied to by a volley of pistol shots. The flag bearers ran for their life and escaped with one or two wounds. For a half an hour afterwards, there was much firing into the air which caused a general stampede. The day was a Democratic victory. The Radical hosts were discouraged, and their leaders went home to take no further part in the campaign.

In the *Press & Banner,* June 28, 1916, J. M. Conner of Cokesbury recalled how he as a boy of fifteen saw the event:

The "Big Tuesday" in Abbeville was a memorable day as well as an exciting time. The Radicals were marching down town with their flags flying and drums beating, when about 500 Red Shirts rode into them and shot down the flags and perforated the drums. The procession broke and fled pell mell in every direction. This created a panic among them, No one was killed. This was carrying out the plan of frightfulness inaugurated at that time.

"Big Tuesday" looked very different from the Republican perspective. L. L. Guffin, one of about twenty white members of the party in Abbeville, described his experience on that day to a Congressional investigating committee, as follows:

I might say that the canvass opened . . .when there was a mass meeting appointed at Abbeville Court House at which Governor

Big Tuesday

Chamberlain and other gentlemen were to speak. They came according to appointment. At that time they were met by the democratic clubs from Edgefield, Laurens, and Abbeville. I suppose there were five or six thousand mounted men there--what we call red shirts [Beverly Vance, a black Republican leader from Hodges, testified at the same hearing that white democrats from the town of Abbeville did not wear red shirts, only the men from the country]-*with their pistols. You may say that they broke up our meeting. There was some little joint discussion, but it was all on one side. The democrats circled around the stand on horseback and got the few republicans that were there, what we would call in frontier life, corraled, and would tell them to close up; and they would get them closer and closer, so that it was impossible for them to stay in the crowd, and so a great many of them slipped out and left. The democrats had the meeting all their own way, whenever the democrats would have speaking, they would cheer them, and if a republican got up they would not allow him to speak.*

Following the speaking, Lem Guffin retired to his house near by because a Mr. King warned him that, *he thought from the demonstration being made the meeting was likely to break up in a general row, and my* [Guffin's] *life would not be safe if it did.* Guffin watched the red shirts parade by his house. *My little girl I had in my arms, holding her up to see the cavalry, as they called it, pass, and they taunted me as "the damned radical son of a bitch," and asked me to come out of there and they would make short work of me. I told them I guessed they didn't want to do that. While sitting there they rode up town and commenced shooting. I suppose there were one hundred fifty or two hundred shots fired in the Square. There was quite a large party that looked to me like three thousand five hundred men, at the entrance of the street that I live on- Main Street. They had come down and formed a line. There was a lady in town sent me word that probably I had better get out, as she thought may be they were coming down to my residence, so my brother and myself went over to Widow Hollinshead's, where Governor Chamberlain was staying, and we stayed there a while, in fact we stayed there until night.*

XXIII. ABBEVILLE AT LEISURE IN THE 1870s AND 1880s

1. Baseball Comes to Town, 1873-74

Press & Banner, August 15, 1873

The Abbeville Amateur Base Ball Club having accepted the challenge of the Cokesbury Athlete Club, the game came off on the grounds of the Abbeville Club on last Friday afternoon. Much interest had been taken from several days previous by both the Cokesbury and Abbeville people and large numbers from both places had made preparations to witness the game. Greenwood and other portions of the District were also well represented. On the three o'clock train more than a hundred ladies and gentlemen arrived from Cokesbury at our Depot, where they found a welcome greeting from delegations of our people, who had all the available carriages, buggies, and wagons of the town awaiting to convey to the field of the friendly contest. By this time all the places of business in the town of Abbeville had been closed, and her citizens were assembling en masse, and by half past three o'clock the grove was crowded with spectators.

At the meeting of the clubs it was agreed that Mr. G. M. Hodges of the Cokesbury club should act as the Umpire. Messrs. H. P. Hodges and T. P. Quarles were scorers for their respective clubs, Messrs. J. M. Dickson and W. C. Benet, as captains.

The Abbeville Club went to the bats first, and in the presence of the large assembly each member of the clubs took the place assigned him, either in the field or on the corners. At a few minutes before 4 o'clock the game was commenced and at the first inning the Abbeville club made but two rounds and the Cokesbury club made twenty which gave them prestige and their efforts were redoubled. Second and third innings were much in favor of the Cokesbury club, and at the fourth inning the Abbeville club was "white-washed," they having failed to make a single "round." The fifth inning was also to the disadvantage of the Abbeville club, but at the sixth inning Abbeville came out ahead and played with more spirit and better effect during the remainder of the game.

The whole number of scores made by the Abbeville club was fifty one, while the Cokesbury club ran the number of their scores to eighty six. In justice to the Abbeville club, we would state that they have been only recently organized, whilst their opponents have had much longer practice.

The large number of scores may be accounted for, as owing to the unevenness of the ground, the gullies and the trees.

Much elated at their victory, the Cokesbury people returned to their homes on the extra train which left here at 7 o'clock.

In September, Abbeville played a return game at Cokesbury before

Parson Mountain as a Summer Resort

a crowd of 500 and lost by the score of 43 to 28.

The *Press & Banner*, October 22, 1873, in the middle of a long account of the annual fair held by the Abbeville Agricultural Society had a short account of the second baseball game played in Abbeville and the first one in which the home team was victorious, as follows: *At three o'clock in the afternoon of Wednesday* [October 14], *the match game between Abbeville and Cokesbury was played on the grounds of the Abbeville club and was witnessed by a large number of both sexes. Mr. C. A. C. Waller of Greenwood acted as umpire and after a close and exacting contest, announced a victory for Abbeville--the score standing 54 to 51.*

The *Press & Banner*, July 1, 1874, carried the following story:

Baseball Contest. According to previous announcement, the match game between the Cokesbury Baseball Club and the Resolutes of Abbeville came off here on Friday last, and after a spirited contest the palm of victory was borne off by the Resolutes. The score stood fifty to twenty three. The umpire was Mr. C. A. C. Waller of Greenwood and the scorers were Messrs. T. P. Quarles of Abbeville and E. C. Graydon of Cokesbury. A special train brought up the young men of the Cokesbury club, also a bright array of ladies and gentlemen to witness the attractive game. Abbeville too turned out in full force and lent the potent witchery of bright eyes and ardent sympathy, to stimulate its champions to victory. Both sides put forth their best efforts, but Abbeville bore off the coveted prize. The opposing champions were distinguished by handsome uniforms--the Cokesburians by neat caps trimmed with blue, white shirts and blue knee pants--the Abbevillians by blue shirts and white pants with a blue stripe.

2. Parson Mountain as a Summer Resort, 1883

Press & Banner, August 15, 1883

About fifty or sixty of our citizens are summering at Little [Parson's] *Mountain, some seven miles distant from Abbeville C. H.*

The mineral waters at that place is believed to work wonders in giving tone and vigor to the stomach, and hence the rejuvenating of wearied and sick people. Among those of our people who are now at that place are Mrs. Coogler and family, Dr. E. L. Wilson and family, Mrs. White, Mrs. Branch, Mr. J. B. Rogers and family, Mr. W. T. McDonald and family, Mr. George W. Syfan and family, Mrs. C. V. Hammond and family, Mr. J. Allen Ramey and family, Mr. William McAllister and family, Mrs. William Miller and family, Mrs. Sondley and son, Mr. John McCullough, Miss Annie Boozer of Columbia, Miss Fannie Hammond and her mother.

Many other of our citizens would have gone if houses could have

Parson Mountain as a Summer Resort

been had. Mr. A. M. Hill has returned, very much improved in health. Mrs. McDonald has been greatly benefited. Mr. Rogers is enthusiastic in his praises of the beneficial effects of the water.

Seven house have been built about the spring, and all of them are occupied to their full capacity, and visitors spend a delightful time. At night, music, song and dancing make up a part of the amusement at Little Mountain.

The lodgers at Little Mountain are supplied with vegetables and fowls by the people in the vicinity, who bring their eatables to that place for sale.

The medicinal qualities of the water at Little Mountain has attracted the attention of our medical men, some of whom send vessels daily for rations of the healing water, and some of our business men are daily drinkers from that fountain.

Last Sunday, Mr. G. W. Syfan made a Sunday School address to the children, which was greatly enjoyed by both old and young.

One week later, a correspondent from "Our Mountain Home" wrote, We devote several hours of each day to vocal and instrumental music, dancing, reading, visiting, talking together, sporting and occasionally a ramble through the forest--all vocal with merry songsters, and often times ringing with gay and happy sons of merry children. Sometimes we visit the mountain with our sweetheart and sometimes just with ourselves. Suffice it to say, the days glide rapidly by and never hang heavily upon us. We cannot close our letter without once more bringing before the public and all invalids the "Fountain of Health," in the form of the most magnificent mineral spring extant. Its health giving properties are witnessed by many and acknowledged by all who ever drank of its cooling and delightful waters. . . .

In regard to the accomodations for another season, we learn that the proprietors of this valuable place contemplate building a number of pretty cottages which will be rented to applicants for a nominal sum.

XXIV. SCENES OF VIOLENCE FROM 1880 TO 1900

The quarter century after Reconstruction was marked by several incidents of spectacular violence. Every case had its own distinctive setting, but each was surely influenced by the atmosphere of the time. Among the numerous homicides, there were some which commanded special attention. The first of these, the killing of ex-Sheriff Guffin in 1880, attracted national interest. It will be obvious to the reader that the bias of the *New York Times* in 1880 was toward the Republican Party.

2. "The Killing of Pem Guffin," *New York Times*, October 4, 1880.

Charleston, S. C., Oct. 3. The murder of Pem Guffin in a billiard saloon at Abbeville court house on September 27 has been already briefly announced in the **Times**. *Facts which have since come to light leave no doubt that the crime, instead of being the result of a quarrel over a game of billiards, was a premeditated act to remove a fearless and influential opponent from the road to Democratic success.*

Pem, Lem, and Will Guffin, descendants of one of the oldest Abbeville families, affiliated with the Republican party at the time of its organization in the State. Being well known among the colored people, they accepted them as leaders and elected Pem to the legislature. In 1870, he was elected county commissioner and in 1872 sheriff, which office he held until 1876, when fraud and intimidation wrested the county from the Republicans. From that time until recently, all three of the brothers were engaged in farming. A few months ago, Will Guffin was appointed Special Deputy Collector of Internal Revenue, and Lem obtained an office at the Charleston Custom House.

At the beginning of the present campaign, Pem Guffin again took an active part in politics, and was spoken of as the Republican nominee for sheriff of that county. His energy and pluck contributed much to the well organized condition of the Republicans of that section, and the open defiance with which the latter met the mandates of the Bourbon chiefs on several occasions was attributed to Guffin's teachings. On the Saturday before he was shot, he had given offence to the Democrats at a political gathering and had been warned to be on his guard.

From the evidence given before the coroner's jury, it appears that Guffin entered the billiards saloon with C. Q. McClung and Campbell Martin, with whom he was well acquainted, for a friendly game of billiards. Near the close of the game, Campbell asked the colored man, Lang Goolsley, who was in attendance, to get Guffin's knife from Mr. Norwood [the proprietor of the saloon], *and Goolsley had scarce-*

Scenes of Violence from 1880 to 1900

ly reached the foot of the stairs when he heard two shots fired and saw McClung rushing down the stairs and endeavoring to make his escape in a buggy waiting in the rear of the house.

J. B. Wilson, [an employee of the saloon], *testified that he saw Martin hand McClung a pistol a few minutes before they went into the billiards saloon, and he did not think that they had time to play more than one game before he heard the shooting. A bystander who heard the shots and saw McClung jump into the buggy, caught the mule by the bridle, whereupon the murderer jumped out and endeavored to make his escape on foot. He was overtaken, however, before he had run far and conveyed to jail.*

Several men, on entering the billiards saloon, found Guffin on his knees, at the side of the table, his body bent forward and his face resting against the floor, in a pool of blood. On examination, it was discovered that one shot had entered his right temple, ranging toward the left ear, and the other struck him near the regions of the heart. Either of the shots was sufficient to cause instantaneous death. Martin was subsequently arrested as a participant in the crime. He stated that the murder was committed by McClung in self-defense; that Guffin, during a quarrel about the game, had endeavored to cut McClung.

The story is improbable. Neither Goolsley, who left the room a few seconds previous to find Guffin's knife, nor Wilson, who was sitting near a window adjoining the billiards room at the time of the shooting, heard any altercation.

The Republicans are very much excited over this new exhibition of Democratic deviltry. They believe, and in fact this opinion, it is said, is shared by many Democrats, that Guffin was decoyed into the saloon to be murdered, and that Goolsley was sent after Guffin's knife, while Martin had it still in his pocket, to guard against a witness. The knife was subsequently found on the floor of the billiards saloon where Martin had undoubtedly thrown it.

The victim of this crime leaves several young children, his wife having died two years ago. McClung, a Tennessean by birth, has the reputation of being a drunken desparado, who shrinks from no crime, and who has ever been found a ready tool to wreak vengeance on the hated "Radicals." Will the State authorities punish these men as they deserve to be punished? The experience of the past does not warrant the supposition that they will.

The *Press & Banner*, October 27, 1880, carried an account of the trial. Both Charles McClung and Campbell Martin maintained that in a dispute over the outcome of the billiards game, Pem Guffin had attacked McClung with a knife. McClung's shirt was cut or torn, and there was a cut or abrasion on his chest which was not bleeding when he was arrested. The chief questions at issue were whether Guffin

Scenes of Violence from 1880 to 1900

even had a knife at the time and whether the defendants, McClung and Martin, had planned to kill him.

McClung testified that, *when he arrived in Abbeville from his farm on Saturday, September 27th, the little boy Lang who drives his* [Campbell Martin's] *buggy told me Martin was in town and wanted me to heel a chicken for him.* [Martin was "running" some cock fights]. *I first saw Guffin 1/2 hour after I saw Martin. I saw him coming out the back door of Christian's bar-room. I went to heel chickens full 1/2 hour after I first saw Martin. The first cock fight took place about half past one o'clock p. m. I put gaffs on it. I got Guffin's knife and had it long enough to cut off ends of a string that tied the gaff on. I asked if anybody had a sharp knife or scissors. Someone handed me a knife, but it was dull, and I gave it back, when Guffin took out his knife and said to me, "Here's one which is as sharp as any scissors you ever tried." I took it and cut the strings. I think the knife shown to me* [he was referring to a knife on exhibit which was reputedly found at the scene after the killing] *is the one I got from him or a facsimile of it. I handed Guffin's knife to Martin when I got through with it. The second cock fight took place an hour and a half or an hour and a quarter after the first.*

McClung and Martin had E. B. Gary, D. H. Magill, and Armistead Burt as their defense counsel. The defense obviously feared that the blacks would be more sympathetic to Guffin, and they struck four out of the five blacks whose names were drawn. The jury took somewhat less than two hours to decide what juries in Abbeville County with one exception (Samuel Banks in 1874) had done since 1836 and that was to find on the behalf of a white defendant who was charged with murder.

The newspaper described Charles McClung as *a muscular 6' 2" Tennesseean who had commanded McClung's Battery in* [Nathan Bedford] *Forrest's forces, while Pem Guffin was physically ... weak, but he was a stranger to fear.* Guffin had told a Congressional Committee in the Election of 1876 that he had volunteered for Confederate service when he was only 13 years old, and during the war he was known as "Babe." He had served in the cavalry as *one of Hampton's special "scamps," or independent scouts.*

Guffin's reputation may have swayed the jury. For example, the *Press & Banner*, June 5, 1872, carried the following story: *An Affray. L. P. Guffin and H. Ellison, both members of the Legislature from Abbeville, had a street fight on the public square on Monday last. The quarrel commenced with some angry words pertaining to politics, and resulted, we learn in Guffin striking Ellison who thereupon threw the other down, when Guffin drew a knife and inflicted a slight wound upon Ellison's neck. The fight at one time promised serious results, but no immediate damage was done to either party.*

2. The Benedict Homicide, 1884

Another spectacular homicide occurred on Christmas Eve of 1884 when John C. Ferguson killed Arthur Benedict, a clerk in the store of his Uncle Charles Auerbach. Ferguson was tried four times before he was acquitted, and the case attracted wide attention over the state. The *Press & Banner,* December 31, 1884, carried a detailed account of the homicide, as follows:

This community was shocked and a gloom cast over the Christmas festivities by the shooting of Mr. Arthur Benedict by Mr. John C. Ferguson which sad event occurred in the store of Mr. Charles Auerbach in Abbeville at half past one o'clock, Wednesday, December 24, 1884. The killing was done with what is called a "bull dog" pistol of 38 calibre, the ball breaking the sixth rib and penetrating the left lung immediately below the heart. Death resulted in about fifteen minutes, though the deceased became unconscious in an exceedingly short time.

It was the day before Christmas and the streets and stores were crowded with people. . . . Mr. Auerbach's store was full of customers, and Mr. Benedict was at his usual place of business, intent on serving his employer faithfully, and in the active discharge of his duty to customers, when his slayer entered the store and shot him. Some of the witnesses say he spoke to the deceased, and they heard the deceased acknowledge his presence. Other witnesses who were equally near and had an equal opportunity to hear, testify that they heard no words between them. Beyond report of the affair, we knew nothing, however, and speak only from hearsay.

The deceased, as soon as he was shot, placed his hands over the wound, and going toward the door in great agony, with tearful eyes, and death pictured on his face, said, "My God, I am shot. Hold me," and at once the man who was so recently in full vigor of manhood, was helpless, and began to sink to the earth, but was caught by the persons to whom he spoke, and who were standing near him. He was then carried to his hotel in a dying condition. Almost immediately afterwards he died.

. . . .According to Jewish custom in cases of violent death, the body of Mr. Benedict was placed in his coffin in the clothing which was upon his person at the instant of killing, and he was buried without any change of apparel. . . . Mr. Auerbach took his body aboard the train on Christmas morning, and quite a number of persons, as a mark of respect for the deceased, went to the railroad depot to witness the departure of his remains, which were taken to Columbia, and deposited in the Jewish burial grounds of that city.

Mr. Arthur Benedict, the deceased, was about twenty seven years of age, an unmarried man, a stranger in a strange land. He was a native of Austria, but had been living in Abbeville some four or five years, during which time he had saved some money, and at the time

The Benedict Homicide

of his death he was perfecting arrangements by which he would open a store on his own account at Greenville, Mississippi, about the first of next February. He had made good friends among our people. Retiring and inoffensive in his manners, courteous and warm hearted in his sentiments, his death is much regretted.

Mr. John C. Ferguson is about twenty four years of age, the son of Mr. A. J. Ferguson, a well known farmer of considerable property living some four miles west of Abbeville village. Two or three years ago he was married to a daughter of Mr. W. H. Brooks, a wealthy and much respected citizen of the village. After his marriage he settled on a tract of land which his father bought at the estate sale of T. C. Perrin, and built a house on it with every prospect of a fair success-- his greatest drawback being his love of whiskey.

.... The *Press & Banner*, February 11, 1885, reported on the first trial which was held on the 6th and 7th. Both sides challenged numbers of jurors, and the jury which was chosen included nine white men and three colored men. A large crowd attended the trial with whites on one side of the courtoom and blacks on the other. Judge B. C. Pressley presided.

The prosecution witnesses testified that on Friday or Saturday preceding the shooting, Ferguson had called Benedict a "damned liar" and Benedict replied, "you are another." One witness said that only a few minutes before the shooting while in Reuben Haddon's bar room, he heard Ferguson say to Stark Martin, "Come on down here, if you want to see me kill a damned Jew." Martin begged him not to go to Auerbach's store. Another witness, Mr. Kaliski, a fellow Jewish merchant who said that he was not a friend of Auerbach and had not spoken to Benedict for a year, reported that just before Ferguson performed the fatal shooting, he had come into his store to purchase cartridges for his pistol. When the merchant found that he did not have the size Ferguson needed, the latter said it did not matter for "I have enough to kill a man."

The defense emphasized Ferguson's history of "faints" or "spells" from childhood. Martha Wharton testified that as an eight year old slave who belonged to the Ferguson family, she had tended young John from the age of one until he was five years old. She said that he frequently fell down and could not learn to tell his age. His mother, Mrs. Susan Barksdale Ferguson, said that although the family had understandably tried to keep it quiet, her family had a history of mental instability, and two of her uncles had suffered severe breakdowns. The defense called upon Dr. F. F. Gary who said that some of Ferguson's reputed symptoms could indicate temporary insanity.

The prosecution produced a number of witnesses who had grown up with John Ferguson and had never heard or noticed any such

The Benedict Homicide

aberration in his behavior. They also produced doctors, including the family doctor in his childhood, who reported no knowledge of any such unusual behavior.

John's father, A. J. Ferguson, testified that his son "had been drinking heavily for the last three years" and that he had seen a jug of whiskey in the buggy the day before the shooting. He also said that John had carried a pistol for "perhaps a year." The defense attorneys were able to elicit testimony from Mr. Kaliski that many other men had come into his store to buy cartridges and had engaged in boastful language about what they planned to do with the pistols they were carrying. In fact, he said that several had done this since the shooting. Ferguson's chief attorney, Scottish-born W. C. Benet, told a Charleston newspaper reporter that carrying guns on one's person was still a common practice in Abbeville despite the state law forbidding it, and he estimated that at least a dozen spectators in the courtroom during the trial were carrying concealed pistols.

Perhaps only coincidentally it was brought out that John C. Ferguson had himself worked as a dry goods clerk in Abbeville for three or four years, and his last employer had been Charles Auerbach. Auerbach himself was present at the trial, but he was so emotionally upset that he could not stand examination. Soon after the trial ended, he committed himself to the State Asylum since he was unable to sleep or work.

The jury refused to convict; in fact, they voted 10 to 2 to acquit him. N. G. Gonzales, the reporter who covered the trial for the Charleston *News & Courier* and later was a founder of the Columia *State*, reported that he was told that the pro-Ferguson jurors had held a caucus during the trial. The State tried Ferguson three more times with resulting mistrials twice and acquittal in June, 1886. The defense strategy was to avoid jurors from the town of Abbeville, and this proved successful. Less than two months after Ferguson was cleared by jury action, the incident claimed an additional victim. Benedict's uncle, Charles Auerbach, died in the State Asylum, and the *Abbeville Medium*, August 5, 1886, made a terse comment that "the cause of his sad death is well known."

Abbeville became known for its homicides and even better known for its tolerance for those charged with committing them. Hugh Wilson, the editor of the *Press & Banner*, wrote November 1, 1893, in reference to the success of defense counsel in moving a murder case to Anderson for trial, *the counsel for the defense erred in not removing the trial to Abbeville. If the case had been tried before an Abbeville jury, we have no doubt that he would have come clear.* He angrily declared that "human life is the cheapest thing in the county" and that his newspaper had ceased to carry the details of murder cases, because there was no longer any suspense as to the outcome.

Lynching of Dave Roberts

Wilson could have been referring to the June session of the criminal court in Abbeville. Of the nine men charged with murder which were before the court in the Summer of 1893, none were convicted of murder.

In June, 1907, Abbeville juries convicted two white men of manslaughter, and Editor Wilson commented (*Press & Banner*, June 12, 1907) *There have been many homicides in this county since 1877, but as far as we can now recall this is the first instance of conviction of a white man for manslaughter.*

This tradition continued into the 20th century. In September, 1920, there were fourteen cases of murder on the docket (this was after both Greenwood and McCormick counties had been created). On the first day of court, the *Press & Banner*, September 8, reported that in the first four cases, all of the defendants had been cleared of murder. All of the victims were black, and two of the accused were black. The court found the latter two guilty of carrying concealed weapons.

Many reasons were given for both the prevalence of murder and the failure to convict the perpetrators. One reason was the tradition of defending one's personal honor by resort to fighting which often led to the use of deadly weapons. Blacks and less well-off whites followed the example of the ante bellum gentlemen. Other reasons included the skill of the Abbeville bar, the widespread practice of carrying concealed weapons, and the persistence of intemperance. As an example of the latter, in 1885, Abbeville County had ten bar rooms, and seven of them were in Abbeville, the others in Hodges. In December, 1882, when the town of Abbeville voted on "license" or "no license," (wet or dry) the former won by 175 to 94.

3. The Lynching of Dave Roberts (1882) and the Rescue of Charles Hall (1896)

Blacks accused of crimes faced the prospect of extra-legal as well as legal punishment. Sometimes authorities gave up prisoners to angry mobs who were in search of vengeance, and in at least one instance the authorities were able to rescue a prisoner from an angry mob. The *Press & Banner*, January 3, 1883, carried the following account of the lynching of Dave Roberts who was being held for assault on Dr. H. G. Klugh:

Last Sunday night being the last of the year, many devout persons in this village set up. . . . About half-past one o'clock, after the conspirators had secured and carried away their victim, some persons of the Public Square were notified of the fact, but at that hour of the night, when people were in the bed, and the livery stables closed, it was too late to undertake to prevent the contemplated murder. The

Lynching of Dave Roberts

murderers would have had ample opportunity to execute their deadly purpose before it would be possible to organize a company of pursuit and recapture of their victim. . . .Rumor hath it, though we know not whether truthfully or not, that Dr. Klugh since his recovery, visited the jail but refused to identify the prisoner as his assailant though there were circumstances which strongly indicated that he was the man who had struck the blow. Dave Roberts was a black man, aged about forty years, and a farmer, or farm hand, who lived near Cokesbury. ... On January 1, 1883, his lifeless body was found in a tree about two miles east of Abbeville on the roadside near Elijah Wilson's wagon shop.

Testimony before the Coroner
    J. F. C. DuPre, being sworn, says:
    That he was woke up about one o'clock; got up at once and went to the front door and found four men coming up the jail steps, and they said, Mr. Sheriff, we have a prisoner here that we wish to lock up. I at once entered my room and obtained the keys; when I returned I could tell that the men were white; I asked who they had; they replied they had a horse thief, who they had followed all day and caught near Ninety Six about dark; I handed my son Willie the keys, he opened the door and went up the stairs; two of the men went up with Willie; the prisoner apparently tied; I asked one of the men what is that man's name; he replied I don't know, they just got me to come along and help them; I said then, who are you; he said I am from Edgefield; by that time we had gotten to the platform in the third story; my son Willie unlocked the wood door; I said to the man with the prisoner, let me have the committment; I was then told, we have no prisoner; we came for Dave Roberts; I told him they could not get him; they replied that they had come for him and that they intended to have him; they told me they were in sufficient numbers to take him; I remonstrated with them about what they were intending to do.
    I asked them to let me go down and put on some clothes; they allowed me to go but two of them followed me; I came out of the jail or the main building of the jail, and as I came out they seized me; they had their pistols out; they kept me there until the men upstairs came down with Roberts; they never released me until the party with Dave Roberts went out the front gate; some of the men were disguised; I did not know any of the parties; I did not see or smell anything that indicated that there was any whiskey in the crowd; they did not get the keys from me; my son Willie had the keys; I cannot say how many men there were , but I think there must have been thirty; they were in and around the walls of the jail and out at the gate; when the prisoner was brought out the men who were holding me were standing in such a position that I did not see Roberts until he was down the steps going toward the gate.

Rescue of Charles Hall

Jan. 1st, 1883   *J. F. C. DuPre, Sheriff, A. C.*

W. C. DuPre, being sworn, says:
Last night after we went up into the third story, I requested the men to let me go down and put on some clothes; they did not let me go further than to the second floor; they asked me for the keys; I told them I did not have them; they then gathered me by the arm and two more of them searched me and found the keys; they then went into the corridor where Roberts was confined and brought him out tied with a small rope; as soon as they left I went up [the] street and tried to get up a crowd to pursue them; I failed to get up a crowd; they took me in a room and kept me there until they found Roberts; I did not recognize any of the party; they were all disguised in some way.
Jan. 1st, 1883   *W. C. DuPre*

Twenty years later, February 6, 1907, the *Press & Banner* observed that many years after this event, another Cokesbury black, Wince McNary, confessed on his death bed that it was he and not Dave Roberts who had struck Dr. H. G. Klugh and knocked him out on that December night in 1882 when he was caught stealing Klugh's cotton. It was for this that Dave Roberts was jailed, and it was for this that he was abducted and lynched by the mob.

In contrast, an Abbeville sheriff, F. W. R. Nance, some fifteen years later was able to use a posse of Abbevillians to take a suspect away from a mob and thus prevent a lynching.

Abbeville Medium, November 17, 1898

Tuesday morning in the lower Long Cane section, Kennedy McCaslan, a young white man, was shot by Charles Hall, colored. The weapon used was a shot gun and the load struck McCaslan in the mouth making a terrible wound. It seems that the two parties were working a crop on shares. Hall had been neglecting his business during election time and since. Tuesday morning McCaslan went over to Hall's house and directed him to get to work and get the cotton out, Hall seized the gun and used it as above stated.

The news spread rapidly through the country and a party started in pursuit of Hall who fled with great speed as soon as he fired the shot. A messenger was sent to Joseph Johnson, who came, with Abbeville's famous "Negro dogs." Hall's track was soon discovered, and the dogs opened their music. Johnson went with the dogs on foot and the crowd came behind, armed and mounted. The hounds held to the trail steadily and as Hall heard them in the distance he strained every muscle to escape, but in vain.

In the afternoon, he was overtaken on our public square in front of the store of G. A. Douglass. He was immediately seized by some of the

Kennedy, Dansby, and Kyle Slaying

pursuing party who started out of town with him. The news of the shooting had only reached Abbeville a few hours before, and nothing was known of it outside of a half dozen of our citizens. This being the fact our people were startled when a band of armed men rode into town in hot haste, seized Hall and began to drag him hastily from the town. A great crowd soon filled the public square, Hall cried out in agonizing shrieks for the police, for the sheriff, and for the Lord. No one present will ever forget the despair of his helpless voice. His captors were not moved by his appeals and the surging mass slowly made its way down Main Street. Someone hit Hall in the mouth with a pistol, and he received a blow or so over the head.

Sheriff Nance commanded the peace and a number of men went to his assistance and finally Capt. J. L. Perrin of the Second Regiment, [local unit in recent Spanish American War] Charles J. Lyon, and Lawton Robertson got possession of the prisoner and carried him to jail.

When the arrest was made, there was not a policeman near at hand and notwithstanding this Hall was not more than 250 yards from where he was seized when he was rescued. Sheriff Nance and Mayor Miller were on hand almost as soon as the man was caught. They were ably assisted by our citizens and the men who captured Hall listened with reason to what was said.

The pursuing party was made up from quiet, orderly, industrious clear headed men descended from those substantial men known as the Long Cane Irish. . . . Out of abundant caution, the jail was guarded by the Home Guards Monday night, and Hall was sent to Greenville Tuesday morning by the early train. . . . Kennedy McCaslan who was shot is the son of R. H. F. McCaslan. He is highly spoken of by everyone. At last accounts, he was still alive, but in a very critical condition, liable to die at any moment.

A Shocking Tragedy. Sheriff Kennedy, U. S. Marshal Dansby, and William Kyle of Massachusetts, Killed.

Two years after the above incident in which the *Medium* writer paid tribute to the "clear headed men descended from those substantial men known as the Long Cane Irish," two descendants of the Long Cane Irish were involved in a particularly tragic shooting episode which led to three deaths.

Abbeville Medium, January 3, 1901

Last Saturday night the people of Abbeville were horrified at a bloody tragedy in which three lives were lost. The trouble began at the Carolina Hotel on Washington Street. The stories of the events of

Kennedy, Dansby, and Kyle Slaying

the night are conflicting and it is hard to get an accurate and satisfactory statement of what occurred.

After supper, as usual, a number of the boarders were congregated in the office of the Carolina Hotel. Some were reading, some talking and several were playing a social game of poker with goobers [peanuts] to keep the score.

About 9:30 o'clock John Dansby walked into the office and to the fire-place. In a little while he stepped to the table and watched the game, standing behind the chair of William Kyle who had a hand in the game. He threw down some money, but it was declined by Mr. Royall. Kyle told Dansby to get away from behind his chair and to get in front of him. Dansby stepped back to the fireplace and stood for a short while. He then returned to where the game was in progress, said he "was a gentleman," and offered his hand to one of the players, and they shook hands.

Dansby then offered his hand to Kyle repeating that he "was a gentleman." Kyle refused to shake hands saying to Dansby, "You are not much of a gentleman from the way you talked to me this morning," or something to that effect. Dansby stepped back to the fireplace and and some harsh words passed between the two. Dansby finally called Kyle "a damned son of a bitch," Kyle threw down his cards, rose from the table with his hands raised, gesturing while talking to Dansby and advanced to within eight feet of him. Dansby drew a pistol with his left hand, but was seized by the proprietor of the Hotel and as if returning the weapon to his hip-pocket he changed it to his right hand behind his back, brought it into position and fired from his hip. The ball struck Kyle in the abdomen, ranged downward, passing out from the hips, ploughed through the brace of a chair and rolled across the floor.

Dansby then retired from the office walking backward with pistol in hand. The proprietor of the hotel ran out and gave the alarm, and the police hurried to the scene. Dansby went by the colored Baptist church to the Cotton Mills. Police Johnson and O'Bryant came up with him near Miller's store, and he warned them not to come nearer for while he was a friend to both of them he would kill them if they did. They separated and telephoned to town for assistance. O'Bryant went back to town but soon returned with Sheriff Kennedy, both mounted. Chief of Police Riley followed on foot with Aug. W. Smith, Wyatt Aiken, J. Hayne McDill, and others.

In the meantime Dansby reached the house of his father-in-law, Thomas Creswell. He said he had been in a difficulty and was being followed. He asked Mr. Creswell to take charge of his little son and raise him up properly so that he would not come to the same condition that he was in just at that time. The policemen reached the house and took their stations around it. Sheriff Kennedy went to the

Kennedy, Dansby, and Kyle Slaying

front door and called for Dansby addressing him as "John" for they had long known each other. Dansby answered and came out of the front door. Sheriff Kennedy told Dansby he must come with him. Dansby replied that he would not do so and immediately firing began. Perhaps twenty five shots were fired.

Sheriff Kennedy and Dansby were facing each other a few steps apart. When the firing ceased, it was found that both were mortally wounded. A ball from a Colt's Army calibre 45 entered the breast of Sheriff Kennedy two inches above the left nipple and passed entirely through his body. Dansby was shot through the chest and the left thigh.

Sheriff Kennedy fell into the arms of A. W. Smith, who with Chief Riley had reached the spot. He suffered intensely. He was carried to the house of J. J. Blanchett and lingered for about two hours. His mother and wife and little boy reached him.

Dansby walked about fifty steps when his pistol was wrested from him and he fell to the ground. He never spoke after he fell although he lived long enough to be hauled to the jail. If he suffered, he gave no sign of it.

. . . . Dansby and Kennedy were both buried at Lower Long Cane Monday. Early Monday morning, Rev. T. W. Sloan went to the home of Mr. Creswell and conducted funeral services which consisted of reading the scriptures and prayer. About 9 o'clock the hearse of J. W. Sign left the city with the body of Mr. Dansby.

Funeral services were held over the body of Sheriff Kennedy at 10 o'clock Monday morning in the A. R. P. Church which was filled to its limit. Immediately after, McDill & Lyon's hearse began the journey to Lower Long Cane with the body of Sheriff Kennedy.

The Dansby cortege reached the cemetery first and the interment was over before the others arrived. The hearses met and passed each other about an eighth of a mile from the cemetery. A large crowd was present and they stood around both graves. No ill feeling was apparent. The two dead men had always been friendly.

XXV. DAYS OF CELEBRATION AND DEDICATION

From 1903 to 1908, there were four significant additions to the Abbeville public square: the Eureka (later Belmont Inn), the Confederate monument in the center of the square, the municipal building with the opera house, and the new court house. Each was dedicated with appropriate fanfare.

1. The Eureka (*Press & Banner*, August 26, 1903)

The formal opening of the Eureka, under the management of that prince of hotel men, Mr. W. T. McFall, an event that had been looked forward to with no little interest by our people, was signalized by a sumptuous dinner on last Wednesday evening [the 19th], *at which were the Board of Directors and their wives, besides a number of invited guests . . . .* [total of fifty].

Dinner was served at 7 p. m., consisting of quite a number of courses and embracing so many substantial and dainty dishes and exhilerating potions as put it beyond the power of anyone short of an expert in such matters to describe, and therefore we are forced to forego the undertaking--suffice it to say, however, that in our opinion it could not have failed to satisfy the taste and cravings of the most pronounced epicure.

The beautiful parlor and spacious dining room fairly ablaze with scores of incandescent lights, and with every nook and corner filled with lovely begonias, palms, ferns and various potted flowers, presented within themselves, truly, an enchanting scene; but when to this was added the presence of quite a number of Abbeville's loveliest ladies, the combination far surpassed our descriptive powers.

The Eureka differs altogether from the ordinary style of hotel buildings. It is of Spanish architecture, and with its broad and extended verandas, its wide spreading roof, reaching some six or eight feet beyond the outer walls of the building, makes it highly suggestive of restfulness, ease and comfort.

The interior is most fittingly arranged, having large airy rooms handsomely furnished, and with a number of bath rooms and other modern conveniences on each floor.

Along with the other numerous attractions at the Eureka is "The Eureka News and Cigar Stand," in the hands of Mr. Thomas H. Cobb, who will supply you with cigars, cigarettes, tobacco, and books of the highest grades at the lowest prices.

Cooks: First Cook, A. R. Rook; Second Cook, Robert Jackson
Waiters: James Thomas (Head Waiter), Jos.Wright, Richard Gantt
Bell Boys: John Griffin, Luther Davis

The Confederate Monument

Abbeville Medium, August 27, 1903

Grand Ball and Banquet at the Eureka on Friday Evening [the 21st]. *Wurm's orchestra of Atlanta furnished the music which was the very latest and the best. . . . . Dancing began promptly at 10:30 o'clock and continued until 12:30 without any intermission. Then the ladies and gentlemen formed in line and went in procession to the temporary dining hall in the lower story of the Hotel where supper was served. . . .*

The supper continued until 2:30 o'clock when all returned to the ball room and finished the dances on the card. At 4:30 o'clock, the orchestra played "Home Sweet Home" and soon the lights were out and all was quiet at the Eureka.

The dance program consisted of thirteen waltzes, six two-steps, and "Home Sweet Home."

2. Confederate Monument

The *Abbeville Medium*, August 30, 1906, in a story on the unveiling of the Confederate monument recounted the history of the U. D. C. (United Daughters of the Confederacy) in Abbeville. The first U. D. C. chapter was organized in 1896. The real push to sponsor a Confederate monument on the public square was during the presidency of Mrs. Lucy Calvert Thomson. The chapter presented numerous entertainments to raise the funds, and on the evening of August 22nd, it celebrated its success with *a reception on the lawn of the Stark Mansion. . . for all the adult citizens of Abbeville and their visitors. It was largely attended, but a rain made it necessary to serve the punch on the spacious walk on the Main Street side. There was room enough and the refreshments were enjoyed by every one.*

The First Artillery Band [which Congressman Wyatt Aiken had secured from its base near Charleston] *was seated on the Main Street portico and discoursed the sweetest music throughout the evening. . . . The grounds were brilliantly illuminated with electric lights. . . . There were twenty five lights around the tables.*

The *Press & Banner*, August 29, 1906, described the events of the following day, as follows:

Last Thursday, August 23, 1906, was a "Red Letter" day for Abbeville, the occasion being the unveiling of the Confederate Monument [39 1/2 feet high] *which marks another glorious and grand epoch in the history of our city.*

The day arose threateningly with low murky clouds floating through the sky, but the rain was withheld and the clouds only served as a partial covering from the rays of the sun.

Long before the hour [11 a. m.] *announced for the unveiling of*

New City Hall and Opera House

the monument, crowds were pouring in from every avenue to the city until the public square was filled with a seething mass of human beings watching and waiting for the hour to arrive.

Soon the sound of martial music was heard and all eyes turned to the upper part of the square and as the parade drew near a company of 15 young ladies uniformed in white with red sashes, upon each of which was written the name of the state the wearer represented. These were preceded by the officers of the day and the First Artillery Band of the U. S. Army, while the old veterans brought up the rear under the command of that gallant and brave officer, J. Fuller Lyon.

As the column neared the Monument, the band struck up **Dixie** *causing the "old rebel yell" to be given lustily.*

This parade marched in and encircled the Monument, when the exercises were opened with prayer by Rev. Preston B. Wells of the Methodist church, after which Mrs. Lucy Calvert Thomson, President of the Abbeville Chapter of the U. D. C.'s was introduced, and standing upon the base of the Monument she presented it to the city in a few well chosen words appropriate to the occasion.

Dr. G. A. Neuffer [the mayor] *was then introduced and in a happy style and appropriate remarks received the Monument in behalf of the city. Then it was that Miss Mary Klugh and Miss Lucy White, daughters respectively of Judge J. C. Klugh and Mr. Charlie White, pulled the strings that unveiled the Monument, and the 15 young ladies representing the 15 states* [the twelve Confederate states plus, Missouri, Kentucky, and Maryland] *sang that beautiful patriotic air, "The Bonny Blue Flag" which called forth lusty cheers.*

The exercises around the monument being over the crowd moved to the band stand in the pretty shaded park just in front of the Eureka . . . [where R. R. Hemphill spoke, and Miss Jessie Boyce of Due West recited the poem, "Conquered Banner"].

At the conclusion of the addresses, the veterans were invited to the Court House where a sumptuous repast was in waiting. . . . In the afternoon a match game of ball [baseball] *was played at the Abbeville diamond between Greenwood and Due West in the presence of a large crowd. The game was hotly contested from start to finish and wound up 6 to 4 in favor of Greenwood whose team played only 8 innings. . . . The day's pleasure concluded with a ball at the Eureka Hotel in the evening. The large hall was crowded and all had a happy time.*

3. New City Hall and Opera House

Abbeville Medium, October 1, 1908

The City Hall is a large three story building and is made up of twenty offices for renting purposes, a mayor's office, a clerk's office, a

New City Hall and Opera House

council chamber, the Opera House, a box office, fourteen stage dressing rooms, a basement to be used for heating purposes, a number of toilets, and several baths.

The woodwork in the hallways of the municipal building is of bog oak and is of heavy substantial appearance. The wainscoting is about three feet deep and is of red quarry tile, imported from Wales.

The Opera House is a handsome affair. The seating capacity is about one thousand, the dress circle seating about four hundred. The boxes are six in number and have a seating capacity of ten each. The stage is one of the finest in the State, being forty two by seventy feet. About fifteen sets of curtains and scenery have been put in position and are ready for the opening night. An asbestos curtain has been put up for fire protection.

The colorings in the Opera House are most harmonious. The walls and ceiling being canary while the wood work is in old ivory. In the offices and hallways, rich ochres and siennas with contrasting woodwork have been used.

Five hundred lights will be used in the Opera House alone. The hallways of the building will have large bowl globes while the offices will have drop cord lights, something over a hundred lights being used. The offices are all communicating rooms, the average being sixteen by sixteen.

Six fire escapes of the latest improved design are a part of the municipal building. The entrance to the stage is from the court which separates the two buildings [this building and the adjoining new court house]. There are also two fire escapes which open on this court.

The city government at present is composed of the following gentlemen: James L. McMillan, mayor, Albert Henry, mayor pro tem, J. C. Ellis, H. G. Smith.

The county grand jury in the Spring of 1905 (*Abbeville Medium*, March 2, 1905) declared, *The last Grand Jury recommended that the stage now in the Court House be taken out, but we find it still in use, and we insist that it be taken out immediately after the present term of the Court and that in the future the court room not be used for theatrical purposes. Not taking into consideration the danger from fire, etc., we think that the damage to the building and to the furniture more than over balances all money received for the rent of the same.*

Abbeville Medium, October 14, 1908

"The Great Divide." *The first show to be given in the Opera House was "The Great Divide." The show was far above the average show that hails this way. The plot is an interesting one, and the acting was high class in every detail. The stars were backed by the best actors in minor parts.*

New City Hall and Opera House

The staging in the second act was superb. It was a graphic representation of the Great Divide. The scenery in the second act approached the sublime.
A good house witnessed this initial play.

Abbeville Medium, October 21, 1908

"The Clansman." This play was presented last Thursday night at the Opera House. Every seat was sold and some would-be buyers of tickets were turned away. The play was not in any sense offensive, as we thought it would be. The atrocities of what we believe to be the facts of the Ku Klux Klan were so slightly presented as to be rather pleasing--pleasing to us to get off so lightly. The play kept up the interest of hearers and spectators throughout.

The tickets, as we understand, were as follows: In the pit or first floor, $1.50; in the first gallery, $1.00; in the third gallery, 75 cents; in the boxes, $2.00.

No colored people attended, as far as we are informed.

The show people are pronounced in their admiration for our opera house. One man said that he had been in many parts of the country, and he had not seen a better opera house or court house than ours.

Press & Banner, March 3, 1909

Hugh Wilson editorially commented that the Opera House drew a 1,000 gate for *The Clansman* with tickets from $.75 to $2.00. He obtained the figures from the Opera House books for the first two months of 1909, and, omitting two nights when the weather was particularly bad, the total paid admissions were:

Jan. 2--199   Feb. 20--433
14---224   23--238
15---288   27--150

Another news item indicated that the city fire bell's new home was atop the Opera House, and an Opera House advertisement declared that the Burgner & Alton Stock Company with a cast of 20 persons would begin a week's engagement at the "Grand Opera House" with a presentation of "On the Frontier." Prices ranged from 10 cents to 30 cents. The company promised that the bill would change each night in the week.

About a half century before the Opera House was built, Abbeville had a popular amateur dramatic group of young men who took the name, "the Thespian Corps."

Independent Press, October 17, 1856

New City Hall and Opera House

The Thespian Corps. We are sorry that our limited space in the present issue restricts us to a brief notice of the performance of this amateur company, during the past week. She Stoops to Conquer and The Irish Lion; Pizarro and The Stage Struck Yankee; The Gamester and The Rough Diamond were performed on three successive nights to crowded houses and much to the gratification of a highly intelligent audience. We have heard but one opinion expressed of the character of the performances.

Independent Press, December 19, 1856

The Thespian Corps. The house was crowded; the front seats by youth and beauty, whose encouraging smiles lent inspiration to the performers; while in the rear the sterner sex were prepared to reward somewhat more noisy demonstrations of approval.

The program began with the two act farce, **Naval Engagements** *and concluded with "an after-piece" titled* **Raising the Wind.** The Thespian Corps had its own hall located in the Marshall House and admission was 50 cents.

The reporter praised the performances of each of the young men, but especially of "Tony Lumpkin" who "made many good hits, which brought down the house," yet in his opinion "the character provided too limited a scope for the exercise of his peculiar abilities."

Also, in the writer's opinion, *by way of interlude we had an Irish song from Mr. J., and some excellent performances on the violin by that accomplished musician, Mr. Rothschild, who evoked the most rapturous applause, and enthusiastic encores.*

Less than a year after the end of the war, the *Abbeville Press,* February 2, 1866, described the return of the amateur theater, as follows:

"Private Theatricals." One of the most pleasant entertainments of the season was presented for the gratification of a small audience on Thursday evening last, in the shape of a number of very attractive plays, in which the characters were personated by several of the young ladies and gentlemen of our village. It was a revival of the very popular amusement contributed by the "Thespians" before the war, with this novel feature, and very decided improvement, that the female characters were represented by ladies. Men at best can furnish only an inadequate representation--a "counterfeit presentment" . . . . A charm of these "Village Theatricals" arises from the sympathy which exists between the performers and the audience. . . .

The first piece of the very attractive programme of the evening's entertainment was **The Dead Shot,** *so well known to those of us who have seen it performed by the "Thespians" of old. Louisa was personated by Miss Jane T.; Chatter by Miss Rosa B.*

4. The New Court House
Abbeville Medium, October 1, 1908

In the Court House the same excellent good taste in architecture, coloring, and arrangement prevails as in the City Hall. In both buildings, the aim has been artistic simplicity and while the fronts of both are entirely different, the basic principles of art have been preserved. The entrance to the City Hall is through an arched doorway of handsomely carved stone while the front of the Court House is made more imposing by the portico, two buttresses and four massive columns of stone. These columns are three feet at the base and two and a half feet at the top. The buttresses are of stone and will be ornamental with two handsome electriliers of sixteen lights each.

The spacious porticos are to each side of the building. They are massive affairs of stone and are set off by floors of red tile. In the interior the flooring is all of red tiling ornamented with a Grecian key design in cream and black. Red tile wainscoting with a wood finishing in bog oak is also used in all the corridors.

The Clerk of Court's office is first on the right hand as you enter and is a large and comfortable looking room. On the left hand a wide staircase leads up to the court room.

The county offices are all on the first floor, and each office is especially designed for the convenience of the officer occupying the same. Each doorway is finished off with triangular heads, simply but artistically designed. Each office is fitted out with a fireproof vault.

The record room is two stories high and is absolutely fireproof. A small balcony runs around the room and this is reached by a spiral staircase. Two large casement windows with wire glass furnish a subdued light which is further augmented by an electrilier of six lights. This will be one of the handsomest rooms in the whole building when completed.

The Treasurer's and Auditor's offices are most convenient, being communicating rooms fitted out with metal railings, oak counters, and money drawers to be used at tax paying times. A wide space between the two railings is nicely tiled and is for the conveniences of the tax payers. The colorings in these rooms are rich green, ornamented with gilt.

The furniture in all the offices is of highly polished oak. An office table, chairs, and roll top desks are in each office.

In the basement are the Coroner's and Magistrate's offices, several store rooms, the heating arrangements, and a toilet room.

Upstairs the court room is a thing of beauty and something that every Abbeville born person can feel proud of. The room is large, high ceiling, and most conveniently arranged. The Judge's bench is on a raised platform of three steps while to either side are the jury boxes, comfortable, convenient, and handsomely set off with brass railings. The prisoner's box is in the center of the railing, fronting the

The New Court House

Judge, and in full view of the spectators.

The colorings in the court room are soft and harmonious. The walls are a chocolate, the ceiling a deep cream, and the pilasters a soft white. The wood work is bog oak, and the wainscoting a soft grey, highly polished marble. Six large casement windows furnish light and ventilation.

The electriliers are three in number of ten globes each, with ten wall fixtures of two lights each. The room is fitted out with opera chairs of the latest and most comfortable designs.

Back of the court room are two jury rooms, one on each side. In the center is a large room to be used for eating and sleeping purposes when a jury is locked in. There is a private retiring room for the Judge and a consulting room for the lawyers and a retiring room for the women who find it necessary to attend court.

These magnificent buildings were erected by Frederic Minshall, contractor, and one of the most popular and energetic citizens of Abbeville. . . .A great part of the credit and responsibility for the new Court House rested on Captain G. N. Nickles, county supervisor. Other members of the Court House Commission were W. H. Jones, secretary, J. L. McMillan, G. A. Neuffer, J. Allen Smith, Sr., M. G. Donald, S. J. Wakefield, J. M. Morrah, and T. J. Britt.

Press & Banner, October 7, 1908

Thursday [October 1] was a Epoch making day for Abbeville. The Epoch has been made and Thursday was its celebration, the dividing line between the old Abbeville and the new.

The square does not look like the same place since the material left from building has been removed. There is much more room for watermelon wagons, cotton wagons, apple wagons, etc. than ever before. The Eureka Hotel is more in evidence now, and on the whole there is not a prettier square in the whole country.

The mayor had constructed a band stand to play for the Grand reunion. . . and on Wednesday evening the band gave a concert for an hour, rendering beautiful, classical music as well as patriotic songs. At the end of the concert the band played **Dixie** *and the vast audience did the rest.*

Thursday morning dawned bright and clear, and it was not long before the square was packed. At 11 o'clock the ceremony of laying the corner stone took place. This was an interesting feature of the day. The ceremonies were under the direction of Mr. J. L. Michie, Grand Master, A F M Jurisdiction of South Carolina. The Abbeville Lodge met and asembled in front of the new Court House and took part in the ceremonies, prominent among whom were Dr. F. E. Harrison and Mr. H. G. Smith. . . .

The Shadow of the Dispensary

At 11 o'clock, court was called. Judge Klugh was appointed to hold special court for this day. There was a new Bible, a new docket, a new calendar.

The roll of the Grand Jury was then called by the clerk. Their names were: James A. Gilliam, foreman, F. H. Corn, L. D. Wells, Lawrence Ashley, J. L. Cannon, J. A. McIlwain, W. R. Ellis, T. O. Price, J. P. Sharpe, T. E. Deason, C. S. Gilbert, J. A. Stevenson, R. L. Winn, R. L. Mabry, F. Henry, T. G. White, J. R. Glenn, W. S. Stewart.

When the names of the grand jurors had been called by the clerk, it was found that the foreman was absent. Accordingly the name of "Jas. A. Gilliam" was called three times from the balcony by the veteran court crier. Mr. Gilliam, whose name was the first to be cried from the new court house, later came in.

Capt. G. N. Nickels [usually spelled Nickles], the chairman of the building committee, then presented the keys of the building to Judge Klugh. After receiving the keys, Judge Klugh declared that it must be obvious to all that the commission had done its duty well.

At the conclusion of his charge, the keys were turned over to the foreman. The grand jury retired and brought in a special presentment accepting the building, commending the commission, and delivering the keys to the custodian, Capt. "Jack" Perrin, clerk of court. No county in this State can boast of a more efficient or accomodating officer than is Capt. Perrin. His father and grandfather were clerks of this county, and all of them have not only been good officers, but they have always and under all circumstances measured up to the mark of best citizenship. The keys of Abbeville Court House are in good hands.

After the presentation of the keys, court adjourned for a short while. By this time the savory flavor of hash began to penetrate the olfactories of many of the vast concourse assembled and straight way took themselves in the direction of Genl. Pickens' favorite spring, where Messrs. James and Dave Gilliam, Andrew Bass, and Wm. DuPre had cooked to a queen's taste about 500 gallons of hash. It must have been good for not one complaint was heard from the thousands who ate it. There was an abundance of it. 3,000 loaves of bread were served with the hash and the man who went away hungry that day did so from pure contraryness [sic].

5. The Shadow of the Dispensary

The building of the new court house and the new opera house/municipal building in 1908 was indirectly financed by the Abbeville Dispensary. Abbeville had a branch of the South Carolina Dispensary during the fifteen years in which the state operated a state owned whiskey business. The Abbeville branch was one of the more

The Shadow of the Dispensary

successful. For example, in 1903, it was ninth in sales among the ninety three units in the state. In 1905, the Cary-Cothran Act provided that the S. C. Dispensary be converted into county operated units with the provision for local option prohibition. By 1908, the dry forces had been so successful that the Abbeville Dispensary was the only one still open above Columbia, and it was generating heavy profits. The Cary-Cothran Act provided that 1/3 of the profits went to the county, 1/3 went to the town in which the dispensary was located, and 1/3 went into the public school funds of the county. During the last four months of 1908, the Abbeville Dispensary had gross sales of about $60,000, and the net profits for the year were about that amount.

Prohibitionists considered such profits immoral, and they angrily declared that the new buildings were being paid for at great human cost. Others pointed out that the money earned by the dispensary was earmarked for operating costs and therefore could not be used to pay for the new public buildings. While this was literally true, the county and the town could operate with dispensary money and use property taxes to pay for the new buildings. For the county particularly, the dispensary money allowed veteran county supervisor G. N. Nickles to replace the many wooden bridges destroyed by the great August flood of 1908 with steel bridges.

However, as early as August, 1908, there were signs that the prohibition sentiment was turning public opinion versus the dispensary. Renwick Bradley, a member of the family which had purchased the *Press & Banner* from Hugh Wilson, summarized that view in an article for that paper on August 5, 1908. He said that when the question was finally put to the Abbeville voters, in his opinion, they would vote the dispensary out for three reasons. First, "the Abbeville Dispensary is making too much money. . . . The average citizen says he prefers to pay his taxes himself rather than to have them paid by the Dispensary." Both sides agreed that the profits generated by the Abbeville Dispensary were probably two or three times as much as the county or city derived from property taxes. The second reason he cited was that whereas there were many in the county who did not believe that prohibition would work, they were tired of being looked upon by their neighbors, such as those in Anderson and Greenwood, as unfairly preventing their efforts at prohibition from having a chance to work. Lastly, he said, many farmers saw the Dispensary as too great a temptation for their black laborers.

In January, 1909, the *Anderson Daily Mail* carried a long article on the Abbeville Dispensary, which it noted was the only one still operating above Columbia. The newspaper said that while this dispensary was supported by some of "the best people" in Abbe-

The Shadow of the Dispensary

ville, and its profits were appreciated by the county leaders there was strong resentment among many over the image of irresponsibility that it brought to Abbeville.

In May, 1909, W. N. Graydon, the Abbeville state senator, told the same paper (reprinted in the *Press & Banner,* June 2, 1909) that "we cannot afford to vote it [the dispensary] out. There is too much money in it for us. Our dispensary sold $9,000 worth of liquor in April, and half of that was profit. We expect to make at least $60,000 out of it this year." He added that the Abbeville Dispensary was shipping a lot of liquor out of the state to North Carolina and Georgia, both of which were now dry states. Legally, he said, Abbeville could not ship to dry counties within the State, but there was nothing to prevent outsiders from coming to Abbeville to buy, and it sold "a great deal of whiskey to Greenwood, Laurens and Anderson County people."

After several previous efforts had failed, the prohibitionists forced a referendum on the question of the dispensary on August 17, 1909. Although the town of Abbeville voted to retain its dispensary by a vote of 213 to 186, the county voters rejected it by a margin of 749 to 516. While the vote total was less than half of that of a typical primary turnout, its margin was nonetheless decisive.

On November 17, 1909, the *Press & Banner* noted that the last furniture and stock of goods had been sold from the old dispensary site on the square, and that *A new-comer Greek will occupy the storeroom formerly occupied by the dispensary. He will open a restaurant* [the Dixie Cafe] *where the hunger may be satisfied, while allowing the stomach to continue to thirst for that which brings men victorious over all the ills of life.*

XXVI. HOPE AND TRAGEDY: THE STORIES OF HARBISON COLLEGE AND ANTHONY CRAWFORD

In 1871, the state census taker for the town of Abbeville wrote, *there is too strong a tendency among our colored people everywhere in the state, and perhaps nowhere more so than in our District, to leave the farm and the workshops, the settled industry and remunerative labor of the country, and to seek a precarious, hand to mouth living in the town or village.* An examination of the 1880 census indicates that while some Abbeville blacks worked on nearby farms, a large number had to be content to work as domestics. Opportunities to advance were limited, and unfortunately, efforts for improvement often failed. In the following two examples, the attempts to develop black colleges came to a tragic end; and, when the most successful black farmer became too wealthy, he lost his life.

Abbeville's Black Colleges

On March 23, 1910, the *Press & Banner* reported that, *on last Thursday morning* [March 17] *about three o'clock the alarm of fire was sounded in the city of Abbeville, when it was discovered that the main remaining building at Harbison College located near Abbeville* [about a mile from the square on the Due West highway] *was in flames. The walls of the building were already falling in before persons from the town could reach the place to render assistance to the inmates. There were some thirty to forty colored boys in the building, three of whom were burned to ashes.*

Three or four others suffered painful and serious injuries from jumping from the second story. The three Negro boys who perished in the flames were: Carl Duckett of Charlotte, N. C., Samuel Jenkins of Carlisle, S. C. and Edward Dubose of Lamar, S. C. The last named was about thirteen years of age.

The fire was undoubtedly incendiary as evidenced by the fact that kerosene was also poured on the back door of the President's house, and it was also set afire. This was extinguished before any serious damage could be done.

It seems that kerosene had been poured over practically the entire lower floor of the main building, as the fire, when discovered, seemed to be burning in all parts of the building at the same time.

That afternoon there was a mass meeting at the Court House of the people of Abbeville who strongly condemned the act of arson and offered a $100 reward for information leading to the arrest of the arsonist. In reporting this, the *Press & Banner* added its editorial comment that "not since history was in the making has such a hellish crime been perpetrated in Abbeville County."

This was not the first serious loss by fire at Harbison College.

Harbison College

Three years earlier the original building on the campus had burned with no loss of life since at the time the college was closed.

The report of the *Press & Banner*, January 23, 1907, was that, *The burning of the Ferguson Hall was not known in the city until the next morning. The building was discovered on fire at half past ten o'clock in the night. The night was unusually dark owing to the dense fog. This was one of four valuable brick structures on a sixty acre lot fronting the Due West road and the city of Abbeville. The building which was destroyed was the first one built out there. Including the mansard roof it was three stories, and was used as a home for the president and the female teachers, and as a dormitory for the boarding school girls. The Hall was possibly 60 by 100 feet, with an ell about 60 by 80 feet. The ell was one story and was used as a cook room and dining hall.*

The loss of the building is estimated at $10,000. The value of the furniture and other things which were destroyed is unknown. The furniture in five out of eight rooms in the second floor was saved. All the furniture or other goods in the third floor were destroyed, as were nearly all the goods in the cook room and dining hall. The property is owned by the Northern Presbyterians, whose Board of Freedmen's Mission has its headquarters at Pittsburgh, Pa. Dr. Henry D. Lindsay, formerly of Due West, is one of the directors on the board. . . .

The agitation of the race question has awakened and intensified the race prejudice which seemed dormant or which had not until recently come to the surface in a pronounced form. The president of Harbison [Rev. C. M. Young] *is a native born Negro* [from Due West], *and one who seems to be acceptable to a majority of our people, but he has not opened the school this year. His predecessor* [Rev. Thomas Amos] *was a Northern Negro, who was objectionable to some of our people. He left and the school closed last August or September, and is still closed.*

A week after the fire, President Young sent the local newspapers a letter explaining that the fire was likely accidental. He wrote, *We have stated to our many anxious inquiring friends, white and colored, in Abbeville and elsewhere, that there was no fire in the room over which the fire caught and destroyed Ferguson Hall and contents on Wednesday night, 16th instant. It develops today* [the 24th] *that beyond question a fire had been kindled in a stove in said room on the morning of the same day by inmates of the building and that furthermore the flue was defective to some extent.*

Out of deference to fairness and justice to the community in which the unfortunate affair has occurred, and especially under the existing circumstances, I regard it a very important and indispensable duty for me, as president of the college, to make this very significant and timely correction.

Harbison College

The combination of the two fires and the controversies which had surrounded the school for nearly two decades led the Northern Presbyterians to move Harbison to Irmo, S. C. in the fall of 1910. In later years, the school grounds were leased to the state of South Carolina and today the name Harbison is borne by a planned town near Irmo.

The cause of the 1910 fire was never discovered, and it was suggested that it may have been set by disaffected blacks instead of whites as it was generally supposed. The school had long been the center of controversy for blacks as well as whites.

At the time of the Ferguson Hall fire, the *Press & Banner*, June 30, 1886, recounted the events which had led to the beginning of the construction of Ferguson Academy (later Ferguson Hall). It was, as follows:

In 1868, the Negro Methodists built a good school house, erected a large and commodious house of worship, [St. James, A. M. E.] and put up a comfortable parsonage. In after years, the Negro Presbyterians, namely, Shedrick Lesley, George M. Richey, George W. Smith, Lewis Richey, William Pope, George Barr, Alfred Foster, and others, under the lead of the Rev. E. W. Williams in 1881, sought to establish a form of worship which would more nearly conform to their religious beliefs and . . . to establish a separate school.

Mr. Williams went north [he had come from Washington, D. C.] *in December of the same year, and after three months of labor among the white Presbyterians of the North, succeeded in securing the sum of $1500 which was supplemented by $500 from the Board of Church Erection in the City of New York. This sum was further supplemented by gifts received from white and colored people at home. With this money a handsome church and school house combined was built on a suitable lot in town.*

The building was finished and opened one year after the organization of the congregation. The school was opened in January, 1882 by Mrs. Williams, the wife of the pastor, who before her marriage had a large and extended experience as a teacher in the public schools of Washington, D. C. The school has been thoroughly graded, and this year . . .[attracted] *a daily average attendance of about sixty five scholars. . . .*

The object at first was simply to sustain a small parochial school as an auxiliary to their church, but the success of the school under Mrs. Williams' most excellent management has been so great that the McClelland Presbytery, comprising twelve counties in the upper part of the state, has decided to make Abbeville an educational centre for Negro children of both sexes. To further this end, Mr. Williams went North again in 1885 to raise money to assist in erecting a school building of more extensive dimensions. About $1,000 was subscribed

Harbison College

in the North, and it is hoped that the remaining necessary money may be secured as the work progresses. The building which they contemplate erecting will be of brick 45 x 60 feet, and will be located on the church lot. While it is not expected to finish the building this winter, it is hoped, however, that sufficient money will be secured to cover it in, and that by another year the whole building will be finished. The foundation has been dug. A hundred thousand bricks have already been burnt for the work.

It is proposed to accomodate at least three hundred children of both sexes. In the Academy there will be a boarding and industrial department, where children may do something to earn their way in an institution.

The Rev. Williams enjoyed such success that the *Press & Banner*, January 10, 1890, took notice of the fact that *a splendid three story structure with mansard roof now stands on the church lot--a monument to the zeal of his race and the liberality of his Northern sympathizers. . . . The institution is practically out of debt and the work in the college, and on the farm which is connected with the school, progresses in a satisfactory manner.*

He offended the Board of Freedmen's Missions of the Northern Presbyterian church, however, and was removed from the direction of the institution which he had founded. He was replaced by the Rev. Thomas Amos of Baltimore. The *Press & Banner*, April 26, 1893, reported that, *For some months past there has been friction between the Ferguson Academy and the Colored Presbyterian Church at this place. The pastor, the Rev. E. W. Williams, was removed from the presidency of the college over which he had presided since its erection, but has been retained by the congregation as pastor of the church.*

Ever since he was superseded in the college by another, he and his congregation have been subjected to various petty annoyances. It is reported to us that Rev. Williams undertook last week to carry on a protracted meeting, when the church lamps were broken, and because of this fact, and threats, the meeting was abandoned. . . . The school house, or college, is on the same lot with the church, and the buildings are only a few feet apart.

A week later, the same paper gave an update on the Williams-Amos controversy, as follows: *McClelland Presbytery sent a committee to Abbeville on April 27 to investigate contention in the Second Presbyterian church. In a congregational meeting, those members present voted 48 to 46 to dissolve the pastoral relationship with Rev. Williams. The committee also determined that it would be in the best interest of the Ferguson Academy and the Second Presbyterian church for the Rev. Thomas Amos, the president of the Academy, to be transferred, because "intentionally or unintentionally* [he has] *been associated and involved with these serious troubles."*

Rev. Williams presented his side of the controversy in a letter to the Abbeville community in which he declared, *In the twelve years that I was in charge of the work, I never had any trouble or friction with the officers of the church until last October. The Board of Missions . . . revoked my commission as pastor of the church and turned over the school work to Rev. Thomas Amos.*

A year later, the *Press & Banner*, March 7, 1894, recounted the story from Rev. Williams' point of view, *A little more than a year ago the Rev. E. W. Williams, who for nearly thirteen years has labored for the elevation of the colored people at and about Abbeville, wrote an editorial concerning the management and control of the general work under the Board of Missions for Freedmen. The wisdom and expediency of Rev. Williams' editorial was questioned by the Board . . . . [which] at once sought from him a retraction of the offensive words. Failing to get a retraction from him even on the condition that he be allowed to hold his position as president of Ferguson Academy, the Board then offered all possible inducement to Rev. Williams to leave Abbeville.*

He refused and now, he has a large and flourishing school for which a handsome and commodious brick building has been erected during the winter. A majority of the members of the original congregation, which was divided by the action of the Board of Missions still follow him, which fact seems to foreshadow the organization of a new congregation and the erection of another house of worship in the near future.

The new college building is nearly finished and will probably be occupied before the close of the present month. The new building has accomodation for about fifty boarding students and is provided with a large dining room, kitchen and a storeroom. Thus it is seen that Rev. Williams has been instrumental in the erection of one good church and two splendid three story college buildings.

The new Ferguson and Williams College was dedicated in June, 1894. The following year, Williams' new church, the Third Presbyterian Church of Abbeville, became the first black congregation to join the South Carolina Presbytery of the Southern Presbyterians. In 1897, he was dismissed to form the Independent Colored Presbytery of Abbeville. His school, the Ferguson and Williams College for girls, was sponsored by the Southern Presbyterians for the next two decades. In 1919, the building was acquired by Abbeville County which converted it into the Abbeville Memorial Hospital.

In 1901, the Board of Missions for the Freedmen of the Northern Presbyterians secured a charter from South Carolina which converted the old Ferguson Academy into Harbison College for Colored Youth. Samuel P. Harbison of Pittsburgh became its chief benefactor, and he

Anthony Crawford

secured a farm of 209 acres (on the Lowndesville road) for its use and financed the construction of a new main building which was burned in 1910. On July 8, 1903, the *Abbeville Medium* reported that during the preceding year Harbison College had 337 students with 187 of them boarding students. In its Industrial department during the past year, forty boys had been able to earn their own way. Contributions from all sources during the 1902-1903 school year exceeded $10,000 with $4,000 of that coming from the students.

Its success brought renewed strains on relations with the Rev. Williams' followers and increasing hostility from some elements of the white community. Rev. Amos never won any acceptance from the latter and he decided to resign in September, 1906.

. . . . Later events proved that Amos was not the issue, since there was no apparent friction with President C. M. Young who was serving at the time of the fires. The actual cause of the fire in 1910 which took the lives of three students has continued to be one of the unsolved crimes of Abbeville, but the poisonous atmosphere which led to this tragedy was no mystery.

2. Lynching of Anthony Crawford

The lynching of Anthony Crawford in October, 1916, attracted national attention to Abbeville. *The Independent,* a news weekly published in New York, sent a journalist to Abbeville who covered the event under the guise of being a real estate agent. His story created a sensation in the town when it appeared, despite the general consensus that it was accurate in most of its details.

Roy Nash, "Lynching of Anthony Crawford," *The Independent,* December 11, 1916.

Cotton Seed was selling at ninety cents a bushel on Saturday morning, October 21. A wealthy Negro named Anthony Crawford drove into Abbeville, South Carolina with two loads [of cotton] to be baled; and while waiting his turn at the gin, went into the store of W. D. Barksdale to sell a load of seed.

As to just how the dispute started, no one knows but Mr. Barksdale. The version current on the Abbeville curb is that Barksdale offered eighty five cents for his cotton seed. Crawford told him he had already received a better offer and Barksdale called him a liar. Whereupon, (and from this point the evidence all tallies) Crawford curst the storekeeper and accused him of trying to beat him out of his money. Barksdale turned back into the store and left Crawford giving full play to his temper outside until a clerk came flying out with an ax handle in his hand. Crawford backed off toward the square and was

Anthony Crawford

promptly arrested. By the time the policeman and the Negro reached the municipal building a hundred yards distant, the crowd was streaking across the place from every store around the market place, intent on giving the Negro a whipping for daring to curse a white man. This crowd dispersed without having laid hands on Crawford, and when they had gone Chief of Police Johnson collected fifteen dollars bail and let the Negro out a side door. Crawford started toward the gin a short hundred yards back of the municipal building, where his two bales of cotton were waiting.

There was a second rush toward the square when some one spied him going toward the gin. He probably would have gotten off with a good beating if he had been an humbler sort, but Anthony Crawford was a successful farmer worth over twenty thousand dollars, far richer than most of those who pursued him, and proud. He once said to a friend, "the day a white man hits me is the day I die." When he heard the hue and cry behind him, Crawford made for the boiler room of the gin, down in a partially covered pit, where he took off his coat, picked up a four pound hammer, and waited. McKinney Cann, a rough chap who sells buggies and feed for J. S. Stark, led the rabble. As they closed in on him, Crawford smashed in Cann's skull, and would have killed him had not someone grabbed his arm as he aimed the blow, then a rock from above caught the Negro in the head and he went down. To their credit be it said, the superintendent of the gin and two furniture dealers, W. A. Calvert and son John, tried to prevent what followed. These citizens of Abbeville took Crawford into the road where everybody could get to him. Under their ministrations, the Negro regained consciousness, got on his feet, and fought his way for fifty feet up the road before a knife was plunged into his back again. While he was down into unconsciousness--We spare you the rest.

Enter the law.

The police, as soon as they turned Crawford out of the municipal building, had urgent business further up the street; but Sheriff [R. M.] Burts ran to the gin as soon as the fight started. He begged the boys not to kill the Negro; he pleaded, he cajoled, he entreated his constituents to consider him and his duty, he explained that they were putting him into a terrible hole; and at the end of forty five minutes, by promising Leslie and Jack Cann and their followers that he would not remove the Negro from the county jail nor make any other move until they were sure their brother had not been fatally hurt, the sheriff persuaded them to permit him to arrest the mass of pulp lying there in the road and cart it half a block to the county jail.

At the jail, after the sheriff had summoned a doctor to patch him up for the next round, Crawford told John Scoven to get his coat from the gin and give his bank book to his son; and during the afternoon

Anthony Crawford

he talked rationally to a trusty. "I thought I was a good citizen," he said.

What is the evidence on this point? Anthony Crawford's life and character embodied most of the things that Booker T. Washington held to be virtuous in a Negro. His father, freed from slavery, acquired a cotton patch seven miles northwest of Abbeville. Anthony, born in January, 1865 [actually May, 1860], used to walk that seven miles to school in the morning and back at night, so eager was he to educate himself. At his father's death, Anthony fell heir to the clearing and by dint of hard work and thrift increased his holding to four hundred and twenty seven acres of the prettiest cotton land in the county; as his family increased to twelve sons and four daughters, nine of whom are now married and settled in homes of their own, near enough to their father's house so that all could hear his voice when he called from the front porch. For nineteen years their father was secretary of [Cypress] Chapel AME Church, and as its chief financial prop he was undoubtedly something of a dictator; but aside from that, three days of diligent conversation did not unearth another tangible thing against Crawford's character.

While he lay on his couch of pain in the jail, the afternoon wore peacefully on in Abbeville. For all who arrived on the noon train could see, no tragedy was impending more imminent than the boll weevil a hundred miles away over in Georgia--not up to three forty five. Then some evil tongue turned loose the rumor, "the sheriff is fixing to take the nigger away on the four o'clock train."

No such concept of his duty was in the sheriff's mind; indeed, the mob was making for the jail as quickly as he, for Sheriff Burts is not built for speed. They swarmed in the front door to meet him coming in the rear. Neither he nor Jailer Foster McLain [McLane] made effective protest when they took away their guns and keys. Up the three flights of stairs the leaders rushed as fast as they could unlock doors (for the Abbeville jail is unusually well built) and let themselves into the cell where the magnificent vitality of Crawford was battling with death. They dragged his broken body down and threw it to the cheering throng at the door. Thru the Negro quarter they dragged Crawford by his neck as a hint to "good niggers" to continue so, but on coming into a white residential district they threw their victim on the top of a passing load of slabs, and so passed in triumph through the streets of this city of handsome homes, surrounded by lawns adorned with late-blooming marigolds and the lovely old fashioned princess feather.

Altho he was dead before they reached the fair grounds, they hanged Crawford to the solitary great pine that stands in the row of junipers at the gate, and expended a couple of hundred cartridges in firing at his body. Coroner F. W. R. Nance led a jury up the hill at

Anthony Crawford

sunset, good men and true, who, without going thru the formality of taking evidence, announced their verdict that Anthony P. Crawford came to his death at the hands of parties unknown to the jury.

That Saturday night the boys were drunk and a proposition to go out and clean up Crawford's fifteen children and kin met with such a hearty response that, as one eminent citizen said, "I knew if they ever started, they'd shoot every nigger along that seven miles of road." So three or four leading business men intervened and postponed the party by suggesting a meeting on Monday to settle the fate of the Crawford family.

The Monday meeting proved as big an attraction as the Democratic primary, even Anderson County, twenty miles to the north, being well represented. The boys were all for immediate action. Things were looking so ugly that Jack Perrin, for thirteen years clerk of the court and one of the most respected men in Abbeville, hurried over to the bank and persuaded its president, Mr. J. Allen Smith, to assert his influence that they would try to get an agreement with the Crawford boys to quit the State quietly by November 15. Captain Perrin, Mr. Smith and J. S. Stark, a dealer in the town, thereupon jumped into a machine [automobile] and drove out to the Crawford place.

A solemn deliberative assembly was called in the court house upon their return, attended by several hundred people. The three committee men reported that the Crawford boys were very polite and took off their hats as "good niggers" should; and that they agreed to abandon twenty thousand dollars worth of property and quit the State any time the white citizens of Abbeville requested it, altho they would prefer to stay in the home of their father and of their father's father. . . . At the end of the deliberations it was voted unanimously to order the immediate family of Anthony Crawford to wind up their business affairs and leave the State by November 15, 1916.

A portion of those attending were not satisfied, and after the meeting proceeded to close up all the Negro establishments in Abbeville. . . . And on November 6, at a meeting in the court house attended by practically every business man of the city, war was declared on those who had decided to run out the Crawford family on the 15th, in resolutions which decried lawlessness, pledged physical support of the officers of the law, suggested the formation of a local company of militia, assured the protection of the men at the meeting to all citizens regardless of condition or color, and called for a meeting of representatives of the law-abiding elements of the whole county for noon on Monday, November 13, two days before the Crawfords were to be expelled. The second peace conference differed on ways and means of maintaining law and order, but endorsed the resolutions of the first meeting and appointed a conciliation commit-

Anthony Crawford

tee of twelve, two from Abbeville, two from the towns other than Abbeville, and eight from the rural districts who shall "take up with the citizens the matters discussed in the meeting and endeavor to bring about a proper understanding between the people of the county." The Crawfords were not expelled on the 15th. . . ..

Until October, 1916, not only had Anthony Crawford lived by the philosophy espoused by Booker T. Washington, but his life story might have earned the same title as that of Washington, *Up from Slavery.* From the census records, other public records, and a few newspaper notices, it is possible to reconstruct something of his back ground and that of his family. The 1900 census listed his birth date as May, 1860. His father, Thomas Crawford, was fifty-one years old at the time of emancipation, and Thomas' father, Charles, was still living in 1880 (in Thomas' household) at the age of 100.

Anthony Crawford's father, Thomas, bought the first part of the family lands in 1873 when he purchased 181 acres on Penny Creek from General Samuel McGowan. Anthony inherited part of his father's lands and acquired additional lands until 1903 when he owned 427 acres which included some very good farmland. He and his family gained a reputation for hard work and enterprise.

The *Abbeville Medium* on August 17, 1888, reported that *Anthony P. Crawford has sold 3 wagon loads of splendid melons in town this season and finds that there is as much money in them as in cotton.* On December 15, 1904, it had a much longer article, as follows: *Anthony P. Crawford, colored, sold a load of splendid corn of his own raising in the city last week. His fat mules, good wagon and prosperous appearance led us to inquire particularly about his crop. He farms and owns the old Belcher place. He holds in his own right 500 acres of land in three tracts, paid for by his own labor. This year his corn crop was 1,000 bushels, of which he sold 250. He made 200 gallons of syrup and 48 bales of cotton. November 26th he sold $662.08 worth of cotton and has made other sales. He has six horses, 12 head of cattle, 18 hogs, two good wagons, a McCormick rake, and a new top buggy. He also has a good bank account and a family of thirteen children.*

The *Press & Banner* ran a notice on September 19, 1908, which indicated that his family had been engaged in some type of disagreement with one of his white neighbors. It was, as follows: *A Card of Thanks. I wish to thank my white friends for their kindness and sympathy towards me and my family during the late unpleasantness that happened by a misunderstanding between my boys and Mr. James Rogers and to assure the public, that no one deplores the unfortunate occurrence more than I. And it will be the highest endeavor of our lives, to strive to make as good citizens in the future as we have in the past and to those who opposed and differed*

Anthony Crawford

with us, I have nothing but a friendly feeling. For individuals as well as nations sometimes differ. But it is mete and right to settle their differences, legally and amicably. A Citizen, Anthony P. Crawford.

In the days immediately following the Crawford lynching, region-wide attention and the fear that Negro out-migration might be acclerated by such an incident led to vigorous efforts by Governor Richard I. Manning and Solicitor Robert Cooper to prosecute the lynchers. Manning sent a special investigator to secure evidence, and on December 5th at the preliminary hearing at the local magistrate's court, sixteen men were brought into court, including McKinney Cann's brothers, as leaders of the lynch mob. Many of the witnesses, however, denied that they had recognized any members of the mob, and it was on the sheriff's own testimony that fifteen men were ordered bound over for grand jury action. The grand jury considered the case in February, 1917, and indicted no one for the lynching.

Anthony Crawford's children did not leave the county, at least not for some years, and most never did. The six who remained at the home place in 1923 secured a mortgage on the home place from the People's Saving Bank in Abbeville. The farm depression which hit the entire South in the Twenties prevented the Crawfords from paying any of the mortgage payments and also led to the failure of the bank. In 1929, Anthony Crawford's once valuable farm was sold at public sale and it brought only $504.

XXVII. ABBEVILLE ARTISTS

The most recognized art inspired by Abbeville was the series of paintings which an Atlanta artist, Wilbur G. Kurtz, did in 1921-22. These five paintings were designed to symbolize the history of the town and were commissioned by the National Bank of Abbeville to be placed on the walls of its building when it was being renovated.

This building was first put up in 1860 when the town was at its peak of prosperity. The directors of the state-owned Bank of the State of South Carolina decided to build a branch in the northwestern part of the state, and Abbeville proudly won the competition for the branch with Anderson and Greenville. The branch opened in 1860 and lasted through the war years.

Lewis Perrin, the cashier of the National Bank of Abbeville and an Abbeville native who was a zealous student of local traditions, was responsible for orienting Kurtz in his subject. He later recalled that he went to Atlanta several times and that Kurtz came to Abbeville on a number of visits while the project was under way. It took a year and a half before the paintings were publicly unveiled in the late summer of 1922.

Kurtz was originally from Illinois, but he had married a woman from Atlanta a decade before this. He was a history buff with special interest in the Civil War and the campaigns around Atlanta. Early in his career, he supervised the restoration of the Atlanta Cyclorama, and in the decades after his Abbeville work, he served as technical advisor for such classic films as Margaret Mitchell's *Gone with the Wind* and the Uncle Remus epic, *Song of the South.* Despite his Northern birth, his sympathies with the South were very evident.

His paintings for Abbeville were very large; four of which were four feet by eight, and one, depicting the Jefferson Davis war council scene, was ten feet long. The *Press & Banner*, August 9, 1922, described the scenes, as follows:

The first shows the first Secession meeting which was held in 1860 on the hill back of Mr. Richard Sondley's home on Magazine Street. An ardent Secessionist is addressing a group of men in frock coats and women in hoop skirts.

The second of the paintings is a Square scene in Abbeville. In the background is a group of buildings among which are the old National Bank and the former home of P. B. Speed. Two covered wagons drawn by oxen and other cotton-laden vehicles driven by Negroes are features. In the central foreground stand L. W. White, G. A. Visanska, and W. Joel Smith, who were among the first directors of the National Bank.

The next picture is a portrait of General Andrew Pickens. He is mounted on a white horse and is stationed, gun in hand, before the old Block House which is said to have been a stronghold against the

Artists

Indians during the Revolutionary War. This fort is said to have been stationed in that section of town now called Fort Pickens in honor of the subject of the painting.

Another of the five shows John C. Calhoun standing near a stage coach before leaving for his home. Calhoun is in an impressive attitude with hand on hip and with a long cape draped over his shoulder. In the background is the old wood burner engine of the Abbeville Division, whose smoke stack looks rather larger than the engine itself. A traveler carrying a carpet bag, an oak watering trough, and an "old-time slavery Uncle" give touches which bring to mind glimpses of the old South.

The last painting, somewhat larger than the others, represents the last meeting of the Confederate Cabinet which was held in the Burt house, now occupied by J. S. Stark. President Davis is standing and the members of his cabinet and Generals in attendance are seated around him. The details of the picture are correct. The fireplace and the mantel of the room, the quaint old arm-chairs, the shaded lamp are all as they were then. A picture of John C. Calhoun above the mantel is not historically accurate, but was added for effect.

While Abbeville had rarely been the residence of artists before the Kurtz paintings, two men of diverse backgrounds deserve special notice. Clarage H.(usually called C. H.) Kingsmore was a doctor, portrait painter, and commercial photographer in the middle of the 19th century; and Marcus Ammen, a Virginia artist who was General J. E. B. Stuart's map maker during the Civil War, spent his last years in Abbeville in the early 20th century. Although he never lived in Abbeville, George F. E. Wenck, a German emigrant who became a doctor, painted a view of the ruins of the great fire on the Square in 1873. See the article on the fire in Chapter XXII.

Kingsmore was born in Savannah, and his family moved to Abbeville early in his life. His father, John C. Kingsmore, was active in village politics as a prohibition leader and served on the town council. C. H. was educated in medicine in Vermont and returned to practice in Abbeville. Whether he was successful or not, in August, 1846, he began running an advertisment in the *Abbeville Banner*, as follows: *To Physicians. Having exchanged the practice of medicine for a more congenial employment, I offer for sale my entire stock of Medicine, Shop Furniture, Saddle-Bags, and excellent case of Surgeon's Pocket Instruments, etc.*

The "more congenial employment" was portrait painting, but apparently Kingsmore did not find that he could quit his medical practice. By the following March, he was running the following notice in the *Banner: Dr. C. H. Kingsmore having made arrangements to locate in the village of Due West, would respectfully offer his services as a Physician to the citizens of the village and adjacent country.* While in Due West, he combined painting with his practice, and among the portraits which he painted there was one of Dr. R. C. Grier, President of Erskine College.

By the time of the Census of 1850, he had returned to the village of Abbeville, and his occupation was listed as "Portrait painter." In a few years, he had moved his studio to Newberry, and C. C. Puckett, editor of the *Independent Press* in 1855 wrote, *As we returned from our late visit North, tarrying a few hours at the village of Newberry, we called at the studio of Dr. Kingsmore to gain his acquaintance and see his paintings. We had seen years ago, a few of his maiden efforts to sketch the "human face divine," and occasionally an allusion by the press to his later performances. . . . He exhibted to us several portraits which we unhestitatingly adjudge the finest (and so far as we are acquainted with the originals) the most correct we have ever seen.*

After he left Abbeville, Dr. Kingsmore went to Italy to study painting, and his work became much more contrived. Puckett wrote that *The one most attractive to us, representing a little babe, which had recently died, ascending a stairway of clouds to the home of the angels, was as beautiful in execution as it was appropriate in design.* Kingsmore exhibited his work in the annual Charleston Institute or fairs.

When he died in 1873, the *Press & Banner*, May 28, 1873, commented on his early life in Abbeville and his death in Augusta at the age of 53. It said, *He was quite a successful painter, and a number of his works in our communiity and elsewhere attest his merit as an artist.*

Marcus Ammen, a much more noted artist who had painted both portraits and landscapes during the Civil War, lived and worked in Abbeville from 1903 to 1912. His daughter, Blanche, was teaching in the Williamston Female College when she married Senator John R. Blake of Abbeville, and Ammen came to live with them on North Main Street. The *Press & Banner*, October 10, 1912, carried the following story.

News was received in Abbeville of the sudden death at Greenwood of Mr. Marcus Ammen, for some years a resident of Abbeville, but who removed to Greenwood something more than a week ago with the family of his son-in-law, Mr. John R. Blake. Mr. Blake was in Abbeville when the sad news was received and he hastened to Greenwood on the afternoon train.

Modest and retiring by nature, but possessed of a warm heart, Mr. Ammen was beloved by all with whom he came in contact during his residence in Abbeville, and many friends were shocked at the news of his sudden death.

Mr. Ammen was an artist of rare ability and the fidelity of his

Artists

reproduction from life made him excel particularly in portrait work. His last work, a portrait of Dr. Boyce, late president of the Female College at Due West, was regarded by those who enjoyed Dr. Boyce's acquaintance and had seen the portrait, as a masterpiece of delineation, life-like in its faithful reproduction of the noble features of that goodly man.

Perhaps the most ambitious work ever undertaken by Mr. Ammen was his "Elaine." "The Lily Maid of Astolat, who pines and dies for love of Lancelot," was depicted by him in a manner which showed a conceptive genius of a high order and a skill in execution which makes this work take high rank in the world of art. The canvas has received much favorable comment from capable critics.

.... Mr. Ammen was 82 years old at the time of his death. He was a native of Fincastle, Va., and served in the Confederate army throughout the War Between the States, being severely wounded on two occasions. He was a topographical artist in the war and served on the staffs of Gens. Beauregard, Johnston, and Lee, receiving high praise for his accuracy in detailed drawings of the topography of the country in which the army operated.

Mr. Ammen received his education in art in the city of Baltimore, afterwards teaching art in Washington and Lee University, in Williamston Female College, and later in the cities of Philadelphia and Baltimore.

The obituary writer neglected to mention that Marcus Ammen first came to Abbeville in May, 1865 with the Confederate Treasure Train. At that time, he was a member of the faculty of the Confederate Naval Academy, and therefore when the young midshipmen were assigned the task of guarding the shipment southward of the Confederate treasure, the somewhat older Ammen marched along with them. Thus he came to Abbeville along with Mrs. Jefferson Davis, and traversed the same route from Abbeville to Washington, Ga., to Augusta and back to Washington and Abbeville. Under his initials "M.A.," he wrote an account of his experiences which was published as "The Confederate Treasure" in the *Press & Banner*, May 4, 1904. As he left Abbeville to walk back to his home in Virginia in May, 1865, he and some of his fellows drew an allowance of rations from the Abbeville Confederate commisary which they later found filled with worms.

XXVIII. ALL AMERICAN HERO, TOM HOWIE

In the long history of the village of Abbeville, there have been many sons and daughters who have displayed great courage, but the only one ever cast in the national spotlight as a hero was Major Thomas D. Howie at the Battle of St. Lo, July 17, 1944. The son of Mr. and Mrs. T. V. Howie, he had been an outstanding student at Abbeville High School and The Citadel; and when the Second World War broke out, he was teaching at Staunton Military Academy in Virginia.

A well known war correspondent, Hal Boyle, filed the following account from Normandy on July 23rd:

"The Major of St. Lo" was Thomas D. Howie of Staunton, Va., one of the best loved battalion leaders in the American Army. He was killed July 17, the day before the city fell, after he broke through the Nazi wall to relieve another battalion of this regiment [116th Infantry] *which was encircled on the outskirts. On the day St. Lo was taken, the dead major was carried through the streets in state in an ambulance and his flag draped body was placed in a pile of rubble besides the shell wrecked church of Ste. Croix. The storming force passed in review through an artillery barrage thrown by the withdrawing Germans.*

Howie was in his middle thirties. He formerly taught English literature and coached boxing and football at Staunton Military Academy. He was an athletic star himself earlier at The Citadel, military academy in Charleston, S. C.

A wiry, muscular officer, the native of Abbeville, S. C., was popular with all ranks in the division from the lowest private to the commanding officer who personally ordered his body taken into St. Lo by the combat force as a gesture honoring him and his battalion. By taking the high ground dominating the approaches to the city, his men sealed its fall.

"He had given up an operations post at regimental headquarters to take over the battalion only five days before," said Capt Charles R. Cawthon of Murfreesboro, Tenn., executive officer of the cut-off battalion to whose relief Howie and his troops came after they had been almost three days with no fresh rations or ammunition supplies. "We have many officers in the army, but you can't say of all that they are gentlemen, Major Howie was the finest gentleman I ever knew."

Thirty years later, Cawthon wrote the lead article in the *American Heritage* (June, 1944), "July, 1944: St. Lo." Cawthon said of Major Howie that, *he alone among the shadowy figures in this account is to be called forth by name, and this is because he combined to an uncommon degree the kindness and courage that would have better become us all. In mourning Tom Howie I mourn all for whom life and laughter ended at St. Lo and, by some projection, those for*

The Major of St. Lo

whom it has ended since. Tom Howie had made a vow as he launched the attack which cost his life that he would reach the city. News stories and photographs followed, and Tom Howie became the Major of St. Lo--the nation's symbol of the battle. Many who grieved for the fallen soldier at the time may now [1974] have forgotten, and the new generations may never have heard of him at all, but the story stirred America to no small degree in that July of 1944. . . .The Major of St. Lo inspired editorial tributes and one of the few poems of merit to come out of the war, unimportantly in error on some points.

The poem was "Incident At Saint Lo" which was carried in *Life Magazine*, September 18, 1944, with a number of Auslander's "war poems," as follows:

> *They rode him in, propped straight and*
> *   proud and tall*
> *Through St. Lo's gates. . .He told the*
> *   lads he led*
> *That they would be the first at St. Lo's*
> *   fall--*
> *But that was yesterday--and he was*
> *   dead:*
> *Some sniper put a bullet through his*
> *   head,*
> *And he slumped in a meadow near*
> *   a wall;*
> *And there was nothing further to be*
> *   said;*
> *Nothing to say-- nothing to say at all.*
>
> *Ride soldier in your dusty dizzy jeep,*
> *Grander than Ceasar's chariot! O ride*
> *Into the town they took for you to*
> *   keep,*
> *Dead captain of their glory and their*
> *   pride!*
> *Ride through our hearts forever,*
> *   through our tears,*
> *More splendid than the hero hedged*
> *   with spears!*
>   __Joseph Auslander, 1898-1965

XXIX. ROLL OF ABBEVILLE CITIZENS (MALE)
MAY, 1859

Hugh Wilson's memory roll of Abbeville citizens when he came to the village in May, 1859 and what had happened to them since, from the *Press & Banner*, May 14, 1884.

J. A. Allen, merchant, died 24th March, 1868.
J. Clark Allen, at school, killed at Moultrie House, Sullivan's Island, 14th February, 1861, being the first man to lose his life in the war.
Charles Henry Allen, druggist, moved to Fernandina, Fl., died 1870.
Warren Allen, lives in Spartanburg.
John Allen, stone cutter at Chalmers' marbleyard, left Abbeville and died.
Godfrey C. Bowers, carpenter, moved to Columbia.
S. Henry Beard, surgeon dentist, moved to Murfreesboro, Tenn.
Ames Baker, plasterer, still living in Abbeville.
William W. Belcher, moved to Shreveport, La.
Isaac Branch, physician and druggist, died in Abbeville.
W. T. Branch, at school, still lives in Abbeville.
R. E. Bowie, law student, moved west and died.
J. Gamble Baskin, lawyer & magistrate, died in war.
George Buchanan, clerk for Wm. Hughey, died in army.
A. Brussels, merchant, still a merchant in Charleston.
W. R. Buchanan, cabinet workman, Cokesbury preacher.
Thomas Browning, harness maker, returned to his home in Tenn.
George W. Brown, carpenter, returned to his home in another state.
D. S. Benson, physician, still a farmer near Abbeville.
Joe Bergin, carpenter, died in poor house.
Eccles Cuthbert, plasterer, now correspondent of the New York *Herald*.
Robert N. Chatham, teacher, killed in battle near Atlanta, 1864.
E. Cobb, proprietor of The Marshall House, took laudanum and died, 1859.
William Champlain, bricklayer, returned to Charleston.
Jack Champlain, bricklayer, returned to Charleston.
F. Cownover, builder and contractor, returned to his home in the North at the outbreak of the war.
Matthew Cochran, deputy sheriff, went to Illinois and died.
James D. Chalmers, dealer in marble, still lives in Abbeville.
T. B. Crews, printer and editor of the *Abbeville Banner*, now editor of Laurensville *Herald*.
James C. Calhoun, lawyer & magistrate, moved to Memphis, died from exposure on Texas plains.
James H. Cobb, merchant, dead.
John Coumbe, plasterer and bricklayer, fell from scaffold on brick building on Washington Street and died from injuries.
Charles Cox, manufacturer of buggies, wagons, etc., died of consumption.
Thomas M. Christian, dealer in shoes, still lives.
Thos. R. Cochran, ex-Sheriff, died before war.
J. S. Cothran, lawyer, still lives in Abbeville.
W. Norwood Calhoun, still lives in Abbeville.
James Cobb, silversmith, died during war.
John A. Calhoun, farmer, dead.
A. B. Cobb, lives in Texas.
Bunyan Crawford, livery stable business, dead.
Charles Dendy, owner of tanyard & farmer, died in 1859.
J. D. Daly, architect, went to Richmond before the war.
Stephen C. DeBruhl, lawyer, moved to Fla., dead.
W. C. Davis, lawyer & editor of the *Banner*, killed in battle.
N. Jefferson Davis, farmer, died 1875.

Abbeville Male Citizens, 1859

John G. Edwards, merchant, still lives in Abbeville.
John Enright, ginwright, died of consumption.
A. W. (Whit) Edwards, clerk at Allen's store, moved to Ga.
O. J. Farrington, tailor, moved West, 1867.
James W. Fowler, clerk at Weir & Lythgoe's store, merchant in St. Joseph, Mo.
Waddy Fowler, clerk at Weir & Lythgoe's store, dead.
R. A. Fair, lawyer, Presbyterian minister, Newberry.
William Godfrey, saw mill hand, killed in war.
John Gray, merchant, lives in Columbia.
Rueben Golden, harnessmaker, went to Fla., dead.
Benjamin P. Hughes, chief clerk at White's store, died 1866.
J. R. Hamlin, mail carrier & butcher, lives in Greenville.
John A. Hunter, merchant, died soon after the war.
Clem Hamilton, printer, *Press* office.
Robert E. Hill, on a trip to Ireland, lives in Abbeville.
William Hill, Ordinary, lives on farm near Abbeville.
Cicero Hughes, lives in Abbeville.
William Hughey, proprietor Abbeville Hotel & dealer in whiskey, dead.
T. A. Hoyt, pastor Presbyterian church, Presbyterian minister, Louisville, Ky.
Samuel Henry, carpenter, left the state.
James M. Hughey, brick layer, lives in county.
A. M. Hill, deputy Sheriff & assistant Census taker for Abbeville District.
M. Israel, merchant, lives in Charleston.
F. Ives, tailor & town marshal, dead many years ago.
Cincinnati Jones, law student, died in war.
Robert Jones, merchant.
H. A. Jones, lawyer, moved west in 1860, dead.
D. F. Jones, lawyer, died since war.
David Junkin, miller.
Robert Junkin, printer, *Press* office, last known address, Augusta.
D. A. Jordan, druggist & physician, died in West before the war.
Benjamin Johnson, rector Trinity Episcopal church, preacher in Ga.
Elihu Kernel, employed in steam mill, killed in war.
William Knox, blacksmith, still lives in Abbeville.
John Knox, merchant, still lives in Abbeville.
Nathaniel Knox, merchant, killed while carrying the colors of his regiment.
Louis Kernel, saw mill hand, killed in war.
H. S. Kerr, merchant, died 1880.
Robert P. Knox, clerk for J. & N. Knox, dead.
John H. Ligon, photographer, now lives on farm near Charleston.
Benjamin Lichenstein, lives in New York.
A. J. Lythgoe, merchant, killed at battle of Murfreesboro, 1862.
H. T. Lyon, physician, lives in Abbeville.
L. H. Lomax, lawyer, lunatic asylum, Columbia.
J. F. Livingston, physician, died 1867.
H. W. Lawson, tinner and dealer in tinware, dead.
W. James Lomax, lives in Ga., near Lowndesville.
J. F. Livingston, Jr., lives in Abbeville.
J. W. Livingston, law student, lives in Seneca.
W. B. Lackey, plasterer.
W. A. Lee, lawyer, lives in Abbeville.
John Moreem, house painter.
Luther Martin
John Martin, dead
Thomas Martin, dead
Robert A. Martin, tailor, dead.

Abbeville Male Citizens, 1859

W. C. Moore, merchant, lives in Abbeville.
James Moore, local preacher & conductor on Abbeville branch railroad, dead.
E. W. Moore, clerk for R. H. Wardlaw & Son.
Joseph T. Moore, Sheriff, dead.
William Mooney, carpenter, moved off.
J. Foster Marshall, lawyer, killed in war.
J. W. W. Marshall, physician, lives in Abbeville.
C. Murchison, Methodist preacher, still in S. C. Conference.
Israel Myers
Wm. Motes, printer, *Press* office.
W. J. Marshall, went to Washington.
Geo. McD. Miller, farmer near Ninety Six.
John A. Murrill, house painter
S. McGowan, lawyer, lives at Abbeville.
Matthew McDonald, Clerk of Court, dead.
Donald McLaughlin, druggist, returned to N. C.
Benja. McLaughlin, drug clerk, returned to N. C.
John McLaughlin, drug clerk, returned to N. C.
John McBryde, assistant postmaster, lives in Columbia.
John McLaren, postmaster, dead.
Robert McBryde, junior, in Va. preaching.
John M. McBryde, dead
T. W. McMillan, brickyard, lives in Abbeville.
John McCrae, lives in Miss.
Harvey McCrae, dead.
Wm. McGhee, wheelwright, went to Miss.
A. H. McGowan, law student, dead.
E. Noble, lawyer, lives at Abbeville.
Stephen Norrell, harness maker, lives in Abbeville.
John T. Owen, silversmith, Cartersville, Ga.
Moses T. Owen, silversmith, died of wounds in war.
Patrick O'Keefe, shoemaker, moved off.
John O'Conner, bricklayer & plasterer, lives in New York.
Patrick Owens, tailor, died in Anderson, 1883.
Barney O'Conner, stone mason, lives in Abbeville.
W. T. Penney, clerk at Moore & Quaife's, druggist in Abbeville.
A. Paul, physician, died during war.
James M. Perrin, lawyer, killed at Chancellorsville, May, 1863.
Thos. C. Perrin, lawyer, dead.
W. H. Parker, lawyer & Commissioner in Equity in Abbeville.
W. H. Perrin, dead.
Rockingham Perry, well digger, dead.
L. W. Perrin, lawyer, lives in Abbeville.
Thomas Perrin, killed in war.
C. F. Quaife, merchant.
J. T. Robertson, merchant, farmer in Abbeville.
L. H. Russell, owner, livery stable & dealer in whiskey, lives in Abbeville.
P. W. Rutledge, owner of livery stable and mail contractor, lives in Spartanburg.
Samuel O. Russell, killed in war.
Johnson Ramey, chief clerk at B. M. & S. A. Winstock, dead.
E. Roche, shoe maker and dealer, lives in Abbeville.
Joseph Roofe, clerk at J. A. Allen's store, returned to Ireland.
Wm. F. Rifford, contractor & builder, returned home.
Thomas J. Robertson, clerk at Gray & Robertson, dead.
J. William Robertson, wheelwright at Cox's shop.
T. C. Seal, coach painter at Cox's carriage shop.

Abbeville Male Citizens, 1859

Henry Stevenson, clerk at Allen's store, died 1883.
D. B. Smith, carpenter, lives in Abbeville.
A. M. Smith, carpenter, died Richmond, 1863.
George Smith, lives in Abbeville.
James Shillito, senior, tailor, dead.
James Shillito, junior, tinner, coroner in Abbeville.
George Syfan, engineer on railroad, lives in Abbeville.
John Scanlon, carpenter, returned to his home.
Thomas Shehan, ginwright, died of consumption.
John Small, at school, moved West, dead.
Andrew Small, clerk at McLaughlin's drug store, dead.
John Sign, carpenter.
D. R. Sondley, depot agent, dead.
R. C. Starr, clerk at Kerr's store, moved to Ga., died.
E. J. Taylor, maker of carriages, wagons & buggies, moved to Fla. and died.
Ezekiel Tribble, dead.
Jesse Tribble, printer, *Press* office, killed in battle of Lookout Mountain, 1863.
Wat. Thomas, carpenter
H. T. Tusten, jeweler, lives in Abbeville.
Thomas Thomson, lawyer, dead.
John Thomson, dead.
Joseph W. Trowbridge, clerk for R. H. Wardlaw & Son, lives in Anderson.
James Verell, house painter, moved to Texas.
John Wilson, dealer in liquors, lives in Abbeville.
A. A. Williams, merchant, dead.
A. J. Woodhurst, plasterer & bricklayer, lives in county.
R. H. Wardlaw, merchant, lives in Abbeville.
John G. Willson, insurance & collection agency, dead.
W. H. Wilson, publisher of *Independent Press*, moved to Lake City, Fla.
Hugh Wilson, successor to W. H. Wilson, lives in Abbeville.
Patrick Wilson, printer, *Banner* office.
E. Westfield, saddle & harness maker, lives near Abbeville.
Robert J. White, merchant, died in Louisiana.
John White, merchant, dead.
Leroy J. Wilson, engineer on railroad, lives at Abbeville.
Clark Wardlaw,
James H. Wardlaw, merchant, died 1862.
W. H. White, principal, male academy, killed Second Manassas.
W. C. Wardlaw, assistant teacher, male academy, lives in Augusta.
George White, clerk at White's store, lives in Abbeville.
L. W. White, clerk at White's store, lives in Abbeville.
Hugh Wilson, senior, owner of steam mill, lives at Donalds.
B. M. Winstock, merchant, lives at Charleston
S. A. Winstock, merchant, died in Abbeville, 1862.
Robert Wilson, dead.
J. H. Wilson, lawyer, dead
J. A. Weir [Wier], merchant, lives in Greenville.
Robert H. Wardlaw, junior, died of wound in war.
G. Allen Wardlaw, law student, dead.
Lewis A. Wardlaw, law student, dead.
Ezekiel White, owner of wagon shop, dead.
D. L. Wardlaw, judge, dead.

The Citizens of Abbeville, April, 1884

Hugh Wilson's selected list in *Press & Banner,* May 14, 1884, with names also on 1859 list in bold face.

J. E. Agnew, coach printer at Seal, McIlwaine & Co. carriage shop.
R. E. Agnew, wheelwright at Seal, McIlwaine & Co. carriage shop.
Charles Auerbach, merchant, clothing.
Charles D. Allen, deputy sheriff
T. W. Adams, printer, *Press & Banner.*
B. S. Barnwell, collection & insurance agency.
W. C. Benet, lawyer.
B. K. Beacham, architect & builder.
Thomas Beggs, dealer in wagons, buggies & harness.
D. F. Bradley, jeweler.
Arthur Benedict, clerk in Miller Bros.
W. E. Bell, clerk in Wardlaw & Edwards.
M. L. Bonham, lawyer and Master.
L. K. Bowie, clerk in L. H. Russell.
W. H. Brooks, farmer.
J. M. Brooks, farmer.
W. O. Bradley, clerk at McGettigan's.
W. T. Branch, commercial tourist.
C. E. Bruce, boot and shoe maker.
Jerry Bradley, clerk at McGettigan's.
R. W. Cannon, merchant & agent for sale of steam engines.
G. McD. Cater, clerk at White Bros.
S. C. Cason, lawyer.
E. B. Calhoun
R. A. Calhoun, clerk at White Bros.
J. S. Cothran, circuit judge.
T. P. Cochran, lawyer.
Wade S. Cochran, merchant and drugs.
G. C. Cobb, painter.
W. J. Cobb, painter.
J. D. Chalmers, merchant, furniture & marble.
James Chalmers, lawyer, merchant and furniture.
Thos. M. Christian, merchant, liquors.
John L. Clark, jeweler.
John L. Clark, jr., farmer.
Jas. R. Cunningham, general merchandise.
W. G. Chapman, manufacturer and repairer of wagons, buggies, etc.
A. D. Calhoun, clerk, White Bros.
O. T. Calhoun, lawyer.
Wm. P. Calhoun, lawyer.
Frank Cunningham, dealer in whiskey.
Thos. G. Coogler, telegraph operator.
M. P. DeBruhl, lawyer.
J. F. C. DuPre, Sheriff
J. H. DuPre, clerk at Wardlaw & Edwards.
W. C. DuPre, farmer.
W. O. Dundas
G. A. Douglass, general merchandise.
Lucius Douglass, clerk at G. A. Douglass.
W. S. Dansby, carpenter.
John G. Edwards, general merchandise.
Eugene B. Gary, lawyer.

Citizens of Abbeville, 1884

Frank B. Gary, lawyer.
F. F. Gary, doctor.
John M. Gambrell, clerk at White Bros.
Ellis G. Graydon, lawyer.
William N. Graydon, lawyer.
James M. Giles, clerk at White Bros.
George W. Garrick, merchant, liquors.
Charles R. Garrick, clerk for G. W. Carrick.
B. F. Galphin, clerk for R. M. Haddon & Co.
C. V. Hammond, depot agent.
J. S. Hammond, public weigher.
Henry S. Hammond, superanuated.
R. L. Harper, superanuated Methodist preacher.
R. M. Haddon, merchant & millinery.
R. B. Haddon, merchant & liquors.
John A. Harris, clerk at White Bros.
Robert R. Hemphill, lawyer & editor of *Abbeville Medium*.
W. H. Hanckel, rector, Trinity Episcopal Church.
A. M. Hill, merchant, liquors and lesse Central Hotel.
Richard Hill, merchant, liquors & livery stable business.
Henry Hill, merchant, liquors & livery stable business.
R. E. Hill, farmer.
R. M. Hill, general merchandise.
L. T. Hill, doctor.
Cicero Hughes, copying clerk for office, Mesne Conveyance.
Francis Henry, general merchandise.
J. Y. Jones, farmer.
A. W. Jones, painter.
B. W. Jones, painter.
D. J. Jordan
Thos. Jackson, octogenarian.
M. Kaliski, clothing merchant.
John Kirby, street overseer.
John Knox, general merchandise.
Jacob Kurz, tanner and shoe maker.
J. C. Klugh, lawyer.
David W. Keller, clerk at White Bros.
E. M. Keaton, dealer in stoves, clocks, sewing machines.
Thomas Kellar, carpenter.
G. Link, clerk at Quarles & Thomson.
W. A. Lee, lawyer.
Jas. M. Lawson, merchant, tin and stoves.
Wm. D. Lomax, clerk at Parker & Hill's.
J. Fuller Lyon, Probate Judge.
J. F. Livingston, Jr., general merchandise.
S. L. Lowry, merchant, drugs.
John T. Lyon, merchant, drugs.
W. A. Lyon, clerk for Probate Judge.
W. T. McDonald, merchant, confectionery.
Samuel McGowan, judge, Supreme Court.
W. C. McGowan, lawyer.
Thomas McGettigan, merchant, liquors.
H. P. McIlwaine, manufacturer & repairer of wagons, buggies, etc.
J. W. W. Marshall, doctor.
Thomas J. Mabry, doctor.
J. L. Martin, pastor, Presbyterian church.

Citizens of Abbeville, 1884

James W. Martin, printer, *Press & Banner*.
Jones F. Miller, merchant.
J. C. Miller, merchant.
Wm. L. Miller, lawyer.
W. C. Moore, painter & paper hanger.
G. H. Moore, merchant.
A. B. Morse, clerk of W. Joel Smith & Son.
George Murbach, book keeper.
J. A. Millwee, printer, *Press & Banner*.
T. W. McMillan, owner of mill and brick yard.
James McMillan
William McMillan
Edward Noble, senior, lawyer.
Edward Noble, junior, lawyer.
Stephen B. Norrell, harness maker.
Wesley Norrel, printer, *Abbeville Medium*.
Barney O'Conner, stone mason.
Edwin Parker, doctor.
W. H. Parker, lawyer.
E. F. Parker, merchant.
J. T. Parks, Auditor.
W. T. Penney, merchant, drugs.
L. W. Perrin, County lawyer.
J. W. Perrin, County Treasurer.
T. C. Perrin
John L. Perrin, clerk for White Bros.
James S. Perrin, law student.
Wm. Perry, marble cutter, Chalmers' yard.
R. N. Pratt, pastor, Baptist church.
G. H. Parks, clerk for County Auditor.
T. P. Quarles, general merchandise.
Wm. Riley, town marshal.
H. D. Reese, jeweler.
J. T. Robertson, farmer.
J. E. Rushton, pastor, Abbeville circuit.
W. J. Rogers, merchant, flour, bacon, corn.
P. Rosenberg, general merchandise.
L. H. Russell, merchant, liquors & dealer in mules & horses.
J. W. Rykard, merchant & liquors.
W. Richardson, Methodist minister.
E. Roche, farmer.
N. T. Sassard, clerk at R. B. Haddon & Co.,
S. M. Scott, fireman on railroad.
T. C. Seal, manufacturer of carriages, wagons & buggies.
James A. Shillito, Coroner.
George A. Shillito, tinner.
D. R. Smith, contractor and builder.
W. F. Smith, carpenter.
Charles Smith, carpenter.
W. Joel Smith, general merchandise.
J. Allen Smith, general merchandise.
L. W. Smith, lawyer.
A.W. Smith, manufacturer of wagons, carriages & buggies, also farmer.
John W. Sign, undertaker.
James H. Simmons, tinner, dealer in tin ware, stoves, lamps, etc.
P. B. Speed, merchant, drugs.

Citizens of Abbeville, 1884

G. W. Syfan, engineer on railroad.
G. W. Syfan, trainman.
Thomas Syfan, conductor on railroad.
Jesse Sprnell, wheelwright at Seal & McIlwaine Co. carriage shop.
Richard Sondley, farmer.
Charleton Sondley, farmer.
James W. Simpson, carpenter.
Lewis Seal, coach painter at Seal, McIlwaine & Co.'s carriage shop.
W. A. Templeton, general merchandise.
A. H. Templeton, clerk for Cunningham & Templeton.
S. G. Thomson, dentist.
J. W. Thomson, law student.
James Taggart, wheelwright at Seal, McIlwaine & Co.'s carriage shop.
H. T. Tusten, jeweler.
S. C. Turner, clerk at Cunningham & Templeton.
David W. Thomas, general merchandise.
Walter Tusten, apprentice.
G. A. Visanska, general merchandise.
Julius Visanska, clerk at P. Rosenburg & Co.
Charles Volkening, baker.
A. B. Wardlaw, general merchandise.
W. P. Wardlaw, farmer.
H. T. Wardlaw
Robert H. Wardlaw, superanuated.
J. B. Wilson, clerk at Knox & Co.'s.
L. J. Wilson, auctioneer.
Willie Wilson, clerk at Knox & Co.,'s.
H. D. Wilson, dentist.
Hugh Wilson, editor, *Press & Banner.*
W. H. Wilson, Hugh Wilson's predecessor.
R. C. Wilson, clerk at Knox & Co.'s.
E. L. Wilson, dentist.
J. A. Watkins, painter.
Joel C. Weir , clerk at W. Joel Smith & Son's.
L. W. White, general merchandise.
George White, general merchandise.
Charles S. White, farmer.
J. W. Wells, contractor and builder.
Samuel Wallingford, stock dealer.
M. G. Zeigler, Clerk of Court.
Charles Zbiden, tanner at Kurz's tanyard.

XXX. NAMING OF STREETS (1883) & BUSINESS DIRECTORY (1894)

The *Press & Banner*, January 9, 1884, reported that on December 23, 1883, the town council adopted fifteen ordinances as the basic law of the village. One of the ordinances concerned the names of the public streets, as follows:

First--the street passing in front of the Court House from east to west is called <u>Main Street.</u>
Second--the street leading by the Abbeville Hotel to the Depot is called <u>Washington Street.</u>
Third--the street from the Public Square by Mrs. White's is called <u>Pickens Street.</u>
Fourth--the street leading from the Public Square by McMillan's Mill across the railroad to the branch on the Cambridge road is called <u>Branch Street.</u>
Fifth--the street leading from Main Street by Mrs. Allen's via Knox's brick residence is named <u>Pinckney Street.</u>
Sixth--the street leading from Main Street via the Academy to R. H. Wardlaw's is called <u>Wardlaw Street.</u>
Seventh--the street leading from Main Street between the lots of Mrs. Jones and J. M. Gambrell is called <u>Cherry Street.</u>
Eighth--the street leading from Main Street up by Mrs. McDonald's is called <u>Magazine Street.</u>
Ninth--the street leading from Main Street via the Tan Yard up into the Vienna road is called <u>Walnut Street.</u>
Tenth--the street leading from Branch Street in front of the Jail to where it intersects the Augusta road is called <u>Poplar Street.</u>
Eleventh--the street diverging from Poplar Street near Alfred Ellison's and leading to Pin Hook is called <u>Pine Street.</u>
Twelfth--the street leading from the Depot across Magazine Street and in front of R. E. Hill's is called <u>Depot Street.</u>
Thirteenth--the street running from a point on Branch Street near the corner of McGettigan's lot up in front of Dr. Marshall's is called <u>Buena Vista Street.</u>
Fourteenth--the street leading from the Baptist church to the Episcopal church and in the rear of Mrs. White's to Walnut Street shall be known as <u>Church Street</u>.
Fifteenth--the street leading from the Cambridge road west of the Depot up into the Greenville road at W. H. Parker's is called <u>Chestnut Street.</u>
Sixteenth--the streets or roads leading from the Public Square or Main Street to Vienna, Moseley's Ferry, Anderson or Greenville Court House, Cambridge or Augusta are called respectively, <u>Vienna Street</u>, <u>Moseley's Ferry Street</u>, <u>Anderson Street</u>, <u>Greenville Street</u>, <u>Cambridge Street</u> and <u>Augusta Street.</u>

Abbeville Business Directory, 1894
(*Press & Banner,* June 13, 1894)

<u>Old Firms</u>
   W. Joel Smith (also A. B. Morse & A. M. Smith), White Brothers
      P. Rosenberg & Co., J. G. Edwards, R. W. Cannon
<u>Millinery Stores</u>
   R. M. Haddon & Co., W. E. Bell, Mrs. Mary Taggart
<u>Banks</u>
   National Bank of Abbeville (J. Allen Smith, B. S. Barnwell & others), Farmers Bank (W. H. Parker & Julius DuPre)
<u>Druggists</u>
   P. B. Speed, Dr. W. T. Penney, Harrison & Game, G. A. Douglass
<u>Livery Stables</u>
   A. M. Hill & Son, Wallingford & Russell, Stark & Cothran
<u>Furniture</u>
   McDill & Tolly, J. D. Kerr
<u>Jewelers</u>
   Reese & Dupre, R. C. Berneau, J. W. Rykard
<u>Shoe and Harness Factory</u>
   C. P. Hammond, Charles E. Bruce
<u>Door, Sash & Blinds Factory</u>
   J. H. Latimer, Smith & Wellington, R. M. Hill, D. K. Beacham
<u>Tinner</u>
   James M. Lawson
<u>Dry Goods</u>
   M. T. Coleman, W. A. Templeton, G. W. Lomax, Thomas P. Thomson, W. B. Groves
<u>Groceries</u>
   Jones F. Miller, J. L. Perrin, J. F. Livingston
<u>Photographers</u>
   Gallaghers Bros., Andrew Willingham
<u>Gunsmiths</u>
   John L. & Mack Clark
<u>Carriages</u>
   James Taggart
<u>Colored Brothers</u>
   W. H. Lomax--confectionary, Pope & Patton--restaurant, Emanuel McKellar--restaurant, Richard Gantt--barber, R. B. Barfield--barber, C. J. Hurst--barber, Armstead Hardy--barber, E. F. Gilliard--tailor, Hutson Butler--blacksmith; Robert Watt--blacksmith, Richard Romans--blacksmith, George Bacon- blacksmith, Robert Adams--blacksmith, C. M. Jones--shoe maker, Henry Titus--shoe maker, Shack Moseley--shoe maker, Russell Robertson--shoe maker, Wm. Shives--shoe maker, Thomas Wilson--restaurant, Mrs. Harriett Adams--restaurant, Mrs. Frances Lomax--boarding house.

XXXI. ABBEVILLE PRESBYTERIANS

In 1854, the Rev. McNeil Turner made the suggestion from the pulpit that those members of the Upper Long Cane Presbyterian Church who resided in the village of Abbeville should have their own church or at least a chapel. Particularly in bad weather, many found themselves unable to drive out to Upper Long Cane which was at least a mile out in the country. Strangely enough, the country members of the congregation received the proposal favorably; it was the village Presbyterians who thought it impractical. In fact, this reaction to his idea may have been the decisive reason why Turner left the congregation in that year. Ironically, it was at this time that the congregation erected a brick chapel or church in the village on the site later occupied by the First Baptist Church. From 1855, services were held there twice a month with the pastor dividing his time between the two places of worship. In 1868, when the Rev. Turner returned to Abbeville, the congregation divided with the village church under his charge as its first pastor.

In 1887, the building was burned when a disastrous fire began in the Perrin-McGowan house nearby (See Golden Age, Chapter IX). A new church was constructed in 1888 a few hundred yards nearer the public square on the west side of Main Street. The *Press & Banner*, November 28, 1888, described the appearance of the the new church as follows: *The new Presbyterian Church fronts on Main Street 58 feet and is 103 feet long. This building is of brick from the foundation, painted in brick color, pencilled in black and trimmed with ornamental stone. Its roof is covered with slate and ornamental cresting; the cornices are of galvanized iron and painted granite color. The roof is divided or constructed of four gables and two transept gables. The chimneys,* [are] *two in number, one on the left rear corner contains three flues, two for grates and one for the Sunday School furnace. The other is on the right, sixty feet from the front, with two flues, one for the auditorium and the other for ventilation purposes, and both chimneys run up to the height of the ridge with heavy cornice tops.*

There are two towers to this building, one about midway on the roof for ventilation which is seventy six feet high from grade line; the other is on the left front and is eighty one feet high. This is used for the bell above and for the entrance to the auditorium with a set of fine granite steps; on the left sixty feet from the front is a beautiful flight of granite steps which leads into the Sunday School department with a head gable over the entrance. Still further along is the entrance to the basement, provided with windows all around except the front.

In the same story, the *Press & Banner* carried a list of the church's members for its first twenty years, as follows:

Abbeville Presbyterians

Roll of Membership, 1868-88

Pastors

Rev. D. McNeil Turner, D. D., April 22, 1868-Dec., 1869.
Rev. Jas. L. Martin, M. D., D. D., Sept. 2, 1870-Oct. 31, 1884.
Rev. J. Lowrie Wilson, Feb. 28, 1886-

Elders

Thomas Chiles Perrin, April 22, 1868; died May 14, 1878.
Robert Henry Wardlaw, April 22, 1868; died July 18, 1887.
Robert A. Fair, April 22, 1868; ordained to ministry, 1874.
George McDuffie Miller, April 22, 1868; dismissed March 8, 1874.
Thomas Thomson, Sept. 24, 1871; died May 5, 1884.
William A. Templeton, June 21, 1874.
Lewis Wardlaw Perrin, April 6, 1879.
James Sproul Cothran, April 26, 1886.
Andrew Bowie Wardlaw, April 26, 1886.
Leonard Waller White, June 19, 1887.
Thomas Perrin Quarles, June 19, 1887.

Deacons

John T. Owen, April 26, 1868; dismissed July 25, 1869.
William C. Wardlaw, August 9, 1868; dismissed July 7, 1872.
Leonard W. White, August 9, 1868; became elder.
John M. Richmond, August 9, 1868; dismissed March 3, 1872.
Lewis W. Perrin, Sept. 3, 1879; became elder.
William A. Templeton, April 7, 1872; became elder.
Thomas P. Quarles, Dec. 15, 1872; became elder.
R. Marshall Haddon, Dec. 15, 1872.
Andrew B. Wardlaw, July 18, 1880; became elder.
Joel Allen Smith, July 3, 1887.
James Mason Giles, July 3, 1887.
Amos B. Morse, July 3, 1887.
George White, July 3, 1887.

Communicants

Mrs. Fannie Allen, widow of James A. Allen, April 22, 1868.
Robert A. Archer, M. D., 1868; died Oct. 1, 1872.
Mrs. Fannie E. Archer, wife of R. A. Archer, April 22, 1868; died Sept.27,1885.
Miss Ida Dendy Allen, wife of Mr. Long, April 22, 1868; dismissed to Peoli church, Ga.
Miss Mary Elise Allen, wife of Mr. Carlisle, April 22, 1868; dismissed to Methodist church, Spartanburg.
Miss Hattie Allen, wife of S. C. Cason, July 6, 1873; dismissed to Methodist church, Abbeville.

Abbeville Presbyterians

Charles Dendy Allen, July 18, 1875.
Miss Fannie Allen, April 7, 1878.
Miss Jane Allen, August 17, 1878.
Miss Rosa Allen, April 14, 1883.
James Albert Allen, July 20, 1884.
Mrs. Nancy Jane Bowie, April 22, 1868; dismissed to Sumter church, Dec., 1872.
Miss Eliza Ayer Bowie, April 22, 1868; dismissed to Spartanburg Presbyterian church.
Mrs. Elizabeth Buchanan, April 22, 1868; died Dec. 24, 1872.
Isaac Branch, M. D., April 22, 1868; died March 19, 1872.
Mrs. Fannie Branch, wife of Dr. Isaac Branch, April 22, 1868; died Nov. 28, 1871.
Miss Louisa H. Branch, wife of R. Marshall Haddon, April 22, 1868; died July 8, 1872.
James A. Bowie, Sept. 5, 1875; dismissed to Spartanburg church, Jan. 10, 1886.
Mrs. Annie Branch, wife of W. T. Branch, Sept. 11, 1875.
Miss Elizabeth Burns, wife of Joel C. Wier, Oct. 10, 1877.
Mrs. Ann Brooks, wife of W. H. Brooks, July 23, 1882.
Miss Lilly W. Brooks, wife of R. C. Wilson, July 23, 1882; dismissed to Warrenton church, Jan., 1885.
Miss Alice P. Brooks, wife of J. C. Ferguson, July 23, 1882; dismissed to Upper Long Cane, 1883.
Miss Maggie W. Brooks, Sept. 24, 1884.
Miles C. Brooks, Sept. 19, 1885.
William H. Burns, Nov. 14, 1886.
Miss Ella Bell, Nov. 14, 1886.
Mrs. Ann Eliza Cox, wife of Charles Cox, April 22, 1868; dismissed to Upper Long Cane, Aug. 5, 1883.
Mrs. Emma Chiles Cothran, wife of J. S. Cothran, April 22, 1868.
Miss Lucie Calvert, widow of John A.Thomson, April 22, 1868.
Miss Eliza P. Cater, Feb. 4, 1872.
Miss Martha A. Cater, Feb. 4, 1872.
Miss Rebecca D. Cater, Feb. 4, 1872.
James S. Cothran, April 22, 1868.
Thomas Perrin Cothran, Sept. 12, 1875.
Miss Mary Jervey Cater, March 31, 1877.
Miss Rebecca C. Cothran, wife of J. Allen Smith, Oct. 17, 1875; died Jan. 8, 1883.
Miss Hannah Clarke Cothran, Jan. 12, 1878.
Wade S. Cothran, Aug. 17, 1878.
Miss Elizabeth C. Cater, Nov. 28, 1880; died March 7, 1886.
McDuffie M. Cater, July 17, 1884.
James S. Cothran, Jr., Sept. 19, 1885.
James Chalmers, Sept. 19, 1885.
James N. Dendy, Jan. 24, 1869; dismissed to Troy church, June 25, 1882.
Robert A. Fair, April 22, 1868; ordained in ministry June 15, 1871; now member of Mecklenburg Presbytery, N. C.
Mrs. Amanda Fair, wife of R. A. Fair, April 22, 1868; dismissed to Aveleigh church (Newberry) Dec. 27, 1868.
James Livingston Fair, April 22, 1868; died Feb., 1871.

Abbeville Presbyterians

James Young Fair, April 22, 1868; ordained in ministry; now pastor 2nd Presbyterian church, Charlotte, N. C.
Mrs. Dorothy Ann Farrington, Aug, 22, 1868; dismissed to Albany, Ga., April 7, 1872, wife of O. G. Farrington.
James Mason Giles, April 22, 1868.
Robert Marshall Haddon, Jan. 7, 1871.
Mrs. Hannah T. Haddon, May 24, 1874; wife of R. M. Haddon.
Mrs. Mary T. Hill, Oct. 19, 1879; died Feb. 17, 1885, wife of R. E. Hill.
Robert Emmet Hill, Nov. 2, 1879.
Miss Jane W. Harrison, March 5, 1882.
Thomas Perrin Harrison, March 5, 1882; dismissed the 2nd church, Charleston, S. C., 1886.
Lod T. Hill, M. D., Aug. 1, 1887.
Mrs. George C. Hodges, June 13, 1886; dismissed to Greenwood church, March 27, 1887.
Miss Mary Hill, Aug. 7, 1887
Daniel Jones Jordan, Aut. 21, 1881; died July 20, 1886.
Mrs. Elizabeth Jordan, Aug. 21, 1881; dismissed to Greenwood church, March 18, 1886.
Miss Lilly Lee Jordan, July 15, 1884; dismissed to Greenwood church, March 18, 1888.
Miss Rosa Jordan, Sept. 19, 1885; dismissed to Greenwood church, March 18, 1888.
Miss Eliza N. Kyle, May 31, 1874.
J. M. Kirby, July 10, 1880.
Mrs. Lula Kirby, July 10, 1880.
Mrs. Margaret J. Lythgoe, April 22, 1868.
Miss Sarah Livingston, April 22, 1868; wife of W. Joel Smith.
William C. Latimer, April 25, 1869; dismissed to Baptist church.
Mrs. M. Fanny Livingston, Oct. 31, 1869; wife of J. Frazier Livingston.
John W. Lesly, May 31, 1874.
Mrs. Lou Jane Lesly, May 31, 1874; wife of John W. Lesly.
Alpheus E. Lesly, Aug. 16, 1874.
Mrs. Virginia C. Lesly, Aug. 16, 1874; wife of A. E. Lesly.
Miss Sarah Livingston, April 3, 1875; wife of P. D. Mazyck.
Miss Meta Lythgoe, Sept. 4, 1875.
Miss Harriet Lythgoe, Sept. 5, 1875; died March, 1878, wife of E. G. Graydon.
George B. Lythgoe, March 31, 1878.
John Frazier Livingston, Jr., Sept. 19, 1885.
John Frazier Livingston, Sr., Sept. 11, 1886.
William E. Lesly, Sept. 19, 1885.
Robert S. Link, Jan. 8, 1888.
Jenner Link, Jan. 8, 1888.
Mrs. Mary C. Miller, April 22, 1868.
Mrs. Mary Thomson McDonald, April 22, 1868; wife of T. P. Quarles.
Mrs. Fannie J. Marshall, April 22, 1868; dismissed to Episcopal church, wife of Dr. J. W. W. Marshall.
George McDuffie Miller, April 22, 1868; dismissed to Ninety Six Presbyterian church, March 8, 1874.

Abbeville Presbyterians

Mrs. Martha Virginia Miller, April 22, 1868; dismissed to Ninety Six Presbyterian church, March 8, 1874, wife of G. M. Miller.
Mrs. Henrietta J. Martin, July 2, 1871; dismissed to Alabama church, Memphis, 1885, wife of Rev. J. L. Martin.
Miss Leonora C. L. Martin[? see third entry below] , July 2, 1871; dismissed to Smyrna church, Newberry County, April 4, 1873, wife of J. B. Piester.
Amos B. Morse, Oct. 5, 1873.
Thomas S. Martin, May 25, 1879; dismissed to Alabama Street church, Memphis, 1885.
Miss Leonora C. L. Martin, May 25, 1879; dismissed to Alabama Street church, Memphis, 1885.
Augustus Griffin Miller, May 25, 1879; dismissed to Ninety Six church, Sept. 4, 1881.
Thomas J. Mabry, M. D., May 16, 1887.
Thomas Virgil Miller, July 24, 1887..
Miss Mary McCaw, July 24, 1868; dismissed to Episcopal church.
Miss Julia McCaw, July 24, 1868.
Miss Mollie McCoy, April 4, 1872; dismissed to 2nd church, Memphis, April 7, 1873.
William S. McCoy, April 7, 1872; dismissed to 2nd church, Memphis, April 7, 1873.
Moses Oliver McCracken, Jan. 16, 1887.
Mrs. M. E. Nance, Oct. 16, 1881; dismissed to New Bern, N. C. church, 1883.
Miss Florence Nance, Oct. 16, 1881; dismissed to New Bern, N. C. church, 1883.
Mrs. Sarah Eleanor Owen, April 22, 1868; dismissed to Cartersville Presbyterian church, July 25, 1869, wife of John T. Owen.
John T. Owen, April 22, 1868; dismissed to Cartersville church, July 25, 1869.
Thomas Chiles Perrin, April 22, 1868; died May 14, 1878.
Mrs. Jane Eliza Perrin, April 22, 1868; died Sept. 9, 1881, wife of T. C. Perrin.
Mrs. Mary J. Perrin, April 22, 1868; died Jan. 29, 1874, wife of J. W. Perrin.
Miss Hannah Clarke Perrin, April 22, 1868.
Mrs. K. C. Perrin, April 22, 1868.
Miss Sarah E. Perrin, April 22, 1868; wife of George White.
Mrs. Narcissa A. Pursley, Jan. 23, 1869; dismissed to Warrenton church, April 16, 1888.
Mrs. Nancy Pursley, Oct. 17, 1869; died May 4, 1874.
Lewis Wardlaw Perrin, Sept. 12, 1869.
George Clopton Perrin, Dec. 14, 1873.
Miss Ivy W. Perrin, April 5, 1874; dismissed to Episcopal church, wife of Rev. Jno. C. Glass.
Mrs. Ellen Watkins Perrin, Aug. 4, 1875; dismissed to 1st church, Richmond, Va., July 2, 1880, wife of Joel S. Perrin.
Miss Eunice C. Perrin, Sept. 5, 1875; died Aug. 10, 1885.
Miss Sarah Amanda Perrin, Jan. 12, 1878; wife of J. Wm. Thomson.
Thomas Chiles Perrin, March 23, 1878.
James Wardlaw Perrin, Aug. 12, 1878.
John Livingston Perrin, Aug. 17, 1878.
Miss Emma Perrin, Nov. 27, 1881.
Miss Kitty Tilman Perrin, Jan. 14, 1883.

Abbeville Presbyterians

Mrs. Mary McCaw Perrin, Sept. 28, 1884; wife of Lewis W. Perrin.
James Wardlaw Perrin, Jr., Sept. 19, 1885.
Thomas Perrin Quarles, Jan. 7, 1871, from Baptist church.
Miss Eliza Thomson Quarles, Sept. 19, 1885.
Miss Agnes Quarles, Oct. 26, 1888.
John M. Richmond, M. D., April 22, 1868; dismissed to St. Joseph, Mo. Presbyterian church, March 3, 1872.
Mrs. E. T. Richmond, April 22, 1868; dismissed to St. Joseph, Mo. Presbyterian church, March 3,1872, wife of Dr. J. M. Richmond.
Mrs. Marie Antoinette Russell, May 18, 1872; wife of L. H. Russell.
Miss Josephine Russell, April 30, 1882.
Mrs. Sarah Russell, Oct. 9, 1883; died Nov., 1885.
Miss Marie Antoinette Russell, Sept. 27, 1884.
Miss Adelaide Russell, April, 1888.
Mrs. Ione Smith, April 22, 1868; died Nov. 3, 1879, wife of W. Joel Smith.
David Richard Sondley, April 22, 1868; died July 15, 1870.
Mrs. Mary Frances Sondley, April 22, 1868; died May 20, 1872, wife of D. R. Sondley.
Mrs. Lavonia Seal, July 2, 1871; wife of T. C. Seal.
George B. Sondley, March 3, 1872; dismissed to Washington Street, Greenville, March 27, 1873.
Miss Mary Lou Smith, July 4, 1875.
Miss Virginia E. Sondley, Sept. 11, 1875; dismissed to 2nd church, Charlotte, N. C. April 16, 1882.
Miss Jane Amanda Smith, July 9, 1876; wife of A. B. Morse.
Miss Ione Smith, July 9, 1876; died July 29, 1887, wife of T. P. Cothran.
W. Joel Smith, Aug. 13, 1878.
Miss Nannie Seal, May 9, 1879.
Thomas C. Seal, May 9, 1879.
Mrs. Margaret Sondley, July 2, 1880.
Miss Ann Scoggins, March 26, 1882.
Mrs. Mary B. Smith, Feb. 20, 1886; wife of J. Allen Smith.
William H. Smith, Sept.. 12, 1886.
Miss Lucia Seal, March 25, 1888.
Miss Grace Smith, Oct. 28, 1888.
Thomas Thomson, April 22, 1868; died May 5, 1884.
Mrs. Margaret M. Thomson, April 22, 1868; died Nov. 8, 1884, wife of Thomas Thomson.
Miss Jane Thomson, April 22, 1868; dismissed to Spartanburg Presbyterian church, Jan. 10, 1886, wife of Jas. A. Bowie.
Mrs. Helen Talmadge, Aug. 22, 1868; dismissed to church in Connecticut, April 15, 1876.
Mrs. Harriet D. Turner, Aug. 22, 1868; dismissed to Homer, La., 1884; wife of Rev. D. McNeil Turner.
Miss Fannie Douglass Turner, Aug. 22, 1868; dismissed to Corpus Christi, Texas, April 4, 1880.
Miss Susan Emma Templeton, March 28, 1869; wife of Jas. M. Giles.
John Shropshire Thomson, March 28, 1869; dismissed to Washington Street Greenville, S. C., Feb. 7, 1878.

Abbeville Presbyterians

William Augustus Templeton, Jan 23, 1869.
Mrs. Eliza A. Templeton, Jan. 20, 1872; wife of W. A. Templeton.
Mrs. Agnes A. Tusten, March 30, 1873; wife of H. T. Tusten.
Mrs. Jane E. Thomson, Oct. 10, 1875; dismissed to Washington Street, Greenville, Feb. 7, 1878, wife of J. S. Thomson.
Alexis H. Templeton, April 12, 1877; dismissed to Lebanon church, Houston County, Miss., Aug. 8, 1880.
William L. Templeton, M. D., Aug. 25, 1878; died June 3, 1882.
Mrs. Mary Taggart, Oct. 1, 1882; wife of James Taggart.
Samuel C. Turner, Nov. 5, 1882; dismissed to Bennettsville church, S. C. 1886.
Miss Florence Templeton, July 16, 1884.
Miss Cleora Thomson, Sept. 19, 1885.
Walter Davis Tusten, Sept. 19, 1885; dismissed to Oxford church, Miss., 1886.
Joseph James Wardlaw, M. D., April 22, 1868; dismissed to Walhalla church, July, 1872; died July, 1873.
Robert Henry Wardlaw, April 22, 1868; died July 18, 1887.
Mrs. Eliza Wardlaw, April 22, 1868; died Aug. 9, 1883; wife of R. H. Wardlaw.
Mrs. Mary Ann Wardlaw, April 22, 1868; dismissed to Walhalla church, July, 1872; wife of J. J. Wardlaw.
Mrs. Eliza Lucretia Wardlaw, April 22, 1868; now wife of J. T. Lyon.
Mrs. Lucy White, April 22, 1868; wife of John White.
Miss Lucy White, April 22, 1868.
Mrs. Sarah White, April 22, 1868; dismissed to Rocky Mount, Bozzier Parish, La.; wife of R. J. White.
Miss Nancy Amelia White, April 22, 1868; wife of A. B. Wardlaw.
Mrs. Susan M. Weir [Wier], April 22, 1868; dismissed to Washington Street church, Sept., 1878; wife of J. A. Weir [Wier].
Mrs. Mary Josephine Wardlaw, April 22, 1868; dismissed to Augusta 1st church, July 7, 1872; wife of W. C. Wardlaw.
Miss Nancy T. Wardlaw, March 28, 1869; dismissed to Winnsboro church, Sept. 25, 1874; wife of J. G. McCants.
Miss Marie W. Wardlaw, April 4, 1869; dismissed to Aveleigh church, Newberry, S. C., April 3, 1875; wife of T. S. Moorman.
Mrs. Sarah Elizabeth Wardlaw, April 1, 1871; died Feb. 13, 1885; wife of A. B. Wardlaw.
Miss Kate C. Weir [Wier], May 12, 1872; dismissed to Washington Street, Greenville, Sept., 1878.
Mrs. Mary Helen White, May 18, 1872; wife of L. W. White.
Patterson Wardlaw, Jan. 4, 1874; dismissed to Columbia 1st church, March 18, 1888.
Miss Emma Wilson, April 4, 1874; dismissed to Mt. Zion, Feb., 1878; died Sept., 1878; wife of T. C. Ligon.
Miss Euphemia Wilson, April 4, 1874; died Jan. 6, 1882.
Miss Eliza H. Wardlaw, April 4, 1874; wife of D. Lucien Mabry.
Andrew Bowie Wardlaw, April 1, 1871.
Leonard Waller White, April 22, 1868.
William C. Wardlaw, April 22, 1868; dismissed to 1st church, Augusta, Ga., July 7, 1872.
George White, April 22, 1868.
Miss Mary E. White, April 6, 1878; dismissed to Rocky Mount church, Bozzier

Abbeville Presbyterians

Parish, La., July 27, 1881.
Mrs. Sarah A. Wilson, Jan. 9, 1881.
Richard Courtney Wilson, Oct. 8, 1882.
Miss Sarah T. Wardlaw, March 11, 1883.
Francis Harper Wardlaw, Sept. 19, 1885.
William D. Wilson, Nov. 22, 1885.
Mrs. Minnie Wilson, April 14, 1887.
Miss Mary Josephine Wardlaw, July 14, 1884.
Mrs. M. C. Waldrop, June 13, 1886; dismissed to Greenwood
   church, March 27, 1887.
Miss Jane W. White, April 1, 1888.
Miss Lucy White, Oct. 7, 1888.
Miss Mary White, Oct. 7, 1888.

XXXII. ABBEVILLE METHODISTS

As early as 1826, the Rev. Joseph Travis, a Methodist circuit rider, began to preach regularly at the Abbeville court house, and in 1828 the little congregation built the first church in the village. James Moore, a shoe maker from Charleston, and his wife Ann were the first converts. James became the first resident minister; and Ann, who according to tradition was raised as a Catholic, became the main force behind the drive to build a new church building.

The *Press & Banner*, March 14, 1888, recounted the story, as follows: *She made personal application to the citizens for subscriptions, and the gentlemen in those days were like the gentlemen of today. They could not refuse a lady whose appeal was in behalf of a good cause. She secured $450, and with the money a plain, unpretentious frame house was built on the lot adjoining the spring, across the street in front of the Abbeville Hotel . . . .Also, she taught the first Sunday School that was organized in the town. . . .*

The house which Mrs. Moore built was used for divine services until the erection of a larger and more commodious house on Main Street in the year 1839 on a lot given to the Methodist church by Mr. James Alston who, though not a member of the church, was a warm friend to the cause of religion, and especially to the Methodist church.

The first house was sold at public auction. Silas Anderson bought it from the purchaser at that sale, and used it as a bar-room, which act of desecrating a holy temple greatly incensed many of the members of the chuch, and the act was the cause of some bitterness of feeling, in censuring those who may have been more or less instrumental in effecting the sale to Mr. Anderson. Afterwards it was fitted for a dwelling house, and finally, after the war, it was used as a carriage shop by Messrs. Seal, Sign and Robertson. It was accidentally destroyed by fire in October, 1867.

In the absence of written records of the earliest members of this congregation, Hugh Wilson made up a memory roll of the earliest members and printed it with the above, as follows:

James Moore and his wife Ann were the first.
Mrs. Robert Key, sister of Paschal Klugh, from Coronaca.
Robert Key, merchant from Edgefield, whose place of business was on the east
  side of Square in the "Old Red House."
John A. Calhoun and his wife Sarah were added to the congregation in 1830.
  Later they moved to the Episcopal church.
William Lomax, widower, and his daughter Miss Harriet Lomax, also joined in
  1830. He died in 1840. She married Thos. Graves of Edgefield and moved
  to Greenville, Ala. in 1840.
Mrs. Susan Wilson, wife of J. S. Wilson, joined in 1830. Moved to Episcopal
  church, left Abbeville in 1850, and died in 1884.

Abbeville Methodists

Dr. Franklin Branch and his wife joined in 1830. She was Matilda Vashti Wilson, sister of John H.Wilson, Esq., and they were married Dec. 16, 1830. He was licensed as local preacher, but left town in the 1850's for Tampa, Fla. where he died Aug. 21, 1882.

Dr. Isaac Branch was on the building committee which erected the second sanctuary. He and his wife moved to the Presbyterians. He died in 1872 and she in 1871.

Samuel Branch and his wife Elizabeth Wilson Branch joined in 1831. Following his death in 1840, she married a Mr. Navy, a journeyman carriage maker and moved to Augusta [See Chapter VIII].

Miss Mary Ann Branch, daughter of Samuel Branch, was a member of the church. She married Eli Holliday, a carriagemaker, and moved to Ga.

Miss Sarah Branch, second daughter of Samuel Branch, married A.Markee, carriage maker, and moved to Charlotte where she died in 1884.

Miss Sarah Downey, widow, built and lived in the house now owned by James A. McCord. She was one of the first members. Her large means enabled her to give liberally to the church. She married and moved away to Ga.

Mrs. Parmelia Shillito, widow of George Shillito, was also a member of the first church.

Mrs. Edna Tusten, mother of H. T. Tusten, was a regular attendant.

Donald Douglass, at one time Sheriff of the County, was a member who moved to the country.

Mrs. Drucilla Douglass, widow of Donald Douglass, now widow of Thomas Aiken, lived at Abbeville and was a faithful member of the church. She died Nov. 16. 1887 in her ninety second year.

Lewis H. Davis, grandson of Andrew Hamilton, was one of the first converts, and he proved to be a useful worker. An accident when in his fourteenth year, cost him his eyesight. A colored man afterward acted as his guide and took him from place to place, and gave him every assistance possible. He became a preacher of unusual force and power, more from his goodness of heart and the earnestness with which he pressed his cause than any extraordinary intellectual ability. He was mainly instrumental in raising the money with which the second church was built. He and his family, however, moved to Tennessee before it was completed.

Mrs. Mahala Shillito, wife of James Shillito, was a member of the church in its early history and until her death.

Miss Ann Jackson, who afterwards in the Episcopal church, was a one time member.

Miss Jane Davis, sister of Lewis Davis, was an exceedingly useful member of the first church. She left Abbeville in 1835 and is now living in Mississippi.

Charles Dendy and his wife A. Ella, were among the members of the first church. Mr. Dendy died in 1859, and Mrs. Dendy is still living.

Mrs. Nancy Hanley, a sister of Charles Dendy, was also a member of the first church. She and her husband moved to Georgia before the second church was built.

John A. Donald was one of the first members of the second church.

Jefferson Weems was one of the first class leaders in the second church.

Jefferson Douglass and his wife Elizabeth became members of the first church only shortly before the second church was built.

Mrs. Elizabeth Spierin, wife of Thos. P. Spierin, was a member of the first church. She moved to Yazoo City in 1859 and died in 1870.

American Methodists

Miss Leontina Moore, daughter of Rev. James Moore and widow of H. S. Kerr, joined the church in her childhood. She has been a Sunday School teacher for about forty years.

Dr. A. B. Arnold and his wife were among the early members.

Additional Memory Roll

Mrs. Martha Atkins, died March 1884.
James Wash. Boyd, March 15, 1872, married Miss Fannie Sharp, Nov. 8, 1877, moved to Francis Street M. E. Church, St. Louis, Mo., May, 1874.
Mrs. Annie K. Bowie, wife of L. D. Bowie, b. in Abbeville in 1863, joined church in 1877 from Westminster, S. C., married June 7, 1881.
Mrs. Annie Branch, wife of W. T. Branch, b. in Cokesbury, April 15, 1855, joined Abbe. church 1870, married, Jan. 7, 1870, dismissed to Presbyterian church, Sept. 11, 1875.
Mrs. Mary Jane Bowie, b. Abbeville Co., 1838, joined church 1862, married L. D. Bowie, 1867, dismissed to Gilgal .
Mrs. Mamie Burke, wife of Henry Burke, b. Abbeville village, Feb. 12, 1866, joined church 1879, married, March 26, 1885, dismissed in 1886 to Greenville, S. C.
Miss Annie Lee Boarman, grand-daughter of Mrs. H. S. Kerr, b. Macon, Ga., March 3, 1876, joined Abbeville church, 1885.
Kerr Belcher, grandson of Mrs. H. S. Kerr, b. Abbeville, 1870, joined church in 1879, removed to New York City.
Harry S. Belcher, grandson of Mrs. H. S. Kerr, b. Tuskegee, Ala., Aug., 1873, joined Abbe. church, 1887, removed to New York City.
William E. Bell, by letter from Salem, 1876.
Mrs. Elvira Baxter, removed January, 1880.
Miss Kate Bruce, daughter of C. E. Bruce, received Oct. 10, 1886.
Miss Mamie Calhoun, wife of R. A. Calhoun and daughter of Maj. M. G. Zeigler, b. Cokesbury, joined Abbe. church, Nov., 20, 1881, married, Dec. 11,1884, transferred to Shreveport, La..
Mrs. Sallie R. Capers, wife of Rev. W. T. Capers, pastor of Abbe. church, 1872-74, born in Columbia, Nov. 13, 1842, dismissed Jan.,1875 to Spring Street church, Charleston.
Miss Willie T. Coogler, daughter of Mrs. Fannie D. Coogler, b. Columbia, Feb. 3, 1865, joined Abbe. church, Sept. 2, 1877, married E. L. Wilson, April 13, 1882.
William G. Chapman, b. Philadelphia, Tenn., March 4, 1859, joined Abbe. church, Sept. 1, 1886, married Miss Belle Wilkinson, April 22, 1883.
Mrs. Belle W. Chapman, wife of above, b. Ninety Six, Oct. 24, 1861, joined Abbe. church 1881.
Thomas Wells Coogler, Jr., b. Columbia, Dec. 17, 1866, joined Abbe. church, Sept. 2, 1877.
Miss Katie D. Coogler, b. Hodges Depot, June 16, 1871, joined the Abbe. church, Oct., 1886.
Miss Bessie G. Coogler, b. Hodges Depot, July 13, 1873, joined the Abbe. church, October, 1885.
Thomas W. Coogler, Sr., b. April 12, 1831, joined Abbe. church, Sept. 2, 1877,

Abbeville Methodists

married Fannie D. Wilson, June 10, 1863.
James D. Chalmers, b. Newberry, June, 1834, joined the Abbe. church, 1870, married Christiana T. Ramey, Dec. 11, 1856.
Mrs. Christiana T. Chalmers, wife of above, b. Abbeville, joined the Abbe. church, 1855.
Mrs. Caroline Cobb, wife of James H. Cobb, born Abbeville.
Henry S. Cason, transferred to Zoar.
Mrs. Mary J. Cason, wife of H. S. Cason, transferred to Zoar.
Samuel C. Cason, born Abbeville Co., Sept. 13, 1852, joined Abbe. church by transfer from Shiloh in 1870, married Miss Hattie Allen, Oct. 7, 1880.
Miss Janie E. Cason, daughter of H. S. Cason, transferred to Zoar, Nov. 23, 1873.
Miss Sallie J. Cason, daughter of H. S. Cason, joined 1873; rtansferred to Zoar, Nov. 23, 1873.
Mrs. Hattie Allen Cason, b. Abbeville, Oct. 10, 1857, joined 1887 from Presbyterian church, died Sept. 19, 1887.
Mrs. W. A. Clark, received by letter January, 1876, transferred.
Mrs. F. D. Coogler, widow of Thos. W. Coogler, received by letter from Hodges, May, 1876.
Frederick Cason, son of H. S. Cason, joined May 7, 1886.
Mrs. Mary Esther DuPre, mother of J. F. C. DuPre, born Charleston, Aug. 22, 1805, joined Abbe. church 1875, married C. Portuvine DuPre, 1826, died July 5, 1882.
Miss Mary DuPre, daughter of J. F. C. DuPre, b. Abbeville, joined church in 1884.
A. Mason DuPre, son of J. F. C. DuPre, b. Abbeville, joined church in 1886.
Frank C. DuPre, son of J. F. C. DuPre, joined Abbe. church 1886.
Eugene McSwain DuPre, son of J. F. C. DuPre, b. Lowndesville, joined Abbe. church about 1875, married Annie K. McKellar, 1882, membership ceased in 1885 by removal.
William C. DuPre, son of J. F. C. DuPre, b. Lowndesville, joined Abbe. about 1883, married Sallie W. Shillito, 1886.
Mrs. M. Josie DuPre, wife of J. H. DuPre, daughter of A. M. Hill, joined church, Aug. 18, 1872.
Mrs. Mary DuPre, wife of J. F. C. DuPre, b. Cokesbury, joined Abbe. church, 1867 by transfer from Smyrna, married, 1856.
Julius F. C. DuPre, b. Anderson Co., Aug. 31, 1831, joined Abbe. church from Smyrna, 1867, married Mary P. Huckabee, 1856.
Mrs. Susan E. DeBruhl, wife of Stephen C. DeBruhl, joined the Abbe. church from Washington Street, Columbia, 1859, died June, 1878.
Marshall P. DeBruhl, b. Abbeville, joined Abbeville church, 1866, married Miss Kate P. Calhoun of Augusta, Ga., Jan. 23, 1858.
Mrs. Kate C. DeBruhl, b. Abbeville Co., joined Abbe. church, April, 1885 from First Presbyterian church, Augusta.
Mrs. Mamie Dorn, wife of John C. Dorn and daughter of J. F. Osborn, b. Hamburg, S. C., June 7, 1859, married April 3, 1877, lately joined Baptist church with husband.
Miss Rebecca Davis, b. Hodges Depot, 1840, joined church in 1859.
Miss Mary C. Davis, daughter of I. B. Davis, b. Augusta, Ga., Dec. 4, 1868, joined Abbe. church, Sept. 26, 1886. from Trinity, Charleston.
Miss Julia L. Davis, daughter of I. B. Davis, b. Augusta, Ga., March 25, 1867,

American Methodists

joined Abbe. church, Sept. 26, 1886 from St. James, Augusta.
Mrs. Martha H. Davis, wife of I. B. Davis, b. Savannah, Ga., Oct. 3, 1829, joined Abbe. church, Sept. 26, 1886 from St. James, Augusta., married June 9, 1851.
Isaac B. Davis, b. Savannah, Ga., Dec. 16, 1818, joined Abbe. church, 1886 from St. James, Augusta, married Martha H. Sassard, June 9, 1851.
Kate E. Delph, b. Hamburg, S. C., joined Abbe. church, Sept., 1886.
Charles N. Dendy, removed.
Mrs. A. E. Dendy, widow of Charles Dendy.
Mrs. Eliza Dearing, received and transferred by certificates.
Mrs. Lavinia Duncan, received in 1872.
James S. Dickerson, received by certificate, Nov. 20, 1881, transferred to Madison, Fla., 1882.
J. Virginia Delph, b. Verdery, joined Abbe. church, Sept., 1886.
Mrs. Matilda D. Douglass, first wife of Thos. J. Douglass, b. near Smithville, Abbeville Co., about 1814, joined Abbe. church, 1832, married 1832, died 1848.
George Archibald Douglass, b. Abbeville, Oct. 30, 1837, joined Abbe. church, 1858, married Lizzie C. Wilson, Oct. 15, 1863 and M. E. Lyon, Dec. 20, 1884.
Thomas Jefferson Douglass, b. Douglass Mills, Abbeville Co., about 1806, married Matilda D. Lomax 1832 and Emily J. Atkins, 1852, died 1870.
Mrs. Emily Douglass, wife of above, b. 1832, joined Abbe. church, 1851 from Asbury, died 1884.
Mrs. Eugenia M. Douglass, wife of John C. Douglass, b. near Abbeville,1853.
Miss Essie Douglass, daughter of T. J. Douglass, b. Abbeville, 1856, joined Abbe. church, 1870, died 1884.
Miss Emma Douglass, daughter of T. J. Douglass, b. Abbeville, Dec. 17, 1865, joined Abbe. church, May, 1884, married John E. Agnew, Feb. 24, 1887.
Miss Georgia Edwards, daughter of John G. Edwards,b. Abbeville, Aug. 21, 1878, joined Abbe. church, June 26, 1887.
James Edmund Edwards, son of J. G. Edwards, b. Abbeville, March 30, 1877, joined Abbe. church, Aug. 21, 1887.
Hollis E. Edwards, son of Nathan A. Edwards, b. Abbeville Co., April 2, 1870, joined Abbe. church, June 26, 1887.
John Gibson Edwards, b. Abbeville Co., Feb. 14, 1832, joined Abbe. church, Dec., 1878, married Jennie A. Bell, Oct., 1867.
Miss Hannah E. Edwards, daughter of J. G. Edwards, b. Abbeville, March 3, 1873, joined Abbe. church, October, 1885.
Andrew Edwards, son of J. G. Edwards, b. Columbia, July 20, 1869, joined Abbe. church, March, 1883.
Robt. O. Edwards, son of John G. Edwards, b. Abbeville, June 8, 1874, joined Abbe. church, June 26, 1887.
Mrs. Jennie Edwards, wife of J. G. Edwards, b. Abbeville Co., Oct. 3, 1846, joined Abbe. church, July, 1870, from Washington Street, Columbia.
W. H. Ewart, joined by letter, April 8, 1883, transferred to Spartanburg, 1884.
Mrs. Sarah E. Ewart, joined by letter, April 8, 1883, transferred to Spartanburg, 1884.
Miss Sallie Ewart, joined by letter, April 8, 1883, transferred to Spartanburg, 1884.
Miss Mary A. Ewart, joined by letter, April 8, 1883, died July, 1883.
William C. Evans, removed in 1872.

Abbeville Methodists

Mrs. Drucilla Eakin, widow of Thos. Eakin, received by letter, died Nov. 16, 1887, age of 92.

James W. Fowler, b. Union District, April 9, 1838, joined Abbe. church, 1869, married Ceceila Chalmers, April 10, 1860, and Ella V. Sharp, March 1,1880, on Feb.1, 1874 dismissed with wife below.

Samuel Waddy Fowler was a member up to his death in 1861, and had been a member about two years.

Mrs. Ella Fowler, wife of James W. Fowler, b. Panola Co., Miss., Feb. 22, 1851, joined Abbe. church about Feb. 1, 1874, dismissed Francis St. M. E., St. Louis, Mo., died May 1, 1878.

Mrs. John W. Fell, daughter of Thomas J. Douglass, b. Abbeville Co.,1857, joined Abbe. church, 1870, married, 1876, moved to Asbury, 1886.

Rev. D. A. Foxworth, received by letter, June, 1872, transferred by certificate, 1874.

Mrs. S. A. Foxworth, wife of above, received by letter, 1872, transferred by certificate, 1874.

John M. Gambrell, b. Toney Creek, Anderson Co., Aug. 10, 1846, joined Abbe. church, May 25, 1873 from Williamston church, married Miss Eliza C. Clinkscales, Jan. 15, 1871, .

Mrs. Eliza C. Gambrell, wife of above, b. Temple of Health, Abbeville Co., April 13, 1846, joined Abbe. church, May 25, 1873.

Claudius C. Gambrell, son of J. M. Gambrell, b. Temple of Health, March 2, 1872, joined Abbe. church, March, 1883.

George C. Gambrell, son of J. M. Gambrell, b. Williamston, July 18, 1878, joined Abbe. church, Oct., 1885.

Miss Ellen C. Gambrell, daughter of J. M. Gambrell, b. Batesville, Miss., May 26, 1878, joined Abbe. church, June 26, 1887.

Frank F. Gary, b. Cokesbury, Nov., 1829, joined Abbe. church from Cokesbury church, 1885, married Miss Mary C. Blackburn, Oct. 20, 1853, died Dec. 31, 1887.

Mary M. Gilmer, received by certificate, transferred by certificate.

Christian V. Hammond, b. Abbeville Co., Oct. 1, 1843, joined Abbe. church, 1864 from Sharon, married Mary F. Rutledge, Nov. 1, 1866.

Miss Mary F. Hammond, wife of above, b. Greenville, July 10, 1845, joined Abbe. church in 1860 from Asheville church.

Charles Percy Hammond, son of above, b. Abbeville, Aug. 27, 1870, joined Abbe. church, 1882.

Arthur Spencer Hammond, son. of C. V. Hammond, born Abbeville, May 25, 1872, joined Abbe. church, 1883, died Sept. 11, 1886.

Miss Ida Virginia Hammond, daughter of C. V. Hammond, b. Abbeville, April 10, 1874, joined Abbe. church, 1884.

Miss Nora Hammond, daughter of C. V. Hammond, b. Abbeville, Sept. 28, 1876, joined Abbe. church, 1886.

George C. Hodges, b. Abbeville, joined Abbe. church, 1885 by letter from Ninety Six, married Miss Corinne Waldrop, 1880, removed to Greenwood, 1887.

William H. Hammond, b. Abbeville Co., Aug. 24, 1841, joined Abbe. church 1866 from Sharon, married Sarah C. McCord, March 11, 1866, dismissed to M. E. church, Clinton.

Mrs. Kate Hammond, b. Mt. Carmel, joined Abbe. church, Sept. 1875 by letter from Zoar, married Joseph S. Hammond, May 25, 1875.

Abbeville Methodists

Joseph S. Hammond, b. Abbeville Co., Dec. 27, 1854, joined the Abbe.church, Sept. 1875 by letter from Sharon, married Miss Kate Scott, above.

Henry S. Hammond, b. Abbeville Co., Nov. 10, 1817, joined the Abbe. church, 1872 from Sharon, married Jane T. Barnes, Oct. 23, 1840, died June 17, 1884.

Mrs. Jane T. Hammond, wife of above, b. Abbeville Co., Jan. 31, 1818, joined Abbe. church from Sharon, 1872, dismissed to Piedmont.

Miss Fannie M. Hammond, daughter of above, b. Abbeville Co., Aug. 24, 1860 joined Abbe. church, 1872, from Sharon, married James Latimer, dismissed to Piedmont church, Greenville.

Albert B. Hammond, son of H. S. Hammond, b. Abbeville Co., Feb. 8, 1851, joined Abbeville church by certificate from Sharon, married Miss Fannie Lane, Columbia.

Miss Alice E. Hammond, daughter of H. S. Hammond, b. Abbeville Co., Sept. 26, 1862, joined Abbe. church, 1872 from Sharon, married Mr. Wannamaker in 1886, dismissed to Piedmont church.

Mrs. Mary C. Hill, wife of R. M. Hill, daughter of Wm. C. Moore, joined March, 1879.

Mrs. Jane E. Hill, wife of A. M. Hill and daughter of J. Allen Ramey, received by letter from Sharon, 1884, died July, 1887.

William E. Hill, son of above, joined May 2, 1884.

James A. Hill, son of A. M. Hill, joined Sept. 6, 1865.

Mrs. Hattie C. Harper, wife of Rev. R. I. Harper, received by certificate, January, 1882, transferred to Mississippi, 1884.

Edward K. Hardin, received by certificate, transferred.

Mrs. Ida C. Hardin, wife of above, received by certificate, transferred.

Miss Orene Hughes, daughter of Cicero Hughes.

Miss Minnie Hughey, daughter of James Hughey, joined March 7, 1886.

Mrs. Susan A. Ivey, wife of John Ivey and daughter of Stephen B. Norrell, b. Greenwood, Jan. 7, 1861, joined Abbe. church, 1875, married 1876, dismissed to Augusta, Ga.

Adolphus W. Jones, b. Abbeville, April 12, 1857, married Miss Celia T. Miller, Dec. 19, 1878.

Miss Anna Jones, daughter of Robert Jones, Sr., b. Abbeville, 1863, joined the Abbe. church, 1885.

Robert Jones, Sr., b. Lowndesville, joined the Abbe. church, 1859, married Mary Davis, 1850.

Mrs. Mary Jones, widow of Robert Jones, Sr., b. Hodges Depot, November, 1831, joined the Abbe. church, 1850.

Joshua Y. Jones, b. near Greenwood, Aug., 1853, joined Abbe. church, 1863.

Joseph E. Jones, b. Abbeville, September, 1870, joined the Abbe. church, June, 1887.

Robert Jones, Jr., son of Robert Jones, joined June 1, 1879, transferred to Texas, Dec., 1880.

H. S. Kerr, b. Lincolnton, N. C., March, 1824, joined the Abbe. church, 1848, married Leontina Moore, January, 1846, died February, 1881.

Mrs. Leontina Kerr, widow of above, b. Abbeville, joined Abbe. church, 1835.

Mrs. Emma E. Klugh, wife of P. D. Klugh, b. Abbeville, Sept. 1, 1857, joined Abbe. church, 1871, married, Oct. 13, 1881.

Mrs. E. Catherine Kurz, widow of Jacob Kurz, b. Hemp Co., Ga., July 7, 1825,

Abbeville Methodists

joined the Abbe. church, 1868, married June 23, 1864 in Augusta, Ga.
Miss E. Catherine Kennedy, b. Abbeville, joined Abbe. church, Aug. 12, 1882 by certificate from Baptist church.
Pascal D. Klugh, b. Abbeville, Dec. 3, 1856, joined Abbe. church, 1886 by certificate, married Miss Emma E. Syfan, Oct. 13, 1881.
James C. Klugh, b. at Cokesbury, April 30, 1857, joined Abbe. church , June, 1886 from Bethlehem.
James Fraser Lyon, b. Verdery, Oct. 13, 1871, joined the Abbe. church, September, 1886.
J. Fuller Lyon, b. Verdery, April 1, 1842, joined the Abbe. church, January, 1877 by certificate, married Mrs. M. Louise Delph, Nov. 21, 1866.
Mrs. Mary Louise Lyon, , b. Chapel Hill, N. C., joined Abbe. church, January, 1877 by certificate from Asbury.
William Andrew Lyon, b. Verdery, Oct. 16, 1867, joined Abbe. church, September, 1886.
William Lyon, b. Abbeville Co., Aug. 8, 1808, joined Abbe. church, January, 1877 on certificate from Asbury, died June 10, 1881.
Hiram W. Lawson, Sr., died April 12, 1881.
Mrs. Fannie J. Lawson, widow of H. W. Lawson, Sr.
Mrs. Harriet B. Lyon, widow of Dr. H. T. Lyon.
H. Thomson Lyon, joined May 11, 1879, died May 29, 1886.
A. W. Lynch, received by certificate, Oct. 22, 18-5 [sic]. transferred.
Maurice Lynch, transferred.
Miss Annie Magruder, b. Madison Co., Miss., joined Abbe. church July, 1879, dismissed to Anderson church, May,1887.
Mrs. Frances Martin, widow of Robert A. Martin, b. Cedar Hill, Abbeville Co., Nov. 4, 1830, joined Abbe. church, 1870, married, March 11, 1851, dismissed to Baptist church.
Mrs. Lalla Marshall, wife of James B. Marshall, daughter of Maj. M. G. Zeigler, b. Cokesbury, joined the Abbe. church, March 25, 1879 by certificate from Cokesbury, married, June, 1882, removed to Greenville.
Miss Fannie Martin, daughter of above, b. Abbeville, joined Abbe. church,1879.
S. Tompkins Mabry, son of Dr. T. J. Mabry, b. Lebanon, Jan. 17, 1870, joined Abbe. church, October, 1885.
Robert L. Mabry, son of Dr. T. J. Mabry, b. Lebanon, March 9, 1866, joined Abbe. church, October, 1885.
Miss Willie Moore, daugher of W. C. Moore, b. Abbeville, joined Abbe. church, September, 1887.
Henry D. Moore, son Rev. James Moore, b. Abbeville, 1838, joined Abbe. church, 1847, married Miss Carrie B. Thomason,1859,dismissed to Marion Street, Columbia , became Methodist minister in Florida and Alabama, in Montgomery, 1888.
John W. McCulloch, b. Guilford, N. C., 1837, joined Abbe. church, 1879 by certificate from Covington, Ga., married Caroline A. McKee of Beaufort in 1863, widower since 1867.
James Willard Martin, b. Fort Pickens, Sept. 1, 1862, joined Abbe.church,1887.
Joel Kennedy Milford, son of T. B. Milford, b. Abbeville Co., July 18, 1867, joined Abbe. church, 1887 from Sharon.
William T. McDonald, b. near Cedar Spring, Feb. 11, 1846, joined Abbe. church,

Abbeville Methodists

1858, married Elizabeth V. Rutledge, May 17, 1870, removed to Zoar church, Mt. Carmel, 1887.

Matthew McDonald, b. Cedar Spring, March 13, 1820, joined Abbe. church, 1847, married Martha D. Jackson, April 17, 1845, died.

Mrs. Martha D. McDonald, widow of above, b. Abbeville Co., July 2, 1827, joined Abbe. church, 1839, died May 12, 1884.

Mrs. Elizabeth V. McDonald, wife of W. T. McDonald, b. Greenville, Oct. 26, 1849, joined Abbe. church, 1858.

Mrs. Elizabeth C. Moore, wife of William C. Moore, died Oct. 9, 1886.

William C. Moore, joined March 7, 1886.

Alice F. McCord, withdrew, 1876.

Nancy S. McCord, removed.

Miss Janie McCord, daughter of William M. McCord, received by certificate, 1883.

Miss Seppie McCord, daughter of W. M. McCord, removed and died.

Luther A. McCord, joined June 3, 1876, transferred to Clinton.

Mrs. M. C. Mood, wife of Rev. J. A. Mood, received by letter, January, 1875, removed by certificate, 1875.

Miss Mary Mood, daughter of Rev. J. A. Mood, received by letter, January, 1875, removed.

Russell E. Mood, son of Rev. Mood, received and removed as above.

Miss Emma Means, daughter of James Means, joined June 3, 1876, transferred to Columbia.

E. H. McBride, received by letter, July, 1878, transferred to Jackson, Tenn.

Mrs. Annie McBride, wife of above, transferred to Jackson, Tenn.

Miss Ellen J. Murphy, received by certificate, 1878, removed, 1880.

William McMillan, son of T. W. McMillan, joined May 11, 1879.

Mrs. Lizzie Miller, wife of J. C. Miller, daughter of T. W. McMillan, joined May 11, 1879.

Mrs. Elizabeth W. Moore, widow of Joseph T. Moore, b. Edgefield Co.,1831, joined Abbe. church, 1847, married, 1846.

Miss Mary Moore, b. Abbeville, 1853, joined Abbe. church, 1869, married James H. Simmons, 1873, died December, 1880.

Joseph T. Moore, b. Abbeville, 1825, married Elizabeth W. Ramage, 1846, died November, 1870.

Miss Leola J. Milford, b. Abbeville Co., 1862, joined Abbe. church, 1886 from Shiloh, married G. H. Moore, 1881.

J. Colin Moore, b. Abbeville, 1857, married Minnow B. Howland of Mobile,Ala., 1882, dismissed to Franklin Street church, Mobile.

George Henry Moore, b. Abbeville, 1855, joined Abbe. church, 1886, married Leola J. Milford, January, 1881.

Stephen B. Norrell, b. Greenwood, Nov. 4, 1840 , joined Abbe. church, 1860 from Greenwood church, married Elizabeth Woodhurst, Dec. 28, 1859.

Mrs. Elizabeth Norrell, wife of S. B. Norrell, b. England, March 9, 1838, joined Abbe. church, 1867, died 1880.

Miss Georgia Norrell , daughter of S. B. Norrell, b. Abbeville, March 26, 1868, joined the Abbe. church, 1879

Enoch Nelson, b. in Fairfield, 1814, joined Abbe. church, 1869, married Louisa E. Neel, 1857, removed.

Mrs. Louisa E. Nelson, wife of above, b. Newberry, 1833, joined Abbe. church in

Abbeville Methodists

1858 from Asbury, died 1875.

G. Augustus Neuffer, b. Orangeburg, March 14, 1861, joined Abbe. church, 1885, from M. E. church, Orangeburg Station.

Mrs. Amelia E. Osborn, wife of John F. Osborn, b. Greenville District, Feb. 5, 1831, joined Abbe. church, Spring, 1870, from St. James in Augusta, married, Sept. 17, 1846, dismissed by removal to Ninety Six, 1878.

Miss Annie Osborn, daughter of above, b. Hamburg, S. C., August 20, 1861.

John F. Osborn, b. Mecklenburg Co., N. C., July 16, 1805, joined Abbe. church in Spring, 1870 from St. James in Augusta, married Miss Amelia E. Green, Sept. 17, 1846, removed to Ninety Six, 1878.

William H. Penney, b. Abbeville Co., May 4, 1845, joined the Abbe. church, January, 1875, by certificate from Gilgal, married Miss S. C. Hammond, Nov. 8, 1870, removed to Hodges.

Mrs. Sallie C. Penney, wife of above, b. Abbeville, Oct. 26, 1852, joined Abbe. church, 1875 by certificate from Gilgal, moved to Hodges, 1875.

Mrs. Nancy Jane Perry, wife of John T. Perry, b. Abbeville Co., July 18, 1857, joined Abbe. church, 1874 by certificate from Gilgal, married, December, 1873.

Mrs. Nancy Perry, married Thomas Perry in 1847, membership ceased July 27, 1872.

John T. Parks, b. Lincoln Co., Ga., June 11, 1829, joined the Abbe. church, January, 1882 from M. E. church, South, Greenwood, married Miss Anna Mary Speers, Oct. 11, 1859.

Miss A. Winton Parks, daughter of Capt. J. T. Parks, b. Greenwood, March 8, 1866, joined Abbe. church, January, 1882.

G. Hertford Parks, son of Capt. J. T. Parks, b. Greenwood, Aug. 9, 1869 , joined Abbe. church, January, 1882.

Mrs. Mary B. Pritchard, wife of Rev. C. H. Pritchard, received by letter, July 8, 1885.

Miss Maggie B. Pritchard, daughter of above, received by letter, removed by certificate, March 19, 1886.

Miss Mary C. Pritchard, daughter of Rev. Pritchard, received by letter, removed by certificate, March 10, 1886.

Thos. G. Perrin, joined 1882, moved out West, 1883.

William T. Penney, b. Laurens Co., Jan. 11, 1838, joined Abbe. church, 1857 by certificate from Salem, married Miss Mary A. Shillito, Dec. 13, 1859.

Mrs. Mary A. Penney, wife of above, b. Abbeville, b. Feb. 11, 1838, joined the Abbe. church, 1857.

Miss Martha J. Pennel, removed 1872.

James H. Perrin, died 1876.

H. Middleton Prince, received by certificate, removed June, 1880.

Dr. Lewis Perrin, received by letter, November, 1878, died Oct. 25, 1880.

Mrs. Ella B. Perrin, wife of J. L. Perrin, b. Abbeville, Oct. 4, 1864, joined 1886, married Nov. 23, 1887.

John W. Rykard, b. Smithville, Dec. 18, 1844, joined Abbe. church, Sept., 1885, married Miss Matilda E. Verell, August 18, 1872.

Mrs. Matilda Rykard, wife of above, b. Laurens Co., May 20, 1850, joined the Abbe. church, 1879, removed to Tranquil.

James William Rykard, son of above, b. Smithville, July 10, 1873, joined Abbe. church, September, 1885, removed to Tranquil.

Abbeville Methodists

Mrs. Lucretia Ramey, b. Abbeville, May 13, 1808, married John Ramey, died.
Miss Ann L. Russel, removed to Columbia.
Philip S. Rutledge, joined December, 1868, removed to Spartanburg.
Mrs. Carolina Reeder, joined 1870.
Ella E. Reese, b. Williamston, 1859, joined 1887 from Baptist church, married Henry D. Reese, 1886.
William S. Richardson, received by letter, June, 1872, removed Nov. 28, 1874.
Annie E. Richardson, received by letter, June, 1872, removed Nov. 28, 1874.
Miss Sallie A. Richardson, received by letter, June, 1872, removed Nov. 28, 1874.
Miss Mary M. Richardson, received by letter, June, 1872, removed Nov. 28, 1874.
Andoline A. Rolison, received January, 1873, removed.
Mrs. Annie E. Rogers, wife of W. J. Rogers, joined March, 1879, transferred to Augusta, Oct. 26, 1886.
Henry Dodson Reese, b. Florida, Dec. 24, 1852, joined Abbe. church, 1882, married Miss Ella E. Bradley, July 6, 1876.
P. Brooks Speed, b. Lowndesville, Jan. 11, 1858, joined Abbe. church, April 15, 1884 from Smyrna.
Mrs. E. Alice Simmons, wife of James H. Simmons, b. Abbeville Co., Aug. 18, 1853, joined Abbe. church about 1879, married J. C. Wosmansky, Feb. 13, 1873 and J. H. Simmons, Feb. 1, 1883.
Mrs. Mary M. Simmons, wife of James H. Simmons, daughter of Mrs. Elizabeth W. Moore, b. Abbeville, Feb. 26, 1853, joined Abbe. church, about 1869, married, December, 1873, died Dec. 17, 1880.
James H. Simmons, b. Reading, Pa., Feb. 2, 1846, joined Abbe. church about 1879, married Miss Mary Moore and Mrs. E. A. Wosmansky.
Mrs. Minne E. Syfan, wife of George W. Syfan, b. Abbeville, March 14, 1839, joined Abbe. church, 1851, married, 1861.
George W. Syfan, b. Charleston, May 22, 1821, joined Abbe. church, 1859, married Minnie C. Jackson.
Mrs. S. Talula Scott, wife of S. A. Scott, daughter of S. B. Norrell, b. Abbeville, Jan. 11, 1863, joined Abbe. church, 1875, married W. H. Scott, September, 1876, dismissed to Presbyterian church.
Miss Lillie Jane Scott, b. Mt. Carmel, joined 1882.
Manning Brown Syfan, son of G. W. Syfan, b. Abbeville, March 11, 1869, joined Abbe. church, 1886.
Joseph A. Scott, b. Mt. Carmel, July 30, 1875, joined the Abbe. church, June 26, 1887.
Mrs. F. E. Scott, b. Abbeville Co., joined the Abbe. church, Jan. 26, 1887 from Zoar, married W. A. Scott., Dec. 17, 1872.
Miss Sallie Scott, b. Mt. Carmel, Dec. 18, 1873, joined Abbe. church from Zoar, Jan. 26, 1887.
Kate H. Scott, b. Mt. Carmel, July 22, 1867.
William G. Syfan, son of G. W. Syfan, joined May 11, 1879.
Thomas J. Syfan, son of G. W. Syfan, joined Sep. 19, 1886.
Mrs. Lilly Syfan, wife of Thos. J. Syfan, joined Sept. 19, 1886.
Mrs. Bettie Shillito, wife of Jas. Shillito, Jr.
Mrs. Lizzie Shillito, wife of Geo. A. Shillito.

Abbeville Methodists

Miss Sallie Shillito, daughter of Jas. Shillito.
Mrs. Mahala Shillito, wife of Jas. Shillito, Sr., died 1883.
Mrs. S. C. Simmons, wife of Rev. D. J. Simmons, joined Abbe. church January, 1878, removed January, 1880.
L. J. Scott, received by letter, transferred to Walhalla.
E. L. Seal, received by letter from Ninety Six circuit, Sept. 15, 1886.
Jesse J. Spruel, son of Wm. Spruel, joined Sept. 19, 1886.
Capt. John Sassard, b. Bordeaux, France, 1795, joined Abbe. church, 1864, married Henrietta Davis, died Feb. 12, 1865.
Mrs. Henrietta Sassard, wife of John Sassard, Sr., b. Washington, D. C., Sept. 23, 1806, died Nov. 9, 1879.
Nelson T. Sassard, b. Charleston, Feb., 22, 1833, joined Abbe. church, May 11, 1879, married Margaretta Anna Small, July 11, 1869.
Mrs. Margaretta A. Sassard, wife of Nelson T. Sassard, b. Caracfurgas, County Antrim, March 1, 1854, transferred from Episcopal church, Abbeville, May, 1882.
Miss Georgianna Sassard, daughter of John Sassard, Sr., b. Charleston, Feb. 22, 1847, joined Abbe. church, 1876, d. May 20, 1884.
Miss Roseanna Sassard, b. Charleston, 1843, joined Abbe. church, 1876, died Dec. 3, 1883.
Arthur D. Sassard, son of N. T. Sassard, b. Abbeville, July 16, 1870, joined Abbe. church, April, 1883.
Mrs. A. Sign, wife of J. W. Sign, b. Abbeville, married Oct. 26, 1865.
Lewis Wardlaw Sign, b. Abbeville, 1872, joined the Abbe. church, 1887.
John W. Sign, b. Philadelphia, Pa., Jan. 1, 1839, joined Abbe. church, 1876, married Julia A. Shillito, Oct. 26, 1865.
Benjamin F. Smith, received by letter, removed by certificate, April 1879.
Mrs. B. F. Smith, wife of above, received by letter, removed by certificate, April, 1879.
Miss Mattie Smith, daughter of above, received by letter, removed by certificate, April, 1879.
Mrs. Fannie Smith, received by certificate, Sept. 15, 1880.
W. Tully Sondley, son D. R. Sondley, joined May 11, 1879, removed.
Mrs. Parthenia Stafford, wiife of Rev. A. J. Stafford, received by letter, removed by certificate, January, 1882.
Samuel M. Scott, b. Mt. Carmel, March 13, 1880, joined Abbe. church, 1882 from Zoar.
Mrs. Sarah A. Scott, b. Mt. Carmel, Dec. 21, 1829, joined Abbe. church, 1882 from Zoar, married T. B. Scott, Dec. 16, 1845.
Mrs. Jessie Trowbridge, wife of J. T. Trowbridge, transferred to Anderson, Nov. 20, 1881.
Mrs. Virginia E. Westfield, wife of Edward Westfield, b. Columbia, 1833, joined Abbe. church, July 15, 1852, married January 8, 1852, died Feb. 1, 1855.
Eugene L. Wilson, b. Fort Pickens, Oct. 3, 1857, joined Abbe. church, 1869, married Miss Willie T. Coogler, April 13, 1882.
Edward Westfield, b. County Arnaugh, Ireland, Jan. 13, 1825, joined Abbe. church, Aug. 10, 1855, married Miss Virginia Elizabeth Beard and Miss Sarah J. Walker, dismissed to Gilgal , January, 1873.
Mrs. Sarah Jane Westfield, wife of Edward Westfield, b. Abbeville Co.,1833,

Abbeville Methodists

joined Abbe. church, 1868 from Cedar Spring A. R. P., dismissed to Gilgal.
Miss Ursula Wosmansky, daughter of Mrs. J. C. Wosmansky, now wife of James H. Simmons, b. Abbeville, joined Abbe. church, 1885.
Mrs. Sarah U. Wilson, wife of Leroy J. Wilson, b. near Cedar Spring, March 25, 1847, joined Abbe. church, June 1, 1880 from Bethel, married Nov. 8, 1877.
Mrs. Sallie Williams, wife of David R. Williams, b. Newberry, 1851, joined Abbe. church, 1869, married 1867, died.
Robert D. Westfield, b. Abbeville, 1858, joined Abbe. church, 1868, removed.
Miss Ella V. Westfield, b. Abbeville, 1855, joined Abbe. church, 1868, married H. P. McIlwain, 1874, dismissed to Upper Long Cane.
Mrs. Catherine M. Wilson, widow of Thomas M. Wilson, b. Douglass Mills, joined Abbe. church from Cokesbury, married in 1844.
Mrs. G. A. Wise, daughter of Maj. M. G. Zeigler, married Dr. G. A.Wise,Feb. 5, 1884, transferred to Shreveport, La.
Henry Donald Wilson, b. Abbeville Co., joined 1872 from Greenwood.
Miss Georgia Zeigler, daughter of M. G. Zeigler, b. Abbeville Co. near Cokesbury, joined Abbe. church, March 25, 1879, died June, 1883.
Miss Jennie Zeigler, daughter of M. G. Zeigler, b. Cokesbury, joined Abbe. church, September, 1885.
Miss Sabina Zeigler, daughter of M. G. Zeigler, b. Cokesbury, joined Abbe. church about September, 1886 from Greenville.
Miss Etta Zeigler, daughter of M. G. Zeigler, b. Cokesbury, joined Abbe. church, Jan., 18, 1883, died 1883.
Miss Julia Zeigler, daughter of M. G. Zeigler, b. Abbeville Co., joined Abbe. church, March 25, 1879 from Cokesbury, married Rev. J. C. Chandler.
Mrs. Lavinia Zeigler, wife of M. G. Zeigler, b. Columbia, joined Abbe. church, March 25, 1879 from Cokesbury, married M. G. Zeigler.

XXXIII. ABBEVILLE IN THE FEDERAL CENSUS SCHEDULES

The federal census of 1850 was the first to list names of persons other than heads of household, and it was also the first to mark off the inhabitants of the village of Abbeville. I chose to include it and the 1860 census because they reveal much about the ante bellum town and should be of interest to students of family history.

I did not include the schedules for the 1870 and 1880 censuses largely because of length. It was a hard choice for these are the first census records to include the names of most of the blacks who made up a majority of the population then, however, this would have added at least sixty pages to the volume. I did copy the census of 1880, and I made a careful study of the 1870 record.

The census of 1870 has notorious faults. Many persons were omitted and there were numerous errors. The surnames were indicated only by initials. Strangely enough, even though it was conducted by Hutson J. Lomax, a black, it contained a very deficient record of black as well as white residents. Lomax was elected to the South Carolina Senate, but was killed in November, 1870 in a train wreck on the way to Columbia to be sworn into office.

The *Press & Bonner*, August 24, 1871, carried the totals of a State census conducted by J. F. C. DuPre, the town's intendent, which was, as follows: whites- 613, blacks-835, for a total population of 1,448. His count also included for tax purposes 78 horses and mules, 318 cattle, 367 hogs, and 148 dogs. The 1880 federal census listed 1,543 persons in the town of Abbeville.

An interesting feature of the 1880 census was the presence of so many domestic servants fifteen years after emancipation. For example, there were 104 washerwomen, 60 cooks, 30 nurses, 17 seamstresses, 8 mantua workers, and numerous other servants who were designated as house girls or women, waitresses, butlers, drivers, coachmen, etc.

A comparison of the census of 1860 with that of 1850 shows that the decade of the 1850s was a time of rapid change in the village of Abbeville. The biggest change was in the population totals and character. In 1850, the free population was 372, and the census taker reported that those free inhabitants owned 881 slaves. There is no way to determine how many of these slaves lived in town, but it is likely that the greater number lived on plantations in the country. Judge R. E. Hill in his memoirs said that when his father moved to the village in the 1850s, it contained somewhat less than a thousand inhabitants. The census of 1860 contained 561 inhabitants, an increase of almost 44%.

Undoubtedly, most of the newcomers to town came like the Hills from the nearby countryside, but the prosperity of the district attracted a good number of migrants from far away. In 1850, the village population included 15 persons of foreign birth; in 1860, there

Abbeville in the Federal Census Schedules

were 42 persons of foreign birth. In 1850, 7 of the inhabitants were born in the Northern states; in 1860, 24 of the villagers were of Northern birth.

An analysis of the census of 1860 illustrates the building boom which was taking place in Abbeville at that time. In the 1850 census, there were only 3 persons in town in the building trades, 1 carpenter, 1 tinner, and 1 house painter. In 1860, there were 33 persons in the building trades: 3 master carpenters, 8 other carpenters, 5 house painters, 4 brick layers, 3 stone masons (including 2 who worked with marble), 3 tinners, 2 joiners, 2 plasterers, 1 cabinet maker, and two architects (J. D. Daly and August Bernelle who was not listed as an architect but as a "teacher of French").

In 1850, there was only 1 free black, a free mulatto named Sarah Rous. In 1860, there were 28 free blacks, 25 of whom were mulattoes. Of these, 17 were listed in the household of John H. Wilson, an attorney who was one of the district's delegates to the South Carolina Secession Convention. They were listed under two family names, Greer and Bug. Of the remaining free blacks, most were Donalsons.

The Census of 1850-Village of Abbeville
(Includes place of birth, if not S. C., and Real Estate value)

739.	David L. Wardlaw	50	Judge-Lawyer	$20,000
	Susan C. Wardlaw	22		
	Lucia G. Wardlaw	17		
	Ella C. Wardlaw	14		
	George A. Wardlaw	12		
	Sally M. Wardlaw	10		
	Jane E. Wardlaw	7		
740.	J. Foster Marshall	31	State Senator	$15,000
	Elizabeth Marshall	25		
	William J. Marshall	6		
	Samuel F. Marshall	4		
	J. Foster Marshall	2		
	John L. Marshall	1		
741.	Timothy D. Williams	64	Painter & Glazier (Wales)	
	Esther Williams	65	(Ireland)	
	Samuel Williams	10		
	John Williams	8		
	David Williams	2		
742.	Isaac Branch	49	M. D. (Vt.)	$4,000
	Fanny Branch	44	(Vt.)	
	Mary L. Branch	16		
	Louisa H. Branch	8		
	William T. Branch	5		
743.	Samuel A. Hodges	45	Innkeeper	

1850 Federal Census

	Name	Age	Occupation	Value
	Mary A. D. Hodges	34		
	Gabraella Hodges	16		
	John F. Hodges	14		
	Mary Hodges	12		
	Julia Hodges	10		
	Arnice Hodges	6 (F)		
	Sophronia Hodges	4		
	Henry Hodges	2		
	William A. Giles	21	Merchant Clerk	
	Andrew Paul	24	M. D.	
	Samuel Hodges	9		
	Patrick Owens	22	Tailor (Ireland)	
	George M. Miller	20	Clerk	
	John H. Wilson	35	Lawyer	$500
	John G. Baskin	25	Lawyer	
	William Robinson	30	Hostler	
	John A. Pucket	26	Law Student	
	Augustus Lomax	28		$8,000
	John Lomax	30		$2,100
	James Cochran	27	Lawyer	
744.	Jane L. Allen	50		$6,925
	William A. Allen	20	Clerk	
	Thomas W. Allen	18	Student	
	Louisa J. Allen	16		
	Ione Allen	13		
	Benjamin Y. Martin	35	Lawyer	
	Caroline Martin	26	(Ga.)	
	Banning Martin	5 (M)		
	Mary L. Martin	3		
	Caroline Martin	4/12	(Ga.)	
	John J. Martin	25	Lawyer	
	John Hunter	30	Gin maker	$7,000
	John McIlwain	30	Merchant	$4,500
	Theopolis A. Sale	36	Dentist	
	Samuel McGowan	27	Lawyer	
	Frederick W. Sellic	28	Ordinary (Ga.)	
	Milton Deal	24	Coachmaker	
	John G. Wilson	32	Merchant	
	William Hill	19	Clerk	
	David W. Hawthorn	26	Deputy Sheriff	
	Samuel W. Mabry	25	Teacher	
	James Cunningham	28	Clerk	
745.	John F. Livingston	46	Farmer/M. D.	$14,800
	Margaret A. Livingston	43	(N.C.)	
	John F. Livingston	20	Student	
	Mary J. Livingston	16 (F)		
	Sarah M. Livingston	16 Twins		
	Eliza L. Livingston	13		
	Mary Livingston	75		

1850 Federal Census

	Name	Age	Occupation	Value
	John Anderson	28	Dentist	
746.	Thomas Sanders	50	Manager	
747.	Joseph J. Wardlaw	43	M. D.	$7,000
	Mary A. Wardlaw	30		
	James W. Wardlaw	10		
	Clark J. Wardlaw	9		
	Louis A. Wardlaw	6		
	Mary W. Wardlaw	4		
748.	Jasper Cheatham	24	Overseer	
749.	Susan V. Wilson	36		
	Delphia D. Wilson	15		
	Wm. L. Wilson	13		
	Susan A. Wilson	11		
	Jane E. Wilson	9		
	Martha T. Wilson	7		
750.	James Alston	75	Farmer (N. C.)	$39,620
	Catherine Alston	64		
	Harriett Hamilton	28		
	Josiah Reynolds	72		
751.	James Moore	52	Meth. Clergyman	$2,000
	Ann Moore	50	(England)	
	William C. Moore	17	Student	
	Henry D. Moore	12		
	Edwin W. Moore	10		
752.	Joseph T. Moore	25	Saddler	
	Elizabeth Moore	18		
	James C. Moore	3		
	John Shields	23	Shoemaker (Ireland)	
753.	Johnson Ramey	42	Inn Keeper	
	Lucretia Ramey	43		
	James Ramey	19	Farmer	
	Christiana Ramey	16		
	Rebecca Ramey	12		
	Justina Ramey	10 (F)		
	Ellen Ramey	8		
	Johnson Ramey	3		
	Matilda Ramey	2		
	Alice Hamilton	5		
	John Taylor	35	Blacksmith	
	Samuel Tustin	18	Clerk	
	Sarah Rous	18	(mulatto)	
754.	Henry Kerr	26	Printer (N. C.)	$1,500
	Amanda L. Kerr	26		
	Ann B. Kerr	3		
	Clara F. Kerr	1/12		
	Elihu Johnson	22	Printer	
	Thomas Knox	18	Printer (Ireland)	
755.	John White	42	Merchant	$17,000
	Lucy White	41		

1850 Federal Census

	Name	Age		Occupation	Value
	Robert White	15		Student	
	William White	13			
	George White	10			
	Lucy White	8			
	Leonard White	6			
	Nannie White	4			
	Charles White	1			
	Newton Bullock	22		Clerk	
756.	Matthew McDonald	29		Teacher	
	Martha D. McDonald	25			
	William T. McDonald	5			
757.	Thomas B. Dendy	31		M. D.	$10,000
	Mary J. Dendy	28			
	Elizabeth G. Dendy	5			
	James N. Dendy	4			
	John McDaniel	35		Overseer (Ireland)	
	Robert M. Cheatham	11			
758.	Elizabeth Lyon	60			$4,000
	John Lyon	23		Druggist	
	Joseph W. Lyon	21		Farmer	
	Henry T. Lyon	19		Student	
759.	Benjamin McFarlin	46		Miller	$2,000
	Nancy McFarlin	42			
	Mary E. McFarlin	15			
	Francis M. McFarlin	13	(M)		
	Benjamin D.C. McFarlin	12			
	John W. McFarlin	4			
	Mary A. McFarlin	68			
760.	Robert H. Wardlaw	43		Merchant	$14,000
	Eliza Wardlaw	42			
	Andrew Wardlaw	19		Student	
	James A. Wardlaw	17		Cadet	
	Samuel W. Wardlaw	15		Clerk	
	William C. Wardlaw	13			
	John L. Wardlaw	10			
	Robert H. Wardlaw	9			
	Francis H. Wardlaw	8	(M)		
	David A. Wardlaw	4			
	Thomas P. Wardlaw	3			
	Charles C. Wardlaw	1			
	Rosa A. Gilmer	78			
761.	Charles Dendy	59		Farmer	$16,000
	Absley Dendy	40	(F)		
	William Dendy	17		Student	
	Harriet Dendy	12			
	Sally Dendy	10			
	Charles Dendy	4			
	James A. Allen	24			
	Frances E. Allen	20	(F)		

1850 Federal Census

	Name	Age	Occupation	Value
	Ida Allen	1		
	Samuel A. Goff	65	Cabinetmaker (N.C.)	
	David Goff	25	Dagauretypist (Ga.)	
762.	Thomas C. Perrin	44	Lawyer	$25,000
	Jane E. Perrin	38		
	Mary E. Perrin	18		
	James W. Perrin	17	Student	
	Emma C. Perrin	15		
	Hannah C. Perrin	14		
	William R. Perrin	12		
	Louis H. Perrin	10		
	Sarah E. Perrin	9		
	Thomas L. Perrin	5		
	Francis H. Perrin	3 (M)		
	George C. Perrin	6/12		
763.	Charles H. Allen	29	Editor	$3,000
	Catherine L. Allen	27	(Ga.)	
	James C. Allen	7		
	Eliza Allen	5		
	Eugene Allen	2		
	Dora Allen	2/12		
764.	James M. Perrin	27	Lawyer	$3,500
	Mary E. Perrin	20		
	Joel S. Perrin	4/12		
765.	Benjamin P. Hughes	38	Clerk	$4,000
	Jane C. Hughes	38		
766.	James Shillito	50	Tailor	$3,000
	Margaret M. Shillito	42		
	Elizabeth C. Shillito	16		
	William W. Shillito	15	Tinner's Apprentice	
	Mary A. Shillito	12		
	James A. Shillito	10		
	Julia A. Shillito	8		
	Hugh H. Shillito	6		
	George A. Shillito	4		
	William Alexander	21	Tailor (Ireland)	
767.	Agnes M. Kingsmore	56	England)	$2,000
	Clarage Kingsmore	27 (M)	Portrait Painter/M. D (Ga.)	
	Lizzy A. Courtright	18		
	Mary M. Kingsmore	14		
	Isaac Courtright	30	Tailor (N. J.)	
768.	Martha L. Pope	31		
	Jacob W. Pope	15	Student	
	Helen P. Pope	12		
	Marion Pope	10 (M)		
	Josephine Pope	7		
769.	Foster A. Deal	27	Coachmaker	$3,000
	Mary J. Deal	22		
	Marcus E. Deal	3		

1850 Federal Census

	Name	Age	Occupation	Value
	James E. Deal	1		
	Thomas Christian	23	Coachmaker	
	James L. Deal	22	Coachmaker	
	John W. Franks	20	Coachmaker	
770.	D. McNeil Turner	36	O. S. P. clergyman	
	Harriet D. Turner	29		
	Ann A. Turner	9		
	Fanny D. Turner	7		
	Stringfellow Turner	4		
	Rignell Turner	1		
	Thornton Turner	1/12		
	Joseph Hilhous	30	O. S. P. clergyman	
	Esther Hilhous	23		
	Benjamin Hilhous	26	Teacher	
771.	Martin Crawley	49	Coachmaker (Md.)	
	Eliza Crawley	49		
	Harriet H. Crawley	29	(Ga.)	
	Mary L. Crawley	16	(Ga.)	
	Henry C. Crawley	13	(Ga.)	
	Leroy H. Crawley	12	(Ga.)	
	Sarah LeSett	26	(Ga.)	
772.	Hiram T. Lawson	28	Farmer [N. Y.]	$3,000
	Frances Lawson	20 (F)	(N. Y.)	
	Sally G. Lawson	3	(N. Y.)	
773.	Andrew J. Weems	43	Farmer	$7,000
	Agnes E. Weems	37		
	Caroline O. Weems	17		
	John M. Weems	15	Student	
	William T. Weems	13		
	Lemuel C. Weems	11		
	Francis A. Weems	9 (M)		
	David J. Weems	3		
	Mary J. Weems	1		
	Joseph H. Norwood	12		
	Franklin H. Norwood	9		
	Agnes Weems	68		
	Sarah Paul	20		
774.	John E. Allen	24	Deputy Sheriff	$2,700
	Sarah A. Allen	23		
775.	Mary A. Frasier	77	Farmer (Va.)	$2,515
	Samuel Gilmer	51	Manager	
776.	Henry Darlington	34	Shoemaker (England)	
	Charlotte Darlington	31	(Ga.)	
	John T. Darlington	8		
	Henry M. Darlington	6		
	Joseph J. Darlington	2		
	John T. Wait	37	M. D.	
777.	Alexander J. Wier	33	Merchant	$3,700
	Susan M. Wier	18		

1850 Federal Census

778.	Thomas Jackson	50	Coachmaker (England)	
	Ann R. Jackson	25		
	John M. Jackson	24	Coachmaker	
	Humphrey R. Jackson	20	Coachmaker	
	Lewis E. Jackson	17	Farmer	
	Ellen G. Jackson	15		
	Mary E. Jackson	12		
779.	William A. Wardlaw	32	Merchant	$4,000
	Ivy Wardlaw	28		
	Arthur Wardlaw	5		
	Edward R. Wardlaw	3		
	David L. Wardlaw	6/12		
780.	John Davis	32	M. D.	$4,000
	Mary A. Davis	28		
	William Davis	8		
	Emma Davis	5		
781.	Lucian H. Lomax	28	Lawyer	$7,000
	Mary E. Lomax	22	(Va.)	
	Alice A. Lomax	4		
	James D. Lomax	1	(Va.)	
	Margaret Fains (?)	55		
	Eliza S. Harrison	30		
	Moses Bass	25	M. D.	
782.	Edward Noble	26	Lawyer	
	Mary M. Noble	21		
	Patrick Noble	1		
	Elizabeth B. Noble	18		
	Samuel B. Noble	12	Student	
783.	Thomas P. Spierin	53	Clerk of Court	
	Elizabeth Spierin	44		
	Leonidas Spierin	16	Clerk	
	Maria F. Spierin	15		
	Emma M. Spierin	14		
	Mirabeau C. Spierin	7		
	Claudia L. Spierin	6		
	Thomas P. Spierin	4		
	Eliza Spierin	50		
784.	Thomas Thomson	35	Lawyer (Scotland)	$7,050
	Eliza Thomson	27		
	Mary Thomson	10		
	John A. Thomson	7		
	Jane Thomson	5		
785.	Washington E. Archer	34	Livery Stable Helper	$1,600
	Eliza Archer	30		
	Thomas Archer	13		
	Eliza Archer	11		
	John Archer	9		
	Franklin Russel	20	Clerk	
786.	Silas Anderson	49	Hotel Keeper	$5,500

1850 Federal Census

	Name	Age	Occupation	Value
	Delora Anderson	40		
	James Hodges	15		
	Lewis Delock	27	Groc. Clerk	
787.	William M. Hughey	31	Grocer	$7,192
	Elizabeth J. Hughey	25		
	George Buchanan	21	Groc. Clerk	
788.	Annie McLaren	73	(Scotland)	
	Jannet McLaren	46	(Scotland)	
	John McLaren	36	Postmaster(Scot.)	$2,700
	John McBride	40	(Scotland)	
	John M. McBride	9		
	Robert J. McBride	7		
	Adolphus Williams	22	Clerk (Ga.)	
789.	David Lesley	51	Farmer	$6,000
	Louisa Lesley	47	(Penn.)	
	Eliza Kyle	36		
790.	James H. Tusten	49	Carpenter. (N. Y.)	$1,000
	Edna P. Tusten	46		
	Hiram T. Tusten	21	Silversmith	
	John L. Tusten	13		
	Martha Posey	65	(Maryland)	
	Wesley Posey	30	Farmer	
	Benjamin Posey	28		
	Benjamin W. Posey	1		
791.	Jordan A. Ramey	32	Steward/Poor H.	$2,000
	Jane A. Ramey	25		
	Lucinda Ramey	9		
	Jane E. Ramey	7		
	Lucius B. Ramey	5		
	Louisa M. Ramey	2		
	Ella Ramey	2/12		
	Samuel Benson	13	Pauper	
	Jordan Jenkins	9	Pauper	
	Absolom Campbell	60	Pauper	
	Robert Turnbulll	55	Pauper	
	William Day	40	Pauper	
	Betsy Love	80	Pauper	
	Mary Perry	70	Pauper	
	Sarah Kilpatrick	50	Pauper	
	Francis Franklin	8 M	Pauper (Ga.)	
792.	William L. Richey	30	Blacksmith	$2,132
	Mandina Richey	26		
	William M. Ellis	8		
	John V. Ellis	6		
	James B. Richey	3		
	Samuel C. Richey	1		
793.	Adison Posey	2		
	Florella Posey	21		
	James H. Posey	2		

1860 Federal Census

	Name	Age	Occupation	Value
	Benjamin L. Posey	22		
794.	Lewis Gillespie	36	Farmer	$2,040
	Jane Gillespie	74		
	Mary Gillespie	42		
	Jane Gillespie	40		

Census of 1860-Village of Abbeville
(Includes place of birth, if not S. C., and Real Estate & Personal Property values)

	Name	Age	Occupation	Value
287.	John Enright	42	Gin maker (Ireland)	10,000/7,500
	John R. Enright	5		
	Thos. G. Enright	3		
	Mary H. Enright	9		
	B-------	15	[F] (Ga.)	
	Thos. Enright	10	(Ga.)	
	Thomas Shehan	25	Gin maker (Ireland)	
	Wm. Thomas	30		
	Lewis Kernel	21		
288.	Susan DeBruhl	50		3,000/10,200
	Susan DeBruhl	24		
	Stephen DeBruhl	22	Attorney	/2,000
	Mary DeBruhl	12		
	Marshall DeBruhl	9		
	William Barkaloo	6		
289.	Jno. F. Livingston	56	Farmer	26,000/40,420
	Sarah Livingston	25		
290.	Mrs. Chloe Barksdale	53		/500
	Mary F. Barksdale	23		
	Susan M. Barksdale	19		
	William S. Barksdale	17		
	Jas. H. Barksdale	15		
291.	Louisa Lesley	55	Farmer	6,000/13,100
	Eliza Kyle	45		
	Andrew Kyle	21	Student Divinity (Ala.)	
292.	Mary C. Miller	48	Farmer	
	Geo. Miller	22		
	William Miller	22		
	Sarah C. Miller	21		
	Virginia Miller	20		
	Harriet Miller	18		
	Sarah Miller	17		
	Carrie Miller	14		
	Catherine Miller	12		
	Jane Miller	10		
	Nicholas Miller	7		
293.	Thomas C. Perrin	54	Pres.G&CRailroad	57,000/127,284
	Jane E. Perrin	42		
	Mary C. Perrin	27		

1860 Federal Census

	Name	Age	Occupation	Value
	Harriet C. Perrin	23		
	William Perrin	22	Student of Medicine	
	Sallie Perrin	19		
	Thos. Perrin	13		
	Geo. C. Perrin	10		
	Lewis W. Perrin	20		
294.	David L. Wardlaw	60	Judge	29,600/88,248
	Fannie Wardlaw	18		
295.	Thomas A. Hoyt	31	OSP Clergyman	9,000/40,000
	Mary H. Hoyt	25		
	M. H. Harrison	45		
	Mrs. M. A. Ellison	77		/20,000
	Mary H. Hoyt	8		
	David M. Hoyt	5		
	Anna L. Hoyt	3		
	Laura E. Hoyt	2		
296.	James Moore	62	Meth. Clergyman	2,000/5,000
	Ann H. Moore	60	(England)	
	Edwin Moore	18	Clerk	
297.	Jas. C. Calhoun	34	Attorney	8,000/11,500
	Mrs. M. Calhoun	29	(Mississippi)	
	Jas. A. Calhoun	6		
298.	Benj. P. Hughes	48	Merchant	9,000/26,000
	Jane C. Hughes	48		
	Wm. P. Hughes	10		
	Sarah Hughes	77		
299.	William A. Shillito	21	Farm laborer	
	Robt. J. White	25	Merchant	16,000/2,000
	Sallie A. White	22		
	John White	2/12		
300.	Jno. A. Allen	33	Merchant	8,500/23,900
	Frances C. Allen	28		
	Ida Allen	10		
	Ellis Allen	8		
	Charles Allen	5		
	Harriet Allen	3		
	Ione Allen	10/12		
	Mrs. Worrell	30	Dressmaker(New York)	
	Mary Lester	25	Milliner	
301.	Henry Allen	40	Merchant	/7,500
	Caroline Allen	38		
	Jas. C. Allen	17		
	Eliza Allen	14		
	Edward Allen	11		
	Dora Allen	10		
	Mary Allen	7		
	Edwin Allen	4		
	William Allen	2		
	Joseph Ruff	30	Merchant clerk(England)	

1860 Federal Census

302.	Dr. D. S. Benson	31	Physician	640/4,000
	Mary E. Benson	34		
	Thos. P. Benson	2		
	James W. Child	28	Merchant	/8,000
303.	William Hill	55	Ordinary (Ireland)	8,000/12,000
	Charles Cox	33	Carriage Maker (N. C.)	
	Ann E. Cox	23		
	Ella Cox	2		
	Ann H. Hill	53		
	Robert E. Hill	21	Merchant clerk	
	Sarah Hill	18		
	Sallie E. Hill	16		
	John Hill	11		
304.	Edwin Parker	37	Physician	6,000/30,000
	Eugenia C. Parker	34		
	Thomas Parker	10		
	Martha C. Parker	9	(Mississippi)	
	William C. Parker	5		
	Ellen L. Parker	3		
	Edwin Parker	9/12		
305.	Isaac Branch	59	Physician (Vermont)	3,000/20,000
	Frances Branch	52	(Vermont)	
	Louisa H. Branch	16		
	William T. Branch	15		
306.	D. R. Sondley	33	R.R. agent	3,000/5,960
	Mary F. Sondley	26		
	Geo. B. Sondley	5		
	Harriet R. Sondley	3		
	Jas. R. Sondley	5/12		
307.	Moses T. Owen	34	Jeweller	6,400/19,000
	Martha A. Owen	24		
	John F. Owen	24	Jeweller	/6,000
308.	Augustus J. Lythgoe	30	Merchant	4,000/10,000
	Mary J. Lythgoe	29		
	Mary Lythgoe	5		
	George Lythgoe	3		
	Harriet Lythgoe	1		
	Louisa Lythgoe	18		
309.	John A. Wier	43	Merchant (W. Indies)	7,000/20,000
	Sarah M. Wier	28		
	Kate Wier	8		
	John B. Wier	5		
	Jas. C. Wier	1		
	Saml. W. Fenlas	17	Merchant clerk	
310.	Matthew McDonald	40	Clerk Court	1,200/10,300
	Martha D. McDonald	33		
	William T. McDonald	14		
311.	Davis F. Jones	33	Attorney	3,000/
	Carrie Dawkins	18		

1860 Federal Census

	Name	Age	Occupation	Value
	Ann G. Roulllain	16		
	Theresa Roulllain	10		
	Susan Jones	14		
	T. Eliza Roullain	18		
	Eliza W. Jones	40		
312.	Jos. W. W. Marshall	38	Farmer	175,000/150,000
	Fannie A. Marshall	30		
	William S. Marshall	12		
	Francis Marshall	10		
	Eliza C. Marshall	8		
	Saml. S. Marshall	5		
	Mary L. Cochran	25		
	Lucy P. Wilson	21		
313.	John A. Hunter	45	Merchant	1,200/3,000
314.	Dinah Donalson	45	(mulatto)	
	Lucy Donalson	22	(mulatto)	
	Ann Donalson	3	(mulatto)	
	Caroline Donalson	16	(mulatto)	
	Robt. Donalson	14	(mulatto)	
	Caroline A. Donalson	8	(mulatto)	
315.	Robt. Jones	40	Merchant	1,200/5,000
	Mary Jones	30		
	Benjn. W. Jones	9		
	Jos. Y. Jones	7		
	Andw. W. Jones	3		
	Robt. Jones	1		
	Rebecca Davis	21		
316.	William H. Parker	31	Attorney	6,000/14,000
	Lucia G. Parker	26		
	Edward F. Parker	4/12		
	Mary E. Putnam	25	School teacher (Massachusetts)	
	Eliza S. Wright	19	(Massachusetts)	
317.	Robt. H. Wardlaw	53	Bank Agent	20,000/30,000
	Eliza Wardlaw	51		
	W. C. Wardlaw	22	Student of medicine	
	J. Langdon Wardlaw	21	Clerk	
	Robt. H. Wardlaw	19	Student	
	Frank Wardlaw	18	Student	
	D. A. Wardlaw	14		
	Thos. P. Wardlaw	12		
	Chas. C. Wardlaw	11		
318.	James Perrin	38	Attorney	27,000/55,000
	Kitty C. Perrin	28		
	James S. Perrin	10		
	Mary E. Perrin	7		
	Jane E. Perrin	4		
	Irene Perrin	1		
	Eliza C. Perrin	5/12		
319.	Robt. A. Fair	38	Attorney	4,000/4,000

1860 Federal Census

	Name	Age	Occupation	Value
	Mary A. Fair	33		
	James F. Fair	13		
	Ann Fair	10		
	Jno. Y. Fair	9		
	Thos. B. Crews	28	Publishes newspaper (N. C.)	/3,500
	Eugenia Crews	27		
	William Crews	3		
	Sarah Crews	1		
	Jas. W. Fowler	23	Merchant clerk	
	Cath. Fowler	17		
	Thomas McCaslan	23	School teacher	
320.	S. Henry Beard	26	Dentist (Virginia)	2,000/4,600
	Eliza T. Beard	22		
	W. H. Beard	2		
	Eliza A. Beard	2/12		
	Jas. Cromer	21	Farmer (Virginia)	
321.	S. Henry Jones	30	Master carpenter	2,700/8,000
	Sarah J. Jones	24		
	Robt. H. Jones	3		
322.	Andrew Small	44	Bookeeper (Scotland)	2,000/500
	Margt. Small	36	(Ireland)	
	John Small	18	Merchant's Clerk	
	Margaret Small	16		
	Louisa Small	15		
	Gertrude Small	12		
	Eva Small	5		
	Kate Small	8		
	Mary Small	2		
	Infant Small	1/12		
323.	O. J. Farrington	27	Tailor (New York)	2,500/1,000
	D. Anna Farrington	23	(New York)	
	Mary A. Farrington	5		
	Martha C. Farrington	3		
	Margt. Farrington	1		
324.	William M. Mooney	36	Joiner (Ireland)	1,400/1,400
	Mary Mooney	30	(Ireland)	
	Richd. Calkin	45	Joiner (Ireland)	
	Margt. A. Calkin	35	(Ireland)	
	Patrick O'Keefe	27	Boot & shoemaker (Ireland)	/6,200
	Ann O'Keefe	19	(Ireland)	
	Mary D. O'Keefe	1		
325.	Benjn. Johnson	36	Episcopal clergyman	/500
	Ann C. Johnson	23		
326.	Jehu F. Marshall	42	Attorney	128,700/188,005
	Eliza A. Marshall	33		
	William J. Marshall	16	College student	
	Saml. F. Marshall	14		
	John J. Marshall	12		
	J. Quitman Marshall	10		

1860 Federal Census

	Name	Age	Occupation	Value
	Ida D. Marshall	7		
	Mary F. Marshall	5		
	Ann Wiggins	45		
327.	Mrs. Mary Martin	50	Farmer	18,000/95,000
	Luther Martin	24	Student	
	John Martin	20		
	Thomas Martin	18		
	Sallie Martin	17		
	Stark Martin	15	Student	
	Junius Martin	13		/10,000
	Chisolm Martin	7		
	William Martin	5		
328.	Andrew Edwards	25	Overseer	
329.	Mrs. Elizh. Jones	70		/3,000
	Jane Jones	30		/2,000
	D. Young Jones	22		500/1,300
330.	Frank McCord	27	Butcher	/600
	Sarah C. McCord	26	(N. C.)	
	Lucy McCord	2		
	Ann McCord	1		
	Geo. Reeves	16		
331.	James H. Cobb	49	Merchant	5,100/13,500
	Rebecca C. Cobb	44		/30,000
	James E. Cobb	17	Silversmith	
	Augustus B. Cobb	15	Merchant clerk	
	Thos. H. D. Cobb	12		
	Geo. C. Cobb	9		
	William J. Cobb	6		
	Robt. Lisenben	28	Silversmith (N. C.)	
	William Robertson	23	Coach maker	
	Mrs. C. Zimmerman	60		/12,000
332.	John Coumbe	62	Brick mason (England)	/200
	Sarah Coumbe	51	(England)	
	Caroline Coumbe	14		
	Jno. F. Coumbe	12		
	Danl. B. Smith	28	Carpenter (Rhode Island)	
	Mary A. Smith	25	(England)	
333.	Dr. H. Thos. Lyon	28	Farmer	11,000/23,400
	Harriet Lyon	22		
	W. H. Lyon	1		
334.	Mrs. A. E. Dendy	48		8,000/18,000
	Sarah E. Dendy	29		
	Chas. N. Dendy	14		
335.	Geo. W. Syfan	36	R. R. Engineer	3,000/5,000
	Jno. C. Syfan	10		
	Eliza E. Syfan	3		
336.	Saml. McGowan	40	Attorney	8,400/65,000
	Sue C. McGowan	30		
	Samuel McGowan	4		

1860 Federal Census

	Name	Age	Occupation	Value
	Sue E. McGowan	2		
	Wm. C. McGowan	1		
	Alex. McGowan	25	Attorney	
337.	Edward Roche	38	Shoemaker (Ireland)	1,000/3,500
	Sarah A. Roche	26		
	Pat. A. Roche	4		
	Margt. Roche	2/12		
338.	Enoch Nelson	46	Farmer	12,000/60,000
	Lucy E. Nelson	29		
	Lucy A. Nelson	8		
	Donald McLaughlin	25	Druggist	/10,000
	Mrs. M. McLaughlin	20		
339.	Thomas McCord	25	Overseer	
	Mary McCord	18		
	James McCord	4/12		
	John McCord	4/12		
340.	Robt. A. Martin	52	Tailor	
	Frances Martin	28		
	Robt. A. Martin	8		
	Alexr. P. Martin	3/12		
341.	John G. Wilson	43	Merchant	3,500/1,000
	Sarah A. Wilson	30		
	Andrew Valentine	14	(Black)	
342.	Edward Noble	36	Attorney	9,000/20,000
	Martha Noble	28		
	Patrick Noble	12		
	B. Noble	8		
	Elizah. Noble	5		
	Floride Noble	1		
343.	Geo. C. Bowers	38	Carpenter	500/500
	Frances Bowers	32		
	William Bowers	9		
	Jane Bowers	6		
	John Bowers	3		
	Jas. Bowers	7/12		
344.	John White	53	Merchant	15,000/75,000
	Lucy W. White	52		
	Wm. White	24	Teacher	
	George White	20	Merchant clerk	
	Lucy White	17		
	Leonard White	15		
	Nancy White	13		
	Chas. White	12		
345.	Mrs. Elizah. Cobb	42	Hotel keeper	/4,300
	James Cobb	14		
	Robt. Chatham	22	College student	
	Jno. G. Baskin	38	Attorney	/3,000
	Moses Miles	28	Tinsmith	
	Hugh Wilson	21	Publishes newspaper	/10,000

1860 Federal Census

	Name	Age	Occupation	Value
	J. Bunyan Crawford	28		
	Michael Junkin	20	Painter	
	Nath. Knox	28	Merchant (Ireland)	/5,000
	Mary J. Knox	20		
	John Gray	30	Merchant (Scotland)	/3,500
	W. E. Camplin	40	Brick mason	
	Ann J. Camplin	30		
	Jno. Hodges	16	Painter	
346.	Andw. M. Hill	26	Farmer	/300
	Mary A. Hill	26		
	Richd. Hill	3		
	Jane Hill	2		
	Infant Hill	1/12		
347.	Ezekiel Tribble	51	Confectioner	/2,500
	Eliza Tribble	26		
	Lucy F. Tribble	21		
	Jesse Tribble	15	Printer	
	Jno. C. Tribble	3		
348.	Thos. M. Christian	32	Boot & shoemaker	/3,500
	Martha A. Christian	27		
	Emma Christian	1		
349.	W. C. Moore	26	Merchant	3,000/4,000
	Emily Moore	26		
	Mary Moore	1		
	Spencer	85 (M) (mulatto)		
350.	Philip S. Rutledge	46	Stage contractor	4,000/18,000
	Mary A. Rutledge	44		
	Benjn. C. Rutledge	18	Clerk	
	James Rutledge	17		
	Mary Rutledge	14		
	Ann Rutledge	13		
	Virginia Rutledge	10		
	Sarah Rutledge	7		
	W. Rutledge	5		
351.	Joseph T. Moore	36	Sheriff A. Dist.	10,000/8,000
	Eliza J. Moore	29		
	Louis C. Moore	10		
	Mary Moore	7		
	Henry Moore	5		
	Charles Moore	3		
	W. Moore	1/12		
	Rebecca Wilson	14		
352.	Henry S. Kerr	36	Merchant (N. C.)	/2,000
	Louisa Kerr	37		
	Ann Kerr	13		
	Caroline Kerr	11		
	Henry Wilson	6		
353.	E. White	49	Wagon maker	/300
	Eliza L. White	44		

1860 Federal Census

	Name	Age	Occupation	Value
	Mary C. White	15		
	Sarah M. White	10		
	Robt. N. White	9		
	Mary E. White	7		
	Jos. G. White	5		
	Infant White	1		
354.	Thomas Thomson	46	Attorney (Scotland)	22,250/68,000
	Mary M. Thomson	34		
	Mary Thomson	19		
	Jno. Thomson	16		
	Jane Thomson	14		
	C. Hollingsworth	13		
	Ninian Thomson	8		
	Mary Hollingsworth	7		
	Thos. Thomson	3		
	George Thomson	2		
355.	Jas. S. Cothran	30	Attorney	6,500/22,000
	Eliza C. Cothran	25		
	Rebecca C. Cothran	4		
	Thos. P. Cothran	2		
	Wade S. Cothran	6/12		
356.	Jos. J. Wardlaw	45	Physician	9,000/45,000
	Mary A. Wardlaw	40		
	Jas. W. Wardlaw	20	College student	
	Jos. C. Wardlaw	19	College student	
	Louis A. Wardlaw	16		
	Mary W. Wardlaw	14		
	Nannie F. Wardlaw	10		
	Julia D. Wardlaw	7		
	Frances E. Wardlaw	4		
	J. G. Wardlaw	1 (M)		
	Mary F. Sadler	15		
	Mary M. McCan	16		
	Geo. C. Graves	15		
357.	John McLaren	45	Farmer (Scotland)	60,000/33,000
	Jno. McBryde	50	Comn. Merchant (Scotland)	
	Adolphus Williams	25	Merchant (Ga.)	
	Jane McLaren	58	(Scotland)	
	Jno. McBryde	19	College student	
	Robt. McBryde	16		
358.	Johnson Ramey	52	Hotel keeper	/500
	Lucretia Ramey	52		
	Jane Ramey	18		
	Eliza Ramey	15		
	Jas. D. Chalmers	27	Monument dealer	250/11,700
	Chois Chalmers	27		
	Ann Chalmers	2		
	John Allen	50	Letter cutter marble (New York)	
	John G. Edwards	25	Merchant	

1860 Federal Census

	Name	Age	Occupation	Value
	William C. Davis	29	Editor & lawyer	
	W. A. Lee	29	Editor & lawyer	/8,000
	M. Israel	26	Merchant (Poland)	/17,000
	Rebecca Israel	20	(Florida)	
	Judith Elias	8		
	Jno. Knox	35	Merchant (Ireland)	/5,000
	Robt. Knox	19	Clerk	
	J. Townes Robinson	25	Merchant	
	Thos. Robertson	20	Clerk	
	James T. Mabry	35	Physician	/6,000
	Lew. H. Russell	27	Livery Stable	500/7,300
	C. F. Quaife	30	Merchant (New York)	/3,000
	Jos. D. Daly	40	Architect (Ireland)	
	Edward S. Cuthbert	23	Plasterer (Ireland)	
	Warren Richey	25	R. R. agent	3,500/4,500
	August Bernelle	30	Teacher French (France)	
	Jno. McLaughlin	20	Clerk (No. Ca.)	
	Lewis Speares	19	Marble cutter	/1,200
	William Lockey	20	Plasterer (England)	
	Lewis Davis	23	Teacher	/2,500
359.	Benj. M. Winstock	26	Merchant (Poland)	4,400/28,000
	J Winstock (F)	24	(Poland)	
	J. W. Winstock	2		
	I. H. Winstock	4/12		
	Saml. A. Winstock	26	Merchant (Poland)	
	L. P. Winstock	2		
	M. Winstock	6/12		
	M. Rosenland	38	(Poland)	
	M. Brylaski	20	Merchant clerk (Poland)	
360.	Hiram W. Lawson	38	Tinner (New York)	3,600/12,000
	Frances J. Lawson	31		
	Lucy W. Lawson	10		
	Hiram W. Lawson	7		
	Jas. W. Lawson	3		
	Jas. S. Shillito	19	Tinner	
	Benjn. McLaughlin	21	Druggist	
361.	Jas. A. Wardlaw	26	Farmer	2,000/8,000
	Eliz. S. Wardlaw	23		
	Ella Wardlaw	2/12		
362.	Henry A. Jones	40	Attorney	40,000/75,000
	Sarah F. Jones	16		
	Eliza M. Jones	17		
363.	W. R. Buchanan	29	Cabinet maker (N. C.)	/2,500
	Mary R. Buchanan	28		
364.	Edwin J. Taylor	35	Coach maker (Mass.)	4,000-/3,000
	Ann S. Taylor	31	(Conn.)	
	Chas. Taylor	10		
	Kate Taylor	6		
	Frances Taylor	3		

1860 Federal Census

	Name	Age	Occupation	Wealth
	James Blackman	35	Carriage maker (N. C.)	
	Jos. Z. Blackman	30	Carriage maker (N. C.)	
	Robt. Gordon	22		
	Jno. Aulders	34	Painter (England)	
365.	Andrew Simonds	30	Bank President	9,000/100,000
	Sallie Simonds	21		
366.	Barney O'Connor	46	Bricklayer (Ireland)	2,000/1,075
	Harriet P. O'Connor	46		
367.	John Conner	26	Bricklayer (Ireland)	800/1,000
	Margt. Conner	24	Ireland	
	Thos. Conner	10/12		
368.	James Shillito	59	Tailor	1,500/1,200
	Mary M. Shillito	51		
	Jane A. Shillito	17		
	Henry H. Shillito	13		
	Geo. A. Shillito	11		
	Jno. Shillito	9		
	Wm. T. Penney	22	Merchant clerk	/1,200
	Mary A. Penney	20		
	Patrick Owens	27	Tailor (Ireland)	
	Saml. Harris	20	Clerk	
369.	Edward Westfield	34	Saddler (Ireland)	1,800/8,000
	Sarah J. Westfield	26		
	Eugene V. Westfield	4		
	Richd. D. Westfield	2		
370.	Carrie Russell	35	Mantua maker	/500
	Dora Williams	13		
371.	Wm. N. Knox	37	Blacksmith (Ireland)	500/2,000
	Rachel Knox	37		
	Martha Barrett	7	(Ireland)	
	Jack Donelson	47	(black) Blacksmith	
372.	Jno. W. North	37	Meth. Clergyman	/2,300
	Mary I. North	21		
	Jno. W. North	4		
	Sarah I. North	2		
	Wm. B. North	1		
	Milledge	15	(black)	
373.	Chas. Wrifford	37	Master carpenter (New Jersey)	/500
	Martha Wrifford	28	(Pa.)	
	Martha H. Wrifford	7	(New York)	
	Chas. Wrifford	4	(Pa.)	
	Mary Wrifford	2	(Pa.)	
374.	W. M. Hughey	41	Hotel keeper	4,000/19,125
	Eliza J. Hughey	35		
	M. E. Buchanan	17 (F.)		
	Andrew Paul	34	Physician	
	Fred. Ives	45	Tailor (England)	
	Saml. McGill	22	House Painter (Ireland)	
	John Ligon	21	Merchant clerk	

1860 Federal Census

	Name	Age	Occupation	Value
	Fred. H. Cowner	49	Master carpenter (Pa.)	
	Harriet H. Cownor	41	(Pa.)	
	Saml. A. Henry	22	Carpenter (Pa.)	
	Wm B. Bates	24	Carpenter (Pa.)	
	Jno W. Syme	22	Carpenter (Pa.)	
	Richd. C. Stair	47	Merchant clerk (Ga.)	
	Chas. Scanling	33	Carpenter (Pa.)	
375.	And. B. Hamblin	19	Hotel keeper (N. C.)	4,125/5,000
	Deborah Hamblin	33		
	And. Murrell	25	House Painter (N. C.)	
	Pat Hazzard	33	Stone cutter (Ireland)	
	Allen Lee	23	(mulatto) Barber	
	John Marion	25	Wagoner	
376.	John H. Wilson	55	Attorney	8,000/28,000
	Robt. Bowie	23	Attorney	
	Allen Greer	40	(mulatto) Carpenter	/160
	Mary Greer	38	(mulatto)	
	Dot N. Greer	4	(mulatto)	
	____ Greer	3	(mulatto)	
	____ Greer	2	(mulatto)	
	____ Greer	1	(mulatto)	
	Mary Bug	27	(mulatto) Farm laborer	/25
	____ Bug	4	(mulatto)	
	____ Bug	2	(mulatto)	
	Martha Bug	35	(mulatto) Farm laborer	
	____ Bug	10	(mulatto)	
	____ Bug	8	(mulatto)	
	Lucy Bug	25	(mulatto) Day laborer	
	____ Bug	2	(mulatto)	
	Ben Greer	20	(mulatto)	
	Martha Greer	18	(mulatto)	
	John Greer	30	(mulatto) Carpenter	/100

[M] indicates Male. [F] indicates Female.

XXXIV. ABBEVILLE TOWN OFFICERS, 1833-1989

This list of the Abbeville town officers from its incorporation has been compiled mainly from newspaper files and is as complete as possible.

Year	Intendent (Mayor)	Wardens (Aldermen)
1833	Moses Taggart	
1838-39	John A. Hunter	Franklin Branch, Samuel Branch, James A. Creight, John C. Kingsmore
1839-40	Thomas C. Perrin	
1844-46	J. F. Livingston	Isaac branch, Joseph Hamilton, David Lesley, A. F. Posey
1846-48	John A. Hunter	T. B. Dendy, Johnson Ramey, W. A. Wardlaw, John H. Wilson
1848-49	J. F. Livingston	Isaac Branch, Augustus Hamilton, David Lesley, A. F. Posey
1852-53	J. F. Marshall	John A. Hunter, John McLaren, J. J. Martin, Edward Noble
1853-55	R. H. Wardlaw	John A. Allen, John Enright, B. P. Hughes, H. W. Lawson
1855-56	Samuel McGowan	James A. Cobb, J. W. W. Marshall, John A. Wier, John H. Wilson
1856-57	John G. Wilson	R. A. Fair, J. A. Hunter, M. T. Owen, H. T. Tusten
1857-58	John G. Wilson	J. A. Hunter, S. McGowan, J. F. Marshall, Thomas Thomson
1858-59	W. C. Davis	Edmund Cobb, Robt. Jones, A. J. Lythgoe, Jno. H. Wilson
1859-60	Robert A. Fair	H. W. Lawson, Matthew McDonald, Wm. H. Parker, James M. Perrin
1860-61	D. F. Jones	Jas. S. Cothran, John Enright, Jos. T. Moore, Edward Westfield
1861-62	John F. Livingston	James S. Allen, Benjamin P. Hughes, Augustus J. Lythgoe, John White
1862-63	Armistead Burt	
1865-66	J. S. Cothran	
1866-67	Robert Jones	
1867-68	Robert Jones	Jas. D. Chalmers, John Enright, Jos. T. Moore, Enoch Nelson
1868-69	Robert Jones	Jas. D. Chalmers, J. F. C. DuPre, John Enright, Jos. T. Moore (Jones was replaced by W. H. Parker by Feb., 1869)
1869-70	W. H. Parker	
1870-71	C. W. Guffin	Snowden Brown, Jerry Hollinshead, Samuel Johnson, Henry Titus
1871-72	J. F. C. DuPre	Snowden Brown, T. M. Christian, R. R. Hemphill, Henry Titus
1872-73	L. D. Bowie	T. M. Christian, Thomas Darracott,

Town Officers

	Isaac Kennedy, Mortimer Sanders
1873-74	**L. D. Bowie** T. M. Christian, Thomas Darracott, Isaac Kennedy, W. H. Shives
1874-76	**Robert Jones** T. M. Christian, Isaac Kennedy, Wm. Pope, Wm. H. Shives
1876-78	**W. H. Parker** A. Bequest, J. F. C. DuPre, T. P. Quarles, John W. Sign
1878-81	**H. T. Tusten** S. A. Brazele, Jacob Kurz, W. P. Penny, T. P. Quarles
1881-82	**J. W. Perrin** J. S. Hammond, A. M. Hill, T. P. Quarles, T. C. Seal
1882-84	**E. G. Graydon** W. T. Branch, J. S. Hammond, R. E. Hill, A. W. Jones
1884-86	**J. S. Hammond** T. P. Cothran, G. A. Douglass, H. P. McIlwaine, Jones F. Miller
1886-88	**W. C. McGowan** R. W. Cannon, Thomas McGettigan, Jones F. Miller, T. C. Perrin
1888-90	**Thos. P. Thomson** F. B. Gary, F. Henry, Jones F. Miller, J. W. Sign
1890-91	**A. W. Smith** S. C. Cason, T. P. Cothran, Jones F. Miller, T. C. Seal
1891-92	**A. W. Smith** T. P. Cothran, J. H. DuPre, Jones F. Miller, S. G. Thomson
1892-93	**R. M. Hill** James Chalmers, J. H. Latimer, J. F. Miller, S. G. Thomson
1893-94	**R. M. Hill** James Chalmers, E. B. Gary, J. C. Klugh, James Taggart
1894-95	**R. M. Hill** James Chalmers, J. E. Corrie, J. C. Klugh, James Taggart
1895-97	**R. M. Hill** Julius H. DuPre, Jno. G. Edwards, Jones F. Miller, Amos B. Morse
1896-98	James Chalmers, A. Cohen, J. C. Ellis, James Taggart
1897-99	**R. M. Hill** W. S. Cothran, J. L. McMillan, J. F. Miller, L. H. Russell
1898-1900	**J. F. Miller** J. C. Ellis, Francis Henry, L. T. Miller, G. A. Neuffer (J. M. Gambrell & A. B. Reader for 1 year terms)
1899-1901	C. D. Brown, W. S. Cothran, J. M. Gambrell, A. B. Reader
1900-02	**S. G. Thomson** Julius H. DuPre, J. M. Harden, J. S. Stark, E. A. Thomson
1901-03	J. M. Gambrell, C. A. Haigler, J. E. McDavid, C. A. Milford
1902-04	**J. L. McMillan** J. H. DuPre, J. M. Harden, Albert Henry, E. A. Thomson
1903-05	J. S. Cothran, C. A. Haigler, James A. Hill, W. Hampton Jones
1904-06	**J. L. McMillan** A. G. Faulkner, Albert Henry, L. T. Miller, W. H. White
1905-07	R. W. Cannon (W. H. Jones), C. A. Haigler, G. A. Neuffer, E. A. Thomson
1906-08	**R. W. Cannon** J. R. Glenn, Albert Henry, L. T. Miller, W. H. White
1907-09	J. C. Ellis, W. H. Jones, G. A. Neuffer, H. G. Smith

Town Officers

1908-10	**J. L. McMillan**	C. C. Gambrell, Albert Henry, L. T. Miller, W. H. White
1909-11		J. R. Glenn, J. M. Lawson, G. A. Neuffer, H. G. Smith
1910-12	**J. E. Jones**	C. C. Gambrell, Albert Henry, L. T. Miller, W. H. White
1911-13		J. R. Glenn, C. A. Haigler, J.. M. Lawson, G. A. Neuffer
1912-14	**C. C. Gambrell**	J. S. Cochran, Albert Henry, Geo. Shirley, M. B. Syfan, M. B. Reese
1913-15		J. R. Glenn, C. A. Haigler, L. T. Miller, G. A. Neuffer
1914-16	**C. C. Gambrell**	J. S. Cochran, Albert Henry, G. W. Shirley, M. B. Syfan
1915-17		T. C. Beaudrot, G. W. Godfrey, J. Allen Long, G. A. Neuffer, (short term) T. M. Miller, J. E. Pressly
1916-18	**C. C. Gambrell**	Albert Henry, J. E. Pressly, M. B. Syfan, H. B. Wilson, (short term) W. M. Blanchett, J. R. Nickles
1917-19		W. M. Blanchett, Ben Cochran, J. R. Nickles, M. B. Reese, (short term) Otto Bristow
1918-20	**J. Moore Mars**	Otto Bristow, Albert Henry, M. B. Syfan, H. B. Wilson, (short term) C. L. Evans, W. M. Langley
1919-21		W. M. Langley, T. M. Miller, M. B. Reese, C. L. Evans
1920-22	**J. Moore Mars**	Otto Bristow, Albert Henry, M. B. Syfan, H. B. Wilson
1921-23		C. L. Evans, W. M. Langley, T. M. Miller, M. B. Reese
1922-24	**J. Moore Mars**	J. S. Cochran, J. M. Gambrell, M. B. Syfan, E. R. Thomson
1923-25		E. W. Gregory, W. M. Langley, M. B. Reese, Harry B. Wilson
1924-26	**J. Moore Mars**	J. S. Cochran, W. M. Langley, M. B. Syfan, E. R. Thomson
1925-27		Ben T. Cochran, W. M. Langley, M. B. Reese, H. B. Wilson
1926-28	**J. Moore Mars**	J. S. Cochran, J. M. Gambrell, M. B. Syfan, E. R. Thomson
1927-29		W. M. Langley, J. S. Morse, J. A. Ramey, H. B. Wilson
1928-30	**J. Moore Mars**	J. S. Cochran, C. D. Jackson, M. B. Syfan, E. R. Thomson
1929-31		Prue Blanchett, W. M. Langley, Joel S. Morse, J. A. Ramey
1930-32	**J. Moore Mars**	Jas. S. Cochran, Robert Greene, M. B. Syfan, E. R. Thomson
1931-33		Prue Blanchett, W. M. Langley, Joel S. Morse, J. A. Ramey
1932-34	**J. Moore Mars**	J. S. Cochran, R. H. Greene, W. Joel Smith, E. R. Thomson
1933-35		M. P. Blanchett, W. M. Langley, J. S. Morse, J. A. Ramey
1934-36	**J. Moore Mars**	(resigned Jan., 1935) J. N. Blum, R. H. Greene, Marshall Leach, W. Joel Smith
1935-37	**J. Allen Long**	(one year term) M. P. Blanchett, W. M. Langley, Joel S. Morse, Jordan A. Ramey
1936-38	**J. Allen Long**	W. B. Godfrey, Percy J. Leach, Watson Norrell, W. Joel Smith
1937-39		M. P. Blanchett, W. M. Langley, Joel S. Morse, Jordan A. Ramey
1938-40	**J. Allen Long**	John T. Evans, Percy J. Leach, W. Joel Smith, J. H. Whaley

Town Officers

1939-41	M. P. Blanchett, W. M. Langley, Joel S. Morse, E. Raymond Wilson
1940-42	**Fred D. West** John T. Evans, Percy J. Leach, L. Reese, L. E. Starnes
1941-43	M. P. Blanchett, Joel S. Morse, W. O. Sutherland, E. Raymond Wilson
1942-44	**Fred D. West** G. Alex Hagen, F. L. Reese, A. D. Simpson, Langdon H. Wilson
1943-45	Joe L. Edwards, W. B. Godfrey, Joel S. Morse, E. Raymond Wilson
1944-46	**Fred D. West** M. P. Blanchett, Fuller L. Reese, A. D. Simpson, Langdon H. Wilson
1945-47	W. T. Hughes, Albert A. Morse, Joe Savitz, E. R. Wilson
1946-48	**J. M. Nickles** W. T. Hughes, J. W. Martin, A. D. Simpson, M. W. Walker
1947-49	G. Alex Hagen, Roy Ransom (resigned and replaced by Henry G. Harris in Nov., 1948), Fuller L. Reese, Walton M. Stephens
1948-50	**Fred D. West** W. T. Hughes, R. K. McKenzie (resigned June, 1949 and replaced by S. E. Ligon in July), D. L. Moss (resigned June, 1949 and replaced by T. V. Howie in August), F. B. Swetenburg
1949-51	Vivian Creswell, G. Alex Hagen, Fuller L. Reese, Walton M. Stephens
1950-52	**J. A. Verchot** J. E. McCann, James M. Mann, A. D. Simpson, T. F. Stanfield(resigned February, 1951 and replaced by Cecil McMahan)
1951-53	S. E. Ligon, R. F. Manning, Fuller Reese, D. E. Simmons(Reese and Simmons replaced by R. M. Clark and Joe Hughes in April, 1952)
1952-54	**Henry G. Harris** D. C. Lewis, Cecil McMahan, James M. Mann, A. D. Simpson
1953-55	R. M. Clark, Joe Hughes, S. E. Ligon, Ed Thomas
1954-56	**J. A. Verchot** J. O. Glenn, James A. Lander, Grace H. Rogers, Willis Timms
1955-57	Wiley T. Coleman, Joe W. Hughes, S. E. Ligon, Ed Thomas
1956-58	**Henry G. Harris** Coy Argo, John Allen Free, H. A. Hanks, Ernest Purser
1957-59	Wiley T. Coleman (replaced by J. O.Glenn in 1958), Joe Hughes, S. E. Ligon, Ed Thomas
1958-60	**Joe L. Savitz, Sr.** Jack D. Farmer, John Allen Free, William (Unk) Hall, Harry L. Horton
1959-61	James O. Glenn, Joe W. Hughes, S. E. Ligon, Ed Thomas
1960-62	**Joe L. Savitz, Sr.** Stuart B. Copeland, Jack D. Farmer, William (Unk) Hall, Harry L. Horton
1961-63	Coy Argo (for unexpired term of William Hall), Gene Garrett, James O. Glenn, John W. Harrington, Joe W. Hughes
1962-64	**Joe L. Savitz, Sr.** Coy H. Argo, Stuart B. Copeland, Jack D. Farmer, Harry L. Horton
1963-65	Gene Garrett, J. C. Porter (replaced by Hugh A. Williams in 1964), Ernest R.Purser, James D. Selvey (replaced by T. Donald Sherard in 1964)
1964-66	**Joe L. Savitz, Sr.** Stuart B. Copeland, Jack D. Farmer, Harry L. Horton, James W. (Pete) Smith
1965-67	Gene Garrett, Ernest R. Purser, T. Donald Sherard, Hugh A. Williams
1966-68	**Joe L. Savitz, Sr.** Jack D. Farmer, James W. Knox, Jr., Harry L. Horton, James W. (Pete) Smith

Town Officers

1967-69	Gene Garrett, Ernest R. Purser, T. Donald Sherard, Hugh A. Williams
1968-70	**Joe L. Savitz, Sr.** Jack D. Farmer, James W. Knox, Jr., Harry L. Horton, James W. (Pete) Smith
1969-71	Gene Garrett, W. F. (Teto) Nickles, III, Hugh A. Williams
1970-72	**Joe L. Savitz, Sr.** Jack D. Farmer, Walter L. Sizemore, James W. (Pete) Smith, Ed Thomas
1971-73	Rayford P. Hodges, S. E. Ligon, Bradley A. McCord, W. F. (Teto) Nickles, III
1972-74	**E. L. Thomas** Jack D. Farmer, Mrs. O. H. (Marilyn) Reid, Walter Sizemore, James W. (Pete) Smith
1973-75	Lindsay Baker, Rayford P. Hodges, Bradley A. McCord, Leland S. Scott
1974-76	**J. W.(Pete) Smith** Duncan D. Carmichael, Walter C. Jennings, J. Rivers Mabry, Jr., Joe L. Savitz, Jr.
1975-77	James E. (Jimmy) Davis, Jr., Bradley A. McCord, Leland Scott, Robert M. Strickland
1976-78	**E. Hilliard Thomas** Duncan D. Carmichael, Jack D. Farmer, Legare Kizer, Eugene W.(Gene) Smith
1977-79	Bradley A. McCord, Leland Scott, James W. (Pete) Smith, Robert M. Strickland
1978-80	**J. W.(Pete) Smith** Duncan D. Carmichael, Jack D. Farmer, Legare Kizer, Spencer Phillips, Bradley A. McCord, Eugene W. (Gene) Smith, Robert M. Strickland
1980-82	**J. W.(Pete) Smith** Jack D. Farmer, Bobby R. Fisher, Pat Hodge, Legare Kizer, Spencer Phillips, Robert M. Strickland, Charles R. Williams
1982-84	**J. E.(Jimmy) Davis** Bobby Bailey, Sr., Jack D. Farmer, Edward P. (Buddy) Newell, Archie Nixon, Eugene W. (Gene) Smith, Robert M. Strickland, Charles R. Williams
1984-86	**J. E.(Jimmy)Davis** Bobby R. Fisher, Jack D. Farmer, Steven S. Hawthorne, Buddy Newell, Archie Nixon, Gene Smith, Charles R. Williams
1986-89	**Joe L. Savitz, Jr.** Jack D. Farmer, Bobby R. Fisher, Edward P. (Buddy) Newell (replaced by Steven Hawthorne in 1987), Brent A. Smith, Spencer Sorrow, Robert M. Strickland (replaced by Frankie Allen in 1988), Charles R. Williams
1989-	**Joe L. Savitz, Jr.** Frankie Allen, Jack D. Farmer, Bobby Fisher, Fred Peeler, James (J. J.) Robinson, Spencer Sorrow, James Thomas, Lee Williams

Abbeville Postmasters

John Bowie, July 1, 1795	George Dusenberry, April 4, 1867
James Wardlaw, July 1, 1796	Hiram W. Lawson, Sept. 9, 1868
William Hamilton, April 1, 1800	Frank H. Green, June 28, 1869
Moses Taggart, October 1, 1802	Thos. H. Williamson, July 26, 1869
John McLaren, Jr., June 21, 1831	Hiram W. Lawson, October 26, 1869
L. H. Russell, September 26, 1865	Mrs. F. J. Lawson, April 18, 1881
H. W. Lawson, October 24, 1865	Thomas Tolbert, June 11, 1889
Theo. L. Ransom, August 20, 1866	Robt. S. Link, January 15, 1895
Mrs. Eliza F. Wood, December 3, 1866	Thomas Tolbert, June 29, 1906

Sources on Abbeville History

Frederic Minshall, December 16, 1910
Rachel Minshall, March 11, 1912
J. R. Tolbert, August 15, 1921
Ralph W. Adams, June 24, 1930
C. Lamar Richey, December 31, 1934
C. C. Stewart, 1945
John T. Mabry, December 1, 1954
William R. Powell, Sept. 11, 1976

Sources on Abbeville History

Although most of the public records of Abbeville were burned, the extant Probate Court and Equity Court records are particularly valuable for family history. The original probate records are found in the Abbeville Court House, and microfilm copies of the equity records are available at the Abbeville County Library. Microfilm copies of both sets of records are available at the South Carolina Department of Archives and History where the original equity records are found.

The scarcity of public records means that the most important sources of information about the history of Abbeville are the files of the local papers. The earliest local paper was *The Abbeville Whig or Southern Nullifier*, and the only known surviving issues are a half dozen found in the R. M. Cooper Library at Clemson University. The Abbeville *Banner* was founded in 1844 and *The Independent Press* began in 1854. Both of these papers were suspended during the Civil War and resumed after the war and merged into the *Press & Banner*. *Microfilm copies of* the files of these papers are available at Erskine College, Lander College, and the South Caroliniana Library in Columbia. The South Caroliniana Library also has a file of the *Abbeville Medium* which dates from 1871, and microfilm copies can be found at Erskine College and Lander College.

Unfortunately, few large manuscript collections of private papers were preserved by Abbevillians. Perhaps the best are found at the Perkins Libary at Duke University where the Armistead Burt, Thomas Chiles Perrin, and Hemphill family papers were located about half a century ago. Smaller collections of the papers of such local families as the McGowans are located at the South Caroliniana Library. Despite the scarcity of family papers, there are happily a number of good family histories such as those of the Perrin and Wardlaw families.

Index

Abbeville Hotel, 66, 187, 197
Abbeville Vigilance Committee, 52
Abbeville Whig & Southern Nullifier, 3, 28
Adams, Harriett, 188
    Jesse, 54-57
    Ralph W., 236
    Robert, 188
    T. W., 183
Agnew, Dr. Enoch, 51
    J. E., 183
    John E., 201
    R. E., 183
    Samuel, 51
Aichel, Oscar, 73
Aiken, D. Wyatt, 134, 152
    Thomas, 198
Alexander, Mr., 66
    John & Co., 73
    William, 215
Alford, Pamelia, 4
Allen, Mrs., 51, 124, 187
    Caroline, 220
    Catherine L., 215
    Charles, 220
    Charles Dendy, 183, 191
    Chas. H., 21, 80, 179, 215
    Dora, 215, 220
    Edward, 220
    Edwin, 220
    Eliza, 215, 220
    Ellis, 220
    Eugene, 215
    Fannie, 190, 191
    Frances C., 220
    Frances E., 214
    Frankie, 235(2)
    Harriet, 220
    Hattie, 190, 200
    Henry, 26, 220
    Ida , 215, 220
    Ida Dendy, 190
    Ione, 212, 220
    James Albert, 190, 191, 214
    James Clark, 80, 92, 179, 215, 220
    James S., 231
    Jane, 191
    Jane L., 4, 8, 10, 212
    John, 179, 227
    John A., 2, 10, 14, 25, 26, 27, 67, 179, 220, 231
    John E., 57, 216
    Louisa J., 212
    Mary, 220
    Mary Elise, 190
    Rosa, 191
    Sarah A., 216
    Thomas W., 212
    Warren, 179
    William, 220
    William A., 212
Alston Corner, 9, 128
Alston, Betsy, 6
    Catherine, 25, 29, 213
    James, 4, 9, 13, 21, 34, 35, 36, 57, 197, 213
Ammen, Blanche, 175
    Marcus, 110, 174, 175-176
Amos, Rev. Thos, 163, 165-167
Anderson, Mr., 23
    Delora, 218
    John, 213
    Robert, 23
    Silas, 30-32, 71, 197, 217
Andy, a slave of A. Lites, 50
Archer, Mrs., 9
    Eliza, 190, 218
    Eliza (II), 218
    Fannie E., 190
    John, 216
    Robert A., 190
    Thomas, 218
    Washington E., 218
Ard, Mr., 59
Argo, Coy H., 234 (3)
Arnold, Dr. A. B., 26, 44-45, 199
Aron, Thomas (?), 2
Arsenal, 2, 4, 19-20, 27
Arthur, Thos. S., 71
Artists, 173-176
Asa, a slave of T. E. Owen, 51
Ashley, Lawrence, 159
Atkins, Emily J., 201
    Martha, 199
Atkison, Wm., 4
Auerbach, Chas., 142-144, 183
Aulders, Jno., 229
Auslander, Joseph, 178
Austin, a slave of Mrs. Allen, 51

Bacon, George, 188
Bailey, Bobby, Sr., 235

Index

Baker, Mrs., 33
  Alpheus, 9, 13, 25, 26, 34, 40, 55, 57
  Ames, 179
  Daniel, 40-41
  John, 73
  Lindsay, 235
  Wm., 4
Banks, Samuel, 141
Barfield, R. B., 188
Barkaloo (Barcolow), Wally, 84, 219
Barksdale, Chloe, 219
  Jas. H., 219
  Mary F., 219
  Susan, 219
  W. D., 61, 167, 219
Barnes, Jane T., 203
Barnett, J. W., 74
  John Jack, 7
Barnwell & Co., 127, 128
  B. S., 183, 188
  B. W., 133
Barr, Dr., 13, 30
  George, 164
Barrett, Martha, 229
Baseball, 136-137
Baskin, J. Gamble, 179
  John G., 212, 225
Bass, Andrew, 179
  Moses, 217
Bates, Wm. B., 230
Baxter, Elvira, 199
Beacham, B. K., 183
  D. K., 188
Beard, Eliza A., 223
  Eliza T., 223
  James, 22, 23
  S. Henry, 179, 223
  Virginia Elizabeth, 208
  W. H., 223
Beaudrot, T. C., 233
Beggs, Thomas, 183
Belcher, Harry S., 199
  Kerr, 199
  William W., 179
Bell, Mr., 19
  Ella, 191
  Jennie A., 201
  William E., 183, 188, 199
Benedict, Arthur, 142-144, 183
Benet, W. Christie, 60, 136, 144, 183
Benjamin, Judah P., 78, 80, 107, 113, 114
Benson, D. S., 179, 221
  Mary E., 221
  Samuel, 218
  Thos. P., 221
Bequest, A., 232
Bergin, Joe, 179
Berneau, R. C., 188
Bernelle, August, 59, 70, 211, 228
Bickerstaff, Lieut., 117
Black, George R., 115
  W. C., 4, 28, 29
Blackburn, Mary C., 202
Blackman, James, 229
  Jos. Z., 229
Blake, John R., 175
Blanchett, J. J., 150
  M. P., 233 (5), 234 (3)
  W. M., 233 (2)
Blease & Baxter, 72
Blease, Coleman L., 119
Block House, 8, 21-23, 174
Blum, J. N., 233
Blythe, Solicitor, 128, 129, 130
Boarman, Annie Lee, 199
Bonham, Amanda Wardlaw, 12, 13
  M. L., 75, 183
Boozer, Annie, 137
Boshell (Bochelle), Dr., 9, 44
Bowers, Frances, 225
  Geo. C., 225
  Godfrey C., 179
  Jane, 225
  Jas., 225
  John, 225
  William, 225
Bowie, Mr., 125
  Alexander, 2, 11, 24, 26
  Andr., 8
  Annie K., 199
  Eliza Ayer, 191
  Eliza E., 6
  George, 24
  James A., 191, 194
  Jas. S., 12, 13, 28, 29
  John, 1, 6, 12, 27, 235
  L. K., 183
  Langdon, 13, 28, 29
  Louis D., 125, 199, 230 (2)
  Mary Jane, 199
  Nancy Jane, 191
  R. E., 179
  Rena, 131
  Robt., 230
  Saml. W., 12, 15
Boyce, Dr., 176

Index

Jessie, 153
Boyd, James Wash, 199
Boyle, Hal, 177
Bradley, D. F., 183
  Ella E., 207
  Jerry, 183
  W. O., 183
  W. Renwick, 160
Bragg, Braxton, 98, 100, 101, 103
Branch, Mrs., 137
  Annie C., 191, 199
  Elizabeth Wilson, 198
  Fannie (Fanny), 191, 211
  Frances, 221
  Franklin, 4, 27, 29, 54, 198, 231
  Isaac, 2, 4, 5, 25, 27, 29, 30, 31-32,
    48, 49, 54, 116, 179, 191, 198,
    210, 221, 231 (2)
  "Aunt" Jinny, 49
  John, 57
  Louisa H., 191, 210, 221
  Mary Ann, 198
  Mary L., 211
  Samuel, 2, 4, 17, 25, 27, 50, 54-57,
    198, 231
  Sarah, 198
  William Tully, 127, 179, 183, 199,
    211, 221, 232
Brazele, S. A., 232
Breckinridge, John C., 79, 80, 98, 100-
    105, 107, 112
  W. C. P., 100, 101, 103
Bristow, Otto, 233 (3)
Britt, T. J., 158
Brooks, Mr., 26
  Alice P., 191
  Ann, 191
  J. M., 183
  Lilly W., 191
  Maggie W., 191
  Mary Jane, 191
  Miles C., 191
  W. H., 143, 183, 191
Brown, C. D., 232
  George W., 179
  Lucretia Ellison, 120-121
  Snowden, 230 (2)
Browning, Thomas, 179
Brownlee, John, 75
  R. E., 130
Bruce, Charles E., 183, 188, 199
  Kate, 199
Brussels, A., 67, 179

Bryan, Leander, 13
Brylaski, M., 228
Buchanan, Elizabeth, 191
  George, 179, 218
  M. E., 229
  Mary R., 228
  W. R., 179, 228
Buck, W. T., 60
Bug family, 230
Bug, Lucy, 230
  Martha, 230
  Mary, 230
Bullock, Newton, 214
Burgner & Aiton Stock Co., 155
Burke, Henry, 199
  Mamie, 199
Burns, Elizabeth, 191
  William H., 191
Burt-Stark House, 62-65, 174
Burt, Armistead, 4, 7, 27, 57, 63-65,
    78, 79, 80-81, 89, 92, 96, 97
    101, 104, 105, 107, 110,112
    122, 123, 124, 128, 141,231
  Martha, 63-65, 96
Burts, R. M., 168, 169, 172
Butler, Hutson, 188

Caldwell, J. J., 57
Calhoun, A. D., 183
  Edward B., 65, 183
  J. A., 4
  James C., 75, 179
  James E., 70
  Jas. A., 220
  Jas. C., 220
  John A., 28, 29, 62, 72, 75, 179,
    197
  John C.,8, 21,23-24, 26,63,174
  Kate P., 200
  Mrs. M., 220
  Mamie, 199
  Martha, 63
  O. T., 183
  R. A., 183, 199
  Sallie, 62
  Sarah, 63, 197
  Sarah (Sallie)Norwood, 65
  W. Norwood, 179
  Wm. P., 183
Calkin, Margt. A., 223
  Richd., 223
Calvert, John, 168
  Lucie, 191

Index

W. A., 168
Campbell, Absolom, 218
Camplin, Ann J., 226
  W. E., 226
Cann, Jack, 168
  Leslie, 168
  McKinney, 168, 172
Cannon, J. L., 159
  Robert W., 26, 183, 188, 232(3)
Capers, Sallie R., 199
  W. T., 199
Carlisle, Mr., 190
Carmichael, Duncan D., 235 (3)
Casey, Thomas, 44
Cason, Frederick, 200
  Hattie Allen, 200
  Henry S., 200
  Janie E., 200
  Mary J., 200
  Sallie J., 200
  Samuel C., 183, 190, 200, 232
Cater, Eliza P., 191
  Elizabeth C., 191
  G. McD., 183
  McDuffie M., 191
  Martha A., 191
  Mary Jervey, 191
  Rebecca D., 191
Cawthon, Charles R., 177-178
Chalmers, Ann, 227
  Cecelia, 202
  Chois, 227
  Chrsitana T., 200
  James, 183, 191, 232 (3)
  James D., 67, 72, 127, 179, 183, 200, 227, 231 (2)
Chamberlain, D. H., 132-135
Chambers, Mr., 66
Champlain, Jacob, 179
  William, 179
Chandler, J. C., 209
Chapman, Belle W., 199
  William G., 183, 199
Chatham, Robert N., 179, 225
Cheatham, Jasper, 213
  Robert M., 214
Child, James W., 221
Chiles family, 9
Chiles, John, 11
Chloe, a slave of the Posey family, 47
Christian & Wilson, 125
Christian, Emma, 226
  Martha A., 226

Thomas M., 67, 179, 183, 216, 226, 231 (3), 232
City Hall, 153-154
Clark, John L., Jr., 183
  John Lee, 183, 188
  Mack, 188
  R. M., 234 (2)
  W. A., 200
Clarke, Hannah, 6
Clinkscales, Eliza C., 202
Coan, Capt., 117
Cobb, Augustus B., 179, 224
  Caroline, 200
  Edmund, 57, 66, 179, 224, 231
  Elizh., 225
  Geo. C., 183, 224
  Howell, 45
  James, 179, 225
  James A., 231
  James E., 224
  James H., 200, 224
  Rebecca C., 224
  Thomas H., 151, 224
  William J., 70, 183, 224
Cochran, Ben T., 233 (2)
  James N., 75, 212
  J. S., 233 (8)
  Mary L., 222
  Matthew, 179
  Robert, 28, 38
  Thos. R., 179
Cohen, A., 232
Coleman, M. T., 188
  Wiley T., 234 (2)
Confederate Monument, 152-153
  Seal, 79, 81
  Treasure, 77-78, 83, 96, 101, 102, 106-108, 110-112, 176
Conner, John, 229
  Margt., 229
  Thos., 229
Connor, J. M., 134
Coogler, Mrs., 137
  Bessie G., 199, 200
  Fannie O., 199, 200
  Katie D., 199
  Thomas, Sr., 199
  Thomas W., Jr., 199
  Thos. G., 183
  Willie T., 199, 208
Cooke, Thompson, 130, 131, 132
Cooper, Robert, 172
Copeland, Stuart B., 234 (3)

Index

Corbett, Mr., 59, 73
Corn, F. H., 159
Corrie, J. E., 232
Cothran, Mr., 128
    Eliza C., 227
    Emma Chiles, 191
    J. S. (Sproul), 6, 81, 82-83, 123, 126, 133, 134, 179, 183, 190, 191, 227, 231 (2)
    James S., Jr., 191
    Hannah Clarke, 191
    Rebecca C., 191, 227
    T. P. (Thomas Perrin), 183, 191, 193, 227, 232 (3)
    Wade S., 183, 191, 227, 232 (2)
Cottrell, Eleanor, 29
Coumbe, Caroline, 224
    Jno. F., 224
    John, 179, 224
    Sarah, 224
Court House, 13-15, 26, 157-159, 187
Courtright, Isaac, 215
    Lizzy, 215
Cownover, Harriet H., 230
    Fred H., 59, 60, 179, 2230
Cox, Ann Eliza, 191, 221
    Charles, 179, 191, 221
    Ella, 221
Crawford family, 171-172
Crawford, Anthony P., 167-172
    Charles, 171
    Enos, 22, 23
    J. Bunyan, 179, 226
    John, 23
    Thomas, 171
Crawley, Eliza, 216
    Harriet H., 216
    Henry C., 216
    Leroy H., 216
    Martin, 216
    Mary L., 216
Creight, James A., 4, 57, 231
Creswell, Thomas, 149, 150
    Vivian, 234
Crews, Eugenia, 223
    Sarah, 223
    Thos. B., 179, 223
    William, 223
Cromer, Jas., 223
    West, 23
Cubic, a slave of David Lesley, 62
Cunningham, Frank, 183
    James, 212
    Jas. R., 183
    John, 27, 28, 29, 46, 55-57
Cuthbert, Eccles, 179
    Edward S., 228

Daly, Joseph D., 59, 60, 179, 211, 228
Dansby, John, 148-150
    W. S., 183
Darlington, Charlotte, 216
    Henry, 216
    Henry M., 216
    John T., 216
    Joseph J., 216
Darracott, Thomas, 231 (2)
Dave, a slave, 47
Davenport, Mr., 15
Davis, Mr., 66, 112
    Carrie, 129-132
    Eli S., 2, 9, 25, 27, 29, 34
    Emma, 217
    Henrietta, 208
    Isaac B., 200, 201
    Jane, 188
    Jefferson, 64-65, 78, 79-80, 89, 96-97, 98-114, 173, 174
    James E. (Jimmy), 235 (3)
    John, 217
    Julia L., 200
    Lewis, 198, 228
    Luther, 1151
    Martha H., 201
    Mary, 203
    Mary A., 217
    Mary C., 200
    Mary Stark, 65
    Nathaniel Jefferson, 97, 179
    Rebecca, 200, 222
    Thos. F., 71
    Varina, 64, 80, 88, 96-97, 106-107, 176
    William, 217
    William C., 75, 179, 228, 231
Dawkins, Carrie, 221
Day, William, 218
de la Howe, John, 1
Deal, Foster A., 215
    James E., 216
    James L., 216
    Marcus E., 215
    Mary J., 215
    Milton, 212
Deale, Mr., 67

Index

Dearing, Eliza, 201
Deason, T. E., 159
DeBruhl family, 85
DeBruhl, Kate C., 200
   Marshall P., 183, 200, 219
   Mary, 219
   Stephen C., 179, 200, 219
   Susan, 219
   Susan E., 200, 219
Delock, Lewis, 218
Delph, J. Virginia, 201
   Kate E., 201
   M. Louise, 204
Dendy, Mrs. A. Ella, 198, 201, 224
   Absley, 214
   Charles, 2, 4, 20, 48, 179, 198, 214
   Charles N., 201, 224
   Elizabeth G., 214
   Harriet, 214
   James N., 191, 214
   Mary J., 214
   Sally (Sarah), 214, 224
   T. B., 214, 231
   Thos. D., 25, 27
   William, 214
Dibbrell, Gen., 100, 101-103, 112
Dick, a slave, 21-22, 49
Dickerson, James S., 201
Dickson, J. M., 136
Dispensary, 160-161
Doggett, Mrs., 26
Donald, John A., 198
   M. G., 158
Donalson, Ann, 222
   Caroline, 222
   Caroline A., 222
   Dinah, 222
   Jack, 229
   Lucy, 222
   Robt., 222
Dorn, John C., 200
   Mattie, 200
Douglass, David, 10, 57
   Donald, 4, 198
   Drucilla, 198
   Elizabeth, 198
   Emily, 201
   Emma, 201
   Essie, 201
   Eugenia M., 201
   George Archibald, 68-69, 148, 183, 188, 201, 232

Hutton, 4, 28
   John C., 201
   Lucius, 183
   Matilda D., 201
   Thomas Jefferson, 19, 198, 201, 202
Downey, Sarah, 4, 198
Dubose, Edward, 162
Duckett, Carl, 162
Duels, 44-48
Duke, Basil, 80, 98-101, 102, 103, 112
Duncan, Lavinia, 201
Dundas, W. O., 183
DuPre, A. Mason, 200
   C. Portuvine, 200
   Eugene McSwain, 200
   Frank C., 200
   Julius F. C., 115, 124, 132, 146-147, 183, 188, 200, 231, 232
   J. H., 183, 200, 232 (4)
   M. Josie, 200
   Mary, 200
   Mary Esther, 200
   Wm. C., 146-147, 159, 183, 200
Dusenberry, George, 235

Eakin, Drucilla, 201
   Thomas, 127, 201
Edwards, A. W. (Whit), 180
   Andrew B., 201, 224
   Georgia, 201
   Hannah E., 201
   Hollis E., 201
   James Edmund, 201
   Jennie, 201
   Joe L., 233
   John Gibson, 180, 183, 188, 201, 227, 232
   Nathan A., 201
   Robt. O., 201
Elias, Judith, 228
Ellis, J. C., 154, 232 (3)
   John V., 218
   W. R., 159
   William M., 218
Ellison, Alfred, 118-121, 128, 187
   Bell, 120
   H., 141
   Jim, 120-121
   Lewis, 119
   Mrs. M. A., 220
   Ralph, 118, 119-121

Index

William H., 118, 119
Enright, John, 67, 74, 180, 219, 231 (4)
   John R., 219
   Mary H., 219
   Thomas G., 74, 219
   Thos., 219
Eureka Hotel (Belmont), 151-152, 158
Evans, C. L., 233 (3)
   John T., 233, 234
   William C., 201
Ewart, Mary A., 201
   Sallie, 201
   Sarah E., 201
   W. H., 201

Fains, Margaret, 217
Fair, Amanda, 191
   Ann, 223
   James F., 223
   James Livingston, 191
   James Young, 192
   Jno. Y., 223
   Mary A., 223
   Robert A., 180, 190, 191, 222, 231
Farmer, Jack D., 233 (6), 234 (7)
Farmer's Bank, 188
Farrington, Dorothy Anna, 192, 223
   Margt., 223
   Martha C., 223
   Mary A., 223
   O. J., 180, 192, 223
Faulkner, A. G., 232
Fell, John W., 202
Fenlas, Saml. W., 221
Ferguson Academy, 164-165
Ferguson and Williams College, 166
Ferguson, A. J., 143, 144
   John C., 142-144, 191
   S. W., 100-102, 103, 112
   Susan Barksdale, 143
Finley, Mr., 22
   John, 2, 9-10, 25, 27
   Matthew, 23
Fires, 125-129
Fisher, Bobby R., 235 (4)
Flynn, John, 9
Fogette, E., 74
Fort Pickens, 174
Foster, Mr., 16
   Alfred, 164
Fowler, Cath., 223
   Ella, 202
   James W., 180, 202, 223

Samuel Waddy, 202
   Waddy, 180
Foxworth, D. A., 202
   S. A., 202
Franklin, Francis, 218
Franks, John W., 216
Frasier, Mary A., 216
Free, John Allen, 234 (2)
Fry, General, 108, 109

Gallaghers Bros., 188
Galphin, B. F., 184
Gambrell, Claudius C., 202, 232 (2), 233 (3)
   Eliza C., 202
   Ellen C., 202
   George C., 202
   John M., 184, 187, 202, 232(3)
Gantt, Richard, 151, 183
Gardin, John M., 84-93
Garrett, Gene, 234 (3), 235 (2)
Garrick, Charles R., 184
   George W., 184
Gary, Eugene B., 133, 141, 183, 2?
   Frank B., 183, 232
   Frank F., 143, 184, 202
Gaston, Mr., 69
Gilbert, C. S., 159
Giles, James M., 184, 190, 192, 1
   William A., 212
Gillespie, Jane, 219
   Lewis, 219
   Mary, 219
Gilliam, Dave, 159
   James A., 159
Gilliard, E. F., 188
Gilmer, Mary M., 202
   Mrs. R. A., 8
   Robt., 8, 29
   Rosa A., 214
   Samuel, 216
Glass, Jno. C., 193
Glenn, J. R., 232, 233 (3)
   James O., 234 (3)
Godfrey, G. W., 233
   W. B., 233, 234
   William, 180
Goff, David, 215
   Samuel A., 4, 57, 215
Golding (Golden), Reuben, 67,
Goolsley, Lang, 139-140
Gordon, Robt., 229
Granite Range, 66, 128

Index

Graves, Geo. C., 227
   Thos., 197
Gray, Mr., 66
   John, 180, 226
Graydon, Ellis G., 137, 184, 192, 232
   William N., 161, 184
Green, Amelia E., 206
   Frank H., 235
Greene, Robert H., 233 (3)
Greer family, 230
   Allen, 230
   Ben, 230
   David, 50
   Dot N., 230
   John, 230
   Martha, 230
   Mary, 230
   Sarah, 50
Gregory, E. W., 233
Grier, I. L., 75, 76
   R. C., 175
Griffin, John, 151
Grisham, Mr., 12
Groves, W. B., 188
Guffin, C. B., 121
   Charles (C. W.), 121-123, 139, 231
   Lem (L. L.), 121-125, 139
   Pem (L. P.), 121-124, 139-141

Hadden, Wm. M., 50
Haddon, Hannah T., 192
   R. B., 184
   R. Marshall, 184, 188, 190, 191, 192
   Reuben, 143
Hagen, G. Alex, 234 (3)
Haigler, C. A., 232 (3), 233 (2)
Hall, Lieut., 117
   Charles, 145, 147-148
   William (Unk), 234 (3)
Hamblin, Albert, 122-124
   Andw. B., 230
   Deborah, 230
Hamilton, Alexander C., 2, 9, 16, 40, 41
   Alice, 213
   Andrew, 1, 2, 5, 6, 8, 9, 18, 19, 21, 25, 36, 49, 57, 198
   Clem, 180
   Harriett, 213
   John, 9
   Joseph A. (Gus), 30, 31, 231 (2)
   Robert B., 40-41
   William, 9, 235
Hamlin, J. R., 180

Hammond, Mr., 25
   Albert B., 203
   Alice E., 203
   Arthur Spencer, 202
   C. P. (Charles Percy), 188, 202
   C. V. (Christian), 184, 202
   Mrs. C. V. (Mary), 137
   Fannie, 137, 203
   Henry S., 184, 203
   Ida Virginia, 202
   Jane T., 203
   Jas. S., 231
   Joseph S., 184, 202, 203, 232
   Kate, 202, 203
   Mary F., 202
   Nora, 202
   Miss S. C., 206
   William H., 202
Hampton, Wade, 39, 121
Hanckel, W. H., 184
Hangings, 14-17, 42-43
Hanks, H. A., 234
Hanley, Nancy, 198
Harbison College, 162-164, 166-167
Harbison, Samuel P., 167
Harden, J. M., 232 (2)
Hardin, Edward K., 203
   Ida C., 203
Hardy, Armistead, 188
Harper, Hattie C., 203
   Rev. R. I., 203
   R. L., 184
Harrington, John W., 234
Harris, Henry G., 234 (2)
   John A., 184
   Saml., 229
Harrison & Game, 188
Harrison, Dr., 48
   Burton, 64, 96, 97, 110
   Eliza S., 217
   Dr. F. E., 158
   Jane W., 192
   M. H., 219
   Thomas Perrin, 192
Harry, slave of the Posey family, 47
Haskell, Charles T., 97
Hawthorn, David W., 212
   Steven S., 235 (2)
Hazzard, Pat, 230
Headley, John W., 104-105
Hearst, Dr. J. W., 75
Helm, Capt., 105
Hemphill, R. R., 64, 75-76, 129,

Index

130, 153, 184, 231
Henderson, Edward, 39
   Eleanor Laurens, 36-37
   Francis, Jr., 36-39
   Francis, Sr., 36-37
Hendricks, Mr., 28
Henry, Albert, 154, 232 (3), 233 (7)
   Frances, 159, 184, 232 (2)
   Samuel, 180
   Samuel A., 230
Hester, Sarah, 65
Hilhous, Benjamin, 216
   Esther, 216
   Joseph, 216
Hill, Andw. M., 127, 128, 138, 180, 184, 188, 200, 203, 226, 232
   Ann H., 221
   Henry, 184
   James A., 203, 232
   Jane, 226
   Jane E., 203
   John, 221
   L. T., 184, 192
   Mary, 192
   Mary A., 226
   Mary C., 203
   Mary T., 192
   R. M., 203
   Richard, 56-57, 184, 226
   Robert Emmet, 64, 180, 184, 187, 210, 221, 232
   Robt. M., 184, 188, 192, 232 (5)
   Sallie E., 221
   Sarah, 221
   William, 5, 180, 212, 221
   William E., 203
Hinton, John, 42
Hodge, Pat, 235
Hodges, Arnice, 212
   G. M., 136
   Gabraella, 212
   George C., 202
   Mrs. George C., 192
   H. P., 136
   Henry, 212
   James, 218
   Jno., 226
   John F., 220
   Julia, 212
   Mary, 212
   Mary A. D., 212
   Rayford P., 235 (2)
   Samuel, 212
   Samuel A., 211
   Sophronia, 212
Hoge, Solomon L., 122, 123, 134
Hollingsworth, C., 227
   Mary, 227
Hollinshead, Jerry, 121, 132, 231
   Widow, 135
Holy Rock, 26
Hook & Ladder Company, 126, 128
Horton, Harry L., 234 (5), 235
Houston, F. B., 129-132
Howell, Jeffy D., 96
Howie, T. V., 177, 234
   Mrs. T. V., 177
   Thomas D., 177-178
Howland, Minnow, 205
Hoyt, Anna L., 220
   David M., 2120
   Laura E., 220
   Mary H., 220
   Mary H. (II), 220
   Thomas, 62, 118, 180, 220
Huckabee, Mary P., 200
Hughes, Benjamin P., 130, 131,180 215, 220, 231 (2)
   Cicero, 180, 184, 203
   Jane C., 215, 220
   Joe W., 234 (6)
   Orene, 203
   Sarah, 220
   W. T., 234 (3)
   Wm. P., 220
Hughey, Elizabeth J., 218, 229
   James M., 180, 203
   Minnie, 203
   William M., 66, 180, 218, 229
Humphries, C., 14
Hunter, John A., 57, 66, 180, 212, 222, 231 (4)
   William, 49
Hurst, C. J., 188

Inter-racial marriages, 129-132
Israel, Marshall's slave, 49,85,93
Israel, M., 67, 180, 228
   Rebecca, 228
Ives, Frederick, 66, 180, 229
Ivey, John, 203
   Susan A., 203

Jack, a slave of Sheriff Chiles, 11
Jack, Mary, 7
   Sam, 11

Index

Ann R., 198, 217
C. D., 233
Ellen G., 217
Humphrey R., 217
John M., 217
Lewis E., 217
Martha D., 205
Mary E., 217
Minnie C., 207
Robert, 151
Thomas, 4, 27, 28, 184, 217
Jails, 17-18, 146, 168-169, 187
Jamison, D. F., 81
Jefferson, Arthur, 118
Jenkins, Jordan, 218
    Samuel, 162
Jennings, Walter C., 235
Jillson, J. K., 134
Johnson, Mr., 149
    Adam R., 105
    Ann C., 223
    Benjamin, 64, 71, 73, 180, 223
    Elihu, 213
    Joseph, 147
    Saml., 231
Johnston, General, 101, 102, 103
Jones, Mr., 187
    Dr., 12
    Adolphus W., 184, 203, 232
    Andw., 222
    Anna, 203
    Benj. W., 184, 221
    C. M., 188
    Cincinnati, 180
    D. Young, 224
    Davis F., 180, 221, 231
    Eliza M., 228
    Eliza W., 222
    Elizh., 224
    Henry A., 2, 5, 29, 180, 228
    J. E., 233
    Jane, 224
    Joseph E., 203
    Joshua Y., 184, 203, 222
    Mary, 2, 7, 203, 222
    Robert, 180, 203, 222, 231 (4)
    Robert, Jr., 203, 222
    Robt. H., 223
    S. Henry, 223
    Sarah F., 228
    Sarah J., 223
    Susan, 221
    W. Hampton, 158, 232 (2), 233

Jordan, D. A., 67, 180
Daniel J., 184, 192
Elizabeth, 192
Lilly Lee, 192
Rosa A., 192
Samuel, 57, 76
Josh, a slave, 50
Junkin, David, 180
    Michael, 226
    Robert, 180
Kaliski, M., 143, 144, 184
Kaplan, Mr., 126
Keaton, E. M., 184
Kellar, David W., 184
    Thomas, 184
Kennedy, E. Catherine, 204
    Isaac, 231, 232 (2)
    Robert, 148-150
Kernel, Elihu, 180
    Louis, 180, 219
Kerr, Mr., 48
    Amanda L., 213
    Ann B., 213, 226
    Caroline, 226
    Clara F., 213
    Mrs. H. S., 199
    Henry, 213
    Henry S., 5, 180, 199, 203, 226
    J. D., 188
    Leontina, 203
    Louisa, 226
Key, Robert, 197
    Mrs. Robert, 197
Kilpatrick, Sarah, 218
King, Mr., 135
    J. N., 133
Kingsmore, Agnes M., 215
    Clarage H., 174-175, 215
    John C., 4, 174, 231
    Mary M., 215
Kirby, John M., 119, 184, 192
    Lula, 192
Kitchens, Kindred, 16, 17, 42-43
Kizer, Legare, 235 (3)
Klugh, Emma E., 203
    H. G., 146, 147
    James C., 153, 159, 184, 204, 232 (2)
    Mary, 153
    Pascal D., 197, 204
Knox, Messrs., 66
    Henry, 26
    James W., Jr., 234, 235

Index

John, 9, 52, 125, 180, 184, 228
Mary J., 226
Nathaniel, 52, 180, 226
Rachel, 229
Robert P., 180
Robt., 228
Thomas, 213
William, 180
Wm. N., 229
Kurtz, Wilbur G., 173-174
Kurz, E. Catherine, 203
Jacob, 184, 203, 232
Kyle, Mrs., 12
Andrew, 219
Eliza, 192, 218, 219
James, 8, 10-11, 12, 25, 62
James W., 8
Jane, 8
Louisa Jane, 62
William, 148, 149
Wm. Hunter, 8, 10, 18

Lackey, W. B., 180
Lander, James A., 234
Lane, Fannie, 203
Joe, 107
Langley, Wm., 233 (11), 234
Latimer, A. C., 119
J. H., 188, 232
James, 203
William C., 192
Laurens' Lands, 36
Henry, 37
John, 36
Lawson, Fannie (Frances), 204, 216, 228, 235
Hiram W., 13, 60, 67, 127, 128, 180, 204, 216, 228, 231, 235 (3)
Hiram W. (II), 227
Ida, 129-132
James M., 184, 188, 233 (2)
Jas. W., 228
Lucy W., 228
Sallie G., 216
Lawton, Gen., 79
Leach, Marshall, 233
Percy J., 233 (2), 234
Lee, Allen, 230
Robert E., 95, 96, 103, 111
W. A., 73, 127, 180, 184, 228
Leovy, Henry, 97
LeSett, Sarah, 216
Lesley, Alpheus E., 192

Caroline Frances, 9, 44
David, 10, 30, 32, 44, 61, 62, 218, 231 (2)
Mrs. David, 25
James, 9, 44
Mrs. James, 44
Janet, 8
John, 8
John W., 192
Louisa, 8, 62, 218, 219
Louisa Jane, 192
Shedrick, 164
Virginia C., 192
William E., 192
Wm., 11, 44
Lester, Mary, 220
Lewis, a slave of Mr. Posey, 47
Lewis, D. C., 234
Lichenstein, Benjamin, 180
Liddle, Jared, 22
Ligon, John, 229
John H., 180
S. E., 234 (6)
Lindsay, Henry D., 163
J. O., 80
W. W., 75, 76
Link, G., 184
Jenner, 192
Robert S., 192, 235
Lipscombe, Mr., 24
Lisenben, Robt., 224
Lites, Abram, 50
Livingston, Eliza L., 24
Henry, 2, 8, 10, 13
J. W., 180
Jane L., 14
John F., 4, 8, 10, 16, 26, 28, 30, 31, 61, 67, 75, 180, 188, 192, 212, 219, 231 (2)
John F., Jr., 180, 184, 192, 212
M. Fanny, 192
Margaret A., 212
Mary, 212
Mary J., 212
Sarah, 192, 212, 218
Talo (Toliver), 2, 8, 9
Thomas, 2
Lockey, William, 228
Logan, John H., 21, 75
Lomax, Mrs., 125
Alice A., 217
Augustus, 212
Frances, 188

Index

G. W., 188
Harriet, 197
James, 26
James D., 217
John, 212
Lucian H., 180, 217
Mary E., 217
Matilda, 201
W. H., 188
W. James, 180
Warren, 46-48
William, 2, 26, 29, 197
Wm. D., 184

Long, Mrs., 190
  J. Allen, 233 (4)
Love, Betsy, 218
Lowry, S. L., 184
Lynch, A. W., 47, 204
  Maurice, 204
Lynchings, 145-147, 167-170
Lyon, Charles J., 148
  Elizabeth, 214
  Harriet B., 204, 224
  Henry T., 180, 214
  H. Thomson, 204, 224
  J. Fraser, 204
  J. Fuller, 153, 184, 204
  John, 214
  John T., 184, 195
  Joseph, 214
  M. E., 201
  Mary Louise, 204
  W. H., 224
  W. Andrew, 184, 204
  William, 204
Lythgoe, Augustus J., 66, 92, 93-94, 180, 221, 231
  George B., 192, 221
  Harriet, 192, 221
  Louisa, 221
  Margaret J., 192
  Mary, 221
  Mary J., 221
  Meta A., 192
McAlister, William, 137
Macbeth, Lieut., 109
McBride, Annie, 205
  E. H., 205
McBryde, John, 181, 218, 227
  John M., 49, 181, 218, 227
  Robert J., Jr., 181, 218
  Robt., 227

McCan, Mary M., 227
McCann, J. E., 234
McCants, J. G., 195
McCaslan, Kennedy, 147, 148
  R. H. F., 148
  Thomas, 223
McCaw, Julia, 193
  Mary, 193
McClung, C. Q., 139
  McCollister, Nat, 42
McCord, Alice F., 205
  Ann, 224
  Bradley A., 235 (5)
  Frank, 224
  James, 225
  James A., 198
  Janie, 205
  John, 118, 225
  Lucy, 224
  Luther A., 205
  Mary, 225
  Nancy S., 205
  Sarah C., 202, 224
  Seppie, 205
  Thomas, 225
  William M., 205
McCoy, Mollie, 193
  William S., 193
McCracken, Moses Oliver, 193
McCrae, Harvey, 181
  John, 181
McCraven, John, 26, 28
McCullough, John W., 137, 204
McDaniel, John, 212
McDavid, J. E., 232
McDill & Lyon, 150
McDill & Tolly, 188
McDonald, Gov., 45
  Mrs., 138, 187
  Elizabeth V., 205
  Martha D., 205, 214, 221
  Mary Thomson, 192
  Matthew, 181, 205, 214, 221, 231
  William T., 137, 184, 204, 214, 221
McDuffie, Geo., 15, 35, 42
McElrone, Hugh, 74
McFall, W. T., 151
McFarlin, Benjamin M., 57, 214
  Benjamin D. C., 214
  Francis M., 214
  John W., 214
  Mary A., 214
  Mary E., 214

Index

Nancy, 214
McGettigan, Thomas, 184, 187, 232
McGhee, Wm., 181
McGill, Saml., 229
McGowan, Alex H., 181, 225
    Samuel, 5, 26, 46, 48, 50, 51, 60, 61
        75, 94, 111, 121, 122, 123, 129,
        130, 132, 133, 171, 181, 184,
        212, 224, 231 (2)
    Samuel (II), 224
    Sue C., 224
    Sue E., 225
    Willie C., 61, 184, 225, 232
McIlwain, J. A., 159
    John, 5, 57, 212

McIlwaine building, 127
McIlwaine, H. P., 184, 209, 232
McKee, Caroline A., 204
McKellar, Annie K., 200
    Emmanuel, 188
McKenzie, R. K., 234
McLain, R., 55-56
McLane, Foster B., 169
McLaren family, 26, 28, 32-35, 38, 41, 45
    Adam, 33, 34
    Adam, Jr., 33, 34
    Agnes, 33, 34, 35
    Annie, 218
    Eliza, 33, 34
    Hattie, 39
    Jane, 226
    Janet, 33, 218
    John (Sawney), 2, 4, 9, 28, 33, 34, 39,
        47, 55, 66, 181
    John, Jr., 33, 34, 218, 227, 231, 235
    Robin, 28, 33, 34
    Susan, 29, 33, 34, 35
McLaughlin, Benj., 181, 228
    Donald, 181, 225
    Jno., 228
    John, 181
    Mrs. M., 225
McMahan, Cecil, 234 (2)
McMillan's Mill, 187
McMillan, James, 185
    James L., 154, 158, 205, 232 (3)
    T. W., 5, 181, 185, 205
    William, 2, 185
McMillen, Wm., 2
McMorries, Mr., 28
McNary, Wince, 147
McWhorter, Wm., 8

Mabry, D. Lucien, 195
    J. Rivers, Jr., 235
    James T., 228
    John T., 236
    Robert L., 159, 204
    S. Tompkins, 204
    Samuel W., 212
    Thomas J., 184, 193, 204
Madden, Limoi, 17
Magill, David H., 141
Magrath, A. G., 75
Magruder, Annie, 204
Mahala, a slave of the Posey family, 47
Mallory, Stephen, 79, 112, 113, 114
Mann, Jaames M., 234 (2)
Manning, R. F., 234
    Richard I., 172
Marion, John, 230
Markey (Markee), A., 56, 57, 198
Mars, J. Moore, 233 (9)
Marshall House, 28, 65, 78, 96, 125
    Eliza A., 223
    Eliza C., 222
    Elizabeth, 211
    Fannie A., 68, 222
    Fannie J., 192
    Francis, 222
    Ida D., 84, 91, 224
    J. Foster, 13, 46, 48, 49, 50, 58, 72,
        73, 84, 92, 93, 211, 223, 231 (2)
    Mrs. J. Foster, 84, 89-91, 181, 210
    J. Foster (II), 84, 211
    J. H., 21
    J. Quitman, 84, 223
    J. W. W., 19, 26, 181, 184, 187,
        192, 222, 231
    James B., 204
    John J., 223
    John L., 211
    Lalla, 204
    Mary, 84
    Mary F., 224
    S. S., 50
    Samuel, 35, 84, 90
    Samuel F., 211, 223
    Samuel S., 222
    William, 84, 90
    William J., 181, 211, 223
    William S., 222
Martin, Mr., 67
    Alexr. P., 225
    Banning, 212
    Benjamin Y., 26, 29, 46, 212

Index

Campbell, 139-141
  Caroline, 212
  Chisolm, 224
  Fannie, 204
  Frances, 204, 225
  Henrietta J., 193
  J. W., 234
  James Willard, 184, 204
  Jas. L., 184, 190, 193
  John, 180, 224
  John J., 212, 231
  Junius, 224
  Leonora C. L., 193
  Luther, 180, 224
  Mary, 224
  Mary L., 212
  Robert A., 180, 204, 225
  Robert M., 104-105
  Robt. A. (II), 225
  Sallie, 224
  Stark, 143, 224
  Thomas S., 180, 193, 224
  William, 224
Matthews, Cornelius, 16-17, 19
Mazyck, P. D., 192
Means, Emma, 205
  James, 205
  William, 54
Mercer, Newlin, 131
Methodist church, 10, 26, 28, 50, 197
Michie, J. L., 157
Miles, Moses, 225
Milford, C. A., 232
  Joel Kennedy, 204
  Leola J., 205
  T. B., 132, 204
Milledge, a free black, 229
Miller, Mayor, 148
  Mrs., 26
  Augustus Griffin, 193
  Carrie, 219
  Catherine, 219
  Celia T., 203
  Geo., 219
  George McDuffie, 75, 181, 188, 192, 212
  Harriet, 219
  J. C., 185, 205
  Jane, 219
  Jones F., 185, 188, 232 (7)
  L. T., 232 (3), 233 (2)
  Lizzie, 205
  Martha Virginia, 193
  Mary C., 192, 219
  Nicholas, 219
  Sarah, 219
  Sarah C., 219
  T. M., 233 (3)
  Thomas Virgil, 193
  Virginia, 219
  William, 219
  Mrs. William, 137
  Wm. L., 185
Mills, Robt., 13-14
Millwee, J. A., 185
Minshall, Frederic, 158, 236
  Rachel, 236
Moffett, Mr., 45
Monaghan, Father, 74
Monroe, Judge, 80, 97
Mood, J. A., 205
  Mrs. M. C., 205
  Mary, 205
  Russell E., 205
Mooney, Mary, 223
  William M., 181, 223
Moore, Agnes, 1
  Ann, 197, 213, 220
  Charles, 226
  Edwin W., 181, 213, 220
  Elizabeth, 213
  Elizabeth C., 205
  Elizabeth W., 205, 207
  Emily, 226
  George, 4
  George Henry, 185. 205
  Henry, 225
  Henry D., 204, 213
  James, 2, 4, 28, 57, 181, 197, 199, 213, 220
  James Colin, 205, 213
  Joe, 128
  Joseph T., 181, 205, 213, 226, 231 (3)
  Leontina, 199
  Louis C., 226
  Mary, 205, 207, 226
  Mary (II), 205, 226
  Robert, 1
  W., 226
  William C., 66, 181, 185, 203, 204, 205, 213, 226
  Willie, 204
Moorman, Robert, 119
  T. S., 195
Moreem, John, 180

Index

Morgan, James Morris, 96, 106-110
Morrah, J. M., 158
Morse, Albert A., 234
    Amos B., 185, 188, 193, 194, 232
    Joel S., 233 (6), 234 (3)
Moseley, Shack, 188
Moss, D. L., 234
Motes, Wm., 181
Murbach, George, 185
Murchison, C., 181
Murphy, Ellen J., 205
Murrell, And., 230
Murrill, John A., 181
Myers, Israel, 181

Nance, F. W. R., 147, 148, 170
    Florence, 193
    M. E., 193
Nash, Roy, 167-171
Nat, a slave of Trenholms, 109-111
National Bank, 173, 188
Navy, Mr., 198
Neddiman, Maria, 13
Neel, Louisa A., 205
Nelson, Enoch, 205, 225, 231
    Louisa E., 205
    Lucy A., 225
    Lucy E., 225
Neuffer, G. Augustus, 153, 158, 206
    232 (3), 233 (4)
Newall, Lot, 7
    Saml. Seth, 7
Newell, Edward (Buddy), 235 (3)
Nichols, J. W., 74
Nickles, G. N., 158, 159
    J. M., 234
    J. R., 233 (2)
    W. F., III (Teto), 235 (2)
Nixon, Archie, 235 (2)
Noble, B., 225
    E. P., 63
    Edward, 28, 48, 51, 72, 82, 128
    181, 185, 217, 225, 231
    Edward, Jr., 185
    Elizabeth B., 217
    Elizh., 225
    Floride, 225
    Joseph, 2
    Martha, 225
    Mary M., 217
    Patrick, 2, 4, 9, 17, 24, 25, 26
    28, 29
    Patrick (II), 217, 225

Samuel B., 217
Norrel, Wesley, 185
Norrell, Elizabeth, 205
    Georgia, 205
    Stephen B., 181, 185, 203
    205, 207
    Watson, 233
North, Jno. W., 229
    Jno. W. (II), 229
    Mary I., 229
    Sarah I., 229
    Wm. B., 229
Norwood, Mr., 140
    Franklin H., 216
    James A., 65, 124
    Joseph H., 216
    Sarah Hester, 65
    Williamson, 35

O'Brien, John, 14-16
O'Bryant, Mr., 149
O'Connor, Barney, 126, 181, 185, 229
    Harriet P., 229
    John, 181
O'Keefe, Ann, 223
    Mary D., 223
    Patrick, 181, 223
O'Neall, John Belton, 23-24, 30
O'Neill, Dennis, 125
Opera House, 153-155
Orr, James L., 50, 93, 123
    Sue Marshall, 50
Osborn, Amelia E., 206
    Annie, 206
    John F., 200, 206
Owen, John F., 221
    John T., 181, 190, 193
    Martha A., 221
    Moses T., 67, 181, 221, 231
    Sarah Eleanor, 193
    T. Elford, 27, 51
Owens, Patrick, 181, 212, 229
    Thomas C., 25

Parker, Dr., 116
    Edwd. F., 185, 222, 226
    Edwin, 185, 221
    Edwin (II), 221
    Ellen L., 221
    Eugenia C., 221
    Lucia G., 222
    Martha C., 221
    Thomas, 71, 73, 220

Index

W. H., 106, 110-114
William C., 221
Wm. H., 225, 26, 60, 72, 122, 127, 181, 185, 187, 188, 222, 231 (3), 232
Parks, A. Winton, 206
  G. Hertford, 206
  John T., 185, 206
Patterson, Josiah, 15
Patton, E. L., 82
Paul, Andrew, 181, 212, 229
  Sarah, 216
Peek, Lieut., 111
Peeler, Fred, 235
Pennel, Martha J., 206
Penney, Mary A., 206, 229
  Sallie C., 206
  W. P., 232
  William H., 206
  William T., 181, 185, 188, 201, 229
Perrin-McGowan house, 60-61
Perrin, Eliza C., 222
  Ella B., 206
  Ellen Watkins, 193
  Emma, 193
  Emma C., 215
  Eunice, 94, 193
  Francis H., 215
  George Clopton, 193, 215, 220
  Hannah Clarke, 193, 215
  Harriet C., 220
  Irene, 222
  Ivy W., 193
  J. L., 148, 159, 170, 188, 206
  J. W., 185, 193, 232
  James, 222
  James H., 206
  James M., 26, 29, 52, 60, 61, 92, 93, 94, 181, 215, 231
  James S., 94, 185, 222
  James Wardlaw, 194, 215
  James Wardlaw, Jr., 194
  Jane, 6
  Jane E., 193, 215, 219, 222
  Joel S., 193, 215
  John L., 185
  John Livingston, 193
  Kitty, 16, 26, 193
  Kitty C., 222
  Lewis, 173, 190
  Dr. Lewis, 206
  Lewis Wardlaw, 181, 185, 194, 220

  Louis H., 215
  Mary C., 219
  Mary E., 215, 222
  Mary Jane, 193
  Mary McCaw, 194
  Robt., 12
  Sallie, 220
  Samuel, 94
  Sarah Amanda, 193
  Sarah E., 193, 215
  Thomas, 181
  Thomas Chiles, 4, 6, 9, 13, 28, 29, 58, 75, 80, 81, 89, 94, 181, 190, 193, 215, 219, 231
  Thomas Chiles (II), 232
  Thomas L., 215
  Thos., 12, 220
  Thos. G., 206
  W. H., 181
  William, 220
  William R., 215
Perry, Mr., 123
  Benjamin F., 63
  John T., 206
  Mary, 218
  Nancy, 206
  Nancy Jane, 206
  Rockingham, 181
  Thomas, 206
  Wm., 185
Perryman, W. W., 76
Pettigrew (Petigru), James L., 37
Phillips, J. P., 133
  Spencer, 235 (2)
Pickens, Mr., 11
  Andrew, 1, 8, 21-23, 49, 71, 159, 173-174
  Francis W., 21, 95
Piester, J. B., 193
Pin Hook, 119, 187
Pinchback, William, 26
Pope & Patton, 188
Pope, Helen P., 215
  Jacob W., 215
  Josephine, 215
  Marion, 215
  Martha L., 215
  William, 164, 232
Porcher, Professor, 85-86
  Rev., 131
Porter, Alexander, 22
  Hugh, 22, 23
  J. C., 234

Index

Posey Range, 125
Posey, Addison F., 25, 27-43, 44, 49, 62, 231 (2)
   Adison, 218
   B. L., 4, 10, 27, 57, 219
   Ben Lane, 46-48, 49, 143
   Benjamin W., 218
   Florella, 218
   James H., 218
   Martha, 218
   Wesley, 218
Powder Magazine, 2, 4, 18-19
Powell, William R., 236
Pratt, Robert N., 185
Presbyterian church, 60-61, 189
Pressley, B. C., 143
Pressly, J. E., 233 (2)
Price, T. O., 159
Pritchard, C. H., 206
   Maggie B., 206
   Mary C., 206
Pucket, John A., 212
Puckett, C. C., 175
Purser, Ernest, 234 (3), 235
Pursley, Nancy, 193
   Narcissa A., 193
Putnam, Mary E., 222

Quaife, C. F., 181, 228
Quarles, Agnes, 194
   Eliza Thomson, 194
   T. P. (Thomas Perrin), 26, 136, 137 185, 190, 192, 193, 232 (3)
Quay house, 6
Quay, John, 6

Railroad, Hodges branch, 87, 174
Ramage, Elizabeth W., 205
Ramey, Christiana, 200, 213
   Eliza, 227
   Ella, 218
   Ellen, 213
   J. Allen, 137, 203, 233 (4)
   James, 213
   Jane, 227
   Jane A., 218
   Jane E., 218
   Johnson, 4, 67, 181, 206, 213, 227, 231
   Jordan A., 218, 231 (3)
   Justina, 213
   Louisa M., 218
   Lucinda, 218
   Lucius B., 218
   Lucretia, 207, 213, 227
   Matilda, 213
   Rebecca, 213
Randolph, Peyton, 10-11
Ransom, Roy, 234
   Theo. L., 235
Rapley, Richard A., 1, 25
Reader, A. B., 232 (2)
Reagan, John H., 64, 79, 105, 112
Red House, 10, 26
Reeder, Carolina, 207
Reese & Tolly, 188
Reese, Ella E., 207
   Fuller L., 234 (6)
   Henry Dodson, 185, 207
   M. B., 233 (6)
Reeves, Geo., 224
Reid, Marilyn, 235
Reynolds, B. W., 124
   Josiah, 213
Rhett, B., 127
Richardson, Annie E., 207
   Mary M., 207
   Sallie A., 207
   William S., 185, 207
Richey, C. L., 236
   George M., 164
   James B., 218
   Lewis, 164
   Mandina, 218
   Robert, 11
   Samuel C., 218
   Warren, 228
   William L., 218
Richmond, Mrs. E. T., 194
   John M., 190, 194
Rifford, Wm. F., 181
Riley, (Chief) Wm., 149, 150, 185
Roberts, Dave, 145-147
Robertson, Francis P., 4
   Frank M., 9
   J. Townes, 58, 85, 181, 185, 228
   J. Wm., 181
   Lawton, 148
   Peter R., 9
   Reuben, 76
   Russell, 188
   Thomas J., 181
   Thos., 228
   Wesley A., 76, 82-83
   Wm., 2, 8, 9, 123, 131, 197, 224
Robinson, J. J., 235

Index

Thos., 127
William, 212
Roche, Edward, 66, 74, 181, 185, 225
   Margt., 225
   Pat A., 225
   Sarah A., 225
Rochelle, Captain, 111
Rock House, 68
Rogers, Annie E., 207
   Grace H., 234
   J. B., 137, 138
   James, 171
   W. J., 185, 207
   Wm., 75
Rolison, Andoline A., 207
Romans, Richard, 188
Roofe, Joseph, 181
Rook, A. R., 151
Roosa, James H., 116
Rosenberg, Philip, 185, 188
Rosenland, M., 228
Rothschild, Mr., 156
Roullain, Ann G., 222
   T. Eliza, 222
   Theresa, 222
Rous, Sarah, 213
Royall, Mr., 148
Ruff, Joseph, 220
Runnels, Joseph, 57
Rushton, J. E., 185
Russel, Mr., 26
   Ann, 207
   Franklin, 217
   John, 4
Russell, Adelaide, 194
   Carrie, 229
   Josephine, 194
   Lew (Lou) H., 122, 124, 125, 181, 185, 194, 228, 232, 235
   Marie Antoinette, 194
   Mrs. Marie Antoinette, 194
   Samuel O., 181
   Sarah, 194
Rutledge, Ann, 226
   Benjn., 226
   Elizabeth V., 205
   James, 226
   Mary, 226
   Mary A., 226
   Mary F., 202
   Phil W., 10, 181
   Philip S., 207, 226
   Sarah, 226
   Virginia, 226
   W., 226
Rykard, James W., 185, 188, 206
   James William, 206
   Matilda, 206

Sacred Heart church, 73-74
Sadler, Mary F., 227
Sale, Theopolis A., 212
Sanders, Mortimer, 231
   R. M., 133
   Thomas, 213
Sarah, a freed woman, 116
Sassard, Arthur D., 208
   Georgiana, 208
   Henrietta, 208
   John, 208
   Margaretta A., 208
   Martha H., 201
   Nelson T., 185, 208
   Roseanna, 208
Savitz, Joe L., Jr., 235 (3)
   Joe, Sr., 234 (6), 235 (2)
Scanling, Chas., 230
Scanlon, John, 182
Scoggins, Ann, 194
Scott, Mrs. F. E., 207
   Joseph A., 207
   Kate H., 203, 207
   L. J., 208
   Leland S., 235 (3)
   Lillie Jane, 207
   R. K., 124, 132
   S. A., 207
   S. Talula, 207
   Sallie, 207
   Samuel M., 185, 208
   Sarah A., 208
   T. B., 208
   W. A., 208
   W. H., 207
Scoven, John, 168
Seal, E. L., 208
   Lavonia, 194
   Lewis, 186
   Lucia, 194
   Nanie E., 194
   Thomas C., 123, 131, 182, 185, 194, 197, 232 (2)
Secession meeting, 75-76
Selleck, Frederick, 46, 212
Selvey, James D., 234
Sharp, Ella V., 202

Index

Fannie, 199
Sharpe, J. P., 159
Shehan, Thomas, 182, 219
Sherard, T. Donald, 234, 235
Shields, John, 213
Shillito, Mrs., 27
   Andrew, 22
   Bettie, 207
   Elizabeth C., 215
   George A., 185, 198, 207, 215, 229
   Henry H., 229
   Hugh H., 215
   James, 4, 25, 27, 31, 57, 67, 182, 195, 198, 208, 215, 229
   James A., Jr., 182, 215
   Jane A., 229
   Jas. S., 228
   Jno., 229
   John, 25
   Julia A., 208, 215
   Lizzie, 207
   Mahala, 198, 208
   Margaret M., 215
   Mary, 95
   Mary A., 206, 215
   Mary M., 229
   Parmelia, 198
   Sallie W., 200, 208
   William A., 220
   William W., 215
Shirley, Geo. W., 233 (2)
Shives, Wm. H., 232 (2)
Sign, Mrs. A., 208
   John W., 123, 128, 131, 150, 182, 197, 208, 232 (2)
   Julia A., 208
   Lewis Wardlaw, 208
Simkins, Eldred, 17
   John Calhoun, 92, 95
Simmons, D. E., 234
   D. J., 208
   E. Alice, 207
   James H., 185, 205, 209
   Mary M., 207
   Mrs. S. C., 208
Simonds, Andrew, 62-63, 229
   Sallie, 62, 229
Simpson, A. D., 234 (5)
   James, 54-55
   James W., 186
Sizemore, Walter L., 235 (2)
Sklarz, Mr., 126

Slaves, 49-53
Sloan, T. W., 150
Small, Andrew, 182, 223
   Eva, 223
   Gertrude, 223
   John, 182, 223
   Kate, 223
   Louisa, 223
   Margaret, 223
   Margaretta Anna, 208
   Margt., 223
   Mary, 223
Smallpox, 115-116
Smith & Wellington, 188
Smith, A. M., 182, 188
   A. M. (Augustus Marshall), 60, 72, 73, 75, 92, 93
   Augustus W., 93, 150, 185, 232 (2)
   Mrs. B. F., 208
   Benjamin F., 208
   Brent A., 235
   Charles, 185
   D. B., 182
   D. R., 185
   Danl. B., 224
   Eugene (Gene) W., 235 (4)
   Fannie, 208
   George, 182
   George W., 164
   Grace, 194
   H. G., 154, 157, 232, 233
   Ione, 194
   Isabella Marshall, 92
   J. (Joel) Allen, 9, 17, 26, 158, 170, 185, 188, 190, 191, 194
   James W. (Pete), 234 (2), 235 (6)
   Jane Amanda, 194
   Joel, 35, 92
   L. W., 184
   Mary A., 224
   Mary B., 194
   Mary Lou, 194
   Mattie, 208
   W. F., 185
   W. Joel, 173, 185, 188, 194, 233 (4)
   William H., 194
Sondley, Mrs., 116, 137
   Charleton, 186
   D. R. (David Richard), 116, 173, 182, 186, 194, 208, 221
   George B., 194, 221
   Harriet R., 221

Index

Jas. R., 221
Margaret, 194
Mary Frances, 194, 221
Virginia E., 194
Wm. Tully, 208
Sorrow, Spencer, 235 (2)
Sossimon, Jacob, 2, 26
Speares, Lewis, 228
Speed, P. Brooks, 173, 185, 188, 207
Speers, Anna Mary, 206
Spencer, a free mulatto, 226
Spierin, Claudia L., 217
   Eliza, 217
   Elizabeth, 198, 217
   Emma, 217
   Mirabeau C., 217
   Maria F., 217
   Thomas P. (II), 217
   Thos. P., 2, 27, 29, 198, 217
Sports, 20, 24, 136-138
Sprnell, Jesse, 186
Sproul, C. W., 81
Spruel, Jesse J., 208
   Wm., 208
Stafford, Andrew J., 208
   Parthenia, 208
Stair, Richd. C., 230
Stanfield, T. F., 234
Stark mansion, 152
Stark & Cothran, 188
   Fannie, 65
   J. S., 65, 168, 170, 174, 232
   Mrs. J. S., 65
Starke, W. Pinckney, 23
Starnes, L. E., 234
Starr, R. C., 67, 182
Stephens, Walton M., 234 (2)
Stevenson, Henry, 182
   J. A., 159
Stewart, C. C., 236
   W. S., 159
Stithmire, Jane, 4
Street names, 187
Strickland, Robert M., 235 (6)
Sutherland, W. O., 234
Swetenburg, F. B., 234
Syfan, Eliza E., 224
   Emma E., 204
   George W., 137, 138, 182, 185, 207, 224
   George W., Jr., 186
   John C., 223
   Lilly, 207

Manning Brown, 207, 233 (10)
Minnie E., 207
Thomas J., 186, 207
William G., 207
Syme, Jno. W., 230

Taffy, a slave of J. White's, 51
Taggart, James, 2, 186, 188, 195, 232 (3)
   John, 4, 16, 29, 43
   Lewis, 19, 29
   Mary, 188, 195
   Moses, 2, 3, 4, 7, 8, 12, 13, 25, 26, 27, 28, 29, 231, 235
   Moses, Jr., 2
   Polly, 12
   W. H., 132
Tallmon, Thos. W., 2
Talmadge, Helen, 194
Talman, M. O., 9, 25
   Thos. K., 9
Tan yard, 187
Taylor, Ann S., 228
   Chas., 228
   Edwin J., 67, 182, 228
   Frances, 228
   John, 213
   Kate, 228
Templeton, Alexis H., 186, 195
   Eliza A., 195
   Florence, 194
   Susan Emma, 194
   W. A. (William Augustus), 186, 188, 190, 195
   William L., 195
Thespian Corps, 156
Thomas, David W., 186
   E. Hilliard, 235
   E. L., 234
   Ed., 234 (4), 235
   James, 151, 235
   Kinney, 56-57
   Wat, 182
   Wm., 219
Thomason, Carrie B., 204
Thompson, Waddy, 57
Thomson, Cleora, 195
   E. A., 232 (3)
   E. R., 233 (6)
   Eliza, 217
   George, 227
   J. S., 195
   J. William, 186, 193

Index

Jane, 195, 217, 227
Jane E., 194
John, 182, 227
John A., 191, 217
John Shropshire, 194
Lucy Calvert, 152, 153
Margaret M., 194
Mary, 217, 226
Mary M., 227
Matthew, 22
Ninian, 227
S. G., 186, 232 (3)
Thomas P., 188
Thos., 6, 25, 26, 28, 75, 123, 128, 182, 188, 190, 194, 217, 227, 231, 232
Thos. (II), 227
Timms, Willis, 234
Titus, Henry, 188, 231 (2)
Togno, Joseph, 59, 68-70
Tolbert family, 121
Tolbert, J. R., 236
  Thomas N., 134, 235 (2)
Townes, Samuel A., 3, 26
Townsend, Miss, 34
Travis, Joseph, 197
Trenholm, Fraser & Co., 96
Trenholm, Mr., 96, 107, 112
  Mrs. William L., 109
Tribble, Eliza, 226
  Ezekiel, 182, 226
  Jesse, 182, 226
  Jno. C., 226
  Lucy, 226
Trinity church, 71-73, 93
Trowbridge & Co., 128
Trowbridge, J. T., 208
  Jessie, 208
  Joseph W., 182
Truit, William, 15
Turnbull, Robert, 218
Turner, Mr., 14-15
  Ann A., 216
  D. McNeil, 189, 190, 194, 216
  Fannie Douglass, 194, 216
  Harriet D., 194, 216
  Henry McNeal, 50
  Rignell, 216
  Samuel C., 186, 195
  Stringfellow, 216
  Thornton, 216
Tusten, Agnes A., 195
  Edna P., 198, 218

Hiram T., 66, 75, 182, 186, 195, 198, 218, 231, 232
James H., 218
John L., 218
Walter Davis, 186, 194
Tustin, Samuel, 213

Valentine, Andrew, 225
Van Ness, Mr., 10, 44
Vance, Beverly, 135
Vaughn, Gen., 80, 100, 102, 103, 112
Verchot, J. A., 234 (2)
Verell, Matilda E., 206
Verrell, James, 182
Visanska, G. A., 25, 173, 186
  Julius M., 186
Volkening, Charles, 186

Waddel, Moses, 15
Wait, John T., 216
Wakefield, S. J., 158
Waldrop, Corinne, 202
  Mrs. M. C., 196
Walker, G. E., 72
  M. W., 234
  Sarah J., 208
Waller, C. A. C., 137
Wallingford & Russell, 188
Wallingford, Samuel, 186
Wannamaker, Mr., 203
Wardlaw, Andrew Bowie, 8, 133, 186, 190, 195, 214
  Arthur, 217
  Charles C., 214, 222
  Clark, 182, 213
  D. A., 222
  David (Sr.), 12
  David A., 214
  David Lewis, 2, 4, 6, 7, 25, 26, 28, 29, 31, 38, 57, 75, 76, 79, 81-83, 92, 95, 117, 182, 210, 220
  David L. (II), 217
  Edward R., 217
  Eliza, 195, 214, 222
  Eliza Alice, 9
  Eliza H., 195
  Eliza Lucretia, 195
  Eliza S., 228
  Ella C., 211, 228
  Fannie, 220
  Frances E., 227
  Francis H., 81, 214
  Francis Harper, 196

Index

Frank, 222
George Allen, 182, 211
H. T., 25, 26, 186
Ivy, 217
J. G., 227
J. Langdon, 214, 222
James, 2, 4, 6, 7, 8, 25, 29, 235
James A., 214, 228
James H., 182
James W., 213, 227
Jane E., 211
Jos. C., 227
Joseph J., 4, 16, 26, 28, 127, 195, 213, 227
Julia D., 226
Lewis (Louis) A., 182, 213, 227
Lucia G., 211
Marie W., 195
Mary Ann, 195, 213, 227
Mary Josephine, 195, 196
Mary W., 213, 227
Nancy T., 195
Nannie F., 227
Patterson, 195
R. H. (Robert Henry), 2, 4, 6-20, 25, 27, 29, 44, 67, 125, 182, 186, 187, 188, 195, 214, 222, 231
Robert H., Jr., 182, 214, 222
Sally M., 211
Sarah Elizabeth, 195
Sarah T., 195
Susan C., 211
Thomas P., 214, 222
W. A., 27, 230
William A., 217, 231
William C., 18, 182, 190, 195, 222
Wm. P., 186
Ware, Nathaniel Alcock, 24
Washington, Booker T., 169, 171
Watkins, J. A., 186
Watt, Robert, 188
  Rosey Ann, 8
  Saml., 8, 10, 13, 21
Webster, Daniel, 34
Weems, Mr., 55
  Agnes, 216
  Agnes E., 216
  Andrew J., 216
  Caroline O., 216
  David J., 216
  Francis A., 216
  Jefferson, 198
  John M., 216
  Lemuel C., 216
  Mary J., 216
  William T., 216
Wells, J. W., 186
  L. D., 159
  Preston B., 153
Wenck, George F. E., 126, 174
West, Fred D., 234 (4)
  William, 7
Westfield, Edward, 67, 182, 208, 229, 231
  Ella V., 209
  Eugene V., 229
  Richd. D., 229
  Robert D., 209
  Sarah Jane, 208, 229
  Virginia E., 208
Wetherel, Dr., 25
Whaley, J. H., 233
Wharton, Martha, 143
White Brothers, 10, 18, 25, 188
White, Mrs., 18, 137, 187
  Andrew, 22
  Charles, 213, 225
  Charles S., 186
  Charlie, 153
  E., 226
  Eliza L., 226
  Ezekiel, 182
  George, 15, 182, 186, 190, 193, 195, 214, 225
  Jane W., 196
  John, 4, 22, 27, 29, 51, 67, 182, 195, 213, 220, 225, 231
  Jos. G., 227
  Lemuel W., 2, 26, 133, 173, 182, 186
  Leonard Waller, 190, 195, 214, 225
  Lucy, 25, 26, 153, 195, 196, 213, 214, 225
  Lucy W., 225
  Mary, 196
  Mary C., 227
  Mary E., 195, 227
  Mary Helen, 195
  Nancy, 225
  Nancy Amelia, 195
  Nannie, 214
  Robert J., 60, 67, 182, 195, 214, 220
  Robt. N., 227
  Sallie A., 220
  Sarah, 195

Index

Sarah M., 227
Thos. G., 159
Wm., 214, 225
Wm. Henry, 182, 232 (2), 233 (2)
Whitfield, George, 9
  Tyler, 24
Wier (Weir), Alexander J., 216
  Jas. C., 221
  Joel C., 186, 191
  John A., 66, 94, 182, 195, 221, 231
  John B., 221
  Kate C., 195, 221
  Margaret Isabella, 94
  Sarah M., 221
  Susan M., 195, 216
Wigfall, Louis T., 46, 106-107
Wiggins, Ann, 224
Wightman, Thomas, 4
Wilkinson, Belle, 199
Williams, Mrs., 33
  Adolphus A., 37, 127, 182, 217, 227
  Charles R., 235 (4)
  David, 209, 211
  Dora, 229
  Rev. E. W., 164-165
  Mrs. E. W., 164
  Esther, 211
  Hugh A., 234 (2), 235
  John, 211
  John S., 97, 100
  Lee, 235
  Samuel, 211
  Timothy D., 19, 211
Williamson, Thos. H., 235
Willingham, Andrew, 188
Willson (Wilson), John G., 182, 212, 225, 231 (2)
Wilson, Mr., 128
  Catherine M., 209
  Delphia, 213
  E. Raymond, 234 (4)
  Elijah, 13, 146
  Emma, 195
  Eugene L., 137, 186, 208
  Euphemia, 195
  Fannie D., 200
  Harry B., 233 (6)
  Henry, 226
  Henry Donald, 186, 209
  Hugh, 79-83, 126, 127, 144-145, 155, 160, 179-186, 197-209
  Hugh, Sr., 182
  J. B., 140, 186
  J. Lowrie, 190
  Jane E., 213
  Jas. S., 27, 28, 29, 57, 197
  John B., 182
  John H., 51, 57, 69, 70, 75, 182, 198, 200, 212, 230, 231 (3)
  Josephine C., 117
  Langdon H., 234 (2)
  Leroy J., 182, 186, 209
  Lizzie C., 201
  Lucy P., 222
  Martha T., 213
  Matilda Vashti, 198
  Minnie, 196
  Patrick, 182
  Rebecca, 226
  R. C. (Richard Courtney), 186, 191, 196
  Robert, 182
  Sarah A., 196, 225
  Sarah U., 209
  Susan A., 197, 213
  Susan V., 213
  Thomas, 188
  Thomas M., 209
  W. H., 182, 186
  William D., 196
  Willie, 186
  Wm. L., 213
Winn, R. L., 159
Winstock, Messrs., 66
Winstock, Benj. M., 182, 228
  I. H., 228
  J., 228
  J. W., 228
  L. P., 228
  M., 228
  Saml. A., 182, 228
Wise, Dr. G. A., 209
  Mrs. G. A., 209
Wood, Eliza F., 235
Woodhurst, A. J., 182
  Elizabeth, 205
Wooldridge, Gibson, 16
  Tom, 45
Worrell, Mrs., 220
Wosmansky, Mrs. E. A., 207
  J. C., 209
  Ursula, 209
Wrifford, Chas., 229
  Chas. (II), 229
  Martha, 229
  Martha H., 229

Index

Mary, 229
Wright, Eliza S., 222
    Jos., 151
Yancey, B. C., 13, 24
    Chas. C., 2, 24
    William, 26
Yeldell, Robert, 75, 76
Young, Rev. C. M., 163, 167

Zbiden, Charles, 186
Zeigler, Etta, 209
    Georgia, 209
    Jennie, 209
    Julia, 209
    Lavinia, 209
    M. G., 186, 199, 204, 209
    Sabrina, 209
Zimmerman, Mrs. C., 224

Confederate Monument with a view of the
southwest corner of the Square in 1906

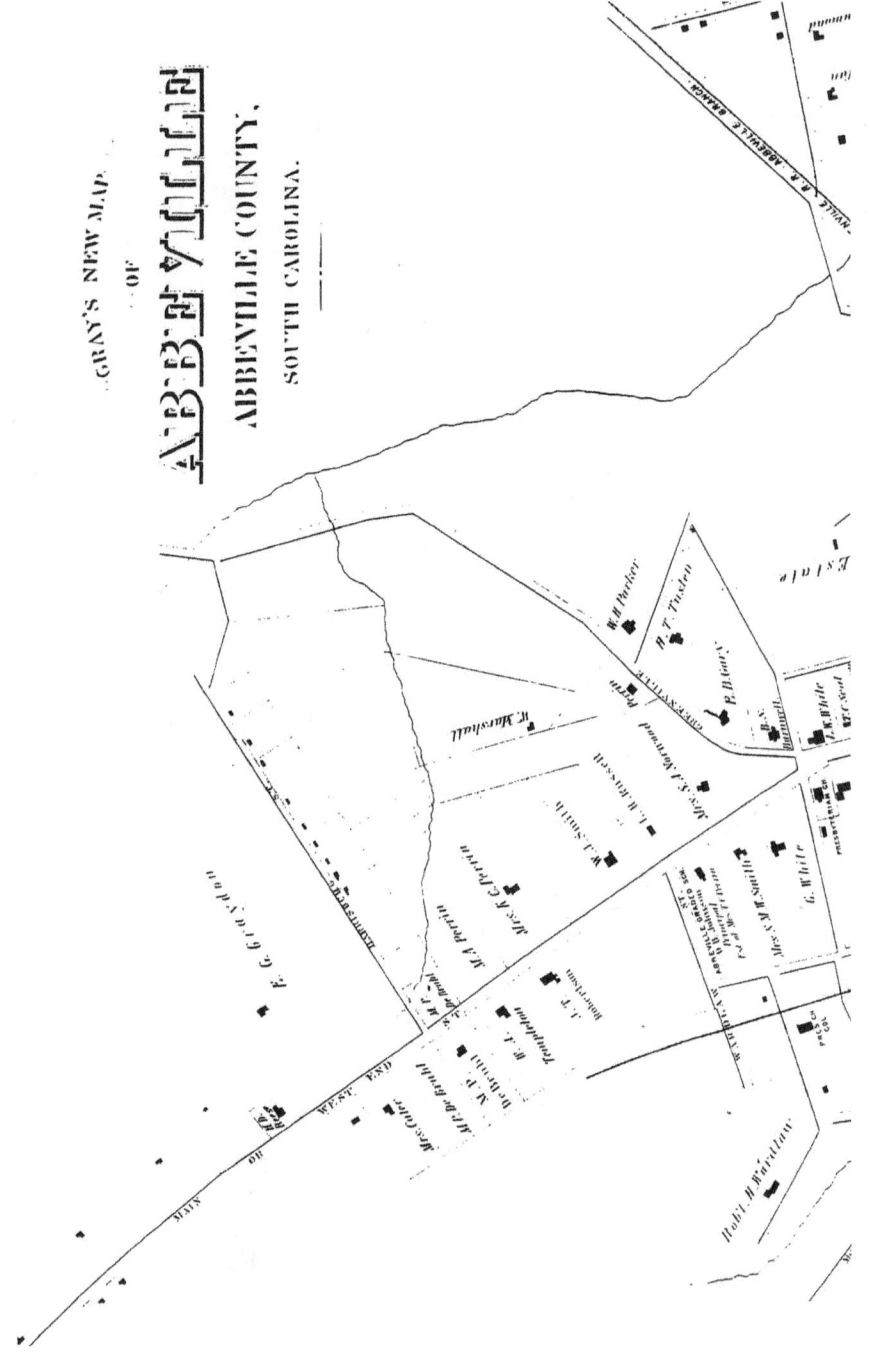

www.ingramcontent.com/pod-product-compliance
Lightning Source LLC
Chambersburg PA
CBHW071424150426
43191CB00008B/1040